Middle School 3-2

기말고사 완벽대비

적중100

영어 기출 문제집

중3

동아 | 윤정미

Best Collection

구성과 특징

교과서의 주요 학습 내용을 중심으로 학습 영역별 특성에 맞춰 단계별로 다양한 학습 기회를 제공하여 단원별 학습능력 평가는 물론 중간 및 기말고사 시험 등에 완벽하게 대비할 수 있도록 내용을 구성

Words & Expressions

Step1 Key Words 단원별 핵심 단어 설명 및 풀이
Key Expression 단원별 핵심 숙어 및 관용어 설명
Word Power 반대 또는 비슷한 뜻 단어 배우기
English Dictionary 영어로 배우는 영어 단어

Step2 실력평가 단원별 수시평가 대비 주관식, 객관식 문제풀이

Step3 서술형 대비 학업성취도 및 수행능력평가 대비 서술형 문제풀이

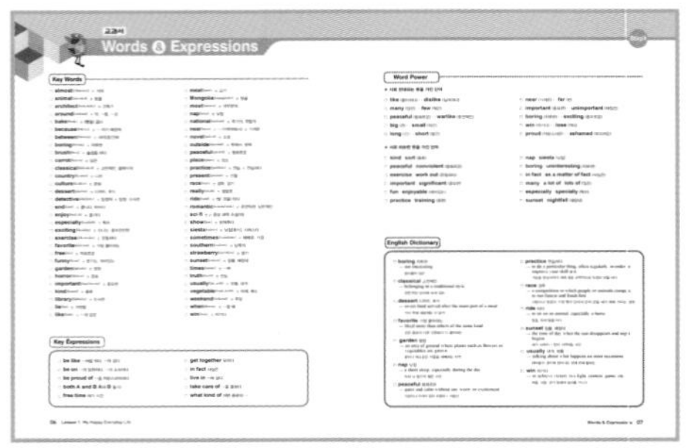

Conversation

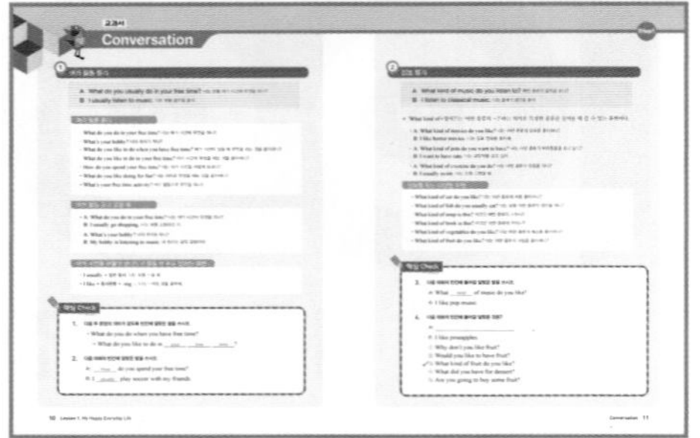

Step1 핵심 의사소통 소통에 필요한 주요 표현 방법 요약
핵심 Check 기본적인 표현 방법 및 활용능력 확인

Step2 대화문 익히기 교과서 대화문 심층 분석 및 확인

Step3 교과서 확인학습 빈칸 채우기를 통한 문장 완성 능력 확인

Step4 기본평가 시험대비 기초 학습 능력 평가

Step5 실력평가 단원별 수시평가 대비 주관식, 객관식 문제풀이

Step6 서술형 대비 학업성취도 및 수행능력평가 대비 서술형 문제풀이

Grammar

Step1 주요 문법 단원별 주요 문법 사항과 예문을 알기 쉽게 설명
핵심 Check 기본 문법사항에 대한 이해 여부 확인

Step2 기본평가 시험대비 기초 학습 능력 평가

Step3 실력평가 단원별 수시평가 대비 주관식, 객관식 문제풀이

Step4 서술형 대비 학업성취도 및 수행능력평가 대비 서술형 문제풀이

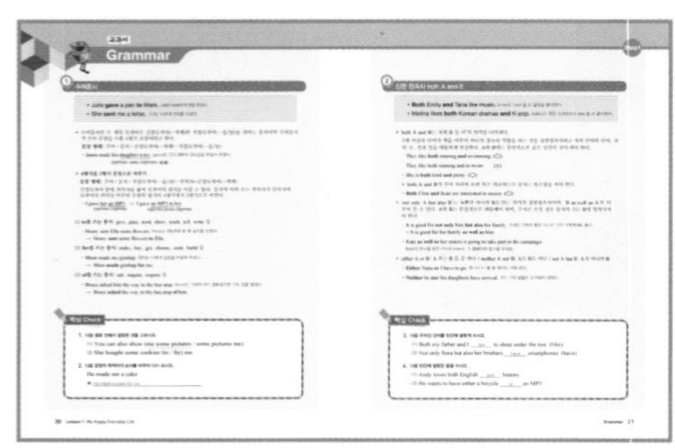

Reading

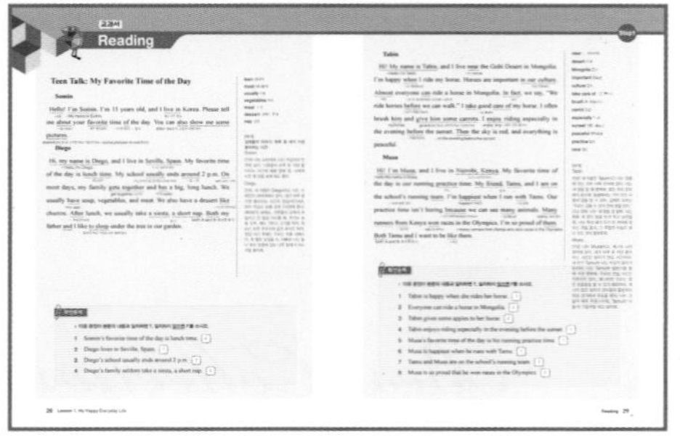

Step1 구문 분석 단원별로 제시된 문장에 대한 구문별 분석과 내용 설명
확인문제 문장에 대한 기본적인 이해와 인지능력 확인

Step2 확인학습A 빈칸 채우기를 통한 문장 완성 능력 확인

Step3 확인학습B 제시된 우리말을 영어로 완성하여 작문 능력 키우기

Step4 실력평가 단원별 수시평가 대비 주관식, 객관식 문제풀이

Step5 서술형 대비 학업성취도 및 수행능력평가 대비 서술형 문제풀이
교과서 구석구석 교과서에 나오는 기타 문장까지 완벽 학습

Composition

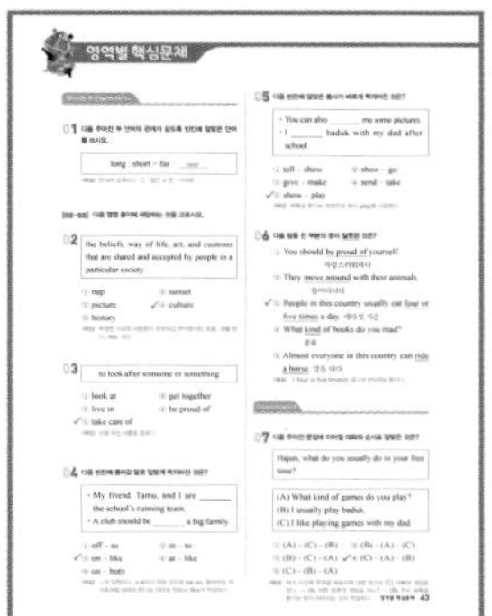

|영역별 핵심문제|

단어 및 어휘, 대화문, 문법, 독해 등 각 영역별 기출문제의 출제 유형을 분석하여 실전에 대비하고 연습할 수 있도록 문제를 배열

|단원별 예상문제|

기출문제를 분석한 후 새로운 시험 출제 경향을 더하여 새롭게 출제될 수 있는 문제를 포함하여 시험에 완벽하게 대비할 수 있도록 준비

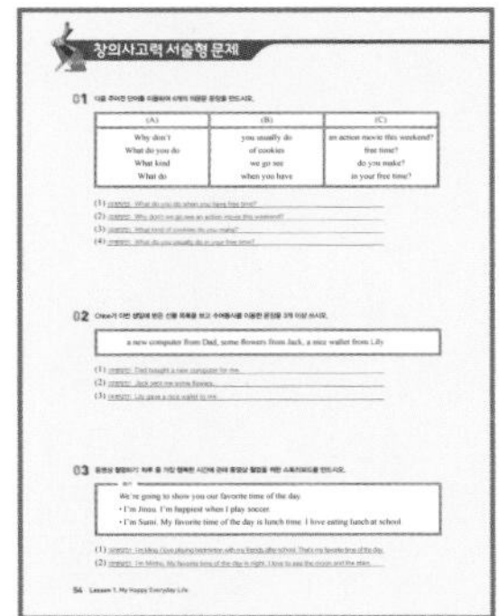

|서술형 실전 및 창의사고력 문제|

학교 시험에서 점차 늘어나는 서술형 시험에 집중 대비하고 고득점을 취득하는데 만전을 기하기 위한 학습 코너

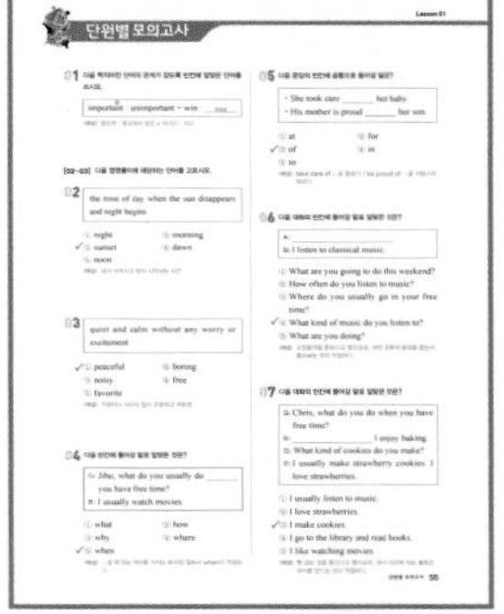

|단원별 모의고사|

영역별, 단계별 학습을 모두 마친 후 실전 연습을 위한 모의고사

교과서 파헤치기

- **단어Test1~3** 영어 단어 우리말 쓰기, 우리말을 영어 단어로 쓰기, 영영풀이에 해당하는 단어와 우리말 쓰기
- **대화문Test1~2** 대화문 빈칸 완성 및 전체 대화문 쓰기
- **본문Test1~5** 빈칸 완성, 우리말 쓰기, 문장 배열연습, 영어 작문하기 복습 등 단계별 반복 학습을 통해 교과서 지문에 대한 완벽한 습득
- **구석구석지문Test1~2** 지문 빈칸 완성 및 전문 영어로 쓰기

이책의 차례

Contents

Lesson 7

Technology in Our Lives

의사소통 기능

- 방법 · 절차 묻고 답하기
  A: Do you know how to return these books?
  B: Sure. First, insert the card. Then put the books in this box.
- 감사 표현하기
  I really appreciate your help.

언어 형식

- 분사구문
  Using various methods, experts analyze big data.
- 접속사 as
  As information and communication technology develops, the amount of data we have is getting much greater than before.

교과서

Words & Expressions

Key Words

- □ **amount** [əmáunt] 명 총계, 총액
- □ **analyze** [ǽnəlàiz] 동 분석하다
- □ **appreciate** [əpríːʃièit] 동 감사하다, 감상하다
- □ **as** [əz] 접 ~함에 따라, ~한 대로, ~ 때문에
- □ **avoid** [əvɔ́id] 동 피하다, 방지하다
- □ **communication** [kəmjùːnəkéiʃən] 명 의사소통, 연락
- □ **complex** [kəmpléks] 형 복잡한
- □ **crime** [kraim] 명 범죄
- □ **database** [déitəbeis] 명 데이터베이스
- □ **develop** [divéləp] 동 성장하다, 발달하다
- □ **endless** [éndlis] 형 끝없는, 무한한
- □ **expert** [ékspəːrt] 명 전문가
- □ **flu** [fluː] 명 독감
- □ **forecast** [fɔ́ːrkæst] 동 예측하다, 예보하다
- □ **further** [fə́ːrðər] 형 더 이상의, 추가의
- □ **huge** [hjuːdʒ] 형 거대한, (크기 · 양 · 정도가) 막대한
- □ **identify** [aidéntəfài] 동 알아보다, 확인하다, 식별하다
- □ **improve** [imprúːv] 동 개선하다, 향상하다
- □ **include** [inklúːd] 동 포함하다
- □ **industry** [índəstri] 명 산업, 공업
- □ **influence** [ínfluəns] 동 영향을 미치다
- □ **insert** [insə́ːrt] 동 삽입하다
- □ **mainly** [méinli] 부 주로
- □ **meaningful** [míːniŋfəl] 형 의미 있는, 중요한
- □ **method** [méθəd] 명 방법
- □ **national** [nǽʃənl] 형 국가의, 전국적인
- □ **performance** [pərfɔ́ːrməns] 명 경기력, 수행, 성과
- □ **predict** [pridíkt] 동 예측하다
- □ **prevention** [privénʃən] 명 예방
- □ **purchase** [pə́ːrtʃəs] 명 구매
- □ **recommend** [rèkəménd] 동 추천하다, 권하다
- □ **rent** [rent] 동 빌리다
- □ **spread** [spred] 명 확산, 전파
- □ **symptom** [símptəm] 명 증상
- □ **trace** [treis] 명 자취, 발자국, 흔적
- □ **traffic** [trǽfik] 명 교통(량)
- □ **unlock** [ənlák] 동 잠금을 풀다
- □ **upload** [ʌplóud] 동 ~을 전송하다, 업로드하다
- □ **various** [vέəriəs] 형 다양한
- □ **wisely** [wáizli] 부 현명하게, 지혜롭게

Key Expressions

- □ **be likely to ~** ~할 것 같다
- □ **be used to+동사원형** ~하는 데 사용되다
- □ **by ~ing** ~함으로써
- □ **get+비교급** 점점 더 ~해지다
- □ **focus on ~** ~에 초점을 맞추다
- □ **for sure** 확실히, 분명히
- □ **help+A(목적어)+동사원형** A가 ~하도록 돕다
- □ **hot spot** 다발 지역
- □ **just as ~** 꼭 ~처럼
- □ **make a decision** 결정하다
- □ **more and more** 점점 더 많이, 더욱 더
- □ **play a role** 역할을 하다
- □ **thanks to ~** ~ 덕분에, ~ 때문에
- □ **the amount of ~** ~의 양/수량
- □ **this kind of+명사** 이런 종류의 ~

Word Power

※ 서로 비슷한 뜻을 가진 어휘

- □ **complex** 복잡한 : **complicated** 복잡한
- □ **forecast** 예측하다, 예보하다 : **predict** 예측하다
- □ **mainly** 주로 : **mostly** 대개, 주로, 보통은
- □ **expert** 전문가 : **specialist** 전문가
- □ **influence** 영향을 주다 : **affect** 영향을 미치다
- □ **various** 다양한 : **diverse** 다양한, 여러 가지의

※ 서로 반대의 뜻을 가진 어휘

- □ **complex** 복잡한 ↔ **simple** 간단한, 단순한
- □ **likely** ~할 것 같은 ↔ **unlikely** ~할 것 같지 않은
- □ **unlock** 잠금을 풀다 ↔ **lock** 잠그다
- □ **include** 포함하다 ↔ **exclude** 제외하다
- □ **meaningful** 의미 있는 ↔ **meaningless** 무의미한
- □ **upload** 업로드하다 ↔ **download** 다운로드하다

※ 접미사 -ful → 명사+-ful

- □ **awe**+**-ful** → **awful** 끔찍한, 지독한
- □ **help**+**-ful** → **helpful** 도움이 되는
- □ **power**+**-ful** → **powerful** 강력한, 영향력 있는
- □ **color**+**-ful** → **colorful** 형형색색의
- □ **peace**+**-ful** → **peaceful** 평화로운
- □ **use**+**-ful** → **useful** 유용한, 쓸모 있는

English Dictionary

□ **analyze** 분석하다
→ to examine something carefully
어떤 것을 주의 깊게 조사하다

□ **avoid** 피하다
→ to stay away from someone or something
어떤 사람이나 사물로부터 떨어져 있다

□ **communication** 의사소통
→ the process by which people exchange information or express their thoughts and feelings
사람들이 정보를 교환하거나 생각, 감정 등을 표현하는 과정

□ **database** 데이터베이스
→ a large amount of information stored in a computer system 컴퓨터 시스템에 저장되어 있는 많은 양의 정보

□ **develop** 발전시키다, 성장하다
→ to grow and change into something bigger, better or more important
더 크고 나은 또는 더 중요한 것으로 변화하고 성장하다

□ **identify** 확인하다
→ to realize who someone is or what something is
어떤 사람이 누구인지 또는 어떤 사물이 무엇인지 알아차리다

□ **industry** 산업
→ the people or companies engaged in a particular kind of commercial enterprise
특별한 종류의 상업적인 기업에 종사하는 사람들 또는 회사들

□ **method** 방법
→ a way of doing something 어떤 것을 하는 방식

□ **performance** 수행, 성과
→ the action or process of accomplishing a task or function 임무나 역할을 완수하는 행위 또는 과정

□ **predict** 예측하다
→ to say that something is going to happen 어떤 일이 일어날 것이라고 말하다

□ **rent** 빌리다
→ to pay someone for the use of something
어떤 사람에게 물건을 사용하는 대가를 지불하다

□ **spread** 확산, 전파
→ the growth or development of something, so that it affects a larger area or a larger number of people
어떤 일의 성장이나 발전이 더 큰 지역이나 더 많은 수의 사람들에게 영향을 주는 것

□ **recommend** 추천하다, 권하다
→ to suggest something to someone
무엇인가를 누군가에게 제안하다

□ **purchase** 구매, 구매품
→ the action of buying something; a thing that has been bought 무언가를 사는 행위; 산 물건

□ **influence** 영향을 주다
→ to change or affect something
어떤 것을 바꾸거나 영향을 미치다

□ **symptom** 증상, 징후
→ something that shows you may have a particular illness
특정한 질병을 갖고 있을지도 모른다는 것을 보여주는 어떤 것

Words & Expressions **시험대비 실력평가** Step2

01 다음 짝지어진 단어의 관계가 같도록 빈칸에 알맞은 말은?

mainly – mostly : specialist – ________

① expert ② purchase
③ crime ④ complex
⑤ amount

서답형

02 주어진 영어 설명에 맞게 문장의 빈칸에 알맞은 말을 쓰시오.

I can ________ big data and draw meaningful results from it.

<영어 설명> to examine something carefully

➡ ____________________

03 밑줄 친 부분의 의미로 알맞지 않은 것은?

① When they make a decision, they depend not on emotion but on reason. (결정하다)
② We arrived just as the musicians were packing up their instruments. (마치 ~하듯이)
③ Thanks to the storm, all flights were canceled. (~ 때문에)
④ Experts say the West Sea will continue to get warmer. (점점 더 따뜻해지다)
⑤ Train fares are likely to remain unchanged. (~할 것 같다)

04 다음 빈칸에 들어갈 가장 알맞은 말을 고르시오.

Telephone is an effective means of ________.

① amount ② transport
③ expert ④ communication
⑤ database

중요

05 다음 <보기>의 단어를 사용하여 자연스러운 문장을 만들 수 없는 것은?

보기
unlock influence predict improve

① There is some hope that things will ________.
② The media has a powerful ________ on public opinion.
③ We will ________ a car for a week and explore the area.
④ I tried to ________ the door, but the key didn't fit.
⑤ It is impossible to ________ what the eventual outcome will be.

06 다음 빈칸에 공통으로 들어갈 말로 알맞은 것을 고르시오.

• Everyone knows about it now, thanks ________ you!
• The test is used ________ diagnose a variety of diseases.

① for ② on ③ at
④ with ⑤ to

01 다음 영영풀이에 알맞은 어휘를 〈보기〉에서 찾아 쓰시오.

보기
identify predict develop database

(1) to grow and change into something bigger, better or more important
(2) a large amount of information stored in a computer system
(3) to realize who someone is or what something is
(4) to say that something is going to happen
➡ (1) ________ (2) ________ (3) ________
(4) ________

중요
02 다음 짝지어진 두 단어의 관계가 같도록 빈칸에 알맞은 말을 쓰시오.

(1) angry – angrily : wise – ________
(2) peace – peaceful : awe – ________

03 다음 우리말에 맞도록 빈칸에 알맞은 말을 쓰시오. (철자가 주어진 경우 그 철자로 시작할 것.)

(1) 그것은 극도로 복잡한 주제에 대한 유용한 입문서이다.
→ It's a useful introduction to an extremely c________ subject.
(2) 그는 학교를 중퇴하자 범죄의 길로 들어섰다.
→ He turned to c________ when he dropped out of school.
(3) 경제가 어디로 향하고 있는지 예측이 되세요?
→ Can you f________ where the economy is heading?
(4) 당신 업무에는 새로운 컴퓨터 시스템을 설치하는 것도 들어간다.
→ Your duties will i________ setting up a new computer system.

고난이도
04 우리말에 맞게 한 단어를 추가하여 주어진 어구를 알맞게 배열하시오.

(1) 저 실험은 수감자들에게만 초점이 맞춰져 있었다. (the prisoners, that test, focused, alone, on)
➡ ________________________________
____

(2) 우리가 견딜 수 있는 고통의 양에는 한계가 있다. (we, a limit, pain, there, the, amount, bear, can, to, of)
➡ ________________________________
____

(3) 점점 더 많은 사람들이 인터넷을 이용하고 있다. (the Internet, people, and, are, more, using)
➡ ________________________________
____

(4) 그가 월요일에 돌아올 것인데 확실히 말할 수는 없다. (I, Monday, he'll, can't, be, say, back, sure, but, on)
➡ ________________________________
____

교과서

Conversation

1 방법 · 절차 묻고 답하기

A Do you know how to use this machine? 이 기계 어떻게 사용하는지 아시나요?
B Yes. First, choose the dish you want. Then touch the ORDER button.
네. 우선 원하는 음식을 고르세요. 그 다음 '주문' 버튼을 누르세요.

- 어떤 일을 하는 방법이나 절차를 물을 때 'Do you know how to ~?', 'Can[Could] you tell me how to ~?', 'Can[Could] you explain how to ~?' 등으로 물을 수 있다. 방법이나 절차를 말할 때 상대방이 이해하기 쉽도록 First, Second, Then 등과 같이 순서를 나타내는 말을 사용하여 설명할 수 있다.
- 다음과 같은 표현을 이용할 수도 있다.
  to begin with(처음에는, 우선, 먼저), secondly(두 번째로[둘째는]), next(그 다음에), also(또한), lastly(마지막으로, 끝으로), finally(마지막으로 (= lastly), 최종적으로) 등
- 절차를 모르는 경우에는 'I'm sorry, I don't know.'라고 말할 수 있다.

방법 · 절차 묻고 답하기

- Do you know how to ~? ~하는 법을 아니?
- Can you tell me how to ~? ~하는 법을 말해 줄래?
- Could you tell me how to ~? ~하는 법을 말해 주시겠어요?
- Can you explain how to ~? ~하는 법을 설명해 줄래?
- Could you explain how to ~? ~하는 법을 설명해 주시겠어요?
- I'm sorry, I don't know. 죄송하지만 전 모릅니다.

핵심 Check

1. 다음 괄호 안의 단어들을 배열하여 문맥에 맞는 문장을 완성하시오.

A: I want to buy a snack. (this machine / you / use / explain / could / how to)?
B: Yes. First, choose the snack you want.
➡ ______________________________

2 감사 표현하기

A I really appreciate your help. 도와줘서 매우 고맙습니다.
B It's my pleasure. 제가 좋아서 한 건데요.

- 상대방에게 어떤 일에 대해 감사를 표현하고 싶을 때 'Thank you so much.'가 일반적이지만 'I really appreciate your help.', 'I can't thank you enough.', 'I'm grateful for ~.', 'I'm thankful for ~.' 등으로 말할 수도 있다.
- 감사 표현에 대한 응답으로 'It's not a big deal.', 'It's my pleasure.', 'Don't mention it.', 'No problem.' 등으로 응답할 수 있다.

감사 표현하기

- Thank you so much. / Thanks a lot.
- I really appreciate your help.
- I'm thankful for helping me out.
- Thank you for your help.
- I'm grateful for your help.

감사에 응답하기

- It's my pleasure. 제가 좋아서 한 건데요.
- You're welcome. 천만에요.
- No worries. 괜찮아요.
- Don't mention it. 별말씀을요.
- No problem. 별거 아냐.

핵심 Check

2. 다음 중 빈칸에 들어갈 것으로 알맞지 <u>않은</u> 표현은?

A: Can you tell me how to make tea?
B: Sure. First, put a tea bag in a cup. Then, pour hot water in the cup and leave it for 3 minutes.
A: I got it. I really appreciate your help.
B: ________________

① I don't mention it.
② It's my pleasure.
③ You're welcome.
④ No problem.
⑤ Don't mention it.

Listen and Talk A 1

B: Excuse me. ❶Can you tell me ❷how to add money to my transportation card?
G: Of course. ❸First, put your card in the machine. Second, choose the amount of money you want to add.
B: OK.
G: Last, insert your money into the machine.
B: That ❹sounds simple. ❺Thanks.

B: 실례합니다. 어떻게 교통카드에 돈을 충전하는지 알려주시겠어요?
G: 그럼요. 우선 기계에 카드를 넣으세요. 둘째로 충전하고 싶은 금액을 고르세요.
B: 네.
G: 마지막으로 기계에 돈을 넣으세요.
B: 간단해 보이는군요. 고맙습니다.

❶ 방법이나 절차를 물을 때 'Can[Could] you tell me how to ~?', 'Do you know how to ~?', 'Can[Could] you explain how to ~?' 등으로 물을 수 있다.
❷ 의문사+to부정사: tell의 직접목적어로 쓰였다.
❸ 방법이나 절차를 말할 때 상대방이 이해하기 쉽도록 First, Second, Then 등과 같이 순서를 나타내는 말을 사용하여 설명할 수 있다.
❹ sound+형용사: ~하게 들리다
❺ 감사를 표현하는 말이다. 'I really appreciate your help.', 'I can't thank you enough.', 'I'm grateful for ~.', 'I'm thankful for ~.' 등으로 말할 수도 있다.

Check(√) True or False

(1) The boy knows how to add money to a transportation card. T ☐ F ☐
(2) The girl explains how to add money to a transportation card. T ☐ F ☐

Listen and Talk A 2

B: I want to buy a snack. ❶Do you know how to use this snack machine?
G: Yeah. First, ❷choose the snack you want.
B: I already ❸did. What's ❹next?
G: Just put in the money. Then take the snack out.
B: ❺Got it. ❻Thanks.

B: 과자를 사고 싶어요. 이 과자 자판기를 어떻게 사용하는지 알려주시겠어요?
G: 네. 먼저 원하는 과자를 고르세요.
B: 이미 했어요. 그 다음은 뭔가요?
G: 돈을 넣으세요. 그러고 나서 과자를 꺼내세요.
B: 알겠어요. 고맙습니다.

❶ 방법이나 절차를 물을 때 'Do you know how to ~?', 'Can[Could] you tell me how to ~?', 'Can[Could] you explain how to ~?' 등으로 물을 수 있다.
❷ choose와 the snack 사이에 목적격 관계대명사가 생략되어 있다.
❸ did는 'chose the snack I want'를 대신하는 대동사이다.
❹ next는 '그 다음에'라는 의미로 순서를 밝히기 위해 사용된다.
❺ 이해했음을 나타내는 표현이다.
❻ 감사를 표현하는 말이다.

Check(√) True or False

(3) The boy wants to know how to use the snack machine. T ☐ F ☐
(4) The girl tells the boy to put in the money first. T ☐ F ☐

Listen and Talk A 3

G: Excuse me. I want to rent a bike. ❶Can you tell me how to use this application?
M: Sure. ❷First, log in to the application. Then find the RENT button and touch it.
G: Then what?
M: Then the application will give you a number ❸to unlock a bike with.
G: Thank you. ❹I really appreciate your help.

❶ 방법이나 절차를 묻는 표현이다.
❷ 방법이나 절차를 말할 때 상대방이 이해하기 쉽도록 First, Second, Then 등과 같이 순서를 나타내는 말을 사용하여 설명할 수 있다.
❸ 형용사적 용법의 to부정사이다.
❹ 감사를 표현하는 말이다.

Listen and Talk B

A: Excuse me. I want to return these books. ❶Do you know how to do it?
B: Sure. It's simple. First, ❷insert the library card into the machine. Second, put the books in this box.
A: OK.
B: Then just ❸take your card out.
A: I really appreciate your help.

❶ 방법이나 절차를 묻는 표현이다.
❷ insert A into B: A를 B에 넣다
❸ take A out: A를 꺼내다

Listen and Talk B

A: Excuse me. I want to ❶add money to my transportation card. Do you know how to do ❷it?
B: Sure. It's simple. First, put your card in the machine. Second, choose ❸the amount of money.
A: OK.
B: Then insert the money.
A: I really appreciate your help.

❶ add A to B: A를 B에 더하다, 추가하다
❷ it은 '교통카드에 돈을 충전하는 방법'을 가리킨다.
❸ the amount of: ~의 양[금액]

Listen and Talk B

A: Excuse me. I want ❶to buy a snack. Do you know how to do it?
B: Sure. It's simple. ❷First, choose the snack. Second, ❸put in the money.
A: OK.
B: Then ❹take the snack out.
A: ❺I really appreciate your help.

❶ want의 목적어로 to부정사가 쓰였다.
❷ 순서를 나타내는 말로 이해를 돕고 있다.
❸ put in the money = put the money in
❹ take out the snack = take the snack out
❺ 감사를 표현하는 말로 'Thank you so much.', 'I can't thank you enough.', 'I'm grateful for ~.', 'I'm thankful for ~.' 등으로 말할 수도 있다.

Listen and Talk C

G: Excuse me, but what's this robot for?
B: Oh, it's a robot ❶that finds books for you.
G: Really? Can you tell me how to use it?
B: Sure. First, ❷place your library card on the robot's screen.
G: OK.
B: Second, type the title of ❸the book you're looking for and then press ENTER.
G: Is ❹that all?
B: Yes. Then, the robot will find the book and take it to the front desk.
G: So I can just go to the front desk and get the book?
B: Right. It's so easy, ❺isn't it?
G: Yes, it's really ❻amazing. Thank you.

❶ that은 주격 관계대명사이다.
❷ place: 두다, 놓다
❸ the book과 you 사이에 목적격 관계대명사가 that[which]이 생략되어 있다.
❹ that은 앞에서 설명한 것을 가리킨다.
❺ 부가의문문으로 'right'로 바꿔 쓸 수 있다.
❻ 감정을 유발하는 것으로 감정을 나타내는 동사의 현재분사형이 쓰이고 있다.

Listen and Talk D

Let me tell you ❶how to use a drink machine. ❷First, insert money into the machine. Then, choose ❸the drink you want. Last, take the drink ❹out of the machine. ❺It's easy.

❶ 의문사+to부정사: tell의 직접목적어로 쓰였다.
❷ 방법이나 절차를 말할 때 상대방이 이해하기 쉽도록 First, Second, Then 등과 같이 순서를 나타내는 말을 사용하여 설명할 수 있다.
❸ the drink과 you 사이에 목적격 관계대명사가 생략되어 있다.
❹ out of = from
❺ It = how to use a drink machine

Talk and Play

A: Do you know how to make tea?
B: Sure. First, ❶put a tea bag in a cup.
A: OK.
B: Then, pour hot water in the cup.
A: And ❷then?
B: Last, take the tea bag out after 3 minutes.
A: ❸I got it. ❹I really appreciate your help.

❶ put A in B: A를 B에 넣다
❷ then 뒤에는 'what should I do' 정도가 생략되어 있다고 볼 수 있다.
❸ I got it = I understand.
❹ 감사를 나타내는 표현이다.

Talk and Play

A: Do you know how to boil eggs?
B: Sure. First, ❶put water and the eggs in a pot.
A: OK.
B: Then, ❷boil the water and eggs for 10 to 12 minutes.
A: And then?
B: Last, ❸take the eggs out and cool them.
A: I got it. I really appreciate your help.

❶ put A in B: A를 B에 넣다
❷ boil: (물이나 액체를) 끓이다
❸ take A out: A를 꺼내다, cool: 식히다, them은 eggs를 가리킨다.

Talk and Play

A: ❶Do you know how to plant a potato?
B: Sure. First, cut the potato into small piece.
A: OK.
B: Then, ❷dig holes in the ground.
A: And then?
B: Third, ❸put the potato pieces in the holes.
A: Then what?
B: Last, cover the holes with ❹dirt.
A: I got it. I really appreciate your help.

❶ how+to부정사: ~하는 방법
❷ dig: (구멍 등을) 파다
❸ put A in B: A를 B에 넣다
❹ dirt: 흙

Review 1

G: Can you tell me how to ❶plant a potato?
B: Sure. First, ❷cut a potato into small pieces. Second, dig holes in the ground.
G: Then?
B: Then put the potato pieces in the holes and ❸cover the holes with dirt.
G: ❹That sounds simple. Thanks.

❶ plant: (나무나 화초 등을) 심다
❷ cut A into small pieces: A를 잘게 썰다
❸ cover A with B: A를 B로 덮다
❹ sound+형용사: ~하게 들리다 simple: 단순한, 쉬운

Review 2

B: ❶Excuse me. Can you tell me how ❷to use this machine?
G: Sure. First, put the paper on the copy machine. Then choose the paper size and ❸ the number of copies.
B: Then ❹what?
G: Press the START button.
B: ❺Thank you. I really appreciate your help.

❶ Excuse me. = I beg your pardon.
❷ '의문사+to부정사'로 명사적 용법이다.
❸ the number of: ~의 수, a number of = many
❹ what 뒤에는 'should I do' 정도가 생략되어 있다고 볼 수 있다.
❺ 감사를 표현하는 말로 'Thank you so much.', 'I can't thank you enough.', 'I'm grateful for ~.', 'I'm thankful for ~.' 등으로 말할 수도 있다.

• 다음 우리말과 일치하도록 빈칸에 알맞은 말을 쓰시오.

Listen and Talk A 1

B: Excuse me. Can you ________ me ________ ________ ________ money ________ my transportation card?
G: Of course. ________, ________ your card ________ the machine. ________, ________ the ________ of money you want to add.
B: OK.
G: ________, ________ your money ________ the machine.
B: That sounds ________. Thanks.

해석

B: 실례합니다. 어떻게 교통카드에 돈을 충전하는지 알려주시겠어요?
G: 그럼요. 우선 기계에 카드를 넣으세요. 둘째로 충전하고 싶은 금액을 고르세요.
B: 네.
G: 마지막으로 기계에 돈을 넣으세요.
B: 간단해 보이는군요. 고맙습니다.

Listen and Talk A 2

B: I want to buy a snack. Do you ________ ________ ________ ________ this snack machine?
G: Yeah. ________, choose the snack you want.
B: I already ________. What's ________?
G: Just ________ ________ the money. Then ________ the snack ________.
B: ________ ________. Thanks.

B: 과자를 사고 싶어요. 이 과자 자판기를 어떻게 사용하는지 알려주시겠어요?
G: 네. 먼저 원하는 과자를 고르세요.
B: 이미 했어요. 그 다음은 뭔가요?
G: 돈을 넣으세요. 그러고 나서 과자를 꺼내세요.
B: 알겠어요. 고맙습니다.

Listen and Talk A 3

G: Excuse me. I want to ________ a bike. Can you ________ me ________ ________ ________ this application?
M: Sure. First, ________ ________ ________ the application. Then find the RENT button and touch ________.
G: Then ________?
M: Then the application will give you a number ________ ________ a bike ________.
G: Thank you. I really ________ your help.

G: 실례합니다. 자전거를 빌리고 싶은데요. 이 앱을 어떻게 사용하는지 알려주시겠어요?
M: 그럼요. 우선 앱에 로그인하세요. 그러고 나서 RENT 버튼을 찾고 터치하세요.
G: 그러고 난 후엔 어떻게 하나요?
M: 그 후에는 앱이 자전거를 잠금 해제하는 번호를 알려 줄 거에요.
G: 고맙습니다. 도와주셔서 정말 감사해요.

Listen and Talk B

A: Excuse me. I want to ________ these books. Do you ________ ________ ________ it?
B: Sure. It's ________. First, ________ the library card ________ the machine. Second, ________ the books ________ this box.
A: OK.
B: ________ just ________ your card ________.
A: I really ________ your help.

A: 실례합니다. 저는 이 책들을 반납하고 싶어요. 어떻게 하는지 아시나요?
B: 그럼요. 간단해요. 우선 도서 대출 카드를 기계에 넣으세요. 둘째로 이 상자 안에 책들을 넣으세요.
A: 알겠어요.
B: 그러고 나서 카드를 꺼내세요.
A: 도와주셔서 정말 고맙습니다.

A: Excuse me. I want to ________ money ________ my transportation card. Do you ________ ________ ________ ________ it?
B: Sure. It's ________. ________, put your card in the machine. ________, choose the ________ of money.
A: OK.
B: ________ ________ the money.
A: I really ________ your help.

A: 실례합니다. 저는 교통카드에 돈을 충전하고 싶어요. 어떻게 하는지 아시나요?
B: 그럼요. 간단해요. 우선 기계에 카드를 넣으세요. 둘째로 금액을 고르세요.
A: 알겠어요.
B: 그러고 나서 돈을 넣으세요.
A: 도와주셔서 정말 고맙습니다.

A: Excuse me. I want ________ ________ a snack. Do you ________ ________ ________ ________ it?
B: Sure. It's ________. ________, choose the snack. ________, put in the money.
A: OK.
B: ________ take the snack out.
A: I really ________ your help.

A: 실례합니다. 저는 과자를 사고 싶어요. 어떻게 하는지 아시나요?
B: 그럼요. 간단해요. 우선 과자를 고르세요. 둘째로 돈을 넣으세요.
A: 알겠어요.
B: 그러고 나서 과자를 꺼내세요.
A: 도와주셔서 정말 고맙습니다.

Listen and Talk C

G: Excuse me, but ________ this robot ________?
B: Oh, it's a robot ________ finds books for you.
G: Really? Can you ________ me ________ ________ ________ it?
B: Sure. First, ________ your library card ________ the robot's screen.
G: OK.
B: Second, ________ the ________ of the book you're looking for and then ________ ENTER.
G: ________ ________ ________?
B: Yes. ________, the robot will find the book and take ________ to the front desk.
G: So I can just go to the front desk and ________ the book?
B: Right. It's so ________, ________ ________?
G: Yes, it's really ________. Thank you.

G: 실례지만, 이 로봇은 용도가 뭔가요?
B: 아, 이 로봇은 당신을 위해 책을 찾아 주는 로봇이에요.
G: 정말요? 어떻게 사용하는지 알려 주실래요?
B: 그럼요. 먼저, 당신의 도서 대출 카드를 로봇의 화면 위에 놓으세요.
G: 알겠어요.
B: 두 번째로, 당신이 찾으려는 책의 제목을 입력하고 나서 ENTER 키를 누르세요.
G: 그게 다인가요?
B: 네. 그러면 로봇이 책을 찾아서 안내 데스크로 가져다줄 거예요.
G: 그러면 저는 그냥 안내 데스크로 가서 책을 받을 수 있나요?
B: 맞아요. 정말 쉽죠, 그렇지 않나요?
G: 그러네요, 정말 놀라워요. 감사합니다.

Listen and Talk D

Let me tell you ________ ________ ________ a drink machine. ________, insert money into the machine. ________, choose the drink you want. ________, take the drink ________ ________ the machine. It's easy.

음료 자판기를 어떻게 사용하는지 알려 줄게. 먼저 기계에 돈을 넣어. 그러고 나서 원하는 음료를 골라. 마지막으로 기계에서 음료를 꺼내. 간단해.

Talk and Play

A: Do you ________ ________ ________ ________ tea?

B: Sure. ________, ________ a tea bag in a cup.

A: OK.

B: ________, ________ hot water in the cup.

A: And then?

B: ________, ________ the tea bag ________ after 3 minutes.

A: I ________ ________. I really ________ your help.

해석

A: 차를 어떻게 만드는지 알고 있니?
B: 물론이지. 우선 컵에 티백을 넣어.
A: 알겠어.
B: 그런 후 컵에 뜨거운 물을 부어.
A: 그러고 나서는?
B: 마지막으로 3분 후에 티백을 꺼내.
A: 알겠어. 도와줘서 정말 고마워.

Review 1

G: Can you tell me ________ ________ ________ a potato?

B: Sure. First, ________ a potato ________ small ________. Second, ________ holes ________ the ground.

G: Then?

B: Then ________ the potato pieces ________ the holes and ________ the holes ________ dirt.

G: That ________ ________. Thanks.

G: 감자를 어떻게 심는지 알려주시겠어요?
B: 그럼요. 우선 감자를 작은 조각으로 자르세요. 둘째로 땅에 구멍을 파세요.
G: 그러고 나서요?
B: 그러고 나서 구멍에 감자 조각들을 넣고 흙으로 구멍을 덮으세요.
G: 간단한 것 같네요. 고맙습니다.

Review 2

B: Excuse me. Can you ________ me ________ ________ ________ this machine?

G: Sure. First, ________ the paper ________ the copy machine. Then choose the paper size and ________ ________ ________ copies.

B: Then ________?

G: Press the START button.

B: Thank you. I really ________ your help.

B: 실례합니다. 이 기계를 어떻게 사용하는지 알려주시겠어요?
G: 물론이죠. 우선 복사기에 종이를 올려놓으세요. 그러고 나서 종이 크기와 복사본 매수를 고르세요.
B: 그러고 나서 어떻게 해요?
G: START 버튼을 누르세요.
B: 감사합니다. 도와주셔서 고마워요.

01 다음 빈칸 (A)에 알맞지 않은 것은?

B: Excuse me. ________ (A) ________ how to add money to my transportation card?
G: Of course. First, put your card in the machine. Second, choose the amount of money you want to add.
B: OK.
G: Last, insert your money into the machine.
B: That sounds simple. Thanks.

① Can you tell me ② Could you tell me ③ Are you explaining
④ Can you explain ⑤ Do you know

02 주어진 어휘를 이용하여 밑줄 친 우리말을 5 단어로 영작하시오.

A: 도와주셔서 정말 감사해요. (appreciate, really)
B: It's my pleasure.

➡ ____________________________

03 다음 대화의 밑줄 친 (a)의 의도와 다르게 쓰인 것을 고르시오.

B: I want to buy a snack. (a)Do you know how to use this snack machine?
G: Yeah. First, choose the snack you want.
B: I already did. What's next?
G: Just put in the money. Then take the snack out.
B: Got it. Thanks.

① Can you explain how to use this snack machine?
② Could you explain how to use this snack machine?
③ Will you show me how to use this snack machine?
④ Can you tell me how to use this snack machine?
⑤ I'd like to tell you how to use this snack machine.

01 다음 중 짝지어진 대화가 어색한 것은?

① A: Do you know how to make tea?
B: Sure. Last, put a tea bag in a cup.
② A: First, choose the snack you want.
B: I already did. What's next?
③ A: Press the START button.
B: Thank you. I really appreciate your help.
④ A: Then put the potato pieces in the holes and cover the holes with dirt.
B: That sounds simple. Thanks.
⑤ A: Excuse me. Can you tell me how to add money to my transportation card?
B: Of course. First, put your card in the machine.

[02~05] 다음 대화를 읽고 물음에 답하시오.

G: Excuse me, but what's this robot ___(A)___?
B: Oh, it's a robot that finds books for you.
G: Really? ___________(B)___________?
B: Sure. First, (a)당신의 도서 대출 카드를 로봇의 화면 위에 놓으세요.(library card, screen, place)
G: OK.
B: Second, type the title of the book you're looking for and then press ENTER.
G: Is that all?
B: Yes. Then, the robot will find the book and take it to the front desk.
G: So I can just go to the front desk and get the book?
B: Right. It's so easy, isn't it?
G: Yes, it's really amazing. Thank you.

02 빈칸 (A)에 들어갈 말을 고르시오.

① in ② for ③ on
④ at ⑤ about

서답형

03 위 대화의 빈칸 (B)에 들어갈 알맞은 말을 주어진 어휘를 배열하여 쓰시오.

you, me, it, how, tell, can, use, to

➡ ______________________

서답형

04 밑줄 친 (a)의 우리말에 맞게 주어진 어휘를 이용하여 영작하시오.

➡ ______________________

중요

05 도서 대출에 관한 위 대화의 내용과 일치하지 않는 것은?

① 로봇은 당신을 위해 책을 찾아 주는 로봇이다.
② 책을 대출하려면 먼저 도서 대출 카드를 로봇의 화면 위에 놓아야 한다.
③ 두 번째는 찾으려는 책의 제목을 입력하고 나서 ENTER 키를 눌러야 한다.
④ 그러면 로봇이 책을 찾아서 안내 데스크로 가져다준다.
⑤ 안내 데스크로 가면 로봇이 책을 건네준다.

서답형

06 대화가 자연스럽게 연결되도록 (A)~(C)를 적절하게 배열하시오.

A: Excuse me. I want to return these books. Do you know how to do it?
B: Sure. It's simple. First, insert the library card into the machine. Second, put the books in this box.
(A) Then just take your card out.
(B) OK.
(C) I really appreciate your help.

➡ ______________

[07~08] 다음 대화를 읽고 물음에 답하시오.

B: I want to buy a snack. ______(A)______ this snack machine?
G: Yeah. First, choose the snack you want.
B: I already __(B)__. What's next?
G: Just put in the money. Then take the snack out.

07 위 대화의 빈칸 (A)에 들어갈 알맞은 말로 가장 적절한 것은?

① Why don't you know how to use
② Shall we know how to use
③ Do you know how to use
④ Do you know when to use
⑤ Will you know how to use

08 위 대화의 빈칸 (B)에 알맞은 대동사를 쓰시오.

➡ ____________________

[09~10] 다음 대화를 읽고 물음에 답하시오.

A: Do you know how to make tea?
B: Sure. First, (a)[pour / put] a tea bag in a cup.
A: OK.
B: Then, (b)[pour / put] hot water in the cup.
A: And then?
B: Last, (c)[make / take] the tea bag out after 3 minutes.
A: I got it. ______(A)______

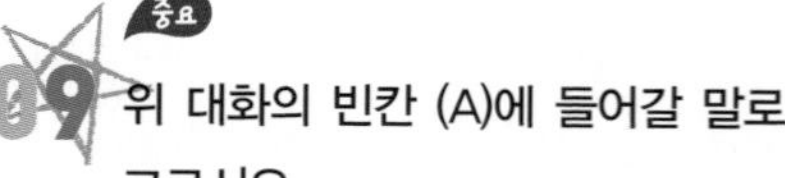

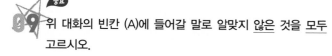

09 위 대화의 빈칸 (A)에 들어갈 말로 알맞지 않은 것을 모두 고르시오.

① I really appreciate your help.
② It's not a big deal.
③ Thank you.
④ It's my pleasure.
⑤ I can't thank you enough.

10 위 대화의 괄호 (a)~(c)에서 알맞은 것을 골라 바르게 짝지은 것은?

	(a)	(b)	(c)
①	put	pour	take
②	put	pour	make
③	put	put	make
④	pour	put	make
⑤	pour	pour	take

[11~13] 다음 대화를 읽고 물음에 답하시오.

A: Excuse me. (①) I want to add money to my transportation card. (②) Do you know how to do it?
B: (③) It's simple. (④) First, put your card in the machine. (⑤) Second, choose the amount of money.
A: OK.
B: Then insert the money.
A: (a)I really appreciate your help.

11 위 대화의 (①)~(⑤) 중 주어진 문장이 들어갈 곳은?

Sure.

① ② ③ ④ ⑤

중요

12 위 대화의 밑줄 친 (a)의 의도로 적절한 것은?

① 절차 표현하기 ② 축하 표현하기
③ 방법 답하기 ④ 유감 표현하기
⑤ 감사 표현하기

서답형

13 위 대화에 나타난 교통카드에 돈을 충전하는 방법의 두 번째 단계를 10자 내외의 우리말로 쓰시오.

➡ ____________________

[01~04] 다음 대화를 읽고 물음에 답하시오.

G: Excuse me, but what's this robot for?
B: Oh, (a)이것은 당신을 위해 책을 찾아 주는 로봇이에요. (a robot, it, find)
G: Really? Can you tell me how to use it?
(A) Second, type the title of the book you're looking for and then press ENTER.
(B) Is that all?
(C) OK.
(D) Sure. First, place your library card on the robot's screen.
B: Yes. Then, the robot will find the book and take it to the front desk.
G: So I can just go to the front desk and get the book?
B: Right. It's so easy, ___ⓐ___?
G: Yes, it's really amazing. Thank you.

01 위 대화의 (A)~(D)를 알맞은 순서로 배열하시오.

➡ ______________________

02 빈칸 ⓐ에 알맞은 부가의문문을 쓰시오.

➡ ______________________

03 괄호 안에 주어진 어휘를 이용하여 밑줄 친 (a)를 8 단어로 쓰시오.

➡ ______________________

04 Where does this conversation happen?

➡ ______________________

[05~06] 다음 글을 읽고 물음에 답하시오.

Let me tell you how to use a drink machine. First, insert money into the machine. Then, choose the drink you want. Last, take the drink (a)out of the machine. It's easy.

05 밑줄 친 (a)out of를 한 단어로 바꿔 쓰시오.

➡ ______________________

06 위 글에 나타난 음료 자판기 사용하는 법 3 단계를 우리말로 쓰시오.

➡ (1) ______________ (2) ______________
(3) ______________

[07~08] 다음 대화를 읽고 물음에 답하시오.

B: Excuse me. Can you tell me how to use this machine?
G: Sure. First, put the paper on the copy machine. Then choose the paper size and the number of copies.
B: Then (a)what?
G: Press the START button.
B: Thank you. I really appreciate your help.

07 위 대화에서 주어진 영영풀이에 해당하는 말을 찾아 쓰시오.

to thank someone in a polite way or to say that you are grateful for something they have done

➡ ______________________

08 밑줄 친 (a)what 뒤에 생략되어 있는 것을 should를 포함한 3 단어로 쓰시오.

➡ ______________________

교과서

Grammar

1 분사구문

- **Using** various methods, experts analyze big data.
  다양한 방법들을 사용하여 전문가들은 빅데이터를 분석했다.

■ 분사구문은 종속접속사가 이끄는 부사절을 분사를 이용하여 간략한 부사구로 바꾼 것이다.

- **While I was walking** along the street, I saw a man with five dogs.
  = **Walking** along the street, I saw a man with five dogs. 길을 걷다가, 나는 개 5마리와 함께 있는 남자를 보았다.

■ 부사구와 주절의 관계에 따라 양보, 동시동작, 이유, 시간, 조건 등의 의미로 쓰인다.

(1) 양보: **Although she is** rich, the woman always buys second-hand goods.
- **Being** rich, the woman always buys second-hand goods. 부유하지만, 그 여자는 늘 중고 물품을 산다.

(2) 동시동작(부대상황): **While he waved** his hand, he walked out of the house.
- **Waving** his hand, he walked out of the house. 손을 흔들며, 그는 집 밖으로 나왔다.

(3) 이유: **Because she was** disappointed with him, Hannah said nothing.
- **Being** disappointed with him, Hannah said nothing. 그에게 실망했기 때문에, Hannah는 아무 말도 하지 않았다.

(4) 시간: **When he works** alone, he uses the special program.
- **Working** alone, he uses the special program. 혼자 일할 때, 그는 그 특별한 프로그램을 사용한다.

(5) 조건: **If you turn** left, you'll see the post office.
- **Turning** left, you'll see the post office. 좌회전하면, 우체국이 보일 것이다.

■ 종속절의 시제가 주절보다 앞선 경우 완료분사구문을 사용한다.

- **As he had read** the book before, Mike lent it to her.
  = **Having read** the book before, Mike lent it to her.

■ 주절과 종속절의 주어가 다를 경우 분사구문의 주어를 남겨 두는 것을 독립분사구문이라고 하며, 일반인이 주어일 경우에는 생략이 가능하다. (비인칭 독립분사구문)

(1) 독립분사구문: **Since it is** windy, I can't play badminton.
= **It being** windy, I can't play badminton. 바람이 불어서, 나는 배드민턴을 칠 수 없다.

(2) 비인칭 독립분사구문: **generally speaking**(일반적으로 말해), **considering**(~를 고려하면)

(3) with+목적어+분사: My uncle fell asleep **with the light turned on**. (불을 켠 채로)

핵심 Check

1. 다음 괄호 안에서 알맞은 말을 고르시오.
(1) With summer (approaches / approaching), it got hotter and hotter.
(2) (Feeling / Felt) nervous, the player drank a glass of water.

2 접속사 as

• **As** information and communication technology develops, the amount of data we have is getting much greater than before. 정보 통신 기술이 발달함에 따라, 우리가 갖고 있는 데이터의 양이 이전보다 훨씬 많아지고 있다.

■ as는 종속접속사로 부사절을 이끈다.

• **As** time goes by, I love her even more. 시간이 지날수록 나는 그녀를 더욱 사랑한다.

• Minho plays the piano **as** his brother sings. 민호는 형이 노래할 때 피아노를 친다.

■ 접속사 as의 역할

(1) '비례' ~함에 따라서

• **As** it gets darker, she became more nervous. 어두워지면서, 그녀는 더 초조해졌다.

(2) '양태' ~하듯이, ~하는 것처럼, ~와 같이

• Do in Rome **as** the Romans do. 로마에서는 로마 사람들처럼 하라.

• She speaks as fast **as** her mother does. 그녀는 엄마만큼 빠르게 말한다.

(3) '이유' ~이기 때문에, ~이므로

• **As** the girl sings well, we will vote for her. 그녀가 노래를 잘해서, 우리는 그녀에게 투표할 것이다.

(4) '시간' ~할 때, ~하는 동안

• She showed up **as** I was talking. 내가 말하고 있을 때 그녀가 나타났다.

(5) '상태' ~인 채로, ~하는 대로

• Leave the thing **as** it is. 그것을 있는 그대로 두시오.

(6) '양보' ~라 할지라도, ~에도 불구하고

• Coward **as** he was, he didn't step back. 비록 겁쟁이였지만, 그는 뒤로 물러서지 않았다.

• Angry **as** she felt, she continued her work. 비록 화가 났지만, 그녀는 일을 계속했다.

■ 전치사 as: ~로, ~로서

• Shanon did well **as** his caretaker. Shanon은 그의 보호자로서 잘 해줬다.

• Mom treats me **as** a baby. 엄마는 나를 아기처럼 대한다.

핵심 Check

2. 다음 빈칸에 공통으로 들어갈 알맞은 단어를 고르시오. (대 · 소문자 구분 안 함)

• ________ I told you, we will meet at dawn at the bus stop.

• The girl got wiser ________ she grew.

• Thank you for your hard work ________ the leader of the team.

① when ② because ③ as ④ until ⑤ before

Grammar 시험대비 기본평가

Step2

01 다음 각 문장의 빈칸에 As[as]를 넣을 때 어색한 것은?

① ________ it was late at night, she went back to her room.
② Stand still ________ I told you.
③ ________ James was very tired, he went to bed early.
④ It's so noisy ________ I can't read my book.
⑤ The boy got wiser ________ he got older.

02 다음 부사절을 분사구문으로 바꿔 쓸 때, 빈칸에 들어갈 말로 가장 적절한 것은?

> As she wanted to buy some snacks, Kay put some money in his pocket.
> → ________ to buy some snacks, Kay put some money in his pocket.

① As she wanting ② She wanting ③ Having wanted
④ Being wanting ⑤ Wanting

03 다음 밑줄 친 부분 중 어법상 어색한 것을 고르시오.

① As Sam was intelligent, we relied on him.
② I was taking a shower as she visited my place.
③ Can you tell me as to use this snack machine?
④ Mary moved as the one in the screen danced.
⑤ As I was tired, I didn't arrange my desk.

04 다음 분사구문을 접속사가 이끄는 부사절로 만들 때, 빈칸에 알맞은 말을 써 넣으시오.

(1) Being absent from school, he couldn't take the test.
➡ As ________ ________ ________ ________ ________, he couldn't take the test.
(2) Watching Utube videos, Susan did her homework.
➡ While ________ ________ ________ ________, Susan did her homework.
(3) Feeling excited, she applied for the position.
➡ As ________ ________ ________, she applied for the position.
(4) Being short, Brian made a dunk shot.
➡ ________ ________ ________ ________, Brian made a dunk shot.

[01~02] 다음 밑줄 친 as 중 나머지 넷과 쓰임이 다른 하나는?

01 ① As I don't know how to add money to my card, I asked her.
② As Lynn talked with Tom, some people waved their hands to her.
③ Emma followed my step as I showed her the basic walking pose.
④ I asked him to recommend me a book as the owner of the bookstore.
⑤ The robot will find the book and take it to you as it is programmed.

02 (중요) ① As IT technology develops, the big data will do much for our society.
② As the CEO of the IT company, Peter Gates has much influence on the government policy.
③ Grace was loved by everyone in my college as she was kind and pretty.
④ Her confidence grew much bigger as she got accustomed to the position.
⑤ As the lady got ready for the party, her husband watched her silently.

[03~04] 다음 우리말을 어법상 알맞게 영작한 것을 고르시오.

03

그녀는 눈을 감은 채로 라디오에서 나오는 음악을 듣고 있었다.

① She was listening to music from the radio her eyes closing.
② She closed her eyes and listening to music from the radio.
③ She listened to music from the radio and closed her eyes.
④ She was listening to music from the radio with closed her eyes.
⑤ She was listening to music from the radio with her eyes closed.

04

많은 사람들을 행복하게 해줬는데도 불구하고, Chad는 외롭게 죽었다.

① Even though he having made many people happy, Chad died lonely.
② Although he making many people happy, Chad died lonely.
③ Having been made happy by many people, Chad died lonely.
④ Though having made many people happy, Chad died lonely.
⑤ He had made many people happy, though Chad died lonely.

05 (중요) 다음 빈칸에 공통으로 들어갈 알맞은 말을 고르시오.

(1) Jane started to exercise ________ she had seen herself in the mirror to be shocked. (2) David felt that it became harder to breathe ________ he tried to climb higher up. (3) The dog followed the movements ________ shown by the trainer.

① because ② as
③ while ④ when
⑤ what

서답형

06 다음 문장에서 어법상 어색한 단어 한 개를 찾아서 고치시오.

> Made sports more exciting, big data is improving the performance of the players.

__________ ➡ __________

07 다음 밑줄 친 as가 어법상 문장 속에서 옳게 쓰인 것을 고르시오.

① As smartphones have changed our lives, allowing us to watch movies on our phones.
② Do you know as to use this snack machine?
③ What happens as information and communication technology develops?
④ Did you know as health professionals can now forecast a disease just as weather experts forecast the weather?
⑤ With the help of this database, as Germany's national soccer team was able to improve its performance and win the 2014 World Cup.

중요

08 다음 밑줄 친 분사구문을 같은 의미의 부사절로 바꿔 쓸 때 적절하지 않은 것은?

① Walking along the street, she saw a man with twelve cats.
→ When she walked along the street,
② Waving her hands, the singer walked out of the train.
→ While she was waving her hands,
③ Eating a chicken sandwich, Tom waited for the bus.
→ As he was eating a chicken sandwich,
④ Using various methods, experts have analyzed big data.
→ As they use various methods,
⑤ Big data improves the performance, making sports more fun.
→ though it makes sports more fun.

09 다음 주어진 문장에서 밑줄 친 as와 가장 가까운 뜻의 as가 쓰인 것을 고르시오.

> Health professionals can now forecast a disease just as weather experts forecast the weather.

① Mina got wiser as she got older.
② As it was late at night, Brian and Kevin went back to their places.
③ You should show up at the bus stop as I told you.
④ All the audience felt too hot as the air conditioning system broke down.
⑤ Would you turn off the TV as you go out this evening?

10 다음 중 밑줄 친 분사구문의 용법이 <보기>와 같은 것은?

보기

> Living in Korea for over 15 years, Brian can't buy a thing at the supermarket.

① Not knowing how long Susan waited for her, Tracy was surprised at her cold face.
② Finishing his homework, Andrew went outside to play basketball.
③ Having nothing unusual to do, the boys lay on the playground.
④ Born in Paris, professor Sean Mika couldn't communicate well in French.
⑤ Turning right at the second corner, you will see the city hall.

11 다음 분사구문이 사용된 문장을 접속사를 이용한 부사절을 이용하여 바꿔 쓸 때, 가장 적절한 것은?

> The virus having come from his country, the Chinese diplomat criticized Korea for a slow response.

① Since the virus came from his country, the Chinese diplomat criticized Korea for a slow response.
② As the virus came from his country, the Chinese diplomat criticized Korea for a slow response.
③ If the virus had come from his country, the Chinese diplomat criticized Korea for a slow response.
④ Though the virus had come from his country, the Chinese diplomat criticized Korea for a slow response.
⑤ Before the virus had come from his country, the Chinese diplomat criticized Korea for a slow response.

서답형

[12~14] 우리말과 일치하도록 괄호 안에 주어진 단어들을 바르게 배열하시오.

12

> 그 축구 시합에서 부상을 당하고 싶지 않았기 때문에, Samuel은 천천히 경기했다.
> → (get, the, to, not, match, in, hurt, wanting, football), Samuel played slowly.

➡ ______________________

13

> 이상하게 들릴지 모르지만, 나는 결코 부자가 되고 싶지 않다.
> → (as, sound, strange, may, it), I never want to be rich.

➡ ______________________

14

> 천 년도 더 전에 건축되었음에도 불구하고, 그 사원은 몇 년 전에 지어진 것처럼 튼튼했다.
> → (been, than, having, more, though, built) a thousand years ago, the temple was as strong as it was built a few years ago.

➡ ______________________

[15~16] 다음 밑줄 친 부분이 어법상 옳지 않은 것을 고르시오.

15 ① As Carla lost her necklace at the hotel, she couldn't leave in time.
② As you lied to me, I could believe you more than ever.
③ As time went by, my uncle changed a lot after he became a lawyer.
④ As the passengers were talking on the road, the driver urged them to get on.
⑤ William took the medicine as he caught a cold.

중요

16 ① You should pay attention to the sensitive person like your mom as your sister does.
② The president is speaking to the young lady as a friend.
③ J. K. Rowling is widely known as the writer of the Harry Potter series.
④ As the couple was sitting down to dinner, someone rang the bell.
⑤ We arrived at the toy store so as they were about to close.

Grammar 서술형 시험대비

01 다음 각 밑줄 친 부분 중 어법상 어색한 것은 고쳐 다시 쓰고, 어색하지 않은 것은 '고칠 필요 없음'이라고 쓰시오.

(1) A little being tired, Timothy went to bed earlier than usual.

➡ ____________________

(2) Found the ring she had lost, I called Sujin to come home early.

➡ ____________________

(3) Having rained the day before, the roads to the concert got all wet.

➡ ____________________

(4) Having not a car, Paul couldn't take his daughter to the interview.

➡ ____________________

(5) Frankly speaking, the prime minster of Japan talks like an idiot.

➡ ____________________

02 중요 다음 <보기>에 있는 접속사를 한 번씩만 사용하여, 각 문장의 밑줄 친 분사구문을 부사절로 바꾸시오. (단, 진행형 불가, 주어는 가능한 대명사로 표현할 것.)

보기: while / because / when / if / though / and

(1) Using various methods, experts analyze big data and draw results from it.

➡ ____________________

(2) Having a problem that you cannot talk to me, try sharing it with a stranger.

➡ ____________________

(3) Being sick through the weekend, I could hand in the report on Monday morning.

➡ ____________________

(4) Not wanting to wake the sleeping baby up, her daddy quietly stood up.

➡ ____________________

____

(5) Big data improves the performance of players, making sports more exciting.

➡ ____________________

(6) Cleaning the windows of the kitchen, Sammy suddenly heard her cat meow from the front.

➡ ____________________

____

03 다음 우리말과 일치하도록 괄호 안에 주어진 단어들을 바르게 배열하여 문장을 완성하시오.

(1) 정보와 통신 기술이 발달함에 따라, 우리가 가진 데이터의 양도 전보다 더 커진다. (develops, and, information, as, technology, communication)

➡ ____________________

____________, the amount of data we have is getting greater than before.

(2) 우리의 몸이 우리의 마음을 변화시키는 것과 같이, 우리의 마음도 우리의 행동을 변화시킨다. (our minds, just, our bodies, as, change)

➡ ____________________, our minds also change our behavior.

(3) 그녀의 반에 친구들이 아무도 없었기 때문에, Jenny는 슬프고 외롭게 느꼈다. (her, friends, any, class, having, in, not)

➡ ____________________, Jenny felt sad and lonely.

(4) 다양한 방법들을 사용해서, 전문가들은 빅데이터를 분석하고 그것으로부터 의미 있는 결과를 이끌어낸다. (experts, using, analyze, methods, various)

➡ ____________________ big data and draw meaningful results from it.

04 다음 각 문장에서 어법상 어색한 단어를 한 개씩 찾아, 다른 한 단어로 고치거나 생략하여 옳은 문장으로 다시 쓰시오.

(1) Did you know that health professionals can forecast a disease just if weather experts forecast the weather?

➡ ______________________

(2) Big data helps companies understand their customers' needs better, as assisting them sell more products.

➡ ______________________

(3) Can you tell me as to add money to my transportation card?

➡ ______________________

(4) Germany's national soccer team was able to improve its performance, won the 2014 World Cup.

➡ ______________________

05 다음 밑줄 친 As로 시작하는 부사절을 알맞은 분사구문으로 전환하여 빈칸을 채우시오.

> As she was singing to the radio music, Riley got a message from downstair.

➡ ______________________ Riley got a message from downstair.

06 다음 그림과 학생들의 발표 내용을 보고, 질문에 답하시오.

> (A)설문 조사에 근거해서 우리는 경주를 골랐습니다. Ten students think that (B)수학 여행지를 고를 때, 가장 중요한 것은 '활동'이다. (C) After we searched for some data online, we found out that there are many things to see and do in Gyeongju.

(1) 밑줄 친 (A)의 우리말에 맞게 다음에 주어진 단어를 알맞은 순서로 배열하시오.
(survey, Gyeongju, on, we, chose, our, based)

➡ ______________________

(2) 밑줄 친 (B)의 우리말에 맞게 다음에 주어진 단어를 활용하여, 총 11 단어로 영작하시오. (동사 형태는 알맞게 변형 가능, 첫 단어는 activities로 시작할 것.)
(choose, be, a field trip place, when, important)

➡ ______________________

(3) 밑줄 친 (C)를 5 단어의 분사구문으로 전환하시오.

➡ ______________________

(4) 위의 발표 내용을 아래와 같이 한 문장으로 요약할 때, 빈칸에 공통으로 들어갈 알맞은 단어를 쓰시오.

> ________ students think it important to do activities, we selected Gyeongju ________ our field trip place.

교과서

Reading

Living with Big Data

Have you ever visited an online bookstore and been surprised by the books that the store recommended for you? Many of them looked interesting to you. So how did the bookstore know what you liked? This is all possible because of big data.

(Have you ever visited: 경험을 나타내는 현재완료 / that = which / what은 의문사로 해석될 수도 있고 선행사를 포함한 관계대명사로도 해석될 수 있다.)

What is big data?

Big data is data sets that are very big and complex. As information and communication technology develops, the amount of data we have is getting much greater than before. This is mainly because almost everything that we do online leaves a trace. For example, the photos you upload on your blog and the records of your purchases at online stores are all part of big data.

(As: ~함에 따라서(접속사) / data we have: 앞에 목적격 관계대명사 which/that 생략 / getting much greater: get+비교급: 점점 더 ~해지다, much로 비교급 강조)

Simply collecting data, however, is not enough. Big data has to be analyzed, and this is done by big data experts. Using various methods, experts analyze big data and draw meaningful results from it. These results then can be used to make decisions or to predict the future.

(collecting data: 주어로 쓰인 동명사구–단수 취급 / Using various methods: 분사구문, 다양한 방법들을 사용하여)

How is big data influencing our lives?

Big data is influencing almost all parts of our lives. It helps companies understand their customers' needs better and helps them sell more products. It helps people avoid heavy traffic. Its uses are endless, and here are some interesting examples.

(It = big data / helps companies understand: help+목적어+목적격보어(to부정사 또는 동사원형): ~가 …하도록 돕다)

communication 의사소통, 연락
develop 성장하다, 발달하다
amount 총계, 총액
trace 자취, 발자국, 흔적
purchase 구매
analyze 분석하다
method 방법
predict 예측하다
influence 영향을 미치다
avoid 피하다, 방지하다
traffic 교통(량)
endless 끝없는, 무한한

확인문제

- 다음 문장이 본문의 내용과 일치하면 T, 일치하지 않으면 F를 쓰시오.

1 Big data is data sets that are very big and complicated. ☐
2 Almost everything that we do offline leaves a trace. ☐
3 The photos you upload on your blog are all part of big data. ☐
4 Simply collecting data is enough. ☐
5 Big data is affecting almost all parts of our lives. ☐
6 The uses of big data are finite. ☐

Disease Forecast

Did you know that health professionals can now forecast a disease just as weather experts forecast the weather? This is possible thanks to big data. For example, when the flu season comes, people will buy more flu medicine. They will also search online about flu symptoms more. If this kind of data is analyzed wisely, the spread of the flu can be predicted.

- just: 꼭
- as: ~하는 것처럼
- when은 부사절을 이끄는 접속사. 'when+주어+동사 ~, 주어+동사' 형태로 주로 쓰임.
- when절에서는 미래의 일이라고 해도 현재시제로 씀.
- is analyzed: 수동태

Improving Performance in Sports

Are you a sports fan? Well, big data is improving the performance of players, making sports more exciting. A famous example is Germany's national soccer team. The team built a database by collecting and analyzing a huge amount of data on players. For example, the data included information about how much each player ran and how long he had the ball. With the help of this database, Germany's national soccer team was able to improve its performance and win the 2014 World Cup.

- making 이하는 분사구문으로 '~ 하면서'
- 전치사 by의 목적어로 쓰인 동명사
- 간접의문문(의문사+주어+동사)으로 전치사 about의 목적어로 쓰인 명사절

Crime Prevention

Thanks to big data, police can now predict crime before it happens. Through the analysis of big data about the type, time and place of crime, police can make a map of crime hot spots. This map identifies when and where crime is most likely to happen. Police can prevent further crime by focusing on the areas and the times this map predicts.

- Thanks to: ~ 덕분에
- police는 단수형이지만 복수 취급
- it: = crime
- 간접의문문(의문사+주어+동사)으로 identifies의 목적어 역할
- 앞에 목적격 관계대명사 which/that이 생략되었음.

Big data has already changed the world greatly. So where will the big data industry go from here? Nobody knows for sure, but experts agree that big data will play a more and more important role in our lives.

- know의 목적어로 바로 앞 문장이 생략되었음.
- play an important role: 중요한 역할을 하다

flu 독감
symptom 증상
wisely 현명하게, 지혜롭게
spread 확산, 전파
improve 개선하다, 향상하다
performance 경기력, 수행, 성과
database 데이터베이스
huge 거대한, (크기 · 양 · 정도가) 막대한
include 포함하다
crime 범죄
prevention 예방
thanks to ~ ~ 덕분에
hot spot 다발 지역
identify 알아보다, 확인하다, 식별하다
be likely to ~할 것 같다
further 더 이상의, 추가의
focus on ~에 초점을 맞추다
play a role 역할을 하다
for sure 확실히

● 다음 문장이 본문의 내용과 일치하면 T, 일치하지 않으면 F를 쓰시오.

1 Health experts can now forecast a disease just as weather professionals forecast the weather. ☐

2 Germany's national soccer team built a database by collecting and analyzing a small amount of data on players. ☐

3 Police can make a map of crime hot spots by analyzing big data about the type, time and place of crime. ☐

4 Big data has not changed the world yet. ☐

Reading 교과서 확인학습 A

• 우리말을 참고하여 빈칸에 알맞은 말을 쓰시오.

1 ________ ________ Big Data

2 Have you ever visited an online bookstore and been surprised by the books that the store ________ ________ you?

3 Many of them ________ ________ to you.

4 So how did the bookstore know ________ ________ ________?

5 This is all possible ________ ________ big data.

6 ________ ________ big data?

7 Big data is ________ ________ that are very big and ________.

8 ________ information and communication technology develops, the amount of data we have is ________ ________ ________ than before.

9 This is mainly because almost everything that we do online ________ ________ ________.

10 For example, the photos you ________ ________ ________ ________ and the records of ________ ________ at online stores are ________ ________ ________ big data.

11 ________ ________ ________, however, is not enough.

12 Big data ________ ________ ________ ________, and this is done by big data experts.

13 ________ various methods, experts analyze big data and ________ meaningful results from it.

14 These results then ________ ________ ________ to make decisions or to predict the future.

15 ________ is big data influencing our lives?

16 Big data is influencing ________ ________ ________ of our lives.

17 It helps companies understand ________ ________ ________ better and helps them ________ ________ ________.

18 It helps people ________ ________ ________.

19 Its uses are ________, and here are some ________ ________.

20 Disease ________

1 빅데이터와 함께 살아가기
2 당신은 온라인 서점을 방문해서 그 서점이 당신을 위해 추천한 책들을 보고 놀란 적이 있는가?
3 그것들 중에 많은 것들이 당신에게 흥미로워 보였다.
4 그 서점은 당신이 무엇을 좋아하는지 어떻게 알았을까?
5 이것은 모두 빅데이터 때문에 가능하다.
6 빅데이터는 무엇인가?
7 빅데이터는 매우 크고 복잡한 데이터 집합이다.
8 정보 통신 기술이 발달함에 따라 우리가 갖고 있는 정보의 양도 이전보다 훨씬 더 많아지고 있다.
9 이것은 주로 우리가 온라인상에서 하는 거의 모든 것들이 흔적을 남기기 때문이다.
10 예를 들어, 당신이 블로그에 올린 사진들과 온라인 상점에서의 구매 기록들이 모두 빅데이터의 일부가 된다.
11 하지만 단순히 데이터를 수집하는 것만으로는 충분하지 않다.
12 빅데이터는 분석되어야 하고, 이것은 빅데이터 전문가들에 의해서 이루어진다.
13 다양한 방법들을 사용하여 전문가들은 빅데이터를 분석하고, 그것으로부터 의미 있는 결과들을 도출한다.
14 그런 다음, 이런 결과들은 결정을 하거나 또는 미래를 예측하는 데 사용될 수 있다.
15 빅데이터는 어떻게 우리 삶에 영향을 미치고 있는가?
16 빅데이터는 우리 삶의 거의 모든 부분에 영향을 미치고 있다.
17 그것은 회사들이 소비자들이 필요로 하는 것을 더 잘 이해하고 그들이 더 많은 상품을 팔도록 도와준다.
18 그것은 사람들이 교통 체증을 피하도록 도와주기도 한다.
19 그것의 활용은 끝이 없고, 여기에 몇 가지 흥미로운 예들이 있다.
20 질병 예측

21 Did you know that health professionals can now forecast a disease ________ ________ weather experts forecast the weather?

22 This is possible ________ ________ big data.

23 For example, when the flu season ________, people ________ ________ more flu medicine.

24 They will also ________ ________ ________ flu symptoms more.

25 If this kind of data ________ ________ ________, the spread of the flu can be predicted.

26 ________ ________ in Sports

27 Are you a ________ ________?

28 Well, big data is improving the performance of players, ________ sports more ________.

29 A famous example is Germany's ________ ________ ________.

30 The team built a database by ________ and ________ a huge amount of data on players.

31 For example, the data included information about ________ ________ each player ran and ________ ________ he had the ball.

32 ________ ________ ________ ________ this database, Germany's national soccer team was able to improve its performance and win the 2014 World Cup.

33 Crime ________

34 ________ ________ big data, police can now predict crime before it happens.

35 ________ the analysis of big data about the type, time and place of crime, police can make a map of ________ ________ ________.

36 This map identifies when and where crime ________ ________ ________ ________ ________.

37 Police can prevent ________ ________ by focusing on the areas and the times this map ________.

38 Big data ________ ________ ________ the world greatly.

39 So where will the big data industry ________ ________ ________?

40 Nobody knows for sure, but experts agree that big data will ________ a more and more important ________ in our lives.

21 당신은 날씨 전문가가 날씨를 예측하는 것과 같이 건강 전문가들이 현재 질병을 예측할 수 있다는 것을 알고 있는가?
22 이것은 빅데이터 덕분에 가능하다.
23 예를 들어서 독감의 계절이 오면, 사람들은 독감 약을 더 많이 구입할 것이다.
24 그들은 또한 온라인상에서 독감 증상들을 더 찾아볼 것이다.
25 만약 이런 종류의 데이터를 지혜롭게 분석한다면, 독감의 확산을 예측할 수 있다.
26 스포츠에서의 경기력 향상
27 당신은 스포츠 팬인가?
28 빅데이터는 스포츠를 더 흥미롭게 만들면서, 선수들의 경기력을 향상하고 있다.
29 유명한 사례로 독일 국가 대표 축구팀이 있다.
30 그 팀은 선수들에 관한 엄청난 양의 데이터를 모으고 분석함으로써, 데이터베이스를 구축했다.
31 예를 들어 데이터는 각각의 선수들이 얼마나 많이 달렸고, 얼마나 오랫동안 공을 소유했는지도 포함했다.
32 이 데이터베이스의 도움으로 독일 국가 대표 축구팀은 경기력을 향상할 수 있었고, 2014년 월드컵에서 우승할 수 있었다.
33 범죄 예방
34 빅데이터 덕분에 경찰은 이제 범죄가 발생하기 전에 범죄를 예측할 수 있다.
35 범죄의 유형, 시간 및 장소에 관한 빅데이터의 분석을 통해, 경찰은 범죄 다발 지역의 지도를 만들 수 있다.
36 이 지도는 범죄가 언제, 어디에서 가장 많이 발생할 것 같은지를 알려 준다.
37 경찰은 이 지도가 예측하는 장소들과 시간대에 집중함으로써, 추가 범죄를 예방할 수 있다.
38 빅데이터는 이미 세계를 크게 변화시켰다.
39 그러면 빅데이터 산업은 여기에서부터 어디로 가게 될까?
40 누구도 확실히 알지는 못하지만, 전문가들은 빅데이터가 우리 삶에서 더욱 더 중요한 역할을 할 것이라는 데에는 동의한다.

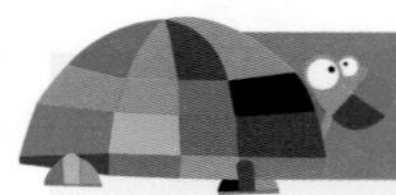

Reading 교과서 확인학습 B

• 우리말을 참고하여 본문을 영작하시오.

1 빅데이터와 함께 살아가기
➡ ______________________

2 당신은 온라인 서점을 방문해서 그 서점이 당신을 위해 추천한 책들을 보고 놀란 적이 있는가?
➡ ______________________

3 그것들 중에 많은 것들이 당신에게 흥미로워 보였다.
➡ ______________________

4 그 서점은 당신이 무엇을 좋아하는지 어떻게 알았을까?
➡ ______________________

5 이것은 모두 빅데이터 때문에 가능하다.
➡ ______________________

6 빅데이터는 무엇인가?
➡ ______________________

7 빅데이터는 매우 크고 복잡한 데이터 집합이다.
➡ ______________________

8 정보 통신 기술이 발달함에 따라 우리가 갖고 있는 정보의 양도 이전보다 훨씬 더 많아지고 있다.
➡ ______________________

9 이것은 주로 우리가 온라인상에서 하는 거의 모든 것들이 흔적을 남기기 때문이다.
➡ ______________________

10 예를 들어, 당신이 블로그에 올린 사진들과 온라인 상점에서의 구매 기록들이 모두 빅데이터의 일부가 된다.
➡ ______________________

11 하지만 단순히 데이터를 수집하는 것만으로는 충분하지 않다.
➡ ______________________

12 빅데이터는 분석되어야 하고, 이것은 빅데이터 전문가들에 의해서 이루어진다.
➡ ______________________

13 다양한 방법들을 사용하여 전문가들은 빅데이터를 분석하고, 그것으로부터 의미 있는 결과들을 도출한다.
➡ ______________________

14 그런 다음, 이런 결과들은 결정을 하거나 또는 미래를 예측하는 데 사용될 수 있다.
➡ ______________________

15 빅데이터는 어떻게 우리 삶에 영향을 미치고 있는가?
➡ ______________________

16 빅데이터는 우리 삶의 거의 모든 부분에 영향을 미치고 있다.
➡ ______________________

17 그것은 회사들이 소비자들이 필요로 하는 것을 더 잘 이해하고 그들이 더 많은 상품을 팔도록 도와준다.
➡ ______________________

18 그것은 사람들이 교통 체증을 피하도록 도와주기도 한다.
➡ ______________________

19 그것의 활용은 끝이 없고, 여기에 몇 가지 흥미로운 예들이 있다.
➡ ______________________

20 질병 예측
➡ ______________________

21 당신은 날씨 전문가가 날씨를 예측하는 것과 같이 건강 전문가들이 현재 질병을 예측할 수 있다는 것을 알고 있는가?

➡

22 이것은 빅데이터 덕분에 가능하다.

➡

23 예를 들어서 독감의 계절이 오면, 사람들은 독감 약을 더 많이 구입할 것이다.

➡

24 그들은 또한 온라인상에서 독감 증상들을 더 찾아볼 것이다.

➡

25 만약 이런 종류의 데이터를 지혜롭게 분석한다면, 독감의 확산을 예측할 수 있다.

➡

26 스포츠에서의 경기력 향상

➡

27 당신은 스포츠 팬인가?

➡

28 빅데이터는 스포츠를 더 흥미롭게 만들면서, 선수들의 경기력을 향상하고 있다.

➡

29 유명한 사례로 독일 국가 대표 축구팀이 있다.

➡

30 그 팀은 선수들에 관한 엄청난 양의 데이터를 모으고 분석함으로써, 데이터베이스를 구축했다.

➡

31 예를 들어 데이터는 각각의 선수들이 얼마나 많이 달렸고, 얼마나 오랫동안 공을 소유했는지도 포함했다.

➡

32 이 데이터베이스의 도움으로 독일 국가 대표 축구팀은 경기력을 향상할 수 있었고, 2014년 월드컵에서 우승할 수 있었다.

➡

33 범죄 예방

➡

34 빅데이터 덕분에 경찰은 이제 범죄가 발생하기 전에 범죄를 예측할 수 있다.

➡

35 죄의 유형, 시간 및 장소에 관한 빅데이터의 분석을 통해, 경찰은 범죄 다발 지역의 지도를 만들 수 있다.

➡

36 이 지도는 범죄가 언제, 어디에서 가장 많이 발생할 것 같은지를 알려 준다.

➡

37 경찰은 이 지도가 예측하는 장소들과 시간대에 집중함으로써, 추가 범죄를 예방할 수 있다.

➡

38 빅데이터는 이미 세계를 크게 변화시켰다.

➡

39 그러면 빅데이터 산업은 여기에서부터 어디로 가게 될까?

➡

40 누구도 확실히 알지는 못하지만, 전문가들은 빅데이터가 우리 삶에서 더욱 더 중요한 역할을 할 것이라는 데에는 동의한다.

➡

Reading 시험대비 실력평가

[01~03] 다음 글을 읽고 물음에 답하시오.

ⓐHave you ever visited an online bookstore and been surprised by the books that the store recommended for you? Many of them looked interesting to you. So ⓑ그 서점은 당신이 무엇을 좋아하는지 어떻게 알았을까? ⓒThis is all possible because of big data.

01 위 글의 밑줄 친 ⓐ와 현재완료의 용법이 같은 것을 고르시오.

① Have you been to the bank yet?
② I have read this novel three times.
③ She has been sick since he came here.
④ He has gone to Seoul.
⑤ He has lived here for ten years.

서답형

02 위 글의 밑줄 친 ⓑ의 우리말에 맞게 주어진 어휘를 알맞게 배열하시오.

the bookstore, you, how, what, know, liked, did

➡ ____________________

서답형

03 위 글의 밑줄 친 ⓒThis가 가리키는 것을 우리말로 쓰시오.

➡ ____________________

____

[04~06] 다음 글을 읽고 물음에 답하시오.

______ⓐ______

Thanks to big data, police can now predict crime before it happens. Through the analysis of big data about the type, time and place of crime, police can make a map of crime hot spots. This map identifies when and where crime is most likely to ⓑhappen. Police can prevent further crime by focusing on the areas and the times this map predicts.

Big data ⓒhas already changed the world greatly. So where will the big data industry go from here? Nobody knows for sure, but experts agree that big data will play a more and more important role in our lives.

중요

04 위 글의 빈칸 ⓐ에 들어갈 제목으로 알맞은 것을 고르시오.

① What is Big Data?
② How to Draw a Map Using Big Data
③ How Is Big Data Influencing Our Jobs?
④ Crime Prevention
⑤ Various Crime Hot Spots

05 위 글의 밑줄 친 ⓑhappen과 바꿔 쓸 수 없는 말을 고르시오.

① occur
② take place
③ arise
④ cause
⑤ come about

중요

06 아래 <보기>에서 위 글의 밑줄 친 ⓒhas already changed와 현재완료의 용법이 다른 것의 개수를 고르시오.

보기

① I have been in Korea for five years.
② I have just finished my homework.
③ I have never seen such a strange thing before.
④ Has she done her homework yet?
⑤ She has lost her bag.

① 1개 ② 2개 ③ 3개 ④ 4개 ⑤ 5개

[07~09] 다음 글을 읽고 물음에 답하시오.

ⓐ ______________________

Big data is influencing almost all parts of our lives. It helps companies understand their customers' needs better and helps them sell more products. It helps people avoid heavy traffic. Its uses are endless, and here are some interesting examples.

Disease Forecast

Did you know that health professionals can now forecast a disease just as weather experts forecast the weather? This is possible thanks to big data. ⓑFor example, when the flu season will come, people will buy more flu medicine. They will also search online about flu symptoms more. If this kind of data is analyzed wisely, the spread of the flu can be predicted.

07 위 글의 빈칸 ⓐ에 들어갈 제목으로 알맞은 것을 고르시오.

① How Does Big Data Help Companies?
② The Benefit of Big Data
③ How to Sell More Products Using Big Data
④ How Is Big Data Influencing Our Lives?
⑤ The Best Way to Avoid Heavy Traffic

서답형

08 위 글의 밑줄 친 ⓑ에서 어법상 틀린 부분을 찾아 고치시오.

__________ ➡ __________

중요

09 Which question CANNOT be answered after reading the passage?

① What is big data influencing?
② How can companies understand their customers' needs better?
③ Can health professionals now forecast a disease?
④ How do weather experts forecast the weather?
⑤ How can the spread of the flu be predicted?

[10~12] 다음 글을 읽고 물음에 답하시오.

ⓐ ______________________

Big data is data sets that are very big and complex. As information and communication technology develops, the amount of data we have is getting much greater than before. (①) This is mainly because almost everything that we do online leaves a trace. (②) For example, the photos you upload on your blog and the records of your purchases at online stores are all part of big data.

(③) Big data has to be analyzed, and this is done by big data experts. (④) Using various methods, experts analyze big data and draw meaningful results from it. (⑤) These results then can be used to make decisions or to predict the future.

10 위 글의 흐름으로 보아, 주어진 문장이 들어가기에 가장 적절한 곳은?

Simply collecting data, however, is not enough.

① ② ③ ④ ⑤

중요
11 위 글의 빈칸 ⓐ에 들어갈 제목으로 알맞은 것을 고르시오.

① The Increasing Amount of Data
② What is Big Data?
③ Our Online Activity Leaves a Trace
④ How to Record the Purchases at Online
⑤ How Is Big Data Influencing Our Lives?

12 According to the passage, which is NOT true?

① Big data is very big and complex data sets.
② Almost everything that we do online leaves a trace.
③ The records of your purchases at the street stalls are included in big data.
④ It is not enough to simply collect data.
⑤ Big data experts analyze big data.

[13~15] 다음 글을 읽고 물음에 답하시오.

Improving Performance in Sports

Are you a sports fan? Well, big data is improving the performance of players, (A) <u>making sports more exciting</u>. A famous example is Germany's national soccer team. The team built a database ___ⓐ___ collecting and analyzing a huge amount of data on players. For example, the data included information about how much each player ran and how long he had the ball. ___ⓑ___ the help of this database, Germany's national soccer team was able to improve its performance and win the 2014 World Cup.

13 위 글의 빈칸 ⓐ와 ⓑ에 들어갈 전치사가 바르게 짝지어진 것은?

① in – By ② by – On
③ by – With ④ in – On
⑤ on – With

서답형
14 위 글의 밑줄 친 (A)를 접속사와 주어, 동사를 포함하는 절로 바꾸시오.

➡ ________________________________

중요
15 위 글의 주제로 알맞은 것을 고르시오.

① the reaction of big sports fans to big data
② the improvement of the team's performance thanks to the database
③ the way to make sports more exciting
④ how to collect and analyze a huge amount of data on players
⑤ the information that can be included in the data

[16~18] 다음 글을 읽고 물음에 답하시오.

Crime Prevention

___ⓐ___ big data, police can now predict crime before ⓑ<u>it</u> happens. (A)[Though / Through] the analysis of big data about the type, time and place of crime, police can make a map of crime hot spots. This map identifies when and where crime is most likely to happen. Police can prevent (B) [farther / further] crime by focusing on the areas and the times this map predicts.

Big data has already changed the world greatly. So where will the big data industry go from here? Nobody knows for sure, but experts (C)[agree / disagree] that big data will play a more and more important role in our lives.

16 위 글의 빈칸 ⓐ에 들어갈 알맞은 말을 <u>모두</u> 고르시오.

① In spite of ② Thanks to
③ Rather than ④ Because of
⑤ Instead of

서답형

17 위 글의 밑줄 친 ⓑit이 가리키는 것을 본문에서 찾아 쓰시오.

➡ ____________________

서답형

18 위 글의 괄호 (A)~(C)에서 문맥이나 어법상 알맞은 낱말을 골라 쓰시오.

➡ (A) ________ (B) ________ (C) ________

[19~21] 다음 글을 읽고 물음에 답하시오.

Improving Performance in Sports

Are you a sports fan? Well, big data is improving the performance of players, ⓐmaking sports more exciting. A famous example is Germany's national soccer team. The team built a database by collecting and analyzing a ⓑhuge amount of data on players. For example, the data included information about ⓒ각각의 선수들이 얼마나 많이 달렸고, 얼마나 오랫동안 공을 소유했는지. With the help of this database, Germany's national soccer team was able to improve its performance and win the 2014 World Cup.

19 아래 <보기>에서 위 글의 밑줄 친 ⓐmaking과 문법적 쓰임이 다른 것의 개수를 고르시오.

보기

① We liked eating pizza.
② I saw Linda crossing the street.
③ My hobby is playing baseball.
④ Walking to school makes me tired.
⑤ She watched TV eating some snacks.

① 1개 ② 2개 ③ 3개 ④ 4개 ⑤ 5개

20 위 글의 밑줄 친 ⓑhuge와 바꿔 쓸 수 없는 말을 모두 고르시오.

① enormous ② tiny ③ vast
④ tremendous ⑤ minute

서답형

21 위 글의 밑줄 친 ⓒ의 우리말에 맞게 주어진 어휘를 알맞게 배열하시오.

each player / had / ran / how much / and / the ball / he / how long

➡ ____________________
____

[22~24] 다음 글을 읽고 물음에 답하시오.

How is big data influencing our lives?

ⓐ빅데이터는 우리 삶의 거의 모든 부분에 영향을 미치고 있다. ⓑIt helps companies understand their customers' needs better and helps them sell more products. It helps people avoid heavy traffic. Its uses are endless, and here are some interesting examples.

서답형

22 위 글의 밑줄 친 ⓐ의 우리말에 맞게 주어진 어휘를 이용하여 10 단어로 영작하시오.

influencing, parts

➡ ____________________

서답형

23 위 글의 밑줄 친 ⓑIt이 가리키는 것을 본문에서 찾아 쓰시오.

➡ ____________________

서답형

24 위 글을 읽고 빅데이터의 활용 사례 3가지를 우리말로 쓰시오.

➡ (1) ____________________
(2) ____________________
(3) ____________________

[01~03] 다음 글을 읽고 물음에 답하시오.

What is big data?

Big data is data sets that are very big and complex. As information and communication technology develops, the amount of data we have is getting much greater than before. This is mainly because almost everything that we do online leaves a trace. For example, the photos you upload on your blog and the records of your purchases at online stores are all part of big data.

Simply collecting data, however, is not enough. Big data has to ___ⓐ___, and this is done by big data experts. Using various methods, experts analyze big data and draw meaningful results from ⓑit. These results then can be used to make decisions or to predict the future.

01 위 글의 빈칸 ⓐ에 analyze를 알맞은 형태로 쓰시오.

➡ ______________________

02 위 글의 밑줄 친 ⓑit이 가리키는 것을 본문의 단어를 변형하여 쓰시오.

➡ ______________________

중요

03 본문의 내용과 일치하도록 다음 빈칸 (A)와 (B)에 알맞은 단어를 쓰시오.

Big data is (A)________ ________ ________ ________ data sets and (B)________ ________ ________ analyze big data and draw meaningful results from it.

[04~06] 다음 글을 읽고 물음에 답하시오.

How is big data influencing our lives?

Big data is influencing almost all parts of our lives. It helps companies understand their customers' needs better and helps them sell more products. It helps people avoid heavy traffic. ⓐIts uses are limited, and here are some interesting examples.

Disease Forecast

Did you know that health professionals can now forecast a disease just as weather experts forecast the weather? This is possible thanks to big data. For example, when the flu season comes, people will buy more flu medicine. They will also search online about flu symptoms more. ⓑIf this kind of data is analyzed wisely, the spread of the flu can be predicted.

고난이도

04 위 글의 밑줄 친 ⓐ에서 흐름상 어색한 부분을 찾아 고치시오.

____________ ➡ ____________ 또는

____

05 How is it possible for health professionals to forecast a disease just as weather experts forecast the weather? Answer in English with 4 words.

➡ ______________________

중요

06 위 글의 밑줄 친 ⓑ를 we를 주어로 하여 능동태로 고치시오.

➡ ______________________

____

[07~10] 다음 글을 읽고 물음에 답하시오.

Improving Performance in Sports

Are you a sports fan? ⓐWell, big data is improving the performance of players, making sports more excited. A famous example is Germany's national soccer team. The team built a database by collecting and analyzing a huge amount of data on players. For example, ⓑthe data included information about how much each player ran and how long he had the ball. With the help of this database, Germany's national soccer team was able to improve ⓒits performance and win the 2014 World Cup.

07 위 글의 밑줄 친 ⓐ에서 어법상 틀린 부분을 찾아 고치시오.

________ ➡ ________

중요

08 위 글의 밑줄 친 ⓑthe data에 포함된 정보 두 가지를 우리말로 쓰시오.

➡ (1) ________________

(2) ________________

09 위 글의 밑줄 친 ⓒits가 가리키는 것을 본문에서 찾아 쓰시오.

➡ ________________

10 How was it possible for Germany's national soccer team to build a database? Fill in the blanks (A) and (B) with suitable words.

> The team (A)________ and (B)________ a huge amount of data on players to build a database.

[11~14] 다음 글을 읽고 물음에 답하시오.

Crime Prevention

ⓐThanks to big data, police can now predict crime after it happens. Through the analysis of big data about the type, time and place of crime, police can make a map of crime hot spots. ⓑThis map identifies when and where crime is most likely to happen. Police can prevent further crime by focusing on the areas and the times this map predicts.

Big data has already changed the world greatly. So where will the big data industry go from here? Nobody knows for sure, but experts agree that big data will play a more and more important ⓒrole in our lives.

11 위 글의 밑줄 친 ⓐ에서 흐름상 어색한 부분을 찾아 고치시오.

________ ➡ ________

고난이도

12 위 글의 밑줄 친 ⓑThis map의 역할 두 가지를 우리말로 쓰시오.

➡ (1) ________________

(2) ________________

13 위 글의 밑줄 친 ⓒrole과 바꿔 쓸 수 있는 한 단어를 쓰시오.

➡ ________________

중요

14 다음 빈칸 (A)와 (B)에 알맞은 단어를 넣어 경찰이 범죄 다발 지역의 지도를 만드는 방법을 완성하시오.

> Police can make a map of crime hot spots by (A)________ big data about the type, time and place of (B)________.

교과서

구석구석

After You Read B Read and Complete

Example 1

Health professionals (= experts) can now forecast the spread of the flu by analyzing (전치사 by의 목적어로 쓰인 동명사) the sales of flu medicine and online searches about flu symptoms.

Example 2

By collecting and analyzing (collecting과 analyzing은 전치사 by의 목적어로 쓰인 동명사) a huge amount of data on players, Germany's national soccer team was able to improve its (Germany's national soccer team을 가리킨다.) performance and win the 2014 World Cup.

Example 3

Through the analysis of big data, police (police는 복수 형태의 명사는 아니지만 복수 취급한다.) can make a map of crime hot spots and use it to prevent (to부정사의 부사적 용법(목적)) further crime.

구문해설 • forecast 예측하다 • spread 확산, 전파 • flu 독감 • symptom 증상 • huge 거대한, (크기 · 양 · 정도가) 막대한 • performance 경기력, 수행, 성과 • crime 범죄 • hot spot 다발 지역 • prevent 예방하다 • further 더 이상의, 추가의

해석

사례 1

건강 전문가들은 독감 약 판매와 독감 증상에 관한 온라인 검색을 분석함으로써 이제 감기의 확산을 예측할 수 있다.

사례 2

독일 국가 대표 축구팀은 선수들에 관한 엄청난 양의 데이터를 모으고 분석함으로써, 경기력을 향상하고 2014년 월드컵에서 우승할 수 있었다.

사례 3

빅데이터의 분석을 통해서 경찰은 범죄 다발 지역의 지도를 만들 수 있고 그것을 추가 범죄를 예방하는 데에 사용할 수 있다.

Around the World

Yuna: We're not late. The bus will arrive in 4 minutes. (in+시간: [경과] (지금부터) ~ 후에)

Computer: Last time, you missed question numbers 3 and 5, so let's review them (= question numbers 3 and 5) first.

Yuna: What's the weather like tomorrow? (= How's the weather tomorrow?)

AI: It's going to rain. Take (= bring) your umbrella.

Yuna: Big data is making my life so much (비교급 수식 (= even, far, a lot, still)) easier!

구문해설 • review: 복습하다 • take: 가지고 가다, 휴대하다

유나: 늦지 않았네. 버스가 4분 후에 도착할 거야.

컴퓨터: 지난번에 당신은 3번과 5번 문제를 틀렸습니다. 그러니 우선 그것들부터 복습해 봅시다.

유나: 내일 날씨가 어때?

AI: 비가 올 예정입니다. 우산 챙기세요.

유나: 빅데이터는 내 삶을 훨씬 더 쉽게 만들고 있구나!

Think and Write

Teens' Free Time Activities

We asked 100 teenagers about their free time activities. The results show that (접속사(명사절)) the free time activity the teenagers (목적격 관계대명사 생략(which/that)) want to do the most is traveling (동명사(보어)). 34% said that they want (시제 일치 예외(현재 사실)) to travel in their free time. However, the free time activity they actually do the most is watching (동명사(보어)) TV. 39% said that they watch (시제 일치 예외(현재 사실)) TV in their free time. Looking at (분사구문(= As/When we look at)) the results, we see (알게 되다(= find, learn)) that there is a big gap between what the teenagers want to do (관계대명사절) and what they actually do in their free time.

구문해설 • actually: 실제로 • gap: 차이 • between A and B: A와 B 사이에

청소년들의 여가 활동들

우리는 100명의 청소년들에게 여가 활동에 관해 질문했습니다. 그 결과 청소년들이 가장 하고 싶은 여가 활동은 여행인 것으로 나타났습니다. 34%는 여가 시간에 여행을 가고 싶다고 답했습니다. 하지만 그들이 실제로 가장 많이 하는 여가 활동은 TV를 보는 것입니다. 39%는 여가 시간에 TV를 본다고 답했습니다. 결과로 봤을 때, 우리는 청소년들이 여가 시간에 하고 싶은 활동과 실제로 하는 활동 사이에 큰 차이가 있다는 것을 알 수 있습니다.

영역별 핵심문제

Words & Expressions

01 〈보기〉의 밑줄 친 identifies와 같은 의미로 쓰이지 않은 것을 고르시오.

보기

This map identifies when and where crime is most likely to happen.

① You should not identify wealth with happiness.
② She was able to identify her attacker.
③ Many of those arrested refused to identify themselves.
④ They identify their members by a distinct smell.
⑤ Can you identify your umbrella among these?

02 다음 영영풀이에 해당하는 단어를 주어진 철자로 시작하여 빈칸에 쓰고, 알맞은 것을 골라 문장을 완성하시오.

- s________: the growth or development of something, so that it affects a larger area or a larger number of people
- i________: the people or companies engaged in a particular kind of commercial enterprise

(1) We hope to slow the ________ of the disease.
(2) His novels are a rich source of material for the movie ________.

03 다음 문장의 빈칸에 〈영영풀이〉의 밑줄 친 this에 해당하는 어휘를 쓰시오.

The team built a database by collecting and analyzing a huge ________ of data on players.

<영영풀이> The this of something is how much there is, or how much you have, need, or get.

04 다음 빈칸 (A)~(C)에 알맞은 말을 쓰시오. (주어진 철자로 시작하여 쓸 것.)

- In this area oxen are (A)u________ to pull carts.
- Some areas are (B)l________ to have rain today.
- He (C)h________ her focus only on her studying.

05 괄호 안에 주어진 어휘를 이용하여 빈칸에 알맞게 쓰시오.

(1) The garden was full of ________ flowers. (color)
(2) He offered some ________ advice. (use)
(3) She talks ________ about her problems. (endless)

Conversation

[06~07] 다음 대화를 읽고 물음에 답하시오.

A: ______(a)______
B: Sure. First, put a tea bag in a cup.
(A) Then, pour hot water in the cup.
(B) Last, take the tea bag out after 3 minutes.
(C) And then?
(D) OK.
A: I got it. I really appreciate your help.

06 위 대화의 빈칸 (a)에 know를 이용하여 7 단어로 알맞은 말을 쓰시오.

➡ ______________________

07 주어진 문장 사이에 나올 대화의 순서로 알맞은 것은?

① (B) – (A) – (C) – (D)
② (C) – (B) – (A) – (D)
③ (D) – (A) – (C) – (B)
④ (D) – (B) – (A) – (C)
⑤ (D) – (B) – (C) – (A)

08 다음 중 짝지어진 대화가 어색한 것은?

① A: Then what?
B: Then the application will give you a number to unlock a bike with.
② A: I want to return these books. Do you know how to do it?
B: Thanks.
③ A: Then insert the money.
B: I really appreciate your help.
④ A: What's this robot for?
B: Oh, it's a robot that finds books for you.
⑤ A: It's so easy, isn't it?
B: Yes, it's really amazing.

[09~10] 다음 대화를 읽고 물음에 답하시오.

G: Excuse me, but what's this robot for?
B: Oh, it's a robot that finds books for you.
G: Really? Can you tell me how to use it?
B: Sure. First, place your library card on the robot's screen.
G: OK.
B: Second, type the title of the book you're looking for and then press ENTER. (①)
G: Is that all? (②)
B: Yes. (③)
G: So I can just go to the front desk and get the book? (④)
B: Right. It's so easy, isn't it? (⑤)
G: Yes, it's really amazing. Thank you.

09 위 대화의 (①)~(⑤) 중 주어진 문장이 들어갈 곳은?

> Then, the robot will find the book and take it to the front desk.

① ② ③ ④ ⑤

10 위 대화를 읽고 답할 수 없는 질문을 고르시오.

① What does the robot do?
② Does the boy know how to use the robot?
③ Should the girl type the title of the book she's looking for?
④ How can the robot find the book and take it to the front desk?
⑤ What does the girl think really amazing?

Grammar

11 다음 문장의 밑줄 친 부사절을 분사구문으로 알맞게 바꾼 것을 고르시오.

> As he didn't have anyone around to help and save him, George Floyd was killed by the police.

① As he having not anyone around to help and save him,
② There being anyone around to help and save him,
③ Having not anyone around to help and save him,
④ As having not everyone around to help and save him,
⑤ Not having anyone around to help and save him,

12 다음 문장의 밑줄 친 as와 의미상 쓰임이 같은 것을 고르시오.

> The experts were analyzing the final data as the professor got ready to present their results.

① Take a rest in this place as you wish.
② As it gets hotter and hotter, my dog became weaker.
③ We were listening to music from the radio as my uncle drove us to the summer house in Seattle.
④ The researchers collected as much big data as they wanted in studying the unique psychology of the people online.
⑤ As I am mistaken for the actor, people often ask me to shake hands.

[13~14] 다음 문장의 밑줄 친 as와 의미상 쓰임이 다른 하나를 고르시오.

13

> As Tony lives alone in that big house, he must feel depressed and lonely.

① Big data can be useful as it helps our society in various ways.
② As almost everything that we do online leaves a trace, the amount of data is increasing much more than before.
③ What does the expert think happens as information technology develops?
④ Big data has to be analyzed as simply collecting data is not enough.
⑤ The spread of the flu can be predicted as people will search online more.

14

> Police use a map of crime hot spots as drivers are careful of the area where accident happens frequently.

① The sales of the product have gone up as the expert predicted.
② The puppies bark at me just as their mom does.
③ You can be happy as your mom and dad used to live happily.
④ She could succeed in the business as she built a database by collecting and analyzing a huge amount of data.
⑤ Health professionals can forecast a disease just as weather experts do.

15 다음 그림을 보고 괄호 안의 단어를 배열하여 빈칸을 알맞게 채우시오.

(1) (more, ate, eat, she, as, to)

➡ She felt too full ______________________ a whole pizza.

(2) (as, were, insects, the spider, caught)

➡ A few ______________________ planned.

Reading

[16~18] 다음 글을 읽고 물음에 답하시오.

What is big data?

Big data is data sets that are very big and complex. As information and communication technology develops, the amount of data we have is getting much greater than before. This is mainly because almost everything that we do online leaves a trace. For example, the photos you upload ___ⓐ___ your blog and the records of your purchases at online stores are all part of big data.

Simply collecting data, however, is not enough. Big data has to be analyzed, and this is done by big data experts. (A)<u>Using</u> various methods, experts analyze big data and draw meaningful results ___ⓑ___ it. These results then can be used to make decisions or to predict the future.

16 위 글의 빈칸 ⓐ와 ⓑ에 들어갈 전치사가 바르게 짝지어진 것은?

	ⓐ	ⓑ		ⓐ	ⓑ
①	for	to	②	on	from
③	in	from	④	for	with
⑤	on	for			

17 주어진 영영풀이에 해당하는 단어를 본문에서 찾아 쓰시오.

a sign that something has happened or existed

➡ ______________________

18 위 글의 밑줄 친 (A)<u>Using</u>과 문법적 쓰임이 같은 것을 <u>모두</u> 고르시오.

① He answered <u>smiling</u> at me.
② The baby stopped <u>crying</u>.
③ <u>Taking</u> a walk, they talked about Bob's birthday.
④ <u>Studying</u> hard, he passed the exam.
⑤ <u>Keeping</u> pets has become popular.

[19~21] 다음 글을 읽고 물음에 답하시오.

How is big data influencing our lives?

Big data is influencing almost all parts of our lives. It helps companies understand their customers' needs better and helps them sell more products. It helps people avoid heavy traffic. Its uses are endless, and here are some interesting examples.

Disease Forecast

Did you know that health professionals can now forecast a disease just as weather experts forecast the weather? ⓐThis is possible thanks to big data. For example, when the flu season comes, people will buy more flu medicine. They will also search online about flu symptoms more. If this kind of data is analyzed wisely, the spread of the flu can be predicted.

19 위 글의 밑줄 친 ⓐThis가 가리키는 것을 본문에서 찾아 쓰시오.

➡ ______________________________

____

20 위 글의 주제로 알맞은 것을 고르시오.

① the way companies use big data
② how to avoid heavy traffic
③ health professionals who can now forecast a disease
④ the influence big data has on our lives
⑤ the effective way to predict the spread of the flu

21 According to the passage, which is NOT true?

① Big data is affecting almost all parts of our lives.
② Big data helps companies understand their customers' needs better.
③ People can avoid heavy traffic thanks to big data.
④ The uses of big data are infinite.
⑤ Health professionals can now cure a disease just as weather experts forecast the weather.

[22~23] 다음 글을 읽고 물음에 답하시오.

Teens' Free Time Activities

We asked 100 teenagers about their free time activities. The results show that the free time activity the teenagers want to do the most is traveling. 34% said that they want to travel in their free time. However, the free time activity they actually do the most is watching TV. 39% said that they watch TV in their free time. Looking at the results, we see that there is a big ___ⓐ___ between what the teenagers want to do and what they actually do in their free time.

22 위 글의 빈칸 ⓐ에 들어갈 알맞은 말을 고르시오.

① agreement
② gap
③ harmony
④ arrangement
⑤ correlation

23 According to the passage, which is NOT true?

① The free time activity the teenagers want to do the most is traveling.
② About a third of the teenagers want to travel in their free time.
③ The free time activity the teenagers actually do the most is watching TV.
④ More than two-fifths of the teenagers watch TV in their free time.
⑤ The survey shows that what the teenagers want to do is different from what they actually do in their free time.

단원별 예상문제

출제율 90%

01 다음 중 짝지어진 단어의 관계가 나머지와 다른 것은?

① include – exclude
② complex – complicated
③ meaningful – meaningless
④ lock – unlock
⑤ borrow – lend

출제율 100%

02 밑줄 친 부분의 의미로 알맞지 않은 것은?

① The people cultivate mainly rice and beans. (주로)
② It is impossible to predict what will happen. (예측하다)
③ If he improved his IT skills, he'd easily get a job. (향상시키다)
④ Prevention plays a central role in traditional medicine. (훼방)
⑤ I would like to get advance purchase discount. (구매)

출제율 95%

03 다음 빈칸에 들어갈 알맞은 말을 쓰시오.

(1) Let your eyes ________ on objects that are further away from you.
(2) He is to ________ an important role in promoting Seoul's charm to the rest of the world.

[04~05] 다음 대화를 읽고 물음에 답하시오.

G: Can you tell me how to plant a potato?
B: Sure. First, cut a potato ___ⓐ___ small pieces. Second, dig holes in the ground.
G: Then?
B: Then put the potato pieces in the holes and cover the holes ___ⓑ___ dirt.
G: That sounds simple. Thanks.

출제율 90%

04 위 대화의 빈칸 ⓐ와 ⓑ에 알맞은 말을 쓰시오.

➡ ⓐ ________________ ⓑ ________________

출제율 100%

05 감자 심기에 관한 위 대화를 읽고 대답할 수 없는 질문을 고르시오.

① Does the boy know how to plant a potato?
② What is the first step?
③ What is the second step?
④ When does the girl plant a potato?
⑤ Does planting a potato seem simple?

[06~07] 다음 대화를 읽고 물음에 답하시오.

B: Excuse me. Can you tell me how to add money ___ⓐ___ my transportation card?
G: ______(A)______ First, put your card in the machine. Second, choose the amount of money you want to add.
B: OK.
G: Last, insert your money ___ⓑ___ the machine.
B: That sounds simple. Thanks.

출제율 95%

06 위 대화의 빈칸 (A)에 알맞지 않은 것을 모두 고르시오.

① Of course. ② I don't know.
③ Why not? ④ Sure.
⑤ Don't mention it.

출제율 90%

07 위 대화의 빈칸 ⓐ와 ⓑ에 알맞은 말을 고르시오.

ⓐ ⓑ ⓐ ⓑ
① at – into ② at – to
③ to – into ④ to – to
⑤ on – in

출제율 100%

08 다음 밑줄 친 부분 중 어법상 어색한 것을 고르시오.

① Being sensitive to the feedback, Mary was carefully checking her research paper.
② Written quickly, the novel has been praised as a masterpiece of all time.
③ It being cold and windy, all fishermen couldn't go fishing this morning.
④ Being no money left in her pockets, Robin started part-time job.
⑤ Wanting to allow him to use his car, Mr. Copper told his son to wait for him.

출제율 100%

09 다음 주어진 문장의 부사절을 분사구문으로 적절히 전환한 것을 고르시오.

> As she had not been invited to the party, the girl stayed at home all day.

① Having not been invited to the party, the girl stayed at home all day.
② As she not being invited to the party, the girl stayed at home all day.
③ As she being not invited to the party, the girl stayed at home all day.
④ Not having been invited to the party, the girl stayed at home all day.
⑤ Not having invited to the party, the girl stayed at home all day.

출제율 95%

10 다음 두 문장을 접속사 as를 활용하여, 한 문장으로 고친 것으로 알맞은 것은?

> • It was cold outside in the morning.
> • I nearly caught cold while running.

① As I nearly caught cold while running, it was cold outside in the morning.
② It was cold outside in the morning as I nearly caught cold while running.
③ As I was running, it was cold outside in the morning so that I nearly caught cold.
④ As it was cold outside in the morning, I nearly caught cold while running.
⑤ I nearly caught cold as running was cold outside in the morning.

출제율 95%

11 다음 중 어법상 옳지 않은 문장을 고르면? (정답 2개)

① Worked hard to complete the report in time, Wendy was exhausted.
② Being looked much bigger than before, the flowers are in bloom.
③ The doctor succeeding in the heart operation, the patients in her clinic became even more dependent on her.
④ Living next door, I seldom see him.
⑤ There being no bus service, the crowd had to walk all the way home.

[12~14] 다음 글을 읽고 물음에 답하시오.

> **What is big data?**
> Big data is data sets that are very big and complex. As information and communication technology develops, the amount of data we have is getting (A)much greater than before.

This is mainly because almost everything that we do online leaves a trace. ___ⓐ___, the photos you upload on your blog and the records of your purchases at online stores are all part of big data.

Simply collecting data, ___ⓑ___, is not enough. Big data has to be analyzed, and this is done by big data experts. Using various methods, experts analyze big data and draw meaningful results from it. These results then can be used to make decisions or to predict the future.

출제율 90%

12 위 글의 빈칸 ⓐ와 ⓑ에 들어갈 알맞은 말을 고르시오.

① For instance – therefore
② For example – however
③ In addition – however
④ However – as a result
⑤ That is – for example

출제율 100%

13 위 글의 밑줄 친 (A)much와 바꿔 쓸 수 없는 말을 고르시오.

① even ② still
③ far ④ very
⑤ a lot

출제율 100%

14 위 글의 주제로 알맞은 것을 고르시오.

① the very big and complex data
② the amount of data which is getting much greater than before
③ the popularity of big data experts
④ how to make decisions or to predict the future effectively
⑤ collecting and analyzing of big data and its use

[15~17] 다음 글을 읽고 물음에 답하시오.

Disease Forecast

(①) Did you know that health professionals can now forecast a disease just (A)as weather experts forecast the weather? (②) For example, when the flu season comes, people will buy more flu medicine. (③) They will also search online about flu symptoms more. (④) If this kind of data is analyzed wisely, the spread of the flu can be ___ⓐ___. (⑤)

출제율 95%

15 위 글의 빈칸 ⓐ에 들어갈 알맞은 말을 고르시오.

① protected ② improved
③ predicted ④ produced
⑤ increased

출제율 95%

16 위 글의 흐름으로 보아, 주어진 문장이 들어가기에 가장 적절한 곳은?

This is possible thanks to big data.

① ② ③ ④ ⑤

출제율 100%

17 위 글의 밑줄 친 (A)as와 같은 의미로 쓰인 것을 고르시오.

① As he was a child, he lived in England.
② As it was getting dark, we soon turned back.
③ Leave it as it is.
④ As rust eats iron, so care eats the heart.
⑤ Woman as she was, she was brave.

[18~20] 다음 글을 읽고 물음에 답하시오.

Crime Prevention

Thanks to big data, police can now predict crime before it happens. Through the analysis of big data about the type, time and place of crime, police can make a map of crime hot spots. ⓐ이 지도는 범죄가 언제, 어디에서 가장 많이 발생할 것 같은지를 알려 준다. Police can prevent further crime by focusing on the areas and the times this map predicts.

Big data has already changed the world greatly. So where will the big data industry go from here? Nobody knows for sure, but experts agree that big data will play a more and more important role in our lives.

출제율 95%

18 위 글의 밑줄 친 ⓐ의 우리말에 맞게 주어진 어휘를 이용하여 12 단어로 영작하시오.

identifies, most likely to, happen

➡ ______________________

출제율 95%

19 According to the second paragraph, what do experts agree about big data? Answer in English in a full sentence.

➡ ______________________

출제율 90%

20 According to the passage, which is NOT true?

① Even now, police can't predict crime before it happens.
② Police can make a map of crime hot spots by analyzing big data about the type, time and place of crime.
③ If the police focus on the areas and the times a map of crime hot spots predicts, they can prevent further crime.
④ The world has already changed greatly thanks to big data.
⑤ Nobody knows for sure where the big data industry will go from here.

[21~22] 다음 글을 읽고 물음에 답하시오.

Teens' Free Time Activities

We asked 100 teenagers about their free time activities. The results show that the free time activity the teenagers want to do the most is traveling. 34% said that they want to travel in their free time. However, the free time activity they actually do the most is watching TV. 39% said that they watch TV in their free time. ⓐ Looking at the results, we see that there is a big gap between what the teenagers want to do and what they actually do in their free time.

출제율 90%

21 위 글의 밑줄 친 ⓐ를 접속사와 주어, 동사를 포함하는 절로 바꾸시오.

➡ ______________________

출제율 100%

22 위 글을 읽고 알 수 없는 것을 고르시오.

① What free time activity do the teenagers want to do the most?
② What percent of the teenagers want to travel in their free time?
③ What free time activity do the teenagers actually do the most?
④ What percent of the teenagers watch TV in their free time?
⑤ Why is it difficult for the teenagers to do what they want to do the most in their free time?

서술형 실전문제

[01~03] 다음 대화를 읽고 물음에 답하시오.

G: Excuse me, but what's this robot for?
B: Oh, it's a robot that finds books for you.
G: Really? Can you tell me how to use it?
B: Sure. First, place your library card on the robot's screen.
G: OK.
B: Second, type the title of the book you're looking for and then press ENTER.
G: Is that all?
B: Yes. Then, the robot will find the book and take it to the front desk.
G: So I can just go to the front desk and get the book?
B: Right. It's so easy, isn't it?
G: Yes, it's really amazed. Thank you.

01 위 대화의 로봇을 이용하여 책을 찾는 3 단계의 방법을 우리말로 쓰시오.

➡ 1. ______________________
2. ______________________
3. ______________________

02 위 대화에서 어법상 어색한 것을 하나 찾아 바르게 고치시오.

__________ ➡ __________

03 What does the robot do for people who are using it? Answer with the words, 'and, them'. (11 words)

➡ ______________________
____

04 다음 우리말에 맞도록 괄호 안에 주어진 어휘를 알맞게 배열하여 빈칸을 채우시오.

(1) 비록 학생들이 선생님의 뜻을 알았지만, 그녀가 말한 대로 하지 않기로 결정했다. (what, meant, though, knowing, the teacher)
➡ ______________________, the students decided not to do as she told.

(2) 그 열차에 남은 좌석이 있다면, 그녀는 다음 날 아침에 부산으로 갈 것이다. (seats, there, the train, left, any, on, being)
➡ ______________________, she will go to Busan next morning.

(3) 집을 청소하고 싶었기 때문에, 나는 일을 하루 쉬겠다고 사장에게 말했다. (clean, wanting, house, to, my)
➡ ______________________, I told the boss that I'd take a day off from work.

05 다음 우리말에 맞도록 괄호 안에 주어진 어휘를 알맞게 배열하여 빈칸을 채우시오.

(1) 그녀가 전에 말했듯이, 빅데이터의 중요성은 더욱 커지고 있다. (the importance, is, said, growing, big data, she, of, before)

➡ As ______________________
______________________ even more.

(2) 빅데이터가 세상을 이미 엄청나게 바꿔버렸기 때문에, 나는 미래가 더욱 궁금하다. (already, the world, big data, changed, greatly, as, has)

➡ ______________________
________ I wonder more about the future.

[06~08] 다음 글을 읽고 물음에 답하시오.

What is big data?

Big data is data sets that are very big and complex. As information and communication technology develops, the amount of data we have is getting much greater than before. This is mainly because almost everything that we do online leaves a trace. For example, the photos you upload on your blog and the records of your purchases at online stores are all part of big data.

Simply collecting data, however, is not enough. Big data has to be analyzed, and this is done by big data experts. ⓐ다양한 방법들을 사용하여 전문가들은 빅데이터를 분석하고, 그것으로부터 의미 있는 결과들을 도출한다. These results then can be used to make decisions or to predict the future.

06 What's big data? Answer in English in a full sentence.

➡ ______________________________

07 Why is the amount of data we have getting much greater than before? Answer in English in a full sentence beginning with "Because".

➡ ______________________________

____

08 위 글의 밑줄 친 ⓐ의 우리말에 맞게 주어진 어휘를 이용하여 13 단어로 영작하시오.

Using, experts, draw, meaningful

➡ ______________________________

____

[09~11] 다음 글을 읽고 물음에 답하시오.

How is big data influencing our lives?

Big data is influencing almost all parts of our lives. It helps companies understand their customers' needs better and helps them sell more products. It helps people avoid heavy traffic. Its uses are endless, and here are some interesting examples.

Disease Forecast

Did you know that health professionals can now forecast a disease just as weather experts forecast the weather? This is possible thanks to big data. For example, when the flu season comes, people will buy more flu medicine. They will also search online about flu symptoms more. If ⓐthis kind of data is analyzed wisely, the spread of the flu can be predicted.

09 How does big data help companies? Answer in English in a full sentence beginning with "It".

➡ ______________________________

____

10 다음 빈칸에 알맞은 단어를 넣어 위 글의 밑줄 친 ⓐthis kind of data가 가리키는 것을 완성하시오.

It is the data about people's behavior during ________ ________ ________.

11 위 글의 내용을 다음과 같이 정리하고자 한다. 빈칸 (A)와 (B)에 들어갈 알맞은 단어를 본문에서 찾아 쓰시오.

The big data is influencing (A)________ ________ ________ of our lives and its (B)________ are endless like health professionals can now forecast a disease thanks to big data.

창의사고력 서술형 문제

01 다음 주어진 단어들 중에 자유롭게 선택하여, 아래의 그림과 연관되는 내용이 되도록 〈보기〉와 같이 ① 접속사 'as를 사용한 부사절'이 들어간 문장을 영작하고, ② 영작한 문장에 쓰인 부사절을 같은 의미의 분사구문으로 전환하여 두 세트 이상 쓰시오.

- read / talk / water / listen to / eat / watch / sit / dance / sing
- a book / plants / a sandwich / TV / music / the radio / a song

보기

① As he talked on the phone, Minsu watched TV.
② Talking on the phone, Minsu watched TV.

(1) ______________________________

(2) ______________________________

02 다음 내용을 바탕으로 정보를 설명하는 글을 쓰시오.

1. The survey is about teens' free time activities.
2. The free time activity the teenagers want to do the most is traveling.
3. 34% of the teenagers want to travel in their free time.
4. The free time activity the teenagers actually do the most is watching TV.
5. 39% of the teenagers watch TV in their free time.
6. The survey shows that there is a big gap between what the teenagers want to do and what they actually do in their free time.

Teens' Free Time Activities

We asked 100 teenagers about their (A)______________. The results show that the free time activity the teenagers want to do the most is (B)_______. (C)_______ said that they want to travel in their free time. However, the free time activity they actually do the most is (D)______________. (E)_______ said that they watch TV in their free time. Looking at the results, we see that there is a big gap between (F)______________________ and (G)________________ in their free time.

단원별 모의고사

01 다음 짝지어진 단어의 관계가 같도록 빈칸에 알맞은 말을 쓰시오. (주어진 철자로 시작할 것.)

> spread – expansion : affect – i________

[02~03] 주어진 영어 설명에 알맞은 어휘를 빈칸에 쓰시오. (주어진 철자로 시작할 것.)

02

> He made a quick exit to a________ meeting her.

> <영어 설명> to stay away from someone or something

➡ ____________________

03

> If you are not satisfied with your p________, we will give you a full refund.

> <영어 설명> the action of buying something; a thing that has been bought

➡ ____________________

04 다음 빈칸에 알맞은 말로 짝지어진 것을 고르시오.

> • Can you ________ a good hotel?
> • An early ________ of the disease is a fever.

① recollect – symphony
② reject – symptom
③ reject – sympathy
④ recommend – symptom
⑤ recommend – sympathy

05 다음 우리말을 주어진 어휘를 이용하여 영작하시오.

(1) 독감에 걸리거나 독감의 확산을 피하기 위해, 여러분은 거리를 두고 집에 머물러야 합니다. (the flu, spreading, catching, keep your distance, avoid, should, stay home)

➡ ______________________________

____

(2) 질문할 때 사용하는 말이 사람들이 대답하는 방식에 영향을 미칠 수 있다. (how, influence, the wording of questions)

➡ ______________________________

____

[06~07] 다음 대화를 읽고 물음에 답하시오.

> G: Excuse me. I want to rent a bike. (a)<u>Can you tell me how to use this application?</u>
> M: Sure. First, (b)<u>앱에 로그인하세요.</u> (log, the application) Then find the RENT button and touch it.
> G: Then what?
> M: Then the application will give you a number to unlock a bike with.
> G: Thank you. I really appreciate your help.

06 위 대화의 밑줄 친 (a)를 me와 explain을 이용하여 바꿔 쓰시오.

➡ ______________________________

____

07 위 대화의 밑줄 친 (b)를 주어진 말을 이용하여 영작하시오.

➡ ____________________

[08~09] 다음 대화의 밑줄 친 부분을 괄호 안에 주어진 어휘를 이용하여 바꿔 쓰시오.

08

A: Excuse me. I want to return these books. Do you know how to do it?
B: Sure. It's simple. First, insert the library card into the machine. Second, put the books in this box.
A: OK.
B: Then just take your card out.
A: I really appreciate your help. (grateful)

➡ ______________________

09

B: I want to buy a snack. Do you know how to use this snack machine? (can, tell)
G: Yeah. First, choose the snack you want.
B: I already did. What's next?
G: Just put in the money. Then take the snack out.
B: Got it. Thanks.

➡ ______________________

[10~11] 다음 대화를 읽고 물음에 답하시오.

A: Do you know how to make tea?
B: Sure. First, put a tea bag in a cup.
A: OK.
B: Then, pour hot water in the cup.
A: And then?
B: Last, take the tea bag out after 3 minutes.
A: I got it. I really appreciate your help.

10 How long do you have to wait before you take out the tea bag? Answer by beginning with the word "We".

➡ ______________________
____

11 위 대화의 내용과 일치하지 않는 것은?

① B는 차를 만드는 법을 알고 있다.
② 차를 만들려면 우선 티백을 컵에 넣어야 한다.
③ 티백을 넣은 후 컵에 뜨거운 물을 부어야 한다.
④ 차를 만드는 마지막 단계는 3분 후에 티백을 꺼내는 것이다.
⑤ B는 A에게 감사하고 있다.

12 다음 각 문장의 밑줄 친 분사구문을 부사절로 바꿀 때 어법상 어색한 것은?

① Someone having broken down her bike, Jessie may not use it this afternoon.
→ As someone has broken down her bike,
② Speaking without a break for 2 hours, the comedian got exhausted.
→ As he spoke without a break for 2 hours,
③ Finding the tablet computer Anne had lost, Jane cried out with joy.
→ As she found the tablet computer Anne had lost,
④ Having heard much about the girl before, he was hardly aware of her.
→ As he had heard much about the girl before,
⑤ Composing the last scene of the film, the writer was visited by a stranger.
→ As he was composing the last scene of the film,

13 다음 각 문장의 밑줄 친 부사절을 분사구문으로 바꾼 것 중 옳은 것은?

① If it rains tomorrow, we can't go to the zoo.
→ Raining tomorrow,

② As William went to bed earlier this evening, he woke up at 3.
→ William going to bed earlier this evening,

③ When they are seen from under water, the trees seem even taller.
→ Seen from under water,

④ While Bentley was eating a beef steak, his little brothers fell asleep.
→ Eating a beef steak,

⑤ If you put a coin on the box, the cat will take it away.
→ Putting a coin on the box,

14 다음 문장에 공통으로 들어갈 알맞은 말을 고르시오. (대·소문자 구분 안 함.)

• ________ I mentioned earlier, you should be careful when you upload the pictures or something private.
• Messy used big data ________ a means of persuading his boss.
• ________ the girl got older, she became a lot wiser than any other educated person.

① what ② as ③ when
④ since ⑤ though

[15~16] 다음 글을 읽고 물음에 답하시오.

Simply collecting data, however, is not enough. Big data has to be analyzed, and ⓐ this is done by big data experts. Using various methods, experts analyze big data and draw meaningful results from it. These results then can be used to make decisions or ⓑto predict the future.

15 위 글의 밑줄 친 ⓐthis가 가리키는 것을 우리말로 쓰시오.

➡ ________________________

16 아래 〈보기〉에서 위 글의 밑줄 친 ⓑto predict와 to부정사의 용법이 다른 것의 개수를 고르시오.

보기

① I was sorry to hear about their problem.
② It is not good to spend so much time playing computer games.
③ He went to the library to study for the final exam.
④ I have so many friends to help me.
⑤ The teacher explained when to begin the test.

① 1개 ② 2개 ③ 3개 ④ 4개 ⑤ 5개

[17~18] 다음 글을 읽고 물음에 답하시오.

Disease Forecast

Did you know that health (A)professionals can now forecast a disease just as weather experts forecast the weather? This is possible thanks to big data. ____ⓐ____, when the flu season comes, people will buy more flu medicine. They will also search online about flu symptoms more. If this kind of data is analyzed wisely, the spread of the flu can be predicted.

17 위 글의 빈칸 ⓐ에 들어갈 알맞은 말을 고르시오.

① Whereas ② Therefore
③ In addition ④ For example
⑤ However

18 위 글의 밑줄 친 (A)professionals와 바꿔 쓸 수 있는 말을 본문에서 찾아 쓰시오.

➡ ______________________

[19~20] 다음 글을 읽고 물음에 답하시오.

_______ⓐ_______

Are you a sports fan? Well, big data is improving the performance of players, making sports more exciting. A famous example is Germany's national soccer team. The team built a database by collecting and analyzing a huge amount of data on players. For example, the data included information about how much each player ran and how long he had the ball. ___ⓑ___ the help of this database, Germany's national soccer team was able to improve its performance and win the 2014 World Cup.

19 위 글의 빈칸 ⓐ에 들어갈 제목으로 알맞은 것을 고르시오.

① How Is Big Data Influencing Our Lives?
② Improving Performance in Sports
③ The Way to Build a Database
④ What is Big Data?
⑤ The Victory of Germany's National Soccer Team

20 위 글의 빈칸 ⓑ에 알맞은 전치사를 쓰시오.

➡ ______________________

[21~22] 다음 글을 읽고 물음에 답하시오.

Crime Prevention

Thanks to big data, police can now predict crime before it happens. (①) Through the analysis of big data about the type, time and place of crime, police can make a map of crime hot spots. (②) Police can prevent further crime by focusing on the areas and the times this map predicts. (③)

Big data has already changed the world greatly. (④) So where will the big data industry go from here? (⑤) Nobody knows for sure, but experts agree ⓐ빅데이터가 우리 삶에서 더욱 더 중요한 역할을 한다는 것을.

21 위 글의 흐름으로 보아, 주어진 문장이 들어가기에 가장 적절한 곳은?

> This map identifies when and where crime is most likely to happen.

① ② ③ ④ ⑤

22 위 글의 밑줄 친 ⓐ의 우리말에 맞게 주어진 어휘를 알맞게 배열하시오.

> our lives / a / that / important role / big data / more and more / will play / in

➡ ______________________________
____

Lesson 8

The Joseon Dynasty Through Paintings

의사소통 기능

- 선호 표현하기
  A: Which food do you prefer, Tteokbokki or Gimbap?
  B: I prefer Tteokbokki.
- 의견 표현하기
  It seems to me that it's more delicious.

언어 형식

- to부정사의 의미상 주어
  It was impossible **for him to catch** any fish.
- 가정법 과거
  It **would** be wonderful **if** I **could** eat fresh fish.

교과서

Words & Expressions

Key Words

- □ **appear** [əpíər] 동 ~하게 보이다, 나타나다
- □ **attitude** [ǽtitjù:d] 명 태도, 자세
- □ **bamboo** [bæmbú:] 명 대나무
- □ **behavior** [bihéivjər] 명 행동
- □ **bend** [bend] 동 굽다, 구부러지다
- □ **bloom** [blu:m] 동 꽃을 피우다, 꽃이 피다
- □ **carp** [kɑ:rp] 명 잉어(단 · 복수 동형)
- □ **cancel** [kǽnsəl] 동 취소하다
- □ **character** [kǽriktər] 명 글자
- □ **curvy** [kə́:rvi] 형 굴곡이 많은
- □ **decoration** [dèkəréiʃən] 명 장식
- □ **despite** [dispáit] 전 ~에도 불구하고
- □ **difficulty** [dífikʌlti] 명 어려움, 고난
- □ **disappointed** [dìsəpɔ́intid] 형 실망한, 낙담한
- □ **dynasty** [dáinəsti] 명 시대, 왕조
- □ **effectively** [iféktivli] 부 효과적으로
- □ **folk painting** 민화
- □ **frozen** [fróuzn] 형 얼어붙은
- □ **greatly** [gréitli] 부 대단히, 크게
- □ **harmony** [hɑ́:rməni] 명 조화
- □ **ill** [il] 형 아픈, 병든
- □ **impossible** [impɑ́səbl] 형 불가능한
- □ **influence** [ínfluəns] 동 영향을 미치다
- □ **justice** [dʒʌ́stis] 명 정의, 공정성
- □ **lotus flower** 연꽃
- □ **loyalty** [lɔ́iəlti] 명 충성, 충실
- □ **melt** [melt] 동 녹다
- □ **muddy** [mʌ́di] 형 진흙투성이의, 탁한, 흙탕물의
- □ **object** [ɑ́bdʒikt] 명 물건, 물체
- □ **pond** [pɑnd] 명 연못
- □ **prefer** [prifə́:r] 동 선호하다, 더 좋아하다
- □ **represent** [rèprizént] 동 나타내다, 보여 주다, 상징하다
- □ **respect** [rispékt] 명 존경, 경의
- □ **society** [səsáiəti] 명 사회
- □ **suddenly** [sʌ́dnli] 부 갑자기
- □ **symbol** [símbəl] 명 상징, 기호
- □ **symbolic** [simbɑ́lik] 형 상징적인, 상징하는
- □ **symbolize** [símbəlàiz] 동 상징하다
- □ **thus** [ðʌs] 부 따라서, 그러므로
- □ **value** [vǽlju:] 명 가치, 중요성
- □ **will** [wil] 명 의지
- □ **wonderful** [wʌ́ndərfəl] 형 아주 훌륭한, 경이로운

Key Expressions

- □ **as follows** 다음과 같이
- □ **because of** ~ 때문에
- □ **for example** 예를 들어
- □ **for this reason** 이런 이유로
- □ **get well** 병이 나아지다, 회복하다
- □ **in particular** 특히, 특별히
- □ **look at ~** ~을 보다
- □ **much more than** ~보다 훨씬 많이
- □ **once upon a time** 옛날에
- □ **remind ~ of ...** ~에게 …을 상기시키다
- □ **right after ~** ~ 직후에
- □ **so ~ that ...** 너무 ~해서 …하다

Word Power

※ 서로 비슷한 뜻을 가진 어휘

- □ **despite** ~에도 불구하고 : **in spite of** ~에도 불구하고
- □ **ill** 아픈 : **sick** 아픈
- □ **object** 물건, 물체 : **item** 물품, 품목
- □ **society** 사회 : **community** 지역사회, 공동체
- □ **difficulty** 어려움, 고난 : **hardship** 곤란, 고충
- □ **loyalty** 충성, 충실 : **fidelity** 충성, 충실, 성실
- □ **represent** 나타내다, 상징하다 : **express** 나타내다, 표현하다
- □ **thus** 그러므로, 따라서 : **therefore** 그러므로

※ 서로 반대의 뜻을 가진 어휘

- □ **appear** 나타나다, 출현하다 ↔ **disappear** 사라지다, 없어지다
- □ **impossible** 불가능한 ↔ **possible** 가능한
- □ **ill** 아픈 ↔ **healthy** 건강한
- □ **justice** 정의, 공정 ↔ **injustice** 불평등, 부당함

※ 과거분사 (동사+ed)

- □ **bore+ed** → **bored** 지루해진
- □ **embarrass+ed** → **embarrassed** 당황한
- □ **fascinate+ed** → **fascinated** 마음을 뺏긴
- □ **shock+ed** → **shocked** 충격 받은
- □ **disappoint+ed** → **disappointed** 실망한
- □ **excite+ed** → **excited** 신이 난, 들뜬
- □ **interest+ed** → **interested** 흥미를 가진
- □ **surprise+ed**→ **surprised** 놀란

English Dictionary

□ **appear** 나타나다
→ to begin to be seen; come into existence or use
보여지기 시작하다; 생기거나 쓰이게 되다

□ **attitude** 태도, 자세
→ the way you think or feel about something
어떤 것에 대해 생각하거나 느끼는 방식

□ **behavior** 행동
→ the things that a person or animal does
사람이나 동물이 하는 것들

□ **bend** 굽다, 구부러지다
→ to shape or force something straight into a curve or angle 어떤 곧은 것을 구부러지거나 각이 지게 만들거나 힘을 가하다

□ **bloom** 꽃을 피우다, 꽃이 피다
→ produce or yield flowers 꽃들이 생기게 하다

□ **despite** ~에도 불구하고
→ although something happens or exists
어떤 일이 일어나거나 존재하기는 하더라도

□ **dynasty** 왕조
→ a period of time during which members of the same family rule a country or region
일가족이 한 나라나 지역을 통치하는 기간

□ **frozen** 얼어붙은
→ made into, covered with, or surrounded by ice
얼음으로 만들어지거나 덮였거나 혹은 둘러쌓인

□ **justice** 정의
→ the quality of being fair and reasonable; fairness in the way people are treated
공평하고 합리적인 특성; 사람들이 대우 받는 방식에서의 공정함

□ **loyalty** 충성, 충실
→ a feeling of support for someone or something
어떤 사람이나 어떤 것에 대해 지지하는 감정

□ **object** 물건, 물체
→ a thing that you can see and touch 보거나 만질 수 있는 것

□ **remind** 상기시키다
→ to make someone remember something
어떤 사람에게 어떤 것을 기억하게 만들다

□ **represent** 나타내다
→ to show or mean something 어떤 것을 보여주거나 의미하다

□ **society** 사회
→ all the people who live in a country, and the way they live 한 국가에 살고 있는 모든 사람과 그들이 사는 방식

□ **symbol** 상징, 기호
→ a sign, picture, object etc. that represents something else 다른 어떤 것을 나타내는 기호, 그림, 물건 등

□ **symbolic** 상징적인
→ representing a particular idea or quality
특정한 생각이나 특성을 나타내는

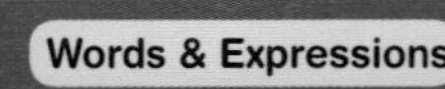

시험대비 실력평가

01 다음 짝지어진 단어의 관계가 같도록 빈칸에 알맞은 말은?

ill – sick : community – ________

① complex ② influence
③ harmony ④ society
⑤ symbol

서답형

02 주어진 영어 설명에 맞게 문장의 빈칸에 알맞은 말을 쓰시오.

Sally's bad ________ began to annoy us.

<영어 설명> the things that a person or animal does

➡ ____________________

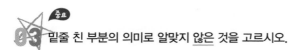

03 밑줄 친 부분의 의미로 알맞지 않은 것을 고르시오.

① Let's take a walk in the bamboo forest. (산책하다)
② Did you figure out if your answers were right after the test? (~ 직후에)
③ Despite the fact that she was wearing a seat belt, she was thrown sharply forward. (~에도 불구하고)
④ Once upon a time there was a beautiful princess. (옛날 옛적에)
⑤ In particular, the museum has many Impressionist paintings. (특히)

04 다음 빈칸에 들어갈 가장 알맞은 말을 고르시오.

You ________ me of your father when you say that.

① remind ② expert
③ chase ④ remember
⑤ memory

05 다음 빈칸에 공통으로 들어갈 말로 알맞은 것을 고르시오. (대 · 소문자 무시)

• There is a similar word in many languages, ________ example in French and Italian. • ________ this reason, experts often compare sports to war.

① to ② at ③ on
④ by ⑤ for

중요

06 다음 〈보기〉의 단어를 사용하여 자연스러운 문장을 만들 수 없는 것은?

보기
object frozen respect bend

① We once walked across a ________ pond at midnight.
② The ________ that he found was old.
③ No charge will be made if you ________ within 10 days.
④ The supports under the bridge were starting to ________.
⑤ We always show our ________ for teachers.

중요
01 다음 영영풀이에 알맞은 어휘를 <보기>에서 찾아 쓰시오.

보기: remind appear bend dynasty

(1) to begin to be seen; come into existence or use
(2) to shape or force something straight into a curve or angle
(3) a period of time during which members of the same family rule a country or region
(4) to make someone remember something

➡ (1) ________ (2) ________ (3) ________
(4) ________

02 다음 빈칸에 주어진 어휘를 알맞은 형태로 쓰시오.

(1) The local history of the area is ________. (fascinate)
(2) I was very ________ with myself. (disappoint)

03 다음 우리말에 맞도록 빈칸에 알맞은 말을 주어진 철자로 시작하여 쓰시오.

(1) 그 노래는 나의 아버지를 생각나게 한다.
→ The song r________ me of my father.
(2) 하트 모양은 사랑을 상징한다.
→ The shape of a heart s________ love.
(3) 학생들은 더운 날씨에도 불구하고 운동회를 즐겼다.
→ The students enjoyed the sports day d________ the hot weather.
(4) 저 분홍 장미는 6월에 꽃이 필 것이다.
→ Those pink roses will b________ in June.

고난이도
04 우리말에 맞게 한 단어를 추가하여 주어진 단어를 알맞게 배열하시오.

(1) 저녁으로 특별히 뭐 먹고 싶은 거 있니? (anything, dinner, there, you'd, is, like, particular, for)
➡ ________________________________

(2) 이런 이유로, 금요일은 결혼식 하기에 좋은 날로 여겨졌다. (Friday, reason, day, weddings, considered, be, was, a, this, good, for, to)
➡ ________________________________

(3) 우리나라 민화에서 호랑이는 자주 등장하는 소재이다. (the tiger, paintings, subject, is, a, Korean, common, in)
➡ ________________________________

(4) 그가 나를 찾아온 이유는 다음과 같다. (he, me, the reason, is, see, came, follows, to)
➡ ________________________________

교과서

Conversation

1 선호 표현하기

A Which food do you prefer, Tteokbokki or Gimbap?
떡볶이와 김밥 중에 어떤 음식을 더 좋아하니?

B I prefer Tteokbokki. 난 떡볶이를 더 좋아해.

- A와 B 두 가지 중 어떤 것을 선호하는지 물을 때 prefer를 사용하여 'Which (one) do you prefer, A or B?'로 표현한다. 같은 표현으로 'Which (one) do you like better, A or B?', 'Which (one) do you like more, A or B?', 'Which one do you want to ~ more?' 등을 쓸 수 있다.
- 대답할 때는 'I prefer ~.' 또는 'I like 목적어 better.', 'I like 목적어 more.'라고 말한다. 'B보다 A를 더 선호한다.'라고 대답할 때는 'I prefer A to B.' 또는 'I like A better than B.', 'I like A more than B.'라고 말한다.

선호 묻고 대답하기

- Which (one) do you prefer, A or B?
- Which (one) do you like better, A or B?
- Which (one) do you like more, A or B?
- Which (one) do you want to ~ more?
- I prefer ~. / I prefer A to B.
- I like 목적어 better. / I like A better than B.
- I like 목적어 more. / I like A more than B.
- I want/would like 목적어 better.
- I want/would like 목적어 more.

핵심 Check

1. 다음 빈칸에 들어갈 알맞은 단어를 쓰시오.

A: ________ painting do you prefer, the one with flowers ________ the one with animals?

B: I prefer the one with flowers ________ the one with animals.

2 의견 표현하기

- It seems to me that it's more delicious. 난 그게 더 맛있는 것 같아.
- It seems that science is more interesting to learn. 과학이 더 배우기가 재밌는 것 같아.
- I think that taking a train is faster than taking a taxi. 택시 타는 것보다 기차 타는 게 더 빠른 것 같아.

■ 자신의 의견을 말할 때 'It seems (to me) that+주어+동사 ~.'로 표현할 수 있다. that 뒤에는 주어와 동사를 갖춘 절로 말한다. 같은 의미의 표현으로 'I think that ~', 'I believe that ~', 'I feel that ~', 'In my opinion, ~(내 의견으로는, ~)', 'From my point of view, ~ (내 관점으로는, ~)' 등을 사용하여 말할 수 있다.

■ 의견에 대해 동의하는 표현으로는 'I agree (with you).' 또는 'I think so.', 'I couldn't agree more.' 등을 쓸 수 있다. 반대로 의견에 동의하지 않는다는 표현으로는 'I disagree (with you).', 'I don't agree (with you).' 등이 있다.

의견 표현하기

- It seems to me that 주어+동사 ~.
- I think (that) 주어+동사 ~.
- I feel (that) 주어+동사 ~.
- In my opinion, 주어+동사 ~.
- I believe (that) 주어+동사 ~.

의견에 대한 동의/비동의 표현

- I think so. 내 생각도 그래.
- I agree (with you). 난 (네 의견에) 동의해.
- I couldn't agree (with you) more. 전적으로 동의해.
- I'm afraid I disagree (with you). 유감이지만 난 (네 의견에) 동의하지 않아.
- I'm sorry but I don't agree (with you). 유감이지만 난 (네 의견에) 동의하지 않아.

핵심 Check

2. 다음 주어진 문장을 자연스러운 대화로 배열하시오.

(A) Of course. And it seems to me that the mask exhibition will be much more interesting.

(B) I prefer the Korean mask exhibition. Is that okay?

(C) There are two exhibitions we can go to. Which do you want to see more?

 ____________________

Conversation 교과서 대화문 익히기

Listen and Talk A 1

G: Minho, look at these two paintings of cats here. Aren't they great?

B: Yes, they are.

G: They ❶both are good, but I like ❷the one on the left more. How about you?

B: ❸I prefer the one on the right. ❹It seems to me that the cat in it is cuter. I also like the bird in it.

G: 민호야, 여기 고양이가 그려진 그림 두 점을 봐. 멋있지 않니?
B: 응, 그러네.
G: 그것들은 모두 멋있지만 난 왼쪽에 있는 그림이 더 좋아. 넌 어때?
B: 난 오른쪽에 있는 그림이 더 좋아. 그림 속 고양이가 더 귀여운 것 같아. 새도 마음에 들어.

❶ both는 대명사로 They와 동격이다.
❷ the one 다음에 which is가 생략되었다고 볼 수 있다.
❸ 선호를 표현할 때 쓰는 말로 문장의 마지막에 'to the one on the left'가 생략된 것이다. 'I like the one on the right more.'로 말할 수 있다.
❹ 자신의 의견을 말할 때 'It seems (to me) that ~'으로 말할 수 있다.

Check(√) True or False

(1) The girl likes the painting on the right more. T ☐ F ☐

(2) The boy thinks the cat in the painting on the right is cuter. T ☐ F ☐

Listen and Talk B

A: ❶Which food do you prefer, Tteokbokki or Gimbap?

B: ❷I prefer Tteokbokki. ❸It seems to me that it's more delicious. How about you?

A: I prefer Tteokbokki, too. / I prefer Gimbap. It seems to me that it's healthier.

A: 떡볶이와 김밥 중에 어떤 것을 더 좋아하니?
B: 난 떡볶이를 더 좋아해. 그것이 더 맛있을 것 같아. 너는 어때?
A: 나도 떡볶이를 더 좋아해. / 난 김밥을 더 좋아해. 그것이 더 건강에 좋은 것 같아.

❶ A와 B 두 가지 중에서 어떤 것을 선호하는지 물을 때 쓸 수 있는 표현이다. 'Which (one) do you like better, A or B?', 'Which (one) do you like more, A or B?', 'Which one do you want more?' 등으로 바꿔 쓸 수 있다.
❷ I like Tteokbokki more.로 바꿔 쓸 수 있다.
❸ 자신의 의견을 말할 때 쓰는 표현이다.

Check(√) True or False

(3) A wants to know if B prefers Tteokbokki or Gimbap. T ☐ F ☐

(4) B thinks Gimbap is more delicious. T ☐ F ☐

Listen and Talk A 2

G: We can have Bibimbap or Galbitang. ❶ Which do you prefer?

B: I prefer Bibimbap. ❷It seems to me that it's ❸the healthier choice.

G: I think so, too. I also like Bibimbap more.

B: Let's order, then. I'm very hungry.

❶ 선호를 묻는 표현이다.
❷ 의견을 말할 때 쓰는 표현이다.
❸ 비교급 앞에 the를 쓴 것은 두 개 중에서 비교하는 것이기 때문이다.

Listen and Talk A 3

G: Look at these two old plates, Steve. Aren't they beautiful?

B: Yes. Which one do you prefer, the green plate or the white plate?

G: Well, it's hard ❶to choose, but I like the green one better. How about you?

B: Me, too. It seems to me that the green plate is more ❷unique.

❶ 부사적 용법의 to부정사이다. 명사적 용법으로 볼 수도 있다.
❷ unique: 독특한

Listen and Talk A 4

G: Junsu, you said you're going to buy a gift for your sister. How about the bags here?

B: They look nice.

G: ❶Which one do you prefer, the one with flowers or the one with animals?

B: I prefer the one with flowers. It seems to me that my sister will like ❷it more.

❶ 선호를 묻는 표현이다.
❷ it은 the one with flowers를 받고 있다.

Listen and Talk B

A: Which painting do you prefer, the one on the left or the one on the right?

B: I prefer the one on the right. It seems to me that the cat in it is cuter. How about you?

A: I prefer the one on the right, too. / I prefer the one on the left. It seems to me that it ❶looks more calm.

❶ looks+형용사(calm): ~하게 보이다

Listen and Talk B

A: Which plate do you prefer, the green one or the white one?

B: I prefer the green one. It seems to me that it's more unique. ❶How about you?

A: I prefer the green one, too. / I prefer the white one. It seems to me that it's simple but beautiful.

❶ How about you? = What about you?

Listen and Talk B

A: Which bag do you prefer, the one with fish or the one with stars?

B: I prefer the one with stars. It seems to me that ❶it's more my style. How about you?

A: I prefer the one with stars, too. / I prefer the one with fish. It seems to me that the fish are cute.

❶ it은 the one with stars를 받고 있다.

Listen and Talk D

I prefer science. It seems to me that ❶it's more fun ❷to learn. I also prefer ❶it because I want to be a great inventor ❸like Edison.

❶ it = science
❷ 부사적 용법의 to부정사이다.
❸ like = such as

Listen and Talk C

G: There are two exhibitions ❶we can go to. Which one do you want to see more, Eric?

B: I prefer the Korean mask exhibition. Is that OK, Somi?

G: Of course. And it seems to me that the mask exhibition will be ❷much more interesting.

B: Do you think so?

G: Yes. Look at this poster. There isn't just an exhibition. There's also a mask dance show at 4:00 and 6:00.

B: Great! I've never seen a mask dance show before.

G: Well, I've seen a show before. I'm sure you'll like it.

B: So where is the show?

G: It's in Dasom Hall, ❸next to the exhibition room.

B: It's 4:30 now, so let's watch the 6 o'clock show.

G: OK. Let's go see the exhibition first.

❶ exhibitions와 we 사이에 목적격 관계대명사가 생략되어 있다.
❷ much로 비교급을 강조하고 있다.
❸ Hall과 next 사이에 '주격 관계대명사 which+is'가 생략되어 있다.

Talk and Play

A: Which do you prefer, Ramyeon or spaghetti?

B: I prefer Ramyeon. It seems to me that ❶it's more delicious. How about you?

A: I prefer Ramyeon, too. / I prefer spaghetti. It seems to me that it's ❷healthier.

❶ it = Ramyeon
❷ healthier는 healthy의 비교급이다.

Review 1

G: Joe, didn't you say you ❶needed to buy a cap? How about these caps here?

B: They look great.

G: Which one do you prefer, the one with triangles or the one with flowers?

B: I prefer the one with triangles. It seems to me that it's more unique.

❶ need는 to부정사를 목적어로 취한다.

Review 2

B: We can have Gimbap or Tteokbokki. Which do you prefer, Jenny?

G: I prefer Gimbap. It seems to me that it's ❶the healthier choice. How about you, Minsu?

B: I'll have Tteokbokki. ❷I heard that the Tteokbokki here is very good.

G: Let's order, then. I'm very hungry.

❶ 두 개 중에서 비교하고 있기 때문에 비교급 앞에 the를 썼다.
❷ I heard = People say

Review 3

John: There are two movies we can see. ❶ Which one do you want to see more, Somi?

Somi: I prefer *Batman*. I saw *Spider-Man* last week. Is this OK, John?

John: Of course. ❷It seems to me that *Batman* will be much more fun.

Somi: Good. Then, let's go and see ❸it.

❶ 선호를 묻는 표현이다.
❷ 의견을 말할 때 쓰는 표현이다.
❸ it = *Batman*

● 다음 우리말과 일치하도록 빈칸에 알맞은 말을 쓰시오.

Listen and Talk A 1

G: Minho, look at these ________ ________ ________ ________ here. Aren't they great?

B: Yes, they ________.

G: They ________ are good, but I like ________ ________ on the left more. How about you?

B: I ________ the one on the right. It ________ to me that the cat in it is ________. I also like the bird in it.

해석

G: 민호야, 여기 고양이가 그려진 그림 두 점을 봐. 멋있지 않니?
B: 응, 그러네.
G: 그것들은 모두 멋있지만 난 왼쪽에 있는 그림이 더 좋아. 넌 어때?
B: 난 오른쪽에 있는 그림이 더 좋아. 그림 속 고양이가 더 귀여운 것 같아. 새도 마음에 들어.

Listen and Talk A 2

G: We can have Bibimbap or Galbitang. ________ do you ________?

B: I ________ Bibimbap. ________ ________ to me that it's the healthier ________.

G: I think ________, too. I also ________ Bibimbap ________.

B: Let's order, then. I'm very hungry.

G: 우리는 비빔밥이나 갈비탕을 먹을 수 있어. 어떤 것이 더 좋니?
B: 난 비빔밥이 더 좋아. 그것이 더 건강에 좋은 선택인 것 같아.
G: 나도 그렇게 생각해. 난 비빔밥을 더 좋아하기도 해.
B: 그럼 주문하자. 난 정말 배고파.

Listen and Talk A 3

G: Look at these two old plates, Steve. Aren't they beautiful?

B: Yes. ________ ________ do you prefer, the green plate or the white plate?

G: Well, it's hard ________ ________, but I like the green one ________. How about you?

B: ________, ________. It ________ to me ________ the green plate is more unique.

G: Steve, 이 두 개의 옛날 접시들을 봐. 아름답지 않니?
B: 응. 초록색 접시와 흰색 접시 중 무엇이 더 좋니?
G: 음, 고르기가 어렵지만 난 초록색 접시가 더 좋아. 너는 어때?
B: 나도. 초록색 접시가 더 독특한 것 같아.

Listen and Talk A 4

G: Junsu, you said ________ ________ ________ buy a gift for your sister. How about the bags here?

B: They look ________.

G: ________ ________ do you ________, the one with flowers ________ the one with animals?

B: I ________ the one ________ flowers. ________ ________ ________ ________ that my sister will like it more.

G: 준수야, 너 여동생 줄 선물을 살 거라고 했잖아. 여기 이 가방들은 어때?
B: 좋아 보인다.
G: 가방에 꽃들이 있는 것과 동물들이 있는 것 중 무엇이 더 좋니?
B: 난 꽃들이 있는 것이 더 좋아. 내 여동생이 그것을 더 좋아할 것 같아.

Listen and Talk B

A: ________ food do you ________, Tteokbokki or Gimbap?
B: I ________ Tteokbokki. It seems to me that it's more delicious. How about you?
A: I ________ Tteokbokki, too. / I ________ Gimbap. It seems to me that it's healthier.

A: ________ painting do you ________, the one on the left ________ the one on the right?
B: I ________ the one on the right. It seems to me that the cat in it is cuter. How about you?
A: I ________ the one on the right, too. / I ________ the one on the left. It seems to me that it looks ________ ________.

A: ________ plate do you prefer, the green one ________ the white one?
B: I ________ the green one. It seems to me that it's ________ ________. How about you?
A: I ________ the green one, too. / I ________ the white one. It seems to me that it's simple ________ beautiful.

A: ________ bag do you ________, the one with fish ________ the one with stars?
B: I ________ the one with stars. It seems to me that it's ________ my style. How about you?
A: I ________ the one with stars, too. / I ________ the one with fish. It seems to me that the fish are cute.

Listen and Talk C

G: There are two exhibitions we can go to. ________ one do you want to see ________, Eric?
B: I ________ the Korean mask exhibition. Is ________ OK, Somi?
G: Of course. And it seems to me that the mask exhibition will be ________ more interesting.
B: Do you think ________?
G: Yes. Look at this poster. There isn't ________ an exhibition. There's ________ a mask dance show at 4:00 and 6:00.
B: Great! I've ________ seen a mask dance show ________.
G: Well, I've seen a show ________. I'm ________ you'll like it.
B: So where is the show?
G: It's in Dasom Hall, ________ ________ the exhibition room.
B: It's 4:30 now, so ________ ________ the 6 o'clock show.
G: OK. Let's go see the exhibition ________.

A: 떡볶이와 김밥 중에 어떤 것을 더 좋아하니?
B: 난 떡볶이를 좋아해. 그것이 더 맛있을 것 같아. 너는 어때?
A: 나도 떡볶이를 좋아해. / 난 김밥을 좋아해. 그것이 더 건강에 좋은 것 같아.

A: 왼쪽 그림과 오른쪽 그림 중 어떤 것을 더 좋아하니?
B: 난 오른쪽 그림을 더 좋아해. 그림 속 고양이가 더 귀여운 것 같아. 너는 어때?
A: 나도 오른쪽 그림이 더 좋아. / 난 왼쪽 그림을 더 좋아해. 그것이 더 평화로워 보이거든.

A: 초록색 접시와 흰색 접시 중 어떤 것을 더 좋아하니?
B: 난 초록색 접시가 더 좋아. 그것이 더 독특하다고 생각해. 너는 어때?
A: 나도 초록색 접시가 더 좋아. / 난 흰색 접시가 더 좋아. 그것이 단순하지만 아름답다고 생각해.

A: 물고기가 있는 가방과 별들이 있는 가방 중 어떤 것을 더 좋아하니?
B: 난 별들이 있는 가방을 더 좋아해. 그것이 더 내 취향이야. 너는 어때?
A: 나도 별들이 있는 가방이 더 좋아. / 난 물고기가 있는 가방을 더 좋아해. 물고기가 귀여운 것 같아.

G: 우리가 갈 수 있는 전시회가 두 곳이 있어. 어느 것을 더 보고 싶니, Eric?
B: 나는 한국의 탈 전시회를 더 선호해. 소미야, 괜찮겠니?
G: 물론이지. 그리고 나도 탈 전시회가 더 흥미로울 것 같아.
B: 그렇게 생각하니?
G: 그래. 이 포스터를 봐. 단순히 전시회만 있는 것이 아니야. 탈춤 공연도 4시와 6시에 있어.
B: 좋아! 나는 전에 탈춤 공연을 본 적이 없어.
G: 음, 나는 전에 본 적이 있어. 네가 분명 좋아할 거야.
B: 그래서 공연은 어디서 해?
G: 전시관 옆 다솜 홀에서 해.
B: 지금 4시 30분이니까 6시 공연을 보자.
G: 그래. 우선 전시회부터 보자.

Listen and Talk D

I ________ science. It seems to me that it's ________ ________ ________ ________. I also ________ it because I want to be a great inventor ________ Edison.

해석

난 과학을 더 좋아해. 그것을 배우는 것이 더 즐거운 것 같아. 난 Edison과 같은 훌륭한 발명가가 되고 싶어서 그것을 더 좋아하기도 해.

Talk and Play

A: ________ do you ________, Ramyeon or spaghetti?

B: I ________ Ramyeon. It seems to me that it's more delicious. How about you?

A: I ________ Ramyeon, too. / I ________ spaghetti. It seems to me that it's healthier.

A: 라면과 스파게티 중 어떤 걸 더 좋아하니?

B: 난 라면을 더 좋아해. 그것이 더 맛있는 것 같아. 너는 어때?

A: 나도 라면을 더 좋아해. / 난 스파게티를 더 좋아해. 그것이 건강에 더 좋을 것 같아.

Review 1

G: Joe, didn't you say you needed ________ ________ a cap? How about these caps here?

B: They look ________.

G: ________ ________ do you ________, the one with triangles ________ the one with flowers?

B: I ________ the one with triangles. It seems to me that it's more unique.

G: Joe, 모자를 사야 한다고 하지 않았니? 여기 있는 이 모자들은 어때?

B: 그것들은 좋아 보인다.

G: 삼각형이 있는 것과 꽃이 있는 것 중 어떤 것이 좋니?

B: 난 삼각형이 있는 것이 더 좋아. 그것이 더 독특한 것 같아.

Review 2

B: We can have Gimbap or Tteokbokki. ________ do you ________, Jenny?

G: I ________ Gimbap. It seems to me that it's ________ ________ ________. How about you, Minsu?

B: I'll have Tteokbokki. ________ ________ that the Tteokbokki here is very good.

G: Let's ________, then. I'm very hungry.

G: 우리는 김밥이나 떡볶이를 시킬 수 있어. 어떤 것이 더 좋니, Jenny?

B: 난 김밥이 더 좋아. 건강에 더 좋은 선택인 것 같거든. 민수야, 넌 어떠니?

G: 난 떡볶이 먹을래. 여기는 떡볶이가 더 맛있다고 들었거든.

B: 그럼 주문하자. 난 정말 배고파.

Review 3

John: There are two movies we can see. ________ ________ do you want to see ________, Somi?

Somi: I ________ *Batman*. I saw *Spider-Man* last week. Is ________ OK, John?

John: Of course. It seems to me that *Batman* will be ________ more fun.

Somi: Good. Then, let's go and see it.

John: 우리가 볼 수 있는 영화가 두 개 있어. 소미야, 어떤 것이 더 보고 싶니?

Somi: 난 "배트맨"이 더 좋아. 난 "스파이더맨"을 지난주에 봤거든. John, 괜찮니?

John: 물론이지. "배트맨"이 훨씬 더 재미있을 것 같아.

Somi: 좋아. 그럼 영화 보러 가자.

01 다음 빈칸 (A)에 알맞지 않은 것은?

G: Minho, look at these two paintings of cats here. Aren't they great?
B: Yes, they are.
G: They both are good, but ______(A)______. How about you?
B: I prefer the one on the right. It seems to me that the cat in it is cuter. I also like the bird in it.

① I like the one on the left more
② I like the one on the left better
③ I'd rather the one on the left
④ I prefer the one on the left
⑤ I think the one on the left is better

02 주어진 어휘를 이용하여 밑줄 친 우리말을 8 단어로 영작하시오.

G: Which cap do you prefer, the one with triangles or the one with flowers?
B: I prefer the one with triangles. 그것이 더 독특한 것 같아. (it, me, unique, seem)

➡ ______________________________

03 다음 대화의 밑줄 친 (a)의 의도와 다르게 쓰인 것을 고르시오.

G: Junsu, you said you're going to buy a gift for your sister. How about the bags here?
B: They look nice.
G: Which one do you prefer, the one with flowers or the one with animals?
B: I prefer the one with flowers. (a)It seems to me that my sister will like it more.

① In my opinion, my sister will like it more.
② I think that my sister will like it more.
③ I feel that my sister will like it more.
④ I believe that my sister will like it more.
⑤ I hope that my sister will like it more.

01 다음 중 짝지어진 대화가 어색한 것은?

① A: Which movie do you want to see more, Somi?
B: I like *Batman*.

② A: It seems to me that the mask exhibition will be much more interesting.
B: Do you think so?

③ A: It seems to me that it's more my style. How about you?
B: I prefer the one with stars, too.

④ A: I like the green one better. How about you?
B: Me, too. It seems to me that the green plate is more unique.

⑤ A: Which do you prefer, dogs or cats?
B: I prefer dogs. It seems to me that dogs are cuter.

[02~04] 다음 대화를 읽고 물음에 답하시오.

G: We can have Bibimbap or Galbitang. ____(A)____? (prefer)
B: I prefer Bibimbap. It seems to me that it's the healthier choice.
G: I think so, too. I also like Bibimbap ___(B)___.
B: Let's order, then. I'm very hungry.

서답형

02 빈칸 (A)에 들어갈 알맞은 말을 주어진 어휘를 이용하여 4 단어로 쓰시오.

➡ ______________

03 위 대화의 빈칸 (B)에 들어갈 말은?

① a lot ② more ③ many
④ much ⑤ less

중요

04 선호하는 것에 관한 위 대화의 내용과 일치하지 않는 것은?

① 여자 아이와 남자 아이는 비빔밥이나 갈비탕을 먹을 수 있다.
② 남자 아이는 비빔밥을 더 좋아한다.
③ 남자 아이는 비빔밥이 더 좋은 선택이라고 생각한다.
④ 여자 아이는 남자 아이의 의견에 동의하고 있다.
⑤ 여자 아이는 정말 배가 고프다.

서답형

05 대화가 자연스럽게 연결되도록 (A)~(C)를 순서대로 바르게 배열하시오.

G: Look at these two old plates, Steve. Aren't they beautiful?
(A) Well, it's hard to choose, but I like the green one better. How about you?
(B) Yes. Which one do you prefer, the green plate or the white plate?
(C) Me, too. It seems to me that the green plate is more unique.

➡ ______________

[06~07] 다음 대화를 읽고 물음에 답하시오.

A: (a)넌 어떤 음식을 더 좋아하니, Tteokbokki ___(A)___ Gimbap?
B: I prefer Tteokbokki. It seems ___(B)___ me that it's more delicious. How about you?
A: I prefer Tteokbokki, too.

06 위 대화의 빈칸 (A)와 (B)에 들어갈 말로 알맞게 짝지어진 것은?

① and – for ② and – to
③ or – to ④ or – for
⑤ at – from

서답형

07 주어진 어휘를 이용하여 밑줄 친 (a)의 우리말을 5 단어로 영작하시오. (which)

➡ ______________________

[08~10] 다음 대화를 읽고 물음에 답하시오.

G: There are two exhibitions we can (a)[go / go to]. Which one do you want to see more, Eric?
B: I (b)[like / prefer] the Korean mask exhibition. Is that OK, Somi? (①)
G: Of course. (②) And it seems to me that the mask exhibition will be much more interesting.
B: Do you think so? (③)
G: Yes. Look at this poster. There isn't just an exhibition. (④)
B: Great! (⑤) I've never seen a mask dance show (c)[ago / before].
G: Well, I've seen a show (c)[ago / before]. I'm sure you'll like it.
B: So where is the show?
G: It's in Dasom Hall, next to the exhibition room.
B: It's 4:30 now, so let's watch the 6 o'clock show.
G: OK. Let's go see the exhibition first.

중요

08 위 대화의 (①)~(⑤) 중 주어진 문장이 들어갈 곳은?

There's also a mask dance show at 4:00 and 6:00.

① ② ③ ④ ⑤

09 위 대화의 괄호 (a)~(c)에서 알맞은 것을 골라 바르게 짝지은 것은?

	(a)	(b)	(c)
①	go to	prefer	before
②	go to	like	before
③	go to	prefer	ago
④	go	like	ago
⑤	go	prefer	ago

10 위 대화의 내용과 일치하는 것은?

① Eric과 소미가 갈 수 있는 전시회는 탈 전시회뿐이다.
② Eric은 탈춤 공연을 더 선호한다.
③ 포스터에는 단순히 탈 전시회만 있었다.
④ 탈춤 공연은 전시관 옆 다솜 홀에서 한다.
⑤ Eric과 소미는 4시 30분 공연을 볼 것이다.

[11~12] 다음 대화를 읽고 물음에 답하시오.

A: Which do you prefer, Ramyeon or spaghetti?
B: I prefer Ramyeon. (a)<u>It seems to me that it's more delicious.</u> How about you?
A: I prefer spaghetti. It seems to me that it's healthier.

11 위 대화의 밑줄 친 (a)의 의도로 가장 적절한 것은?

① 선호 표현하기
② 유감 표현하기
③ 동의하기
④ 감정 표현하기
⑤ 의견 표현하기

중요

12 위 대화를 읽고 답할 수 있는 것을 고르시오. (정답 2개)

① Where are they talking?
② Does A prefer spaghetti to Ramyeon?
③ Why does B like Ramyeon?
④ What does A ask B to do?
⑤ Why does A think spaghetti is healthier?

[01~03] 다음 대화를 읽고 물음에 답하시오.

G: There are two exhibitions we can go to. (a) 어느 것을 더 보고 싶니, (one, see, more) Eric?
B: I prefer the Korean mask exhibition. Is that OK, Somi?
G: Of course. And it seems to me that the mask exhibition will be much more interesting.
B: Do you think so?
G: Yes. Look at this poster. There isn't just an exhibition. There's also a mask dance show at 4:00 and 6:00.
B: Great! I've never seen a mask dance show before.
(A) It's in Dasom Hall, next to the exhibition room.
(B) It's 4:30 now, so let's watch the 6 o'clock show.
(C) So where is the show?
(D) Well, I've seen a show before. I'm sure you'll like it.
G: OK. Let's go see the exhibition first.

중요
01 위 대화의 (A)~(D)를 알맞은 순서로 배열하시오.

➡ ______________

02 괄호 안에 주어진 어휘를 이용하여 밑줄 친 (a)를 8 단어로 쓰시오.

➡ ______________

03 What are they talking about?

➡ ______________

[04~05] 다음 글을 읽고 물음에 답하시오.

I prefer science. It seems to me that it's more fun to learn. I also prefer it because I want to be a great inventor (a)like Edison.

04 밑줄 친 (a)like를 두 단어로 바꿔 쓰시오.

➡ ______________

고난이도
05 Write the two reasons why the writer prefers science.

➡ (1) ______________
(2) ______________

[06~07] 다음 대화를 읽고 물음에 답하시오.

G: Minho, look at these two paintings of cats here. Aren't they great?
B: Yes, they ___(A)___.
G: They both are good, but I like the one on the left more. How about you?
B: I prefer the one on the right. It seems to me that the cat in it is cuter. I also like the bird in it.

06 빈칸 (A)에 알맞은 동사를 쓰시오.

➡ ______________

07 Why does the boy prefer the painting on the right? Write two reasons.

➡ ______________
____

교과서

Grammar

1 to부정사의 '의미상의 주어': 'for+목적격'

- It was impossible **for him to catch** any fish. 그가 어떤 물고기라도 잡는 것은 불가능했다.
- It is nice **of you to help** me. 네가 나를 돕다니 친절하구나.

■ 동작의 행위자(agent): 동사가 행하는 동작을 '누가' 하는지 나타내는 말을 동작의 행위자라고 한다. 주어가 대부분 행위자이지만 그렇지 않은 경우, '의미상의 주어'라고 한다.

- **Philip** wants to ride the car. Philip은 (그가) 그 차를 타기를 원한다.
  : 문장의 주어 Philip이 동사 wants와 to부정사 to ride의 행위자

  → Philip wants **me** to ride the car. Philip은 내가 그 차를 타기를 원한다.
  : me가 to ride의 행위자 = 의미상의 주어

■ 'It' 가주어, 'to' 진주어 문장에서 to부정사의 '의미상의 주어'는 'for+목적격' 형태로 표현한다.

- It is not easy **for me** to move this table. 내가 이 탁자를 옮기는 것은 쉽지 않다.
- It was impossible **for him** to solve the quiz. 그가 그 문제를 푸는 것은 불가능했다.
- It is necessary **for Sumin** to be honest with her friends. Sumin이 그녀의 친구들에게 솔직해지는 것이 필요하다.

■ to부정사의 의미상의 주어가 일반 사람을 가리킬 때는 생략할 수 있다.

- It is healthy **(for us)** to walk regularly. (우리가) 규칙적으로 걷는 것이 건강에 좋다.
- It is difficult **(for people)** to manage time effectively. (사람들이) 시간을 효과적으로 관리하는 일은 어렵다.
- It is easy to make egg scramble. 계란 스크램블을 만드는 것은 쉽다. (일반 사람)

  → It is easy **for my mom** to make egg scramble. 나의 엄마가 계란 스크램블을 만드는 것은 쉽다. (특정인)

■ 사람의 성격, 태도 등을 나타내는 형용사는 'of+목적격' 형태로 의미상의 주어를 표현한다.

- It was **kind of him** to help the blind. 그가 그 맹인들을 도운 것은 친절했다.
- It was **nice of the girls** to find the kid's parents. 그 소녀들이 그 아이의 부모님을 찾아준 것은 착한 일이었다.
- It was **foolish of me** to stay up all night watching foreign dramas. 내가 외국 드라마를 보느라 밤을 새운 것은 어리석은 것이었다.

핵심 Check

1. 다음 괄호 안에서 알맞은 말을 고르시오.

(1) It is stupid (for / of) Mike to spend all the money playing a card game.

(2) It was difficult (for / of) the employee not to fall asleep at work.

2 가정법 과거: 'If+주어+동사 과거형 ~, 주어+would/could+동사원형 …'

- It **would** be wonderful **if** I **could** eat fresh fish.
  신선한 물고기를 먹을 수 있다면, 정말 좋을 텐데.

■ 가정법 과거: '만약 ~라면 …할 텐데'의 뜻으로, 현재 사실을 반대로 가정하거나 실현 가능성이 없는 일에 대해서 가정할 때 쓰며, 'If+주어+동사 과거형 ~, 주어+would/could+동사원형 …'의 형태이다.

- **If** I **knew** his phone number, I **would call** him. 내가 그의 전화번호를 안다면, 그에게 전화할 텐데. (가정법 과거, 현재 사실의 반대 가정)

  = **As** I **don't know** his phone number, I **won't call** him. 내가 그의 전화번호를 모르기 때문에, 나는 그에게 전화하지 않을 것이다.

■ 'be'동사는 주어의 인칭 및 수와 무관하게 'were'를 쓰지만, 1, 3인칭 단수의 경우 현대 영어에서는 'was'를 쓰기도 한다.

- **If** she **were[was]** blind, she **couldn't see** me. 그녀가 눈이 안 보인다면, 나를 볼 수 없을 텐데.

■ 가정법 과거완료는 이미 일어난 과거 사실을 반대로 가정하는 데 사용하며, 'If+주어+had+과거분사 ~, 주어+would/could+have+과거분사 …'의 형태로 나타낸다.

- **If** the teacher **had taught** us, we **would have succeeded**. 그 선생님이 우리를 가르쳐 주셨더라면, 우리는 성공했을 텐데.

■ **가정법의 다양한 표현들**

- **As** the man **is** rich, he **can** buy me the expensive meal. (직설법)

  → **If** he **were not** rich, he **couldn't buy** me the expensive meal. 그가 부유하지 않으면, 그 비싼 밥을 사 줄 수 없을 텐데. (가정법)

  → **Were** he **not** rich, he **couldn't buy** the expensive meal. (If 생략 가능, 도치문으로 가정)

- **Without[But for]** music, the world **would be** a dull place. 음악이 없다면, 세상은 따분한 곳일텐데.

  → **If it were not for** music, the world **would be** a dull place.

  → **Were it not for** music, the world **would be** a dull place. (If 생략 후 도치)

핵심 Check

2. 다음 우리말에 맞게 괄호 안의 단어를 바르게 배열하여 빈칸을 채우시오.

(1) 내가 당신이라면, 나를 뽑을 겁니다. (you, hire, would, were, I, me)

➡ If I ______________________________________.

(2) 돈이 좀 있으면, James는 이사를 가지 않을 텐데. (if, money, move away, would, had, some, he, not)

➡ James ______________________________________.

01 다음 중 어법상 바르지 않은 것은?

① It was considerate of the girl to guide the old visitors.
② It can't be possible for him to learn the difficult yoga move.
③ It was a little easy of him to make such decisions.
④ It is interesting for Sean to take their pictures.
⑤ It is not good for you to live alone.

02 다음 각 가정법 문장에서 어법상 어색한 단어를 한 개씩만 찾아 고치시오.

(1) If we make lots of money, we would help poor children.
______ ➡ ______
(2) If I had a talking teddy bear, I will take it everywhere.
______ ➡ ______
(3) It would be good if he can eat some meat.
______ ➡ ______
(4) I will learn the Chinese characters if I were the boy.
______ ➡ ______

03 다음 문장을 가주어 It과 to부정사를 이용하여 다시 쓰시오.

Riding a bike on the street was not easy for Suji.

➡ ______

04 다음 빈칸에 들어갈 말로 알맞은 것은?

If my mom ______ fresh fish, it would be wonderful.

① can eat ② will eat ③ had eaten
④ could eat ⑤ eats

01 다음 문장의 밑줄 친 단어들 중 어법상 어색한 것은?

> It was ①very wise ②for the student to avoid the fight ③since it ④is hard ⑤to be patient.

02 다음 중 같은 뜻을 가진 문장끼리 짝지어진 것은?

① She could write a letter to the writer of the book if she knew her address.
= She can't write a letter to the writer of the book though she knows her address.

② Brian would hand in the report in time if he had a computer.
= Brian didn't have a computer, so he wouldn't hand in the report.

③ If she studied hard, she could pass the test.
= She doesn't study hard, so she can't pass the test.

④ If Ted saw the car coming, he could avoid the accident.
= Ted didn't see the car coming, so he couldn't avoid the accident.

⑤ If it rains this evening, Amanda would stay at home taking a rest.
= It is raining this evening, so Amanda will stay at home taking a rest.

03 중요 다음 중 빈칸에 들어갈 말이 나머지와 다른 것은?

① It seems easy ________ the soccer team to win the championship this year again.

② It is necessary ________ the thin girl to gain some weight.

③ It's not safe ________ the puppies to play near the stove.

④ It was rude ________ Jimmy to ask his teacher to get out of the room.

⑤ Is it okay ________ us to join you?

04 다음 중 어법상 어색한 문장은?

① If he were polite, he won't do a bad thing to old people.

② If the ants knew the way to their nest, they could cross the stream.

③ If she weren't in Egypt, she could attend her grandmother's funeral.

④ If it were not for the music by the singer, I would not able to live.

⑤ Ailey could be hurt, if the car didn't stop immediately.

05 중요 다음 중 빈칸 ⓐ~ⓕ에 같은 단어가 들어가는 것끼리 바르게 짝지어진 것은?

> • It was wonderful ___ⓐ___ Dr. Jordan to win the award for the research.
> • It wasn't wise ___ⓑ___ the young lady to refuse the job offer.
> • It is possible ___ⓒ___ Pavien to get to the meeting place at 8 tomorrow evening.
> • It was difficult ___ⓓ___ the kids to understand the coach's instruction.
> • It is safe ___ⓔ___ the children to cut the cake with this plastic knife.
> • It is careless ___ⓕ___ Sujin to tell my secret plans to her friends.

① ⓐ, ⓑ, ⓕ　　② ⓐ, ⓒ, ⓕ
③ ⓑ, ⓓ, ⓔ　　④ ⓑ, ⓔ
⑤ ⓑ, ⓕ

서답형

[06~09] 다음 우리말과 일치하도록 괄호 안에 주어진 어구를 바르게 배열하시오.

06

내가 고기를 잡으면, 엄마가 그것을 드시게 할 텐데.
(let, the fish, eat, my mom, would, caught, if, it, I, I)

➡ ______________________________
____

07

문자도가 없었다면, 아이들은 조화의 중요성을 배울 수 없었을 텐데.
(the importance of harmony, couldn't, had, it, have, not, if, learned, been, Munjado, for, children)

➡ ______________________________
____

08

그 소년이 문자도를 사용해서, 한자를 배우는 것은 쉬웠다.
(learn, easy, Munjado, for, it, to, the boy, Chinese characters, was, using)

➡ ______________________________
____

09

그 소녀가 어떤 도움 없이 물고기를 잡는 것은 불가능했다.
(catch, impossible, for, any, without, fish, to, was, the girl, it, help)

➡ ______________________________
____

[10~11] 다음 중 밑줄 친 부분의 쓰임이 나머지 넷과 다른 것은?

10
① It is too cold for the little kids to play outside all day long.
② It's good for the patient to walk for an hour every other day.
③ Isn't it difficult to understand the purpose of the city policy?
④ It is natural for a baby to cry.
⑤ I believe that it is unnecessary for you to go abroad to learn English.

중요

11
① It is fun for her to speak in Chinese.
② It will soon be the lunch time.
③ It is not hard to search for much information on the Internet.
④ It was useful for you to bring the books here.
⑤ It was my pleasure to meet the beautiful person like you.

12 다음 문장의 빈칸 (A)~(C)에 들어갈 말로 가장 적절한 것은?

• If the movie ___(A)___ early, I would help you with the homework.
• Were it not for the air, all the living things in the planet ___(B)___ be dead.
• If I ___(C)___ some money, I could give it to you for helping the poor.

	(A)	(B)	(C)
①	ends	would	have
②	ends	could	have had
③	will end	could	had had
④	ended	would	had
⑤	ended	could	have

서답형

13 다음 대화가 자연스럽게 이루어지도록 주어진 단어를 활용하여 문장을 완성하시오. (어법에 맞게 1 단어를 추가할 것.)

> **Teacher:** Somebody gave so much water to the plants that they all died.
> **Tony:** Oh. I think it must be Jane.
> **Teacher:** ______________________.
> (too, give, careless, to, the plants, much, was, her, it, water)

➡ ______________________

____

14 다음 중 어법상 옳은 문장은?

① It is hard of them to speak Spanish as well as English.
② It was very nice for Timothy to invite her to his presentation event.
③ It was cruel of her to mention his shameful experience in the past.
④ Is it okay for his to get a week off a little earlier than usual?
⑤ It isn't difficult of them to move that heavy furniture inside.

서답형

15 다음 우리말을 조건에 맞게 영작하시오.

> Munjado를 배우면, 그들이 한국을 더 이해할 수 있을 텐데.
> (learn, understand, much, can 활용. If로 시작, 총 9 단어로 할 것, 단어 변형 가능)

➡ ______________________

____

서답형

16 다음 우리말을 영작할 때, 어법상 어색한 문장을 모두 고르시오.

> 사회 질서가 없다면, 우리는 이 세상 속에서 평화롭게 살아갈 수 없을 텐데.

① Without social order, we can't live peacefully in this world.
② If it were not for social order, we couldn't live peacefully in this world.
③ If there is no social order, we couldn't live peacefully in this world.
④ Were it not for social order, we couldn't live peacefully in this world.
⑤ If there were no social order, we couldn't live peacefully in this world.

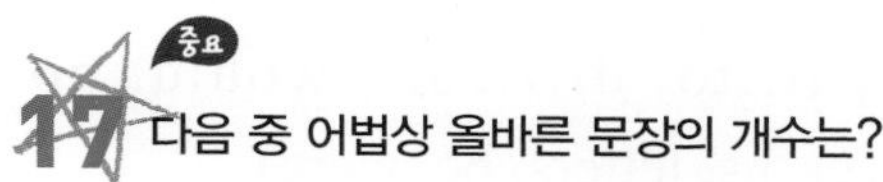

중요

17 다음 중 어법상 올바른 문장의 개수는?

> ⓐ It was pretty importantly for the teacher to make teaching easy to understand.
> ⓑ It was very stupid for Dean to lend money to Kate.
> ⓒ It was wise of Mary not to spend her money buying such a useless thing.
> ⓓ It is clever of Minsu using the equipment.
> ⓔ It is kind of the man to help the old lady to find the way to the subway.
> ⓕ It was impossible for me to arrive at the important business meeting on time.
> ⓖ It is not easy for the girls to pass by that *tteokbokki* restaurant.

① 1개　② 2개　③ 3개　④ 4개　⑤ 5개

서답형

18 다음 문장에서 어법상 어색한 부분을 찾아서 고치시오.

> If the ice didn't melt, the carp wouldn't have come out of the water.

__________ ➡ __________ 또는

__________ ➡ __________

중요

01 다음 우리말과 일치하도록 괄호 안에 주어진 단어들을 바르게 배열하여 문장을 완성하시오.

(1) 그의 어머니가 잉어를 드시면, 곧 건강해질 수 있을 텐데.
➡ If his mother ____________ soon. (could, carp, ate, she, well, get)

(2) 글자가 없다면, 우리가 지식을 전달하는 것이 어려워질 텐데.
➡ If there ____________ ____________ the knowledge. (for, it, to, difficult, would, no, deliver, us, letters, be, were)

(3) 그의 어머니가 자신의 건강을 회복하는 것이 정말로 필요하다.
➡ It's really ____________ ____________. (health, to, for, his, mother, her, necessary, recover)

(4) 이렇게 추운 날씨에 그가 물고기를 잡으려고 하는 것은 매우 어리석었다.
➡ It was ____________ ____________. (try, catch, cold, stupid, this, weather, in, of, to, to, very, him, fish)

고난이도

02 다음 <보기>의 문장과 같은 뜻이 되도록 괄호 안에 주어진 <조건>에 맞게 빈칸을 채우시오.

보기
Without computer, we could not find out much information easily.

(1) ____________ computer, we could not find out much information easily. (it, be동사 활용, 5 단어)

(2) ____________ computer, we could not find out much information easily. (there, no 활용, 4 단어)

(3) ____________ computer, we could not find out much information easily. (it, be동사 활용, 4 단어)

(4) ____________ find out much information easily. (직설법, there, 접속사 as 활용, 6 단어)

03 다음 그림을 보고, 우리말에 맞게 괄호 안의 단어를 활용하여 빈칸을 채우시오.

얼음이 녹지 않았다면, 그가 잉어 세 마리를 잡을 수 없었을 것이다.
→ If ____________ ____________.
(not, melt, catch, carp, ice, can) If 포함하여 총 13 단어, 어형 변화 가능, 축약형 불가)

04 다음 주어진 문장과 뜻이 같도록 빈칸을 알맞게 채우시오. (총 6 단어)

Because Stacy doesn't sleep well enough, she can't be in good condition.
→ If Stacy ____________ in good condition.

05 다음 우리말을 괄호 안에 주어진 단어들을 사용하여 영작하시오. (필요시 단어를 추가하거나 변형할 것)

(1) 전문가들조차 눈이 덮인 산을 등반하는 것은 매우 위험하다.
➡ It is very ______________________ ______________________.
(experts, dangerous, up, with, even, cover, climb)

(2) 당신이 그 짐승을 죽이려고 시도했던 것은 어리석은 일이었다.
➡ It was ______________________ ______________. (attempt, the beast, foolish, kill, to)

(3) 그가 어제 사장님과 파티에 참석했던 것은 재미있었다.
➡ It was ______________________ ______________ yesterday. (his boss, attend, fun, the party)

중요

06 다음 각 가정법 문장에서 어법상 어색한 부분을 모두 찾아 바르게 고치시오.

(1) If I am the superman, I could save the people and defeat the evil aliens.
(2) If it is not for your support, I could not recover from the disaster.
(3) Michelle wouldn't be late for the wedding yesterday if she had caught the subway.
(4) If the girl is lying, I could not understand her situation.
(5) If I have a boy friend, I could go to the concert with him.

➡ (1) ______________ (2) ______________
(3) ______________ (4) ______________
(5) ______________

07 다음 각 문장에서 어법상 어색한 단어를 한 개씩만 찾아 고치시오.

(1) It is necessary for the officers checked all the baggage at the airport.
(2) It was wise for the host of the program to make the actor tell the truth.
(3) It is interesting of Tiffany to meet the boy who could someday be a famous actor.
(4) It was fun for me and my family to sitting around the campfire.
(5) It is not easy for your friends let the eggs stand still.

➡ (1) ______________ (2) ______________
(3) ______________ (4) ______________
(5) ______________

고난이도

08 다음 〈보기〉와 같이 직설법 문장을 가정법으로 고치시오.

보기
As she isn't a dolphin, she can't swim well.
→ If she were a dolphin, she could swim well.

(1) As he is not rich enough, he will go fishing in this cold weather.
➡ ______________________________
____

(2) As Bob isn't in Venice, he isn't happy.
➡ ______________________________
____

(3) As there is no time left, I will cross the road at a red light.
➡ ______________________________
____

(4) As we had Munjado, it was easy for children to learn Chinese characters.
➡ ______________________________
____

교과서

Reading

Munjado, a Window into the Joseon Dynasty

Look at the painting on the right. Do you see the Chinese character, *hyo*(孝)? Do you also see a carp, a geomungo, and a fan? This kind of painting is called (수동태) Munjado, and it is a type of folk painting that (주격 관계대명사: a type of folk painting을 수식) was popular in the late Joseon dynasty. In Munjado, there is usually a Chinese character with (~이 있는) some animals or objects.

One of eight Chinese characters (└ one of+복수 명사: ~ 중 하나, 단수 취급 ┘) appears in Munjado. They are *hyo*(孝), *je*(悌), *chung*(忠), *sin*(信), *ye*(禮), *ui*(義), *yeom*(廉), and *chi*(恥), and they represent the values that (주격 관계대명사: the values를 수식) were important to people of the Joseon dynasty.

The animals or objects in Munjado are not just (= only) decorations. They often are (빈도 부사는 보통 be동사 다음에 나오지만 앞에 나오기도 함.) symbolic. For example, carp in the paintings of *hyo* symbolize (주어인 carp를 복수 취급함.) respect for parents because of (because (×)) an old story. The story goes as follows.

Once upon a time, a man lived with his old mother. One winter, the man's mother became ill (= got ill) and couldn't eat anything. On one very cold day, the mother said to the man, "It would be wonderful if I could eat fresh fish." (가정법 과거: 있을 법하지 않은 일을 가정하여 말할 때 씀.)

dynasty 시대, 왕조
character 글자
carp 잉어(단 · 복수 동형)
folk painting 민화
object 물건, 물체
appear 보이다, 나타나다
represent 나타내다, 보여 주다, 상징하다
value 가치
decoration 장식
symbolic 상징적인, 상징하는
symbolize 상징하다
because of ~ 때문에
once upon a time 옛날 옛적에
ill 아픈
fresh 신선한

확인문제

- 다음 문장이 본문의 내용과 일치하면 T, 일치하지 않으면 F를 쓰시오.

1 There is usually a Chinese character in Munjado. ☐

2 Munjado is a type of folk painting that was popular in the early Joseon dynasty. ☐

3 There are eight Chinese characters that appear in Munjado. ☐

4 The animals or objects in Munjado are only for decorations. ☐

5 The animals or objects in Munjado have meanings. ☐

The man went out to the river, but it was completely frozen. It was
가주어
impossible for him to catch any fish. The man was so disappointed that
의미상의 주어 진주어 some(×) so ~ that ...: 너무 ~해서 …하다
he cried out to the sky, "What should I do? Please help me." Then the
~에 대고 소리치다
ice melted, and three carp suddenly came out of the water. The man
~로부터, 밖으로
went back home and cooked the fish for his mother. Then his mother
= three carp
got well.

There are other examples of symbolic objects in Munjado. They are
other+복수 명사
bamboo in the paintings of the character *chung*(忠) and lotus flowers
in the paintings of *ui*(義). Bamboo does not bend. It stays green in all
= bamboo stay+형용사: ~한 상태를 유지하다
kinds of weather. For these reasons, bamboo came to symbolize loyalty
~하게 되었다(= got to)
to the king. In the case of lotus flowers, they grow in muddy ponds
~의 경우에
but still bloom beautifully. They thus became a symbol of a person's
역접의 의미: 연꽃이 자라는 환경과 꽃을 아름답게 피우는 모습이 대조적임.
will to fight for justice despite difficulties.
형용사적 용법 ~에도 불구하고

Munjado was much more than a painting to people of the Joseon
비교급 more를 수식 (= even, far, a lot, still)
dynasty. It reminded them of important values that greatly influenced
= people of the Joseon dynasty 주격 관계대명사
their behaviors and attitudes. In particular, for children, Munjado was
a study tool. Through it, children in the Joseon dynasty could learn the
= Munjado
importance of harmony in family and society.

frozen 얼어붙은
disappointed 실망한, 낙담한
melt 녹다
suddenly 갑자기
get well 병이 낫다, 회복하다
bamboo 대나무
lotus flower 연꽃
bend 굽다, 구부러지다
for this reason 이런 이유로
loyalty 충성, 충실
muddy 진흙투성이의, 탁한, 흙탕물의
pond 연못
bloom 꽃을 피우다, 꽃이 피다
thus 따라서, 그러므로
will 의지
justice 정의, 공정성
despite ~에도 불구하고
remind A of B A에게 B를 상기시키다
influence 영향을 미치다
behavior 행동
attitude 태도, 자세
in particular 특히
harmony 조화

확인문제

- 다음 문장이 본문의 내용과 일치하면 T, 일치하지 않으면 F를 쓰시오.

1 The man went out to the sea to catch some fish. ☐

2 Three carp suddenly came out of the water in response to the man's cry. ☐

3 Bamboo symbolizes loyalty to the king. ☐

4 Children in the Joseon dynasty could learn the importance of harmony through family and society. ☐

Reading 교과서 확인학습 A

• 우리말을 참고하여 빈칸에 알맞은 말을 쓰시오.

1 Munjado, a Window ________ the Joseon Dynasty

2 Look at the painting ________ ________ ________.

3 Do you ________ the Chinese ________, *hyo*(孝)?

4 Do you also ________ a carp, a geomungo, and a fan?

5 This kind of painting ________ ________ Munjado, and it is ________ ________ ________ ________ ________ ________ ________ ________ in the ________ Joseon dynasty.

6 In Munjado, there is ________ a Chinese character ________ some animals or objects.

7 ________ ________ eight Chinese ________ ________ in Munjado.

8 They are *hyo*(孝), *je*(悌), *chung*(忠), *sin*(信), *ye*(禮), *ui*(義), *yeom*(廉), and *chi*(恥), and they ________ the values ________ ________ ________ ________ people of the Joseon dynasty.

9 The animals or objects in Munjado are not ________ ________.

10 They ________ are ________.

11 For example, carp in the paintings of *hyo* ________ respect for parents ________ ________ an old story.

12 The story ________ ________ ________.

13 ________ ________ ________ ________, a man lived with his old mother.

14 One winter, the man's mother ________ ________ and couldn't eat ________.

15 ________ one very cold day, the mother said to the man, "It ________ ________ ________ ________ ________ ________ ________ fresh fish."

16 The man ________ ________ ________ the river, but it ________ ________ ________.

1 문자도, 조선 시대를 보는 창

2 오른쪽에 있는 그림을 보라.

3 한자 효(孝)가 보이는가?

4 잉어, 거문고, 그리고 부채가 보이는가?

5 이런 종류의 그림은 문자도이며, 조선 시대 후기에 인기 있었던 민화의 한 종류이다.

6 문자도에는 보통 한자 하나가 동물이나 사물과 함께 있다.

7 문자도에는 여덟 개의 한자 중 하나가 나온다.

8 그것들은 효(孝), 제(悌), 충(忠), 신(信), 예(禮), 의(義), 염(廉), 치(恥)이고, 그것들은 조선 시대 사람들에게 중요했던 가치들을 나타낸다.

9 문자도에 있는 동물이나 사물은 단순한 장식이 아니다.

10 그것들은 종종 상징적이다.

11 예를 들어, '효' 그림 속에 있는 잉어는 옛이야기 때문에 부모님에 대한 존경심을 상징한다.

12 그 이야기는 다음과 같다.

13 옛날 옛적에 한 남자가 나이 드신 어머니와 살았다.

14 어느 겨울, 남자의 어머니는 병이 들어서 어떤 것도 먹을 수 없었다.

15 무척 추운 어느 날, 어머니는 남자에게 말했다. "신선한 물고기를 먹을 수 있다면 좋겠구나."

16 그 남자는 강으로 나갔지만, 강은 완전히 얼어붙어 있었다.

17 ________ was impossible ________ ________ ________ ________ ________ fish.

18 The man was ________ ________ ________ he cried out ________ the sky, "What should I do? Please help me."

19 Then the ice ________, and three carp suddenly came ________ ________ the water.

20 The man went ________ ________ and cooked the fish for his mother.

21 Then his mother ________ ________.

22 There are other examples of ________ ________ in Munjado.

23 They are bamboo ________ the paintings ________ the character *chung*(忠) and lotus flowers ________ the paintings ________ *ui*(義).

24 Bamboo does not ________.

25 It ________ ________ ________ all kinds of weather.

26 ________ ________ ________, bamboo ________ ________ ________ loyalty ________ the king.

27 ________ ________ ________ ________ lotus flowers, they grow in muddy ponds ________ ________ bloom ________.

28 They ________ became a symbol of a person's ________ ________ ________ ________ justice ________ difficulties.

29 Munjado was ________ ________ ________ a painting ________ people of the Joseon dynasty.

30 It ________ them ________ important values ________ greatly influenced their behaviors and attitudes.

31 ________ ________, ________ children, Munjado was a study tool.

32 ________ ________, children in the Joseon dynasty could learn the ________ of ________ ________ family and society.

17 그가 그 어떤 물고기라도 잡는 것은 불가능했다.

18 남자는 몹시 낙담해서 하늘에 대고 외쳤다. "제가 어떻게 해야 하나요? 제발 저를 도와주세요."

19 그러자 얼음이 녹았고, 잉어 세 마리가 갑자기 물 밖으로 나왔다.

20 남자는 집으로 돌아가서 어머니를 위해 물고기들을 요리했다.

21 그러자 그의 어머니는 회복되었다.

22 문자도에 있는 상징적인 사물의 또 다른 예가 있다.

23 그것들은 글자 '충(忠)' 그림에 있는 대나무와 '의(義)' 그림에 있는 연꽃이다.

24 대나무는 구부러지지 않는다.

25 그것은 어떤 날씨에서도 푸르름을 유지한다.

26 이런 이유로 대나무는 왕에 대한 충성을 상징하게 되었다.

27 연꽃의 경우, 그것들은 진흙투성이의 연못에서 자라지만 여전히 아름답게 꽃을 피운다.

28 그래서 그 꽃들은 어려움에도 불구하고 정의를 위해 싸우는 사람의 의지를 상징하게 되었다.

29 문자도는 조선 시대 사람들에게 그림 그 이상이었다.

30 그것은 그들에게 자신들의 행동과 태도에 큰 영향을 미치는 중요한 가치를 상기시켰다.

31 특히 아이들에게 문자도는 학습 도구였다.

32 그것을 통해 조선 시대의 아이들은 가족과 사회에서의 조화의 중요성을 배울 수 있었다.

Reading 교과서 확인학습 B

• 우리말을 참고하여 본문을 영작하시오.

1 문자도, 조선 시대를 보는 창

➡ ______________________

2 오른쪽에 있는 그림을 보라.

➡ ______________________

3 한자 효(孝)가 보이는가?

➡ ______________________

4 잉어, 거문고, 그리고 부채가 보이는가?

➡ ______________________

5 이런 종류의 그림은 문자도이며, 조선 시대 후기에 인기 있었던 민화의 한 종류이다.

➡ ______________________

____

6 문자도에는 보통 한자 하나가 동물이나 사물과 함께 있다.

➡ ______________________

7 문자도에는 여덟 개의 한자 중 하나가 나온다.

➡ ______________________

8 그것들은 효(孝), 제(悌), 충(忠), 신(信), 예(禮), 의(義), 염(廉), 치(恥)이고, 그것들은 조선 시대 사람들에게 중요했던 가치들을 나타낸다.

➡ ______________________

____

9 문자도에 있는 동물이나 사물은 단순한 장식이 아니다.

➡ ______________________

10 그것들은 종종 상징적이다.

➡ ______________________

11 예를 들어, '효' 그림 속에 있는 잉어는 옛이야기 때문에 부모님에 대한 존경심을 상징한다.

➡ ______________________

12 그 이야기는 다음과 같다.

➡ ______________________

13 옛날 옛적에 한 남자가 나이 드신 어머니와 살았다.

➡ ______________________

14 어느 겨울, 남자의 어머니는 병이 들어서 어떤 것도 먹을 수 없었다.

➡ ______________________

15 무척 추운 어느 날, 어머니는 남자에게 말했다. "신선한 물고기를 먹을 수 있다면 좋겠구나."

➡ ______________________

16 그 남자는 강으로 나갔지만, 강은 완전히 얼어붙어 있었다.

➡ ____________________

17 그가 그 어떤 물고기라도 잡는 것은 불가능했다.

➡ ____________________

18 남자는 몹시 낙담해서 하늘에 대고 외쳤다. "제가 어떻게 해야 하나요? 제발 저를 도와주세요."

➡ ____________________

19 그러자 얼음이 녹았고, 잉어 세 마리가 갑자기 물 밖으로 나왔다.

➡ ____________________

20 남자는 집으로 돌아가서 어머니를 위해 물고기들을 요리했다.

➡ ____________________

21 그러자 그의 어머니는 회복되었다.

➡ ____________________

22 문자도에 있는 상징적인 사물의 또 다른 예가 있다.

➡ ____________________

23 그것들은 글자 '충(忠)' 그림에 있는 대나무와 '의(義)' 그림에 있는 연꽃이다.

➡ ____________________

24 대나무는 구부러지지 않는다.

➡ ____________________

25 그것은 어떤 날씨에서도 푸르름을 유지한다.

➡ ____________________

26 이런 이유로 대나무는 왕에 대한 충성을 상징하게 되었다.

➡ ____________________

27 연꽃의 경우, 그것들은 진흙투성이의 연못에서 자라지만 여전히 아름답게 꽃을 피운다.

➡ ____________________

28 그래서 그 꽃들은 어려움에도 불구하고 정의를 위해 싸우는 사람의 의지를 상징하게 되었다.

➡ ____________________

29 문자도는 조선 시대 사람들에게 그림 그 이상이었다.

➡ ____________________

30 그것은 그들에게 자신들의 행동과 태도에 큰 영향을 미치는 중요한 가치를 상기시켰다.

➡ ____________________

31 특히 아이들에게 문자도는 학습 도구였다.

➡ ____________________

32 그것을 통해 조선 시대의 아이들은 가족과 사회에서의 조화의 중요성을 배울 수 있었다.

➡ ____________________

[01~03] 다음 글을 읽고 물음에 답하시오.

Munjado a Window into the Joseon Dynasty

Look at the painting on the right. Do you see the Chinese character, *hyo*(孝)? Do you also see a carp, a geomungo, and a fan? This ⓐkind of painting is called Munjado, and it is a type of folk painting that was popular in the late Joseon dynasty. In Munjado, there is usually a Chinese character with some animals or objects.

One of eight Chinese characters appears in Munjado. They are *hyo*(孝), *je*(悌), *chung*(忠), *sin*(信), *ye*(禮), *ui*(義), *yeom*(廉), and *chi*(恥), and ⓑ그것들은 조선 시대 사람들에게 중요했던 가치들을 나타낸다.

01 위 글의 밑줄 친 ⓐkind와 같은 의미로 쓰인 것을 고르시오.

① In the human kind there are varieties in the taste of beauty.
② He is not the kind of person to do things by halves.
③ I know her and her kind.
④ It is very kind of you to lend me the book.
⑤ The periods of kind weather were much too brief.

서답형

02 위 글의 밑줄 친 ⓑ의 우리말에 맞게 주어진 어휘를 알맞게 배열하시오.

they, the Joseon dynasty, the values, people, that, represent, were, important, of, to

➡ ______________________________

____

중요

03 According to the passage, which is NOT true?

① We see the Chinese character, *hyo* at the painting on the right.
② The painting on the right is called Munjado.
③ Munjado is a type of traditional painting.
④ Munjado was popular in the late Joseon dynasty.
⑤ There are usually some animals or objects in Munjado.

[04~06] 다음 글을 읽고 물음에 답하시오.

The animals or objects in Munjado are not just decorations. They often are ____ⓐ____. For example, carp in the paintings of *hyo* symbolize respect for parents because of an old story. The story goes as follows.

Once upon a time, a man lived with his old mother. One winter, the man's mother became ill and couldn't eat anything. On one very cold day, the mother said to the man, "It would be wonderful if I could eat fresh fish."

The man went out to the river, but it was completely frozen. ⓑIt was impossible for him to catch any fish. The man was so disappointed that he cried out to the sky, "What should I do? Please help me." Then the ice melted, and three carp suddenly came ⓒout of the water. The man went back home and cooked the fish for his mother. Then his mother got well.

04 위 글의 빈칸 ⓐ에 들어갈 알맞은 것은?

① characteristic ② objective ③ funny
④ symbolic ⑤ simplistic

05 아래 〈보기〉에서 위 글의 밑줄 친 ⓑIt과 용법이 다른 것의 개수를 고르시오.

보기
① It was windy and chilly yesterday.
② It was hard for me to hide my feelings.
③ When the factory closes, it will mean 500 people losing their jobs.
④ It was very kind of you to visit me when I was ill.
⑤ I make it a rule to get up early in the morning.

① 1개 ② 2개 ③ 3개 ④ 4개 ⑤ 5개

06 위 글의 밑줄 친 ⓒout of와 바꿔 쓸 수 있는 말을 고르시오.

① into ② on ③ at
④ among ⑤ from

[07~09] 다음 글을 읽고 물음에 답하시오.

There are other examples of symbolic objects in Munjado. They are bamboo in the paintings of the character *chung*(忠) and lotus flowers in the paintings of *ui*(義). Bamboo does not bend. It stays green in all kinds of weather. ___ⓐ___, bamboo came to symbolize loyalty to the king. In the case of lotus flowers, they grow in muddy ponds but still bloom beautifully. They thus became a symbol of a person's will to fight for justice despite difficulties.

Munjado was much more than a painting to people of the Joseon dynasty. It reminded them of important values that greatly influenced their behaviors and attitudes. ⓑ특히, for children, Munjado was a study tool. Through it, children in the Joseon dynasty could learn the importance of harmony in family and society.

07 위 글의 빈칸 ⓐ에 들어갈 말로 알맞지 않은 것을 고르시오.

① However ② For these reasons
③ Therefore ④ Thus
⑤ Hence

서답형

08 위 글의 밑줄 친 ⓑ의 우리말을 두 단어로 쓰시오.

➡ ____________________

중요

09 위 글의 앞에 나올 내용으로 적절한 것을 고르시오.

① various Chinese characters that appear in Munjado
② how Munjado developed in the late Joseon dynasty
③ traditional painting skills used in Munjado
④ example of symbolic objects in Munjado
⑤ the use of Munjado

[10~12] 다음 글을 읽고 물음에 답하시오.

Look at the painting on the right. (①) Do you see the Chinese character, *hyo*(孝)? (②) This kind of painting is called Munjado, and it is a type of folk painting ___ⓐ___ was popular in the late Joseon dynasty. (③) In Munjado, there is usually a Chinese character with some animals or objects. (④)
(A)문자도에는 여덟 개의 한자 중 하나가 나온다. (one, eight Chinese characters, Munjado) (⑤) They are *hyo*(孝), *je*(悌), *chung*(忠), *sin*(信), *ye*(禮), *ui*(義), *yeom*(廉), and *chi*(恥), and they represent the values ___ⓐ___ were important to people of the Joseon dynasty.

중요

10 위 글의 흐름으로 보아, 주어진 문장이 들어가기에 가장 적절한 곳은?

> Do you also see a carp, a geomungo, and a fan?

① ② ③ ④ ⑤

11 위 글의 빈칸 ⓐ에 공통으로 들어갈 알맞은 말을 모두 고르시오.

① which ② whom ③ who
④ what ⑤ that

서답형

12 밑줄 친 우리말 (A)를 주어진 어휘를 이용하여 영작하시오.

➡ ______________________________

____

[13~15] 다음 글을 읽고 물음에 답하시오.

> The animals or objects in Munjado are not just decorations. They often are symbolic. ____(A)____, carp in the paintings of *hyo* symbolize respect for parents because of an old story. The story goes as follows.
>
> Once ____ⓐ____ a time, a man lived with his old mother. One winter, the man's mother became ill and couldn't eat anything. On one very cold day, the mother said to the man, "It would be wonderful if I could eat fresh fish."
>
> The man went out to the river, but it was completely frozen. It was impossible for him to catch any fish. The man was so disappointed that he cried out ____ⓑ____ the sky, "What should I do? Please help me." Then the ice melted, and three carp suddenly came out of the water. The man went back home and cooked the fish for his mother. Then his mother got well.

13 위 글의 빈칸 (A)에 들어갈 말로 알맞은 것은?

① However ② Therefore
③ For example ④ In particular
⑤ For these reasons

중요

14 위 글의 빈칸 ⓐ와 ⓑ에 들어갈 전치사가 바르게 짝지어진 것은?

	ⓐ	ⓑ		ⓐ	ⓑ
①	upon	– from	②	upon	– to
③	under	– from	④	under	– to
⑤	on	– at			

서답형

15 What are the animals or objects in Munjado? Answer by using 'not only A but also B', and 'meaning'.

➡ ______________________________

____

[16~17] 다음 글을 읽고 물음에 답하시오.

> There are other examples of symbolic objects in Munjado. They are bamboo in the paintings of the character *chung*(忠) and lotus flowers in the paintings of *ui*(義). Bamboo does not bend. It stays green in all kinds of (A)[weather / whether]. For these reasons, bamboo came to symbolize (B) [royalty / loyalty] to the king. In the case of lotus flowers, they grow in muddy ponds but still bloom beautifully. They thus became a symbol of a person's will to fight (C)[against / for] justice despite difficulties.

서답형

16 What does bamboo stand for in Munjado?

➡ ______________________________

17 위 글의 괄호 (A)~(C)에서 문맥이나 어법상 알맞은 낱말을 골라 쓰시오.

➡ (A) ________ (B) ________ (C) ________

[18~20] 다음 글을 읽고 물음에 답하시오.

Munjado was much more than a painting to people of the Joseon dynasty. It reminded them of important ___ⓐ___ that greatly influenced their behaviors and attitudes. In particular, for children, Munjado was ______ⓑ______. Through it, children in the Joseon dynasty could learn the importance of harmony in family and society.

18 위 글의 빈칸 ⓐ에 알맞은 말을 고르시오.

① values ② tradition ③ habit
④ experience ⑤ experiment

중요

19 위 글의 빈칸 ⓑ에 알맞은 말을 고르시오.

① an entertainment
② a free time activity
③ a playground
④ a study tool
⑤ a stage of practice

서답형

20 What could children in the Joseon dynasty learn from Munjado?

➡ ________________________________
____

[21~23] 다음 글을 읽고 물음에 답하시오.

Look at the painting on the right. Do you see the Chinese character, *hyo*(孝)? Do you also see a carp, a geomungo, and a fan? This kind of painting is called ⓐ<u>Munjado</u>, and it is a type of folk painting that was popular in the late Joseon dynasty. In Munjado, there is usually a Chinese character with some animals or objects.

One of eight Chinese characters appears in Munjado. They are *hyo*(孝), *je*(悌), *chung*(忠), *sin*(信), *ye*(禮), *ui*(義), *yeom*(廉), and *chi*(恥), and they represent the values that were important to people of the Joseon dynasty.

서답형

21 How many Chinese characters appear in Munjado? Answer in a full sentence.

➡ ________________________________
____

서답형

22 다음 빈칸 (A)와 (B)에 알맞은 단어를 넣어, 밑줄 친 ⓐ <u>Munjado</u>에 대한 설명을 완성하시오.

> Munjado is a type of (A)________ painting that was popular in the late Joseon dynasty. In Munjado, there is usually a Chinese character with some animals or objects that represent the (B)________ that were important to people of the Joseon dynasty.

서답형

23 우리가 문자도에서 볼 수 있는 것 두 가지를 본문에서 찾아 쓰시오.

➡ (1) ________________________
(2) ________________________

[01~03] 다음 글을 읽고 물음에 답하시오.

The animals or objects in Munjado are not just decorations. They often are symbolic. For example, carp in the paintings of ___ⓐ___ symbolize respect for parents because of an old story. The story goes as follows.

Once upon a time, a man lived with his old mother. One winter, the man's mother became ill and couldn't eat anything. On one very cold day, the mother said to the man, "___________ⓑ___________"

The man went out to the river, but it was completely frozen. It was impossible for him to catch any fish. The man was so disappointed that he cried out to the sky, "What should I do? Please help me." Then the ice melted, and three carp suddenly came out of the water. The man went back home and cooked the fish for his mother. Then his mother got well.

01 위 글의 빈칸 ⓐ에 알맞은 말을 쓰시오.

➡ ____________________

02 위 글의 빈칸 ⓑ에 'As I cannot eat fresh fish, it is not wonderful.'을 가정법으로 쓰시오. (It으로 시작할 것)

➡ ______________________________

고난이도

03 본문의 내용과 일치하도록 다음 빈칸 (A), (B)와 (C)에 알맞은 단어를 쓰시오.

Carp symbolize (A)_______ _______ _______. In an old story, a man caught (B)_______ _______ in a frozen river and cooked them for his (C)_______ _______.

[04~06] 다음 글을 읽고 물음에 답하시오.

Look at the painting on the right. Do you see the Chinese character, *hyo*(孝)? Do you also see a carp, a geomungo, and a fan? This kind of painting ___ⓐ___ Munjado, and it is a type of folk painting that was popular in the late Joseon dynasty. In Munjado, there is usually a Chinese character with some animals or objects.

One of eight Chinese characters appears in Munjado. They are *hyo*(孝), *je*(悌), *chung*(忠), *sin*(信), *ye*(禮), *ui*(義), *yeom*(廉), and *chi*(恥), and they represent the values that were worthless to people of the Joseon dynasty.

중요

04 위 글의 빈칸 ⓐ에 call을 알맞은 형태로 쓰시오.

➡ ____________________

05 위 글에서 흐름상 어색한 한 단어를 찾아 고치시오.

____________ ➡ ____________

중요

06 위 글에 나타난 문자도의 특징을 '조선 시대 사람'을 반드시 넣어 45자 내외의 우리말로 쓰시오.

➡ ______________________________

____

[07~08] 다음 글을 읽고 물음에 답하시오.

Munjado was ⓐmuch more than a painting to people of the Joseon dynasty. (A)그것은 그들에게 자신들의 행동과 태도에 큰 영향을 미치는 중요한 가치를 상기시켰다. (behaviors and attitudes, values, remind, influence, that) In particular, for children, Munjado was a study tool. Through it, children in the Joseon dynasty could learn the importance of harmony in family and society.

중요

07 위 글의 밑줄 친 ⓐ를 대신해서 쓸 수 있는 것을 3개 이상 쓰시오.

➡ ______________________

08 위 글의 밑줄 친 (A)의 우리말을 괄호 안에 주어진 어휘를 이용하여 13 단어로 영작하시오.

➡ ______________________
____

[09~12] 다음 글을 읽고 물음에 답하시오.

There are other examples of symbolic objects in Munjado. They are bamboo in the paintings of the character *chung*(忠) and lotus flowers in the paintings of *ui*(義). Bamboo does not bend. (A)It stays green in all kinds of weather. For ⓐthese reasons, bamboo ⓑcame to symbolize loyalty to the king. In the case of lotus flowers, they grow in muddy ponds but still bloom beautifully. (B)They thus became a symbol of a person's will to fight for justice despite difficulties.

09 위 글의 밑줄 친 (A)It과 (B)They가 각각 가리키는 것을 본문에서 찾아 쓰시오.

➡ (A) __________ (B) __________

중요

10 위 글의 밑줄 친 ⓐthese reasons에 해당되는 사실 두 가지를 우리말로 쓰시오.

➡ (1) ______________________
(2) ______________________

11 위 글의 밑줄 친 ⓑcame 대신 쓸 수 있는 단어를 쓰시오.

➡ ______________________

고난이도

12 Why could lotus flowers become a symbol of a person's will to fight for justice despite difficulties?

➡ ______________________
____

[13~14] 다음 글을 읽고 물음에 답하시오.

The man went out to the river, but it was completely frozen. ⓐ그가 그 어떤 물고기라도 잡는 것은 불가능했다. The man was so disappointed that he cried out to the sky, "What should I do? Please help me." Then the ice melted, and three carp suddenly came out of the water. The man went back home and cooked the fish for his mother. Then his mother ____(A)____.

13 위 글의 빈칸 (A)에 알맞은 말을 2 단어로 쓰시오.

➡ ______________________

중요

14 위 글의 밑줄 친 ⓐ의 우리말을 it을 이용하여 9 단어로 영작하시오.

➡ ______________________

교과서

구석구석

After You Read B Read and Complete

Paintings of *Hyo*(孝)

Carp symbolize respect for parents. In an old story, a man caught three carp in a frozen river and cooked them for his sick mother.

(symbolize: Carp를 복수 취급함. / them: = three carp)

Paintings of *Chung*(忠)

Bamboo symbolizes loyalty to the king. It does not bend and stays green in all kinds of weather.

(stays green: stay+형용사: ~한 상태를 유지하다)

Paintings of *Ui*(義)

Lotus flowers symbolize a person's will to fight for justice despite difficulties. They grow in muddy ponds but still bloom beautifully.

(fight for: ~을 위해 싸우다 / despite: though(×) / but: 연꽃이 자라는 환경과 꽃을 아름답게 피우는 모습이 대조적임을 나타냄.)

구문해설 • carp: 잉어(단 · 복수 동형) • respect: 존경, 존경심 • frozen: 얼어붙은
• loyalty: 충성, 충실 • will: 의지 • justice: 정의, 공정성 • despite: ~에도 불구하고
• muddy: 진흙투성이의, 탁한, 흙탕물의 • bloom: 꽃을 피우다, 꽃이 피다

해석

'효' 그림

잉어는 부모님에 대한 존경심을 상징한다. 옛이야기에서 한 남자가 얼어붙은 강에서 잉어 세 마리를 잡아 자신의 아픈 어머니를 위해 그것들을 요리했다.

'충' 그림

대나무는 왕에 대한 충성을 상징한다. 그것은 구부러지지 않고 어떤 날씨에서도 푸르름을 유지한다.

'의' 그림

연꽃은 어려움에도 불구하고 정의를 위해 싸우는 인간의 의지를 상징한다. 그 꽃들은 진흙투성이의 연못에서 자라지만 여전히 아름답게 꽃을 피운다.

Around the World

a: This painting shows the harvest time of a countryside in Europe in the 16th century.

(shows: shows 다음에 접속사 that 생략)

b: This painting shows a ssireum competition in the late Joseon dynasty.

(in: 때 · 시간을 나타내는 전치사)

c: This painting shows the marriage of an American farmer's daughter in the 19th century.

(in: 시간을 나타내는 century 앞에 쓰인 전치사)

구문해설 • harvest time: 수확기 • countryside: 시골, 교외 지역 • century: 세기
• competition: 대회 • dynasty: 왕조 • marriage: 결혼, 결혼식

a. 이 그림은 16세기 유럽 교외 지역의 수확기를 보여 준다.

b. 이 그림은 조선 시대 후기의 씨름 대회를 보여 준다.

c. 이 그림은 19세기 미국 농부의 딸의 결혼식을 보여 준다.

Think and Write

My Favorite Painting, *Water Lillies: The Clouds*

My favorite painting is *Water Lilies: The Clouds*. It was painted by Claude Monet. In the painting, I can see the reflection of clouds in the pond as well as water lilies. I like this painting because the colors are beautiful and the scene looks peaceful. I think it was very creative of the painter to draw the pond as a mirror so that the clouds in the sky are reflected in the pond.

(was painted by: 수동태 be+p.p+by(행위자) / as well as: B as well as A = not only A but also B / looks peaceful: look+형용사 보어 peacefully (×) / it: 가주어 / creative of the painter to draw: 사람의 성질+of+의미상 주어+진주어(to 부정사) / so that: ~하도록(목적) / are: 수의 일치 주의 is(×) (the clouds가 주어))

구문해설 • reflection: 반사, 반영, 비친 모습 • B as well as A: A뿐 아니라 B도
• so that: ~하기 위해서, ~하도록

내가 가장 좋아하는 그림, '수련: 구름'

내가 가장 좋아하는 그림은 '수련: 구름'이다. 그것은 Claude Monet에 의해 그려졌다. 그림 속에서, 나는 수련뿐만 아니라 연못에 비친 구름도 볼 수 있다. 나는 색깔도 아름답고, 장면이 평화롭게 보여서 이 그림을 좋아한다. 나는 화가가 연못을 거울로 해서 하늘의 구름이 연못에 비치도록 한 것이 매우 창의적이라고 생각한다.

영역별 핵심문제

Words & Expressions

01 〈보기〉의 밑줄 친 character와 같은 의미로 쓰인 것을 고르시오.

> 보기
> I found that every written character looks balanced and beautiful.

① Before we had our own letters, we had to use Chinese characters.
② The character of the neighbourhood hasn't changed at all
③ Eddie is the funniest character in the show.
④ Character is a habit long continued.
⑤ Just press the button to see your favourite character in action.

02 다음 영영풀이에 해당하는 단어를 주어진 철자로 시작하여 빈칸에 쓰고, 알맞은 것을 골라 문장을 완성하시오.

- a_______: the way you think or feel about something
- t_______: any instrument or simple piece of equipment that you hold in your hands and use to do a particular kind of work

(1) If you want to pass your exams, you'd better change your _______.
(2) Even in small companies, computers are an essential _______.

03 다음 문장의 빈칸에 〈영영풀이〉에 해당하는 어휘를 쓰시오.

They are demanding equal rights and _______.

<영영풀이> the quality of being fair and reasonable; fairness in the way people are treated

04 다음 빈칸 (A)~(C)에 알맞은 말을 쓰시오. (주어진 철자로 시작하여 쓸 것.)

- He goes to his mother and tells her not to worry and to (A)g_______ well soon.
- They might be worth (B)m_______ more than you think.
- You walk (C)s_______ fast that I can't keep up with you.

05 괄호 안에 주어진 어휘를 이용하여 빈칸에 알맞게 쓰시오.

(1) She looked _______ when I told her. (surprise)
(2) It can be very _______ to lose important matches. (disappoint)
(3) His speech was so _______. (bore)

Conversation

[06~08] 다음 대화를 읽고 물음에 답하시오.

B: We can have Gimbap or Tteokbokki. ________(a)________, Jenny?
(A) Let's order, then. I'm very hungry.
(B) I prefer Gimbap. (b)<u>It seems to me that it's the healthier choice.</u> How about you, Minsu?
(C) I'll have Tteokbokki. I heard that the Tteokbokki here is very good.

06 위 대화의 빈칸 (a)에 like를 이용하여 5 단어로 알맞은 말을 쓰시오.

➡ ______________________

07 주어진 문장 다음에 나올 대화의 순서로 알맞은 것은?

① (A) – (C) – (B)
② (B) – (A) – (C)
③ (B) – (C) – (A)
④ (C) – (A) – (B)
⑤ (C) – (B) – (A)

08 위 대화의 밑줄 친 (b)를 think를 이용하여 바꿔 쓰시오. (7 words)

➡ ______________________

09 다음 중 짝지어진 대화가 <u>어색한</u> 것은?

① A: Look at these two old plates, Steve. Aren't they beautiful?
B: Yes. Which one do you prefer, the green plate or the white plate?
② A: I'll have Tteokbokki. I heard that the Tteokbokki here is very good.
B: Let's order, then. I'm very full.
③ A: Which one do you prefer, the one with flowers or the one with animals?
B: I prefer the one with flowers.
④ A: I prefer Tteokbokki. It seems to me that it's more delicious. How about you?
B: I prefer Tteokbokki, too.
⑤ A: Where is the show?
B: It's in Dasom Hall, next to the exhibition room.

[10~11] 다음 대화를 읽고 물음에 답하시오.

John: There are two movies we can see. Which one do you want to see more, Somi?
Somi: I prefer *Batman*. I saw *Spider-Man* last week. Is this OK, John?
John: Of course. It seems to me that *Batman* will be much more fun.
Somi: Good. Then, let's go and see it.

10 위 대화를 읽고 답할 수 <u>없는</u> 질문을 고르시오.

① Does John and Somi want to see a movie?
② What movie did Somi see last week?
③ Does Somi prefer *Batman* to *Spider-Man*?
④ Does John think *Batman* will be much more fun?
⑤ When will John and Somi see *Batman*?

11 위 대화에서 주어진 영영풀이에 해당하는 단어를 찾아 쓰시오.

to like someone or something more than someone or something else, so that you would choose it if you could

➡ ______________________

Grammar

12 다음 중 어법상 올바른 문장의 개수는 모두 몇 개인가?

ⓐ It was exciting for the girl to going abroad to make her dreams come true.
ⓑ It was possibly for me to paint the roof.
ⓒ It is very polite of the baby to say hello to every adult she sees.
ⓓ It's important for the attendants not be late for the event.
ⓔ Was it interesting for they to watch the soccer game between the countries?
ⓕ It is hard of the young ladies to become diligent all the time.

① 1개 ② 2개 ③ 3개 ④ 4개 ⑤ 5개

13 다음 주어진 문장을 가정법으로 바르게 고친 것은?

Since Peterson didn't return the books in time, he couldn't borrow books from the library for a month.

① If Peterson returns the books in time, he can borrow books from the library for a month.
② If Peterson returned the books in time, he could borrow books from the library for a month.
③ If Peterson didn't return the books in time, he could borrow books from the library for a month.
④ If Peterson had returned the books in time, he could have borrowed books from the library for a month.
⑤ If Peterson hadn't returned the books in time, he could not have borrowed books from the library for a month.

[14~15] 다음 우리말에 맞게 영작한 것은?

14

Munjado를 사용하여 자녀를 가르치는 것은 훨씬 더 유용할 것이다.

① It is quite more helpful for you to teach your children using Munjado.
② It will be much more helpful of you to teach your children using Munjado.
③ It is much more helpful for you to teach your children when you will use Munjado.
④ It will be much more helpful for you to teach your children using Munjado.
⑤ It would be quite more helpful for you to teach your children while using Munjado.

15

눈이 충분히 온다면 당신이 스키를 즐길 수 있을 텐데.

① If you have enough snow, you could enjoy skiing.
② Had you snow enough, you can enjoy skiing.
③ If it didn't snow much, you wouldn't enjoy skiing.
④ If it snows enough, you would enjoy skiing.
⑤ If it snowed enough, you could enjoy skiing.

16 다음 문장 중 어법상 어색한 것은?

① If Lucy got up early, she wouldn't be late for the meeting.
② If Jade had worn the coat, she wouldn't have got a cold.
③ If I were the president, I would make a new policy to respect each other.
④ If David told this to her, she would be mad at me.
⑤ If Smith succeeded in catching the school bus this morning, he would not have been late for school.

17 다음 우리말을 주어진 단어를 이용하여 가정법 문장으로 쓰고, 직설법 문장으로도 바꿔 쓰시오.

> 잉어들이 얼음 위로 올라오지 않았더라면, 그의 어머니가 그것들을 먹을 수 없었을 텐데.
> (the carp, come out, eat, can, over the ice)

➡ (1) If ______________________________
______________________________.
(2) 직설법: As ______________________________
______________________________.

Reading

[18~20] 다음 글을 읽고 물음에 답하시오.

> There are other examples of symbolic objects in Munjado. They are bamboo in the paintings of the character *chung*(忠) and lotus flowers in the paintings of *ui*(義). Bamboo does not bend. It stays green in all kinds of weather. ___ⓐ___ these reasons, bamboo came to symbolize loyalty to the king. In the case of lotus flowers, they grow in muddy ponds but still bloom beautifully. They thus became a symbol of a person's will to fight ___ⓐ___ justice despite difficulties.

18 위 글의 빈칸 ⓐ에 공통으로 들어갈 전치사는? (대 · 소문자 무시)

① on ② from ③ in
④ to ⑤ for

19 주어진 영영풀이에 해당하는 단어를 본문에서 찾아 쓰시오.

> to express indirectly by an image, form, or model

➡ ______________________

20 본문의 내용과 일치하도록 다음 빈칸 (A), (B)와 (C)에 알맞은 단어를 쓰시오.

> Bamboo symbolizes (A)________ to the king. It does not (B)________ and stays (C)________ in all kinds of weather.

[21~23] 다음 글을 읽고 물음에 답하시오.

> Munjado was much more than a painting to people of the Joseon dynasty. It remained them of important values that greatly influenced their behaviors and attitudes. In particular, for children, Munjado was a study tool. Through it, children in the Joseon dynasty could learn the importance of harmony in family and society.

21 위 글에서 잘못 쓰인 어휘 하나를 찾아 바르게 고쳐 쓰시오.

______________ ➡ ______________

22 위 글의 주제로 알맞은 것을 고르시오.

① the role of Munjado in the Joseon dynasty
② how to draw Munjado
③ the history of Munjado
④ why people of the Joseon dynasty liked Munjado
⑤ what is Munjado

23 According to the passage, which is NOT true?

① Munjado was much more than a painting to people of the Joseon dynasty.
② People of the Joseon dynasty had some important values.
③ Some important values greatly influenced behaviors and attitudes of people of the Joseon dynasty.
④ Children drew Munjado as a study tool.
⑤ Children in the Joseon dynasty could learn the importance of harmony in family and society through Munjado.

[24~25] 다음 글을 읽고 물음에 답하시오.

Look at the painting on the right. Do you see the Chinese character, *hyo*(孝)? Do you also see a carp, a geomungo, and a fan? This kind of painting is called Munjado, and it is a type of folk painting that was popular in the late Joseon dynasty. In Munjado, there is usually a Chinese character with some animals or objects.

One of eight Chinese characters appear in Munjado. They are *hyo*(孝), *je*(悌), *chung*(忠), *sin*(信), *ye*(禮), *ui*(義), *yeom*(廉), and *chi*(恥), and they represent the values that were important to people of the Joseon dynasty.

24 위 글에서 어법상 <u>어색한</u> 것을 찾아 바르게 고치시오.

__________ ➡ __________

25 What is usually there in Munjado?

➡ ______________________________

____

[26~27] 다음 글을 읽고 물음에 답하시오.

Ssireum was painted by Kim Hong Do. This is one of Kim Hong Do's most famous paintings. It shows two men in a ssireum competition. Many people are watching the competition.

The Country Wedding was painted by John Lewis Krimmel in 1820. The painting shows a wedding. There are two birds above the people getting married. These birds are symbols for peace and happiness.

The Harvesters was painted by Pieter Bruegel the Elder in 1565. It was painted on wood. The painting shows farmers working in the summer. Some workers are taking a rest and some are eating food.

26 What do the two birds above the people getting married in *The Country Wedding* symbolize?

➡ ______________________________

27 Where and when was *The Harvesters* painted?

➡ ______________________________

출제율 95%

01 다음 중 짝지어진 단어의 관계가 나머지와 다른 것은?

① ill – healthy
② represent – symbolize
③ possible – impossible
④ respect – disrespect
⑤ justice – injustice

출제율 100%

02 밑줄 친 부분의 의미로 알맞지 않은 것은?

① You thus need to stay alert and focused. (따라서, 그러므로)
② For this reason, we need signs in this area. (이런 이유로)
③ She puts great value on thrift. (가치, 중요성)
④ The people buried at Stonehenge might have been royalty. (충성, 충실)
⑤ A clover with four leaves is a symbol of luck. (상징)

출제율 90%

03 다음 빈칸에 들어갈 알맞은 어휘를 주어진 철자로 시작하여 쓰시오.

(1) Does this r________ you of the mistake you made last time?
(2) The proposal will go ahead d________ strong objections from the public.

출제율 90%

04 다음 주어진 우리말에 맞게 빈칸을 채우시오. (주어진 철자로 시작할 것)

(1) 그는 선생님들에게 좋은 태도를 보인다.
➡ He has a good a________ towards his teachers.
(2) 조선 왕조는 1392년에 세워졌다.
➡ The Joseon d________ was founded in 1392.

[05~06] 다음 대화를 읽고 물음에 답하시오.

G: Joe, didn't you say you needed to buy a cap? (a)How about these caps here?
B: They look great.
G: Which one do you prefer, the one with triangles or the one with flowers?
B: I prefer the one with triangles. It seems to me that it's more unique.

출제율 90%

05 위 대화의 밑줄 친 (a)를 what과 say를 이용하여 같은 뜻으로 쓰시오.

➡ ________________________

출제율 100%

06 위 대화의 내용과 일치하는 것을 고르시오.

① Joe didn't say he needed to buy a cap.
② These caps here don't look great.
③ Joe prefers the cap with flowers.
④ The cap with triangles seems more unique to Joe.
⑤ The girl prefers the cap with triangles.

[07~08] 다음 대화를 읽고 물음에 답하시오.

G: Look at these two old plates, Steve. Aren't they beautiful?
B: Yes. Which one do you prefer, the green plate or the white plate?
G: Well, it's hard to choose, but I like the green one better. How about you?
B: (a)Me, too. It seems to me that the green plate is more unique.

출제율 90%

07 Why does Steve prefer the green plate? Answer by using "It's because" and "seems to".

➡ ______________________________
____

출제율 95%

08 위 대화의 밑줄 친 (a)Me, too. 대신 쓸 수 있는 것을 고르시오.

① Me, neither.
② Neither am I.
③ Neither do I.
④ So am I.
⑤ So do I.

[09~10] 다음 대화를 읽고 물음에 답하시오.

G: Junsu, you said you're going to buy a gift for your sister. How about the bags here?
B: They look (a)[nice / nicely].
G: (b)[What / Which] one do you prefer, the one with flowers or the one with animals?
B: I prefer the one with flowers. It (c)[appears / looks] to me that my sister will like it more.

출제율 95%

09 위 대화의 괄호 (a)~(c)에서 알맞은 것을 골라 바르게 짝지은 것은?

	(a)	(b)	(c)
①	nice	Which	appears
②	nicely	What	looks
③	nice	What	appears
④	nicely	Which	looks
⑤	nice	What	appears

출제율 90%

10 What do you guess Junsu is going to do? Answer with 12 words.

➡ ______________________________
____

[11~12] 다음 중 어법상 옳은 것을 고르시오.

출제율 95%

11 ① It is impossible for they to master the Chinese grammar in two weeks.
② It was dangerous for the babies to jump on the thin board.
③ It is necessary of those inside the building to breathe in fresh air.
④ It was difficult for the boys to playing on the wet ground.
⑤ It was kind for the principal to help the poor students with his own money.

출제율 100%

12 ① What would Jimin do if it rained on his sister's marathon day?
② If there had been no Chinese characters, it would be difficult for us to communicate.
③ Mary will be sad if I left her.
④ If Nancy were not so hungry, she can share her meal with me.
⑤ Her father would feel happy if Susan makes it to the finals of the competition.

출제율 95%

13 다음 각 문장의 밑줄 친 It[it]이 어떤 용법으로 쓰였는지 〈보기〉에서 기호를 골라 괄호 안에 쓰시오.

보기
ⓐ 가주어-진주어 구문의 It[it]
ⓑ It ~ that 강조 구문의 It[it]
ⓒ 인칭대명사 It[it]
ⓓ 비인칭 주어 It[it]

(1) It is over there. (　　)
(2) It is for his daughters that David has worked so hard day and night. (　　)
(3) It is not true that they will throw a surprise party tonight. (　　)
(4) It is 6 miles from the store to the post office. (　　)
(5) What was it that made the girl decide to lose weight in a short time? (　　)
(6) It is wonderful for your neighbors to gather to celebrate your success. (　　)
(7) It has rained since last weekend. (　　)
(8) It was the graduation present that his uncle bought at the store. (　　)
(9) It is clever of the students to make robots by recycling the waste. (　　)
(10) She overcame her physical weakness, and it made people impressed. (　　)

출제율 90%

14 괄호 안의 조건과 가정법을 이용하여 다음 대화의 빈칸을 알맞게 채우시오.

(1) A: Does he have my phone number?
B: No, but if he ________________, he ____________ you. (have, will, call 활용)

(2) A: Is the man on the right rich?
B: No, but if he ____________, he ____________ the jacket. (be, buy, can 활용)

(3) A: Didn't Amy attend the meeting?
B: Yes, but if she ________________, she ______________ the news. (not, attend, can, hear 활용, 축약형 쓸 것)

[15~17] 다음 글을 읽고 물음에 답하시오.

The animals or objects in Munjado are not just decorations. They often are symbolic. For example, carp in the paintings of hyo symbolize respect for parents because of an old story. The story goes (A)다음과 같이.

Once upon a time, a man lived with his old mother. One winter, the man's mother became ill and couldn't eat anything. On one very cold day, the mother said to the man, "It would be wonderful if I could eat fresh fish."

The man went out to the river, but it was completely frozen. (①) It was impossible for him to catch any fish. (②) The man was so disappointed that he cried out to the sky, "What should I do? (③) Please help me." (④) Then the ice ____ⓐ____, and three carp suddenly came out of the water. (⑤) Then his mother got well.

출제율 90%

15 위 글의 빈칸 ⓐ에 들어갈 알맞은 말을 고르시오.

① froze　② appeared
③ melted　④ heightened
⑤ assembled

출제율 95%

16 위 글의 흐름으로 보아, 주어진 문장이 들어가기에 가장 적절한 곳은?

The man went back home and cooked the fish for his mother.

①　②　③　④　⑤

출제율 90%

17 위 글의 밑줄 친 (A)의 우리말을 두 단어로 쓰시오.

➡ ______________

[18~20] 다음 글을 읽고 물음에 답하시오.

There are other examples of symbolic objects in Munjado. They are bamboo in the paintings of the character (A)*chung*(忠) and lotus flowers in the paintings of (B)*ui*(義). Bamboo does not bend. It stays green in all kinds of weather. For these reasons, bamboo came to symbolize loyalty to the king. In the case of lotus flowers, they grow in muddy ponds but still bloom beautifully. They ___ⓐ___ became a symbol of a person's will to fight for justice despite difficulties.

Munjado was much more than a painting to people of the Joseon dynasty. It reminded them of important values that greatly influenced their behaviors and attitudes. In particular, for children, Munjado was a study tool. Through it, children in the Joseon dynasty could learn the importance of harmony in family and society.

출제율 90%

18 위 글의 빈칸 ⓐ에 들어갈 알맞은 말을 고르시오.

① however ② thus
③ for instance ④ in addition
⑤ that is

출제율 95%

19 위 글의 밑줄 친 (A)와 (B)에 해당하는 그림을 고르시오.

①

②

③

➡ (A) ________ (B) ________

출제율 95%

20 What was Munjado to people of the Joseon dynasty? Fill in the blanks with suitable words.

> Munjado (A)________ them of important (B)________ that greatly influenced their (C)________ and (D)________.

[21~22] 다음 글을 읽고 물음에 답하시오.

Look at the painting on the right. Do you see the Chinese character, *hyo*(孝)? Do you also see a carp, a geomungo, and a fan? This kind of painting is called Munjado, and it is a type of folk painting that was popular in the late Joseon dynasty. In Munjado, there is usually a Chinese character with some animals or objects.

One of eight Chinese characters appears in Munjado. They are *hyo*(孝), *je*(悌), *chung*(忠), *sin*(信), *ye*(禮), *ui*(義), *yeom*(廉), and *chi*(恥), and ⓐ그것들은 조선 시대 사람들에게 중요했던 가치들을 나타낸다.

출제율 95%

21 밑줄 친 ⓐ의 우리말에 맞게 주어진 어휘를 이용하여 13 단어로 영작하시오.

> people of the Joseon dynasty, that, important, represent

➡ ______________________________
____

출제율 100%

22 위 글을 읽고 답할 수 없는 것을 고르시오.

① Can you see the Chinese character, *hyo*(孝) in the painting on the right?
② Are there also a carp, a geomungo, and a fan in the painting?
③ Is Munjado a type of folk painting?
④ Was Munjado popular in the late Joseon dynasty?
⑤ Why does one of eight Chinese characters appear in Munjado?

서술형 실전문제

[01~03] 다음 대화를 읽고 물음에 답하시오.

G: There are two exhibitions we can go to. Which one do you want to see more, Eric?
B: I prefer the Korean mask exhibition. Is that OK, Somi?
G: Of course. And it seems to me that the mask exhibition will be very more interesting.
B: Do you think so?
G: Yes. Look at this poster. There isn't just an exhibition. There's also a mask dance show at 4:00 and 6:00.
B: Great! I've never seen a mask dance show before.
G: Well, I've seen a show before. I'm sure you'll like it.
B: So where is the show?
G: It's in Dasom Hall, next to the exhibition room.
B: It's 4:30 now, so let's watch the 6 o'clock show.
G: OK. Let's go see the exhibition first.

01 Has Somi seen a mask dance show before?

➡ ______________________

02 Before watching the mask dance show what will they do? Answer with 6 words.

➡ ______________________

03 위 대화에서 어법상 어색한 것을 하나 찾아 바르게 고치시오.

__________ ➡ __________

04 다음 우리말과 같은 뜻이 되도록 괄호 안에 있는 단어들을 활용하여, 글자 수에 맞게 영작하시오. (의미에 맞게 주어진 단어들의 형태 변화 가능)

(1) 그들이 호랑이를 잡는 것은 불가능했다. (they, the tiger, catch, possible 활용, 총 9 단어)

➡ ______________________

____

(2) 그 여자들이 커다란 개를 향해 손을 내민 것은 정말로 부주의했다. (woman, care, real, reach out to, a big dog 활용, 총 14 단어)

➡ ______________________

____

05 다음 그림을 보고, 주어진 단어를 알맞게 배열하여 대화를 완성하시오.

Tom: Kim, have you heard of an old story about the carp in Munjado?
Kim: Of course. In a cold day, a man caught the carp to save his mother, right?
Tom: Yeah, that's why the carp symbolized the love for parents.
Kim: Oh. If ______________________.
(in his situation, I, done, have, been, I, the same thing, never, had, could)

➡ ______________________

____

[06~09] 다음 글을 읽고 물음에 답하시오.

The animals or objects in Munjado are not just decorations. They often are symbolic. For example, carp in the paintings of *hyo* symbolize respect for parents because of an old story. The story goes as follows.

Once upon a time, a man lived with his old mother. One winter, the man's mother became ill and couldn't eat anything. On one very cold day, the mother said to the man, "It would be wonderful if I could eat fresh fish."
The man went out to the river, but it was completely frozen. It was impossible for him to catch any fish. ⓐ남자는 몹시 낙담해서 하늘에 대고 외쳤다, "What should I do? Please help me." Then the ice melted, and three carp suddenly came out of the water. The man went back home and cooked the fish for his mother. Then his mother got well.

06 How could the man in the story catch three carp? Fill in the blanks (A) and (B) with suitable words.

When he cried out to the sky, (A)_______ _______ _______, and three carp suddenly (B)_______ _______ _______ the water.

07 Why did the man go out to the river on one very cold winter day? Answer in English in a full sentence with to infinitive.

➡ ______________________________

____

08 Why was it impossible for the man to catch any fish? Answer in English in a full sentence beginning with "Because".

➡ ______________________________

09 밑줄 친 ⓐ의 우리말에 맞게 주어진 어휘를 이용하여 12 단어로 영작하시오.

disappointed, so, cried, the sky

➡ ______________________________

____

[10~11] 다음 글을 읽고 물음에 답하시오.

There are other examples of symbolic objects in Munjado. They are bamboo in the paintings of the character *chung*(忠) and lotus flowers in the paintings of *ui*(義). Bamboo does not bend. It stays green in all kinds of weather. For these reasons, bamboo came to symbolize loyalty to the king. In the case of lotus flowers, they grow in muddy ponds but still bloom beautifully. They thus became a symbol of a person's will to fight for justice ___ⓐ___ difficulties.

10 위 글의 빈칸 ⓐ에 알맞은 한 단어를 쓰시오.

➡ ____________________

11 본문의 내용과 일치하도록 다음 빈칸 (A), (B)와 (C)에 알맞은 단어를 쓰시오.

Lotus flowers symbolize (A)_______ _______ _______ to fight for justice (B)_______ _______. They grow in muddy ponds but still (C)_______ _______.

창의사고력 서술형 문제

01 주어진 표현을 이용하여 〈보기〉와 같이 대화를 완성하시오.

보기

A: Which bag do you prefer, the one with fish or the one with stars?
B: I prefer the one with stars. It seems to me that it's more my style. How about you?
A: I prefer the one with stars, too.

bag / plate / painting / food
the one with fish, the one with stars / the green one, the white one / the one on the left, the one on the right / Tteokbokki, Gimbap
my style / unique / cute / delicious

(1) ____________________

(2) ____________________

(3) ____________________

03 다음 내용을 바탕으로 미술 작품에 대해 감상문을 쓰시오.

1. My Favorite Painting: *Water Lilies*: *The Clouds*
2. name of the painter: Claude Monet
3. details about the painting: I can see the reflection of clouds in the pond as well as water lilies
4. why I like the painting: the colors are beautiful and the scene looks peaceful

My Favorite Painting, (A)____________

My favorite painting is (A)____________. It was painted by (B)____________. In the painting, I can see (C)____________ in the pond as well as (D)____________. I like this painting because (E)____________. I think it was very creative of the painter to draw the pond (F)____________ so that the clouds in the sky are reflected in the pond.

단원별 모의고사

01 다음 짝지어진 단어의 관계가 같도록 빈칸에 알맞은 말을 쓰시오. (주어진 철자로 시작할 것.)

> difficulty – hardship :
> community – s________

[02~03] 주어진 영어 설명에 알맞은 어휘를 빈칸에 쓰시오. (주어진 철자로 시작할 것.)

02

> Soldiers swore their l________ to the country.

> <영어 설명> a feeling of support for someone or something

➡ ____________________

03

> There's a strange o________ in the sky.

> <영어 설명> a thing that you can see and touch

➡ ____________________

04 다음 빈칸에 알맞은 말로 짝지어진 것을 고르시오.

> • Notes ________ musical sounds.
> • The snow was beginning to ________.

① express – bloom
② hide – cancel
③ hide – melt
④ represent – cancel
⑤ represent – melt

05 다음 우리말을 주어진 어휘를 이용하여 영작하시오.

(1) 스트레칭을 할 때 무릎을 구부려라. (your knees, stretch, 6 단어)

➡ ____________________

(2) 그 소년은 나무 뒤에서 갑자기 나타났다. (from, the tree, behind, 8 단어)

➡ ____________________

(3) 비둘기는 평화를 상징한다. (the dove, represent, 4 단어)

➡ ____________________

[06~07] 다음 대화를 읽고 물음에 답하시오.

> **John:** There are two movies we can see. (a) <u>Which one do you want to see more, Somi?</u>
> **Somi:** I prefer *Batman*. I saw *Spider-Man* last week. Is this OK, John?
> **John:** Of course. (b)<u>"배트맨"이 훨씬 더 재미있을 것 같아.</u> (that, fun, me, seem, much)
> **Somi:** Good. Then, let's go and see it.

06 위 대화의 밑줄 친 (a)를 prefer를 이용하여 바꿔 쓰시오.

➡ ____________________

07 위 대화의 밑줄 친 (b)를 괄호 안에 주어진 어휘를 이용하여 영작하시오.

➡ ____________________
____

[08~10] 다음 대화를 읽고 물음에 답하시오.

G: There are two exhibitions we can go to. Which one do you want to see more, Eric?
B: I prefer the Korean mask exhibition. Is that OK, Somi?
G: Of course. And it seems to me that the mask exhibition will be much more interesting.
B: Do you think so?
G: Yes. Look at this poster. There isn't just an exhibition. There's also a mask dance show at 4:00 and 6:00.
B: Great! I've never seen a mask dance show before.
G: Well, I've seen a show before. I'm sure you'll like it.
B: So where is the show?
G: It's in Dasom Hall, next to the exhibition room.
B: It's 4:30 now, so let's watch the 6 o'clock show.
G: OK. Let's go see the exhibition first.

08 What will they do right after the conversation?

➡ ______________________

09 What time will they watch the mask dance show?

➡ ______________________

10 위 대화의 내용과 일치하지 않는 것은?

① Eric은 한국의 탈 전시회를 더 선호한다.
② 소미는 탈 전시회가 더 흥미로울 것 같다고 말한다.
③ 포스터에는 전시회와 탈춤 공연이 나와 있다.
④ 공연은 전시관 옆 다솜 홀에서 한다.
⑤ Eric과 소미는 4시 30분에 탈춤 공연을 볼 것이다.

[11~12] 다음 중 밑줄 친 부분의 쓰임이 다른 것은?

11
① It is nice of the police officer to help those kids cross the road.
② It is very important for you and your friends to manage time effectively.
③ It is foolish of the new staff to make the same mistake twice.
④ It is far from here, and the road is always packed with cars.
⑤ It's very kind of the lady to help my son find his missing kitty.

12
① If a burglar came into my room, I would throw something at him.
② If he were an actor in the film, we could see him at least once.
③ I'd go out to meet the friends if it stopped raining.
④ Dave has no idea if the rumor about Kelly would turn out true.
⑤ If Yuna practiced harder, she would get a full year scholarship.

13 다음 각 문장을 〈보기〉와 같이 바꿔 쓰시오.

보기
To catch any fish was impossible. (the man)
→ It was impossible for the man to catch any fish.

(1) To move the heavy table alone is not easy. (she)
➡ ______________________
____

(2) Taking animals on an airplane is impossible. (he)
➡ ______________________
____

(3) Not showing respect for other players is rude. (Angelina)

➡ ______________________

____

14 다음 중 〈보기〉의 밑줄 친 would와 쓰임이 같은 것은?

보기

Jacob would accept the job offer from the foreign companies if his wife agreed on their suggestion.

① Would you hold my umbrella a little while, please?

② The villagers said that they would visit the land full of honey and milk.

③ My family would go on a picnic to the lake park when my kids were young.

④ All the participants would like to meet the director of the *Academy* award film.

⑤ I would not buy those useless, expensive bags if I were you.

15 다음 중 내용상 〈보기〉의 밑줄 친 부분과 바꿔 쓸 수 없는 것은?

보기

If it were not for the carp from the lake, he could not help her mother to recover.

① Were it not for the carp from the lake

② Without the carp from the lake

③ If there were no carp from the lake

④ But for the carp from the lake

⑤ Had it not been for the carp from the lake

[16~18] 다음 대화를 읽고 물음에 답하시오.

Look at ⓐthe painting on the right. Do you see the Chinese character, *hyo*(孝)? Do you also see a carp, a geomungo, and a fan? This kind of painting is called Munjado, and it is a type of folk painting that was popular in the late Joseon dynasty. In Munjado, there is usually a Chinese character with some animals or objects.

One of eight Chinese characters appears in Munjado. They are ⓑ*hyo*(孝), *je*(悌), *chung*(忠), *sin*(信), *ye*(禮), *ui*(義), *yeom*(廉), and *chi*(恥), and they represent the values that were important to people of the Joseon dynasty.

16 위 글의 밑줄 친 ⓐ에 해당하는 것을 고르시오.

① ② ③ ④ ⑤

17 위 글의 밑줄 친 ⓑ에 대한 설명의 빈칸 (A)와 (B)를 알맞은 말로 써 넣으시오.

They are the eight Chinese characters that (A)________ in Munjado and they represent (B)________ ________ that were important to people of the Joseon dynasty.

18 When was Munjado popular? Answer in English in a full sentence.

➡ ______________________

[19~21] 다음 글을 읽고 물음에 답하시오.

The animals or objects in Munjado are not just decorations. They often are symbolic. For example, carp in the paintings of hyo symbolize respect for parents because of an old story. The story goes as follows.

Once upon a time, a man lived with his old mother. One winter, the man's mother became ill and couldn't eat anything. On one very cold day, the mother said to the man, "It would be wonderful if I could eat fresh fish."

The man went out to the river, but it was completely frozen. It was impossible for him to catch any fish. The man was so ___ⓐ___ that he cried out to the sky, "What should I do? Please help me." Then the ice melted, and three carp suddenly came out of the water. (A)<u>The man went back home and cooked his mother the fish.</u> Then his mother got well.

19 위 글의 빈칸 ⓐ에 들어갈 알맞은 말을 고르시오.

① excited
② delighted
③ disappointed
④ satisfied
⑤ indifferent

20 What happened after the man cried out to the sky?

➡ ________________________________
____

21 위 글의 밑줄 친 (A)를 다음과 같이 바꿔 썼을 때 빈칸에 알맞은 말을 쓰시오.

The man went back home and cooked ____________ his mother.

[22~23] 다음 글을 읽고 물음에 답하시오.

There are other examples of symbolic objects in Munjado. They are bamboo in the paintings of the character *chung*(忠) and lotus flowers in the paintings of *ui*(義). Bamboo does not bend. It stays green in all kinds of weather. For these reasons, bamboo came to symbolize loyalty to the king. In the case of lotus flowers, they grow in muddy ponds but still bloom beautifully. They thus became a symbol of a person's will to fight against justice despite difficulties.

Munjado was much more than a painting to people of the Joseon dynasty. It reminded them of important values that greatly influenced their behaviors and attitudes. In particular, for children, Munjado was a study tool. Through it, children in the Joseon dynasty could learn the importance of

22 위 글에서 흐름상 어색한 부분을 하나 찾아 바르게 고치시오.

____________ ➡ ____________

23 According to the passage, which is NOT true?

① There are some symbolic objects in Munjado.
② Bamboo symbolizes loyalty to the king in Munjado.
③ Lotus flowers in Munjado is a symbol of a person's will to fight for justice despite difficulties.
④ Munjado was just a normal folk painting to people of the Joseon dynasty.
⑤ Children in the Joseon dynasty could learn the importance of harmony in family and society through Munjado.

Lesson

Special

Reading for Fun 3

Finding the Good in Your Friends

교과서

Words & Expressions

Key Words

- □ **accident** [ǽksidənt] 명 사고
- □ **air** [ɛər] 명 공중, 허공
- □ **calm** [kɑːm] 형 침착한, 차분한
- □ **cheerful** [ʧíərfəl] 형 발랄한, 쾌활한
- □ **compliment** [kɑ́mpləmənt] 명 칭찬, 찬사 동 칭찬하다
- □ **confidently** [kɑ́nfədəntli] 부 자신 있게
- □ **creative** [kriéitiv] 형 창의적인, 창조적인
- □ **fair** [fɛər] 형 공평한, 공정한
- □ **hesitate** [hézətèit] 동 망설이다, 주저하다
- □ **hurt** [həːrt] 동 ~을 다치게 하다, 아프다
- □ **list** [list] 명 목록, 명단
- □ **messy** [mési] 형 지저분한, 엉망인
- □ **pause** [pɔːz] 명 (일시적인) 중단
- □ **pick** [pik] 동 뽑다, 따다, 뜯다
- □ **point** [pɔint] 동 가리키다
- □ **scratch** [skræʧ] 동 긁다
- □ **scream** [skriːm] 동 비명을 지르다
- □ **shyly** [ʃáili] 부 수줍게, 부끄러워하며
- □ **still** [stil] 형 가만히 있는, 고요한
- □ **stuck** [stʌk] 형 (~에 빠져) 움직일 수 없는
- □ **worried** [wə́ːrid] 형 난처한, 딱한, 걱정[근심]스러운
- □ **work** [wəːrk] 동 효과가 있다

Key Expressions

- □ **a piece of** 하나의 ~, 한 조각의 ~
- □ **all day long** 하루 종일
- □ **bicycle stand** 자전거 거치대
- □ **come out of** ~에서 나오다
- □ **except for** ~을 제외하고
- □ **Just a minute.** 잠깐만.
- □ **pull out** 빠져나가다[나오다]
- □ **the other day** 일전에, 최근에
- □ **What made you ~?** 무엇 때문에 ~했니?
  = Why did you ~?

Word Power

※ 명사+y: 형용사

□ **messy** 지저분한, 엉망인
□ **stormy** 폭풍우의
□ **foggy** 안개가 낀
□ **milky** 유백색의, 젖의
□ **sleepy** 졸린
□ **dreamy** 꿈같은
□ **cloudy** 구름이 낀
□ **windy** 바람이 부는
□ **salty** 짠, 소금기가 있는
□ **fatty** 지방이 많은
□ **dusty** 먼지투성이의
□ **greedy** 욕심 많은
□ **rainy** 비오는, 비가 많이 내리는
□ **sunny** 햇빛이 잘 드는
□ **oily** 기름의, 지성(脂性)의
□ **spicy** 양념 맛이 강한, 매운
□ **speedy** 빠른
□ **thrifty** 검소한

※ 서로 비슷한 뜻을 가진 어휘

□ **calm** 침착한, 차분한 : **cool** 냉정한, 침착한
□ **fair** 공평한, 공정한 : **just** 올바른, 공정한
□ **point** 가리키다 : **indicate** 가리키다
□ **compliment** 칭찬 : **praise** 칭찬, 찬양
□ **hurt** 다치게 하다 : **injure** 다치게 하다
□ **messy** 지저분한, 엉망인 : **dirty** 더러운

※ 서로 반대의 뜻을 가진 어휘

□ **compliment** 칭찬, 찬사 ↔ **criticism** 비평, 비판
□ **hurt** 다치게 하다 ↔ **heal** 고치다, 낫게 하다
□ **fair** 공평한, 공정한 ↔ **unfair** 불공평한
□ **messy** 지저분한, 엉망인 ↔ **tidy** 단정한

English Dictionary

□ **accident** 사고
→ an unfortunate mishap; especially one causing damage or injury
불운한 일; 특히 손상이나 부상을 일으키는 것

□ **compliment** 칭찬, 찬사
→ a polite remark that you say to someone to show that you like their appearance, appreciate their qualities, or approve of what they have done
누군가에게 당신이 그의 외모를 좋아한다거나 그의 자질을 인정한다거나 그가 한 것을 지지한다는 것을 보여주기 위해 하는 공손한 언급

□ **hesitate** 망설이다, 주저하다
→ to pause or hold back in uncertainty or unwillingness
불확실하거나 내키지 않아서 잠시 멈추거나 억제하다

□ **pause** 중단
→ a short period when you stop doing something before continuing
계속하기 전에 하던 것을 멈추는 잠깐의 기간

□ **point** 가리키다
→ to hold out your finger towards a person or thing in order to make someone notice them
누군가가 그것을 알아채도록 하기 위해 손가락을 사람이나 물건을 향해 내밀다

□ **scratch** 긁다
→ to rub your fingernails against your skin because it is itching
가려워서 손톱을 피부에 대고 문지르다

□ **scream** 비명을 지르다
→ to make a very loud, high-pitched cry
매우 크고 높은 음조로 소리치다

□ **work** 효과가 있다
→ to be successful, effective, or satisfactory
성공적이거나 효과가 있거나 만족할 만 하다

□ **list** 목록, 명단
→ a set of names or addresses which all belong to a particular category, written down one below the other
모두 어떤 특정 범주에 속하는, 하나 밑에 다른 하나가 쓰여 있는 이름이나 주소의 모음

교과서

Reading

The Best Compliment Ever

compliment 칭찬, 찬사; 칭찬하다
all day long 하루 종일
scratch 긁다
list 목록, 명단
except for ~을 제외하고
accident 사고
stuck (~에 빠져) 움직일 수 없는
air 공중, 허공
still 가만히 있는, 고요한
scream 비명을 지르다

Scene 1

It is the last week of school. Each student has just picked a piece of paper with a name on it.

It: 특별한 의미 없이 쓰인 비인칭 주어
paper: 셀 수 없는 명사, 단위를 나타내는 a piece of를 써서 수를 나타낸다.

Ms. Kemp: "Compliments for Classmates" will be our last activity of the school year. Did everyone pick a name?

Class: Yes, Ms. Kemp.

Students are talking to each other.

Beth: So, whose name did you pick?

Lucy: (*smiling*) I got Boyd. I have a lot to say about him. What about you, Beth?

to부정사의 형용사적 용법

Beth: (*looking worried*) Uh, I picked Peter's name.

Lucy: Peter? Oh, no! It won't be easy to find something to compliment him on.

가주어 / 진주어 / compliment+목적어+on ~: ~에 대해 칭찬하다. to compliment: to부정사의 형용사적 용법

Steve: Yeah. He doesn't talk much and just sits at his desk all day long.

Beth: (*scratching her head*) Well, I'll have to find something.

Scene 2

Beth is at home talking with her parents about the activity.

Beth: Everyone has long lists of compliments for other classmates, except for me. I don't know what to compliment Peter on.

everyone: 단수로 취급, 동사: has / ~은 제외하고 / = what I should compliment

Mom: Think carefully. There should be something.

Beth: Well, he's clean. He washes his face every day.

Mom: That's not a compliment. Everybody does that.

= He washes his face every day / everybody: 단수로 취급, 동사: does

Dad: Try again. I'm sure you can find something good to say about him.

I'm sure 다음에 명사절을 이끄는 접속사 that이 생략 / something과 같이 -thing으로 끝나는 대명사는 형용사가 뒤에서 수식 / to부정사의 형용사적 용법

Scene 3

The next day, there is an accident at school. Boyd's foot is stuck in a bicycle stand.

Boyd: (*with arms in the air*) Help! I need help!

Beth: Stay still. I'm trying to pull your foot out.

Boyd: (*screaming*) Ouch! That hurts!

Peter: Let me help. Just a minute.

● 다음 문장이 본문의 내용과 일치하면 T, 일치하지 않으면 F를 쓰시오.

1 Lucy had a lot to say about Boyd. ☐

2 Dad wasn't sure Beth could find anything good to say about Peter. ☐

Peter runs to the school's kitchen and comes back with butter.

Peter: I'm going to put this butter on your foot.

Boyd: What? Butter?

Peter: Just stay calm.

Beth: (*pointing to Boyd's foot*) Wow! It's working! Boyd's foot is coming out of the stand.
It: 발에 버터를 바른 것 / work: 효과가 있다 / come out of: ~에서 나오다

Scene 4

Beth is eating dinner with her parents. She tells them about what happened to Boyd.
= her parents / what이 주어로 쓰인 간접의문문

Beth: There was a little accident at school today. Boyd's foot got stuck in a bicycle stand.

Mom: Oh, no! So how did he get his foot out?

Beth: Peter put butter on his foot and then pulled it out.
동사+부사로 이루어진 구동사. 목적어가 대명사일 경우 동사와 부사 사이에만 올 수 있다. it: his foot

Dad: That was really creative. Messy but creative.
Peter put butter on his foot and then pulled it out.

Beth: Hmm. Creative? Can that be a compliment, Dad?
= being creative

Dad: Sure.

Scene 5

It is the last day of school, and the students are complimenting each other.
비인칭 주어 / 서로

Ms. Kemp: Joanne, what compliment do you have for Beth?

Joanne: Beth, you're always cheerful. You're also kind and fair to everybody.

Beth: Thanks, Joanne. It's so nice of you to say so.

Ms. Kemp: Beth, let's hear from you now. You picked Peter's name.

Beth: (*hesitating*) Well, I think Peter is creative. Peter, you're … uh … creative.
I think 다음에 명사절을 이끄는 접속사 that이 생략

Peter: (*shyly*) Really?
…(목적어)에게 ~하게 하다(사역동사). make+목적어+동사원형의 형태로 씀. What made you think ~? = Why did you think ~?

Ms. Kemp: What made you think Peter is creative?

Beth: (*after a long pause*) When Boyd's foot got stuck in the bicycle stand the other day, Peter got it out by using butter. That was creative.
get out 사이에 대명사 목적어를 씀. it = Boyd's foot / by+-ing: ~함으로써

Boyd: Yeah! Nobody else thought of doing that.
Nobody else ~: 다른 누구도 ~하지 않다 / doing that: 버터를 사용해서 Boyd의 발을 꺼낸 것. 전치사 of 다음에 동명사 사용

Steve: I didn't know that. Well, then, I also think he's creative.

Beth: (*confidently*) Yeah, Peter, you ARE creative!

Peter: Thanks, Beth! It's the best compliment ever!

calm 침착한, 차분한
point 가리키다
messy 지저분한, 엉망인
creative 창의적인, 창조적인
cheerful 발랄한, 쾌활한
fair 공평한, 공정한
hesitate 망설이다, 주저하다
shyly 수줍게, 부끄러워하며
pause (일시적인) 중단
the other day 일전에, 최근에
confidently 자신 있게

확인문제

- 다음 문장이 본문의 내용과 일치하면 T, 일치하지 않으면 F를 쓰시오.

1 Peter put butter on Boyd's foot and then pulled it out. ☐

2 Steve thought Beth was creative. ☐

- 우리말을 참고하여 빈칸에 알맞은 말을 쓰시오.

1 The Best ________ Ever

2 Scene 1

3 *It is the ________ week of school.*

4 *Each student has just picked ________ ________ ________ ________ with a name on it.*

5 Ms. Kemp: "________ ________ Classmates" will be our ________ ________ of the school year.

6 Did everyone ________ a name?

7 Class: Yes, Ms. Kemp.

8 *Students are talking to ________ ________.*

9 Beth: So, ________ ________ did you pick?

10 Lucy: (*smiling*) I ________ Boyd.

11 I have a lot ________ ________ about him.

12 ________ ________ you, Beth?

13 Beth: (________ ________) Uh, I picked Peter's name.

14 Lucy: Peter? Oh, no! It won't be easy to find something to ________ ________ ________.

15 Steve: Yeah. He doesn't talk much and just ________ ________ ________ ________ all day long.

16 Beth: (*scratching her head*) Well, I'll ________ ________ ________ something.

17 Scene 2

18 *Beth is at home ________ ________ her parents about the activity.*

19 Beth: Everyone has long lists of compliments for other classmates, ________ ________ me.

20 I don't know ________ ________ ________ Peter on.

21 Mom: Think ________.

1 최고의 칭찬

2 〈장면 1〉

3 이번 주는 학교의 마지막 주이다.

4 각 학생들은 이름 하나가 쓰인 종이 한 장씩을 막 뽑았다.

5 Ms. Kemp: '학급 친구들 칭찬하기'는 이번 학년 우리의 마지막 활동이 될 거예요.

6 모두 이름을 뽑았나요?

7 Class: 네, Kemp 선생님.

8 학생들이 서로 이야기를 나누고 있다.

9 Beth: 너는 누구 이름을 뽑았니?

10 Lucy: (웃으며) Boyd를 뽑았어.

11 그 애에 관해 할 말이 많아.

12 너는 어때, Beth?

13 Beth: (걱정스러운 표정으로) 어, Peter 이름을 뽑았어.

14 Lucy: Peter? 아, 이런! 그 애에 관해서 칭찬할 것을 찾는 게 쉽지 않을 거야.

15 Steve: 그래. 그 애는 말을 많이 하지 않고 하루 종일 그냥 책상에 앉아만 있잖아.

16 Beth: (머리를 긁적이며) 음, 무언가를 찾아야 해.

17 〈장면 2〉

18 Beth는 집에서 그 활동에 대해 자신의 부모님과 이야기를 나누고 있다.

19 Beth: 저를 제외한 모두가 다른 친구들에 대해 긴 칭찬 목록을 가지고 있어요.

20 저는 Peter에 관해 무엇을 칭찬해야 할지 모르겠어요.

21 엄마: 잘 생각해 봐.

22 There ________ ________ something.

23 Beth: Well, ________ clean.

24 He ________ his face every day.

25 Mom: That's not ________ ________.

26 Everybody ________ ________.

27 Dad: Try ________.

28 ________ ________ you can find something good to say about him.

29 Scene 3

30 *The next day, there is ________ ________ at school.*

31 *Boyd's foot ________ ________ in a bicycle stand.*

32 Boyd: (________ ________ ________ ________ ________) Help! I need help!

33 Beth: ________ ________. I'm trying to pull your foot out.

34 Boyd: (*screaming*) Ouch! That ________!

35 Peter: ________ me help. Just a minute.

36 *Peter runs to the school's kitchen and ________ ________ with butter.*

37 Peter: I'm going to ________ this butter ________ your foot.

38 Boyd: What? Butter?

39 Peter: Just stay ________.

40 Beth: (*pointing to Boyd's foot*) Wow! It's ________!

41 Boyd's foot is ________ ________ ________ the stand.

42 Scene 4

43 *Beth is ________ ________ with her parents.*

44 *She tells them about ________ ________ to Boyd.*

45 Beth: There was ________ ________ ________ at school today.

46 Boyd's foot ________ ________ ________ a bicycle stand.

47 Mom: Oh, no! So how did he ________ his foot ________?

22 뭔가 있을 거야.

23 Beth: 음, 그 애는 깔끔해요.

24 매일 세수를 해요.

25 엄마: 그건 칭찬이 아니야.

26 모든 사람들이 하는 거잖니.

27 아빠: 다시 생각해 보렴.

28 그 아이에 대해 말할 뭔가 좋은 것을 분명히 찾을 수 있을 거야.

29 〈장면 3〉

30 다음 날, 학교에서 사고가 생긴다.

31 Boyd의 발이 자전거 거치대에 끼었다.

32 Boyd: (공중에 양팔을 벌린 채) 도와줘! 도움이 필요해!

33 Beth: 가만히 있어. 네 발을 꺼내려고 노력 중이야.

34 Boyd: (비명을 지르며) 아! 아파!

35 Peter: 내가 도와줄게. 잠깐만.

36 Peter가 학교 주방으로 뛰어가 버터를 가지고 온다.

37 Peter: 네 발에 이 버터를 바를 거야.

38 Boyd: 뭐? 버터를?

39 Peter: 그냥 침착하게 있어.

40 Beth: (Boyd의 발을 가리키며) 와! 효과가 있어!

41 Boyd의 발이 거치대에서 빠져나오고 있어.

42 〈장면 4〉

43 Beth는 부모님과 저녁 식사를 하고 있다.

44 그녀는 부모님께 Boyd에게 일어난 일에 대해 이야기한다.

45 Beth: 오늘 학교에서 작은 사고가 있었어요.

46 Boyd의 발이 자전거 거치대에 끼었어요.

47 엄마: 오, 저런! 그래서 발을 어떻게 뺐니?

48 Beth: Peter put butter on his foot and then ________ ________ ________.

49 Dad: That was really creative. ________ but ________.

50 Beth: Hmm. Creative? Can that be ________ ________, Dad?

51 Dad: ________.

52 Scene 5

53 *It is the last day of school, and the students are* ________ ________ ________.

54 Ms. Kemp: Joanne, ________ ________ do you have for Beth?

55 Joanne: Beth, you're always ________.

56 You're also kind and ________ to everybody.

57 Beth: Thanks, Joanne. It's so nice ________ ________ to say so.

58 Ms. Kemp: Beth, let's ________ ________ ________ now.

59 You ________ Peter's name.

60 Beth: (________) Well, I think Peter is creative. Peter, you're … uh … creative.

61 Peter: (________) Really?

62 Ms. Kemp: ________ ________ ________ ________ Peter is creative?

63 Beth: (*after a long* ________) When Boyd's foot got stuck in the bicycle stand ________ ________ ________, Peter got it out ________ ________ butter.

64 That was ________.

65 Boyd: Yeah! ________ ________ thought of doing that.

66 Steve: I didn't know that. Well, then, I ________ think he's creative.

67 Beth: (________) Yeah, Peter, you ARE creative!

68 Peter: Thanks, Beth! It's ________ ________ ________ ________!

48 Beth: Peter가 그 애 발에 버터를 바르고 나서 발을 당겨서 꺼냈어요.

49 아빠: 정말 창의적이구나. 지저분하지만 창의적이야.

50 Beth: 흠. 창의적이라고요? 아빠, 그것이 칭찬이 될 수 있어요?

51 아빠: 물론이지.

52 〈장면 5〉

53 오늘은 학교의 마지막 날이고 학생들은 서로를 칭찬하고 있다.

54 Ms. Kemp: Joanne, Beth에게 무슨 칭찬을 해 주겠니?

55 Joanne: Beth, 너는 항상 쾌활해.

56 또한 친절하고 모두에게 공정해.

57 Beth: 고마워, Joanne. 그렇게 말해 주다니 친절하구나.

58 Ms. Kemp: Beth, 이제 네 말을 들어 보자.

59 Peter의 이름을 뽑았구나.

60 Beth: (주저하며) 음, Peter는 창의적이라고 생각해요. Peter, 너는… 어… 창의적이야.

61 Peter: (수줍어하며) 정말?

62 Ms. Kemp: Peter가 왜 창의적이라고 생각하니?

63 Beth: (한참 있다가) 일전에 Boyd의 발이 자전거 거치대에 끼었을 때, Peter는 버터를 사용해서 그의 발을 꺼냈어요.

64 그것은 창의적이었어요.

65 Boyd: 맞아! 어느 누구도 그렇게 하는 것을 생각하지 못했어.

66 Steve: 난 몰랐어. 음, 그래, 나도 그가 창의적이라고 생각해.

67 Beth: (자신 있게) 그래, Peter, 너는 창의적이야!

68 Peter: 고마워, Beth! 그건 최고의 칭찬이야!

• 우리말을 참고하여 본문을 영작하시오.

1 최고의 칭찬
➡ ______

2 〈장면 1〉
➡ ______

3 이번 주는 학교의 마지막 주이다.
➡ ______

4 각 학생들은 이름 하나가 쓰인 종이 한 장씩을 막 뽑았다.
➡ ______

5 Ms. Kemp: '학급 친구들 칭찬하기'는 이번 학년 우리의 마지막 활동이 될 거예요.
➡ ______

6 모두 이름을 뽑았나요?
➡ ______

7 Class: 네, Kemp 선생님.
➡ ______

8 학생들이 서로 이야기를 나누고 있다.
➡ ______

9 Beth: 너는 누구 이름을 뽑았니?
➡ ______

10 Lucy: (웃으며) Boyd를 뽑았어.
➡ ______

11 그 애에 관해 할 말이 많아.
➡ ______

12 너는 어때, Beth?
➡ ______

13 Beth: (걱정스러운 표정으로) 어, Peter 이름을 뽑았어.
➡ ______

14 Lucy: Peter? 아, 이런! 그 애에 관해서 칭찬할 것을 찾는 게 쉽지 않을 거야.
➡ ______

15 Steve: 그래. 그 애는 말을 많이 하지 않고 하루 종일 그냥 책상에 앉아만 있잖아.
➡ ______

16 Beth: (머리를 긁적이며) 음, 무언가를 찾아야 해.
➡ ______

17 〈장면 2〉
➡ ______

18 Beth는 집에서 그 활동에 대해 자신의 부모님과 이야기를 나누고 있다.
➡ ______

19 Beth: 저를 제외한 모두가 다른 친구들에 대해 긴 칭찬 목록을 가지고 있어요.
➡ ______

20 저는 Peter에 관해 무엇을 칭찬해야 할지 모르겠어요.
➡ ______

21 엄마: 잘 생각해 봐.
➡ ______

22 뭔가 있을 거야.
➡ ______

23 Beth: 음, 그 애는 깔끔해요.
➡ ______

24 매일 세수를 해요.
➡ ______

25 엄마: 그건 칭찬이 아니야.
➡ ______

26 모든 사람들이 하는 거잖니.
➡ ______

27 아빠: 다시 생각해 보렴.
➡ ______

28 그 아이에 대해 말할 뭔가 좋은 것을 분명히 찾을 수 있을 거야.
➡ ______

29 〈장면 3〉
➡ ______

30 다음 날, 학교에서 사고가 생긴다.
➡ ______

31 Boyd의 발이 자전거 거치대에 끼었다.
➡ ______

32 Boyd: (공중에 양팔을 벌린 채) 도와줘! 도움이 필요해!
➡ ______

33 Beth: 가만히 있어. 네 발을 꺼내려고 노력 중이야.
➡ ______

34 Boyd: (비명을 지르며) 아! 아파!
➡ ______

35 Peter: 내가 도와줄게. 잠깐만.
➡ ______

36 Peter가 학교 주방으로 뛰어가 버터를 가지고 온다.
➡ ______

37 Peter: 네 발에 이 버터를 바를 거야.
➡ ______

38 Boyd: 뭐? 버터를?
➡ ______

39 Peter: 그냥 침착하게 있어.
➡ ______

40 Beth: (Boyd의 발을 가리키며) 와! 효과가 있어!
➡ ______

41 Boyd의 발이 거치대에서 빠져나오고 있어.
➡ ______

42 〈장면 4〉
➡ ______

43 Beth는 부모님과 저녁 식사를 하고 있다.
➡ ______

44 그녀는 부모님께 Boyd에게 일어난 일에 대해 이야기한다.
➡ ______

45 Beth: 오늘 학교에서 작은 사고가 있었어요.
➡ ______

46 Boyd의 발이 자전거 거치대에 끼었어요.
➡ ___

47 엄마: 오, 저런! 그래서 발을 어떻게 뺐니?
➡ ___

48 Beth: Peter가 그 애 발에 버터를 바르고 나서 발을 당겨서 꺼냈어요.
➡ ___

49 아빠: 정말 창의적이구나. 지저분하지만 창의적이야.
➡ ___

50 Beth: 흠. 창의적이라고요? 아빠, 그것이 칭찬이 될 수 있어요?
➡ ___

51 아빠: 물론이지.
➡ ___

52 〈장면 5〉
➡ ___

53 오늘은 학교의 마지막 날이고 학생들은 서로를 칭찬하고 있다.
➡ ___

54 Ms. Kemp: Joanne, Beth에게 무슨 칭찬을 해 주겠니?
➡ ___

55 Joanne: Beth, 너는 항상 쾌활해.
➡ ___

56 또한 친절하고 모두에게 공정해.
➡ ___

57 Beth: 고마워, Joanne. 그렇게 말해 주다니 친절하구나.
➡ ___

58 Ms. Kemp: Beth, 이제 네 말을 들어 보자.
➡ ___

59 Peter의 이름을 뽑았구나.
➡ ___

60 Beth: (주저하며) 음, Peter는 창의적이라고 생각해요. Peter, 너는… 어… 창의적이야.
➡ ___

61 Peter: (수줍어하며) 정말?
➡ ___

62 Ms. Kemp: Peter가 왜 창의적이라고 생각하니?
➡ ___

63 Beth: (한참 있다가) 일전에 Boyd의 발이 자전거 거치대에 끼었을 때, Peter는 버터를 사용해서 그의 발을 꺼냈어요.
➡ ___
___

64 그것은 창의적이었어요.
➡ ___

65 Boyd: 맞아! 어느 누구도 그렇게 하는 것을 생각하지 못했어.
➡ ___

66 Steve: 난 몰랐어. 음, 그래, 나도 그가 창의적이라고 생각해.
➡ ___

67 Beth: (자신 있게) 그래, Peter, 너는 창의적이야!
➡ ___

68 Peter: 고마워, Beth! 그건 최고의 칭찬이야!
➡ ___

서술형 실전문제

[01~02] 다음 빈칸에 공통으로 들어갈 말을 쓰시오.

01

- Come _______ of there, whoever you are.
- The project became so expensive that we had to pull _______.

02

- A car _______ happened last night.
- We met by _______ at the airport.

03 다음 빈칸에 알맞은 단어를 〈보기〉에서 골라 쓰시오.

보기

confidently　air　scratch　hesitate

(1) Smoke hung in the _______ above the city.

(2) He _______ said that he would take all the responsibility.

(3) I didn't _______ for a moment about taking the job.

(4) Dad saw you _______ the car.

04 다음 짝지어진 단어의 관계가 같도록 빈칸에 알맞은 말을 쓰시오.

(1) deep – shallow : criticism – _______

(2) appear – disappear : heal – _______

(3) long – lengthy : cool – _______

05 영영풀이를 보고 빈칸에 알맞은 단어를 주어진 철자로 시작하여 쓰시오.

to be successful, effective, or satisfactory

That medicine didn't w_______ at all.

06 다음 괄호 안의 단어를 알맞은 형으로 바꿔 빈칸에 쓰시오.

그 아이는 밥을 지저분하게 먹어서 자주 꾸지람을 듣는다.

➡ The boy is often scolded for his _______ way of eating. (mess)

07 다음 주어진 어휘를 알맞게 배열하여 우리말에 맞게 빈칸을 채우시오. (단어의 형태는 어법에 맞게 변화 가능함.)

(1) 당신이 누구의 이름을 뽑았는지 궁금하다. (pick, name, wonder, whose, you)

➡ I _______________________.

(2) 나는 David에 대해 무엇을 칭찬해야 할지 모르겠다. (David, on, to, compliment, what)

➡ I don't know _______________ _______.

(3) 너는 왜 Sarah가 창의적이라고 생각하게 되었니? (think, make, what, that, you)

➡ _______________________ Sarah is creative?

(4) 그녀는 부모님께 오늘 Tom에게 무슨 일이 일어났는지에 대해 말한다. (happen, about, what, to, Tom)

➡ She tells her parents _______________ _______________ today.

08 다음 문장에서 어법상 어색한 부분을 찾아 바르게 고치시오.

> It is so thoughtful for Beth to give Peter such a nice compliment.

______ ➡ ______

[09~11] 다음 글을 읽고 물음에 답하시오.

It is the (A)[last / latest] week of school. Each student has just picked a piece of paper with a name on ⓐit.

Ms. Kemp: "(B)[Complements / Compliments] for Classmates" will be our last activity of the school year. Did everyone pick a name?

Class: Yes, Ms. Kemp.

Students are talking to each other.

Beth: So, whose name did you pick?

Lucy: (*smiling*) I got Boyd. I have a lot to say about him. What about you, Beth?

Beth: ((C)[*looking / looked*] *worried*) Uh, I picked Peter's name.

Lucy: Peter? Oh, no! It won't be easy to find something to compliment him on.

Steve: Yeah. He doesn't talk much and just sits at his desk all day long.

Beth: (*scratching her head*) Well, I'll have to find something.

09 위 글의 괄호 (A)~(C)에서 문맥이나 어법상 알맞은 낱말을 골라 쓰시오.

➡ (A) ______ (B) ______ (C) ______

10 위 글의 밑줄 친 ⓐ*it*이 가리키는 것을 본문에서 찾아 쓰시오.

➡ ______

11 Whose name did Lucy pick? Answer in English in a full sentence. (4 words)

➡ ______

[12~14] 다음 글을 읽고 물음에 답하시오.

The next day, there is an accident at school. Boyd's foot is ___ⓐ___ in a bicycle stand.

Boyd: (*with arms in the air*) Help! I need help!

Beth: Stay still. I'm trying to pull your foot out.

Boyd: (*screaming*) Ouch! That hurts!

Peter: Let me help. Just a minute.

Peter runs to the school's kitchen and comes back with butter.

Peter: I'm going to put this butter on your foot.

Boyd: What? Butter?

Peter: ⓑJust stay calmly.

Beth: (*pointing to Boyd's foot*) Wow! It's working! Boyd's foot is coming out of the stand.

12 위 글의 빈칸 ⓐ에 stick을 알맞은 형태로 쓰시오.

➡ ______

13 위 글의 밑줄 친 ⓑ에서 어법상 틀린 부분을 찾아 고치시오.

______ ➡ ______

14 본문의 내용과 일치하도록 다음 빈칸 (A)와 (B)에 알맞은 단어를 쓰시오. (각각 한 단어로 쓰시오.)

> When Boyd's foot became unable to move further in a bicycle stand, Peter put (A)______ on Boyd's foot. It (B)______ and Boyd's foot came out of the stand.

단원별 예상문제

출제율 90%

01 다음 빈칸에 알맞은 단어를 〈보기〉에서 골라 쓰시오.

보기

creative stuck compliment work

(1) We were ________ in a traffic jam.

(2) Let your imagination run wild and be ________.

(3) She took what he said as a ________.

(4) My plan ________ed, and I got them to agree.

출제율 95%

02 다음 단어의 영영풀이가 잘못된 것을 고르시오.

① accident: an unfortunate mishap; especially one causing damage or injury

② pull: to hold out your finger towards a person or thing in order to make someone notice them

③ compliment: a polite remark that you say to someone to show that you like their appearance, appreciate their qualities, or approve of what they have done

④ scream: to make a very loud, high-pitched cry

⑤ hesitate: to pause or hold back in uncertainty or unwillingness

출제율 95%

03 밑줄 친 부분과 바꿔 쓸 수 있는 말을 고르시오.

That's maybe the best compliment of my life.

① indication ② creation

③ thrift ④ pause

⑤ praise

출제율 100%

04 빈칸에 들어갈 접미사가 나머지와 다른 하나를 고르시오.

① The sky looks storm___.

② I can't find anything on this mess___ desk.

③ The hotel staff are friend___ and attentive.

④ The greed___ man asked too much for the bag.

⑤ They have plenty of money now, but they still tend to be thrift___.

출제율 95%

05 다음 우리말에 맞도록 빈칸에 알맞은 말을 쓰시오. (철자가 주어진 것도 있음.)

(1) 약간의 실수를 제외하면 그것은 좋다.

➡ It is good ________ ________ a few mistakes.

(2) 나는 강물을 바라보며 하루 종일이라도 앉아 있을 수 있을 것 같아.

➡ I could sit and watch the river ________ ________ ________.

(3) 아이는 수줍게 웃었다.

➡ The child smiled ________.

출제율 95%

06 빈칸 (A)와 (B)에 들어갈 말로 알맞은 것끼리 짝지어진 것을 고르시오.

- Our team was unable to ___(A)___ out of slump during the first half of the game.
- You have to ___(B)___ calm and patient.

	(A)	(B)
①	push	stay
②	push	keep
③	pull	take
④	pull	stay
⑤	pull	let

출제율 100%

07 다음 중 〈보기〉의 밑줄 친 to부정사와 쓰임이 같지 않은 것은?

보기

Mary has a lot to say about her boyfriend.

① Beth needs a piece of paper to write a letter on.

② Jake had no friends to support him.

③ Please bring the injured soldier some beverage to drink.

④ This is a great chance for you to try many kinds of chocolate in one place.

⑤ Clara was impressed to see Peter pull his foot out of the bicycle stand.

출제율 90%

08 우리말에 맞게 주어진 어구를 알맞게 배열하시오.

(1) 버스는 나무를 들이박고, 모든 사람들이 비명을 지르며 도망간다. (the people, a tree, the bus, all, bumps, run away, scream, and, and)

➡ ______________________________

____

(2) 당신이 수의사를 직업으로 삼을 결심을 하게 된 계기는 무엇이었습니까? (a career, a vet, you, what, decide, made, as, on)

➡ ______________________________

____

(3) 일전에 그 문제에 대해서는 정말 미안해요. (I'm, day, the, that problem, awfully, other, sorry, about)

➡ ______________________________

____

출제율 90%

09 다음 그림을 보고, 우리말에 맞게 괄호 안의 단어를 활용하고 필요한 단어를 추가하여 빈칸을 채우시오.

그녀에 대해 칭찬할 점을 찾기가 쉽지 않을 것이다.
→ It ______________________.
(compliment, something, find, her, easy, will, to, on, It을 포함하여 총 12 단어, 어형 변화 및 축약형 불가)

➡ ______________________________

____

출제율 95%

10 다음 주어진 〈보기〉와 같이 빈칸에 알맞은 단어를 넣어 같은 의미의 문장을 완성하시오.

보기

I don't know what to do next.
→ I don't know what I should do next.

(1) We're sure you will learn how to find something good about others.
➡ We're sure you will learn ________
________________.

(2) Jacob wondered what to put on his foot to pull it out of the bicycle stand.
➡ Jacob wondered ________
________________.

(3) Kate showed me how to open the safe.
➡ Kate showed me ________
________________.

출제율 95%

11 다음 주어진 문장과 의미가 같은 문장을 고르시오.

What makes you think the girl is brave?

① Do you think why the girl is brave?
② How you think is the girl brave?
③ How do you think is the girl brave?
④ Do you think why is the girl brave?
⑤ Why do you think the girl is brave?

출제율 90%

12 다음 주어진 우리말에 맞게 괄호 안의 단어만을 사용하여, When을 포함한 총 15단어로 영작하시오. (어법에 맞게 단어의 형태 변화 가능, 단어 중복 사용 가능)

그녀의 손가락이 병에 끼었을 때, Brian이 버터를 사용해서 빼냈다.
(Brian, get, use, stick, in, out, butter, it, finger, she, the bottle, by)

➡ When ________________
________________.

[13~16] 다음 글을 읽고 물음에 답하시오.

Beth is at home talking with her parents about the activity.

Beth: ⓐEveryone has long lists of compliments for other classmates, including me. I don't know ⓑwhat to compliment Peter on.

Mom: Think carefully. There should be something.

Beth: Well, he's clean. He washes his face every day.

Mom: That's not a compliment. Everybody ⓒdoes that.

Dad: Try again. I'm sure you can find something good to say about him.

출제율 95%

13 위 글의 밑줄 친 ⓐ에서 흐름상 어색한 부분을 찾아 고치시오.

________ ➡ ________

출제율 90%

14 위 글의 밑줄 친 ⓑ를 다음과 같이 바꿔 쓸 때 빈칸에 들어갈 알맞은 말을 두 단어로 쓰시오.

➡ what ________ ________ compliment

출제율 90%

15 위 글의 밑줄 친 ⓒdoes that이 구체적으로 가리키는 것을 우리말로 쓰시오.

➡ ________________

출제율 100%

16 According to the passage, which is NOT true?

① Beth didn't know what to compliment Peter on.
② Beth's mom advised her to think carefully.
③ Beth said Peter was clean.
④ Beth's mom said that it was a good compliment to say Peter washes his face every day.
⑤ Beth's dad was sure she could find something good to say about Peter.

[17~19] 다음 글을 읽고 물음에 답하시오.

The next day, there is an accident at school. Boyd's foot is stuck in a bicycle stand.
Boyd: (*with arms in the air*) Help! I need help!
Beth: Stay ⓐstill. I'm trying to pull your foot out.
Boyd: (*screaming*) Ouch! That hurts!
Peter: Let me help. Just a minute.
Peter runs to the school's kitchen and comes back with butter.
Peter: I'm going to put this butter on your foot.
Boyd: What? Butter?
Peter: Just stay calm.
Beth: (*pointing to Boyd's foot*) Wow! ⓑIt's working! Boyd's foot is coming out of the stand.

출제율 90%

17 위 글의 밑줄 친 ⓐstill과 같은 의미로 쓰인 것을 고르시오.

① I wrote to him last month and I'm still waiting for a reply.
② The next day was still warmer.
③ Still waters run deep.
④ We searched everywhere but we still couldn't find it.
⑤ Do you still live at the same address?

출제율 95%

18 위 글의 밑줄 친 ⓑIt이 가리키는 것을 영어로 쓰시오.

➡ ____________________

출제율 100%

19 Which question CANNOT be answered after reading the passage?

① The next day, what accident was there at school?
② Where was Boyd's foot stuck?
③ Who put butter on Boyd's foot?
④ How did Boyd's foot come out of the stand?
⑤ How did Boyd feel about Peter?

[20~22] 다음 글을 읽고 물음에 답하시오.

Beth is eating dinner with her parents. She tells them about what happened to Boyd.
Beth: There was a little accident at school today. (①)
Mom: Oh, no! (②) So how did he get his foot out? (③)
Beth: ⓐPeter put butter on his foot and then pulled out it. (④)
Dad: ⓑThat was really creative. (⑤) Messy but creative.
Beth: Hmm. Creative? Can that be a compliment, Dad?
Dad: Sure.

출제율 95%

20 위 글의 흐름으로 보아, 주어진 문장이 들어가기에 가장 적절한 곳은?

Boyd's foot got stuck in a bicycle stand.

① ② ③ ④ ⑤

출제율 90%

21 위 글의 밑줄 친 ⓐ에서 어법상 틀린 부분을 찾아 고치시오.

______ ➡ ______

출제율 90%

22 위 글의 밑줄 친 ⓑThat이 가리키는 것을 본문에서 찾아 쓰시오.

➡ ______

______

[23~25] 다음 글을 읽고 물음에 답하시오.

It is the last day of school, and the students are complimenting each other.

Ms. Kemp: Joanne, what compliment do you have for Beth?

Joanne: Beth, you're always cheerful. You're also kind and fair to everybody.

Beth: Thanks, Joanne. ⓐ그렇게 말해 주다니 친절하구나.

Ms. Kemp: Beth, let's hear from you now. You picked Peter's name.

Beth: (*hesitating*) Well, I think Peter is creative. Peter, you're … uh … creative.

Peter: (*shyly*) Really?

Ms. Kemp: ⓑWhat made you think Peter is creative?

Beth: (*after a long pause*) When Boyd's foot got stuck in the bicycle stand the other day, Peter got it out by using butter. That was creative.

출제율 90%

23 위 글의 밑줄 친 ⓐ의 우리말에 맞게 so와 nice를 넣어 8 단어로 영작하시오.

➡ ______

출제율 90%

24 위 글의 밑줄 친 ⓑ를 다음과 같이 바꿔 쓸 때 빈칸에 들어갈 알맞은 한 단어를 쓰시오.

➡ ______ did you think Peter is creative?

출제율 95%

25 본문의 내용과 일치하도록 다음 빈칸 (A)와 (B)에 알맞은 단어를 쓰시오.

> Beth thought Peter is (A)______ because Peter got Boyd's foot out by using butter when it (B)______ ______ in the bicycle stand the other day.

MEMO

MEMO

교과서 파헤치기

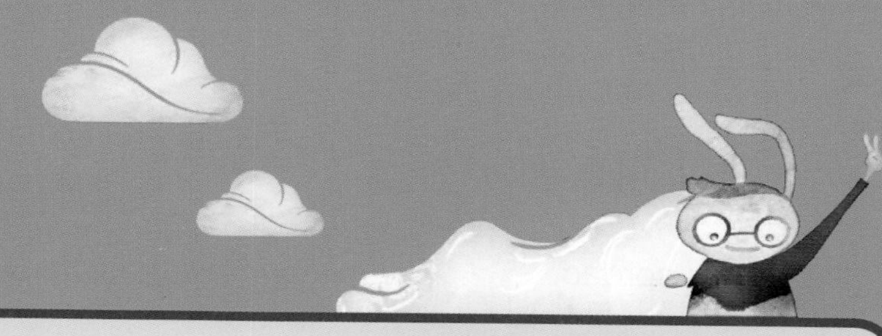

Lesson 7 Technology in Our Lives

Lesson 8 The Joseon Dynasty Through Paintings

Lesson S Finding the Good in Your Friends

단어 Test

Step1

※ 다음 영어를 우리말로 쓰시오.

01 amount ________
02 predict ________
03 influence ________
04 mainly ________
05 complex ________
06 expert ________
07 flu ________
08 insert ________
09 rent ________
10 trace ________
11 forecast ________
12 analyze ________
13 prevention ________
14 crime ________
15 spread ________
16 unlock ________
17 symptom ________
18 meaningful ________
19 industry ________
20 appreciate ________
21 further ________

22 huge ________
23 identify ________
24 purchase ________
25 improve ________
26 develop ________
27 various ________
28 endless ________
29 avoid ________
30 method ________
31 recommend ________
32 upload ________
33 include ________
34 performance ________
35 for sure ________
36 focus on ________
37 by ~ing ________
38 be likely to ~ ________
39 the amount of ~ ________
40 thanks to ~ ________
41 make a decision ________
42 play a role ________
43 be used to+동사원형 ________

단어 Test

Step2

※ 다음 우리말을 영어로 쓰시오.

01 산업, 공업 ____________

02 범죄 ____________

03 전문가 ____________

04 독감 ____________

05 (크기 · 양 · 정도가) 막대한 ____________

06 알아보다, 식별하다 ____________

07 다양한 ____________

08 성장하다, 발달하다 ____________

09 예방 ____________

10 현명하게 ____________

11 개선하다, 향상하다 ____________

12 분석하다 ____________

13 포함하다 ____________

14 총계, 총액 ____________

15 예측하다, 예보하다 ____________

16 교통(량) ____________

17 구매 ____________

18 주로 ____________

19 더 이상의, 추가의 ____________

20 예측하다 ____________

21 끝없는, 무한한 ____________

22 의미 있는, 중요한 ____________

23 삽입하다 ____________

24 피하다, 방지하다 ____________

25 추천하다, 권하다 ____________

26 방법 ____________

27 빌리다 ____________

28 확산, 전파 ____________

29 영향을 미치다 ____________

30 증상 ____________

31 자취, 발자국, 흔적 ____________

32 감사하다, 감상하다 ____________

33 ~을 전송하다 ____________

34 잠금을 풀다 ____________

35 확실히, 분명히 ____________

36 역할을 하다 ____________

37 ~의 양/수량 ____________

38 ~할 것 같다 ____________

39 ~에 초점을 맞추다 ____________

40 결정하다 ____________

41 ~ 덕분에 ____________

42 점점 더 많이 ____________

43 ~하는 데 사용되다 ____________

단어 Test

Step3

※ 다음 영영풀이에 알맞은 단어를 <보기>에서 골라 쓴 후, 우리말 뜻을 쓰시오.

1 __________: a way of doing something: __________

2 __________: to change or affect something: __________

3 __________: to examine something carefully: __________

4 __________: to pay someone for the use of something: __________

5 __________: to stay away from someone or something: __________

6 __________: to realize who someone is or what something is: __________

7 __________: to say that something is going to happen: __________

8 __________: to suggest something to someone: __________

9 __________: the action or process of accomplishing a task or function: __________

10 __________: a large amount of information stored in a computer system: __________

11 __________: the action of buying something; a thing that has been bought: __________

12 __________: something that shows you may have a particular illness: __________

13 __________: the people or companies engaged in a particular kind of commercial enterprise: __________

14 __________: to grow and change into something bigger, better or more important: __________

15 __________: the growth or development of something, so that it affects a larger area or a larger number of people: __________

16 __________: the process by which people exchange information or express their thoughts and feelings: __________

보기

predict	avoid	purchase	database
spread	analyze	develop	recommend
communication	method	identify	performance
symptom	rent	industry	influence

Step1

※ 다음 우리말과 일치하도록 빈칸에 알맞은 말을 쓰시오.

Listen and Talk A 1

B: Excuse me. Can you ________ me ________ ________ ________ money ________ my ________ card?
G: Of course. ________, ________ your card ________ the machine. ________, ________ the ________ of money you want ________ ________.
B: OK.
G: ________, ________ your money ________ the machine.
B: That sounds ________. Thanks.

B: 실례합니다. 어떻게 교통카드에 돈을 충전하는지 알려주시겠어요?
G: 그럼요. 우선 기계에 카드를 넣으세요. 둘째로 충전하고 싶은 금액을 고르세요.
B: 네.
G: 마지막으로 기계에 돈을 넣으세요.
B: 간단해 보이는군요. 고맙습니다.

Listen and Talk A 2

B: I want to buy a snack. Do you ________ ________ ________ ________ this snack machine?
G: Yeah. ________, ________ the snack you want.
B: I already ________. What's ________?
G: Just ________ ________ the money. Then ________ the snack ________.
B: ________ ________. Thanks.

B: 과자를 사고 싶어요. 이 과자 자판기를 어떻게 사용하는지 알려주시겠어요?
G: 네. 먼저 원하는 과자를 고르세요.
B: 이미 했어요. 그 다음은 뭔가요?
G: 돈을 넣으세요. 그러고 나서 과자를 꺼내세요.
B: 알겠어요. 고맙습니다.

Listen and Talk A 3

G: Excuse me. I want to ________ a bike. Can you ________ me ________ ________ ________ this ________?
M: Sure. First, ________ ________ ________ the application. Then find the RENT button and ________ ________.
G: Then ________?
M: Then the application will give you a number ________ ________ a bike ________.
G: Thank you. I really ________ your ________.

G: 실례합니다. 자전거를 빌리고 싶은데요. 이 앱을 어떻게 사용하는지 알려주시겠어요?
M: 그럼요. 우선 앱에 로그인하세요. 그러고 나서 RENT 버튼을 찾고 터치하세요.
G: 그러고 난 후엔 어떻게 하나요?
M: 그 후에는 앱이 자전거를 잠금 해제하는 번호를 알려 줄 거에요.
G: 고맙습니다. 도와주셔서 정말 감사해요.

Listen and Talk B

A: Excuse me. I want to ________ these books. Do you ________ ________ ________ ________ it?
B: Sure. It's ________. First, ________ the library card ________ the machine. Second, ________ the books ________ this box.
A: OK.
B: ________ just ________ your card ________.
A: I really ________ your help.

A: 실례합니다. 저는 이 책들을 반납하고 싶어요. 어떻게 하는지 아시나요?
B: 그럼요. 간단해요. 우선 도서 대출 카드를 기계에 넣으세요. 둘째로 이 상자 안에 책들을 넣으세요.
A: 알겠어요.
B: 그러고 나서 카드를 꺼내세요.
A: 도와주셔서 정말 고맙습니다.

A: Excuse me. I want to ________ money ________ my transportation card. Do you ________ ________ ________ ________ it?

B: Sure. It's ________. ________, put your card in the machine. ________, ________ the ________ of money.

A: OK.

B: ________ ________ the money.

A: I really ________ your ________.

A: 실례합니다. 저는 교통카드에 돈을 충전하고 싶어요. 어떻게 하는지 아시나요?

B: 그럼요. 간단해요. 우선 기계에 카드를 넣으세요. 둘째로 금액을 고르세요.

A: 알겠어요.

B: 그러고 나서 돈을 넣으세요.

A: 도와주셔서 정말 고맙습니다.

A: Excuse me. I want ________ ________ a snack. Do you ________ ________ ________ ________ it?

B: Sure. It's ________. ________, choose the snack. ________, ________ ________ the money.

A: OK.

B: ________ ________ the snack ________.

A: I really ________ your help.

A: 실례합니다. 저는 과자를 사고 싶어요. 어떻게 하는지 아시나요?

B: 그럼요. 간단해요. 우선 과자를 고르세요. 둘째로 돈을 넣으세요.

A: 알겠어요.

B: 그러고 나서 과자를 꺼내세요.

A: 도와주셔서 정말 고맙습니다.

Listen and Talk C

G: Excuse me, but ________ this robot ________?

B: Oh, it's a robot ________ finds books for you.

G: Really? Can you ________ me ________ ________ ________ it?

B: Sure. First, ________ your library card ________ the ________ ________.

G: OK.

B: Second, ________ the ________ of the book you're ________ ________ and then ________ ENTER.

G: ________ ________ ________?

B: Yes. ________, the robot will find the book and take ________ to the ________ ________.

G: So I can just go to the front desk and ________ the book?

B: Right. It's so ________, ________ ________?

G: Yes, it's really ________. Thank you.

G: 실례지만, 이 로봇은 용도가 뭔가요?

B: 아, 이 로봇은 당신을 위해 책을 찾아 주는 로봇이에요.

G: 정말요? 어떻게 사용하는지 알려 주실래요?

B: 그럼요. 먼저, 당신의 도서 대출 카드를 로봇의 화면 위에 놓으세요.

G: 알겠어요.

B: 두 번째로, 당신이 찾으려는 책의 제목을 입력하고 나서 ENTER 키를 누르세요.

G: 그게 다인가요?

B: 네. 그러면 로봇이 책을 찾아서 안내 데스크로 가져다줄 거예요.

G: 그러면 저는 그냥 안내 데스크로 가서 책을 받을 수 있나요?

B: 맞아요. 정말 쉽죠, 그렇지 않나요?

G: 그러네요, 정말 놀라워요. 감사합니다.

Listen and Talk D

________ me tell you ________ ________ ________ a drink machine. ________, ________ money ________ the machine. ________, choose the drink you want. ________, take the drink ________ ________ the machine. It's easy.

음료 자판기를 어떻게 사용하는지 알려 줄게. 먼저 기계에 돈을 넣어. 그러고 나서 원하는 음료를 골라. 마지막으로 기계에서 음료를 꺼내. 간단해.

Talk and Play

A: Do you ________ ________ ________ ________ tea?

B: Sure. ________, ________ a tea bag in a cup.

A: OK.

B: ________, ________ hot water in the cup.

A: And then?

B: ________, ________ the tea bag ________ ________ 3 ________.

A: I ________ ________. I really ________ your help.

A: 차를 어떻게 만드는지 알고 있니?
B: 물론이지. 우선 컵에 티백을 넣어.
A: 알겠어.
B: 그런 후 컵에 뜨거운 물을 부어.
A: 그러고 나서는?
B: 마지막으로 3분 후에 티백을 꺼내.
A: 알겠어. 도와줘서 정말 고마워.

Review 1

G: Can you tell me ________ ________ ________ a potato?

B: Sure. First, ________ a potato ________ small ________. Second, ________ holes ________ the ground.

G: Then?

B: Then ________ the potato ________ ________ the holes and ________ the holes ________ ________.

G: That ________ ________. Thanks.

G: 감자를 어떻게 심는지 알려주시겠어요?
B: 그럼요. 우선 감자를 작은 조각으로 자르세요. 둘째로 땅에 구멍을 파세요.
G: 그러고 나서요?
B: 그러고 나서 구멍에 감자 조각들을 넣고 흙으로 구멍을 덮으세요.
G: 간단한 것 같네요. 고맙습니다.

Review 2

B: Excuse me. Can you ________ me ________ ________ ________ this machine?

G: Sure. First, ________ the paper ________ the ________ ________. Then ________ the paper size and ________ ________ ________ copies.

B: Then ________?

G: ________ the START button.

B: Thank you. I really ________ your help.

B: 실례합니다. 이 기계를 어떻게 사용하는지 알려주시겠어요?
G: 물론이죠. 우선 복사기에 종이를 올려놓으세요. 그러고 나서 종이 크기와 복사본 매수를 고르세요.
B: 그러고 나서 어떻게 해요?
G: START 버튼을 누르세요.
B: 감사합니다. 도와주셔서 고마워요.

대화문 Test

※ 다음 우리말에 맞도록 대화를 영어로 쓰시오.

Listen and Talk A 1

B: ____________________

G: ____________________

____

B: ____________________

G: ____________________

B: ____________________

B: 실례합니다. 어떻게 교통카드에 돈을 충전하는지 알려주시겠어요?
G: 그럼요. 우선 기계에 카드를 넣으세요. 둘째로 충전하고 싶은 금액을 고르세요.
B: 네.
G: 마지막으로 기계에 돈을 넣으세요.
B: 간단해 보이는군요. 고맙습니다.

Listen and Talk A 2

B: ____________________

G: ____________________

B: ____________________

G: ____________________

B: ____________________

B: 과자를 사고 싶어요. 이 과자 자판기를 어떻게 사용하는지 알려주시겠어요?
G: 네. 먼저 원하는 과자를 고르세요.
B: 이미 했어요. 그 다음은 뭔가요?
G: 돈을 넣으세요. 그러고 나서 과자를 꺼내세요.
B: 알겠어요. 고맙습니다.

Listen and Talk A 3

G: ____________________

M: ____________________

G: ____________________

M: ____________________

G: ____________________

G: 실례합니다. 자전거를 빌리고 싶은데요. 이 앱을 어떻게 사용하는지 알려주시겠어요?
M: 그럼요. 우선 앱에 로그인하세요. 그러고 나서 RENT 버튼을 찾고 터치하세요.
G: 그러고 난 후엔 어떻게 하나요?
M: 그 후에는 앱이 자전거를 잠금 해제하는 번호를 알려 줄 거에요.
G: 고맙습니다. 도와주셔서 정말 감사해요.

Listen and Talk B

A: ____________________

B: ____________________

____

A: ____________________

B: ____________________

A: ____________________

A: 실례합니다. 저는 이 책들을 반납하고 싶어요. 어떻게 하는지 아시나요?
B: 그럼요. 간단해요. 우선 도서 대출 카드를 기계에 넣으세요. 둘째로 이 상자 안에 책들을 넣으세요.
A: 알겠어요.
B: 그러고 나서 카드를 꺼내세요.
A: 도와주셔서 정말 고맙습니다.

A:

B:

A:

B:

A:

A: 실례합니다. 저는 교통카드에 돈을 충전하고 싶어요. 어떻게 하는지 아시나요?
B: 그럼요. 간단해요. 우선 기계에 카드를 넣으세요. 둘째로 금액을 고르세요.
A: 알겠어요.
B: 그러고 나서 돈을 넣으세요.
A: 도와주셔서 정말 고맙습니다.

A:

B:

A:

B:

A:

A: 실례합니다. 저는 과자를 사고 싶어요. 어떻게 하는지 아시나요?
B: 그럼요. 간단해요. 우선 과자를 고르세요. 둘째로 돈을 넣으세요.
A: 알겠어요.
B: 그러고 나서 과자를 꺼내세요.
A: 도와주셔서 정말 고맙습니다.

Listen and Talk C

G:

B:

G:

B:

G:

B:

G:

B:

G:

B:

G:

G: 실례지만, 이 로봇은 용도가 뭔가요?
B: 아, 이 로봇은 당신을 위해 책을 찾아 주는 로봇이에요.
G: 정말요? 어떻게 사용하는지 알려 주실래요?
B: 그럼요. 먼저, 당신의 도서 대출 카드를 로봇의 화면 위에 놓으세요.
G: 알겠어요.
B: 두 번째로, 당신이 찾으려는 책의 제목을 입력하고 나서 ENTER 키를 누르세요.
G: 그게 다인가요?
B: 네. 그러면 로봇이 책을 찾아서 안내 데스크로 가져다줄 거예요.
G: 그러면 저는 그냥 안내 데스크로 가서 책을 받을 수 있나요?
B: 맞아요. 정말 쉽죠, 그렇지 않나요?
G: 그러네요. 정말 놀라워요. 감사합니다.

Listen and Talk D

음료 자판기를 어떻게 사용하는지 알려 줄게. 먼저 기계에 돈을 넣어. 그러고 나서 원하는 음료를 골라. 마지막으로 기계에서 음료를 꺼내. 간단해.

Talk and Play

A:

B:

A:

B:

A:

B:

A:

A: 차를 어떻게 만드는지 알고 있니?
B: 물론이지. 우선 컵에 티백을 넣어.
A: 알겠어.
B: 그런 후 컵에 뜨거운 물을 부어.
A: 그러고 나서는?
B: 마지막으로 3분 후에 티백을 꺼내.
A: 알겠어. 도와줘서 정말 고마워.

Review 1

G:

B:

G:

B:

G:

G: 감자를 어떻게 심는지 알려주시겠어요?
B: 그럼요. 우선 감자를 작은 조각으로 자르세요. 둘째로 땅에 구멍을 파세요.
G: 그러고 나서요?
B: 그러고 나서 구멍에 감자 조각들을 넣고 흙으로 구멍을 덮으세요.
G: 간단한 것 같네요. 고맙습니다.

Review 2

B:

G:

B:

G:

B:

B: 실례합니다. 이 기계를 어떻게 사용하는지 알려주시겠어요?
G: 물론이죠. 우선 복사기에 종이를 올려놓으세요. 그러고 나서 종이 크기와 복사본 매수를 고르세요.
B: 그러고 나서 어떻게 해요?
G: START 버튼을 누르세요.
B: 감사합니다. 도와주셔서 고마워요.

※ 다음 우리말과 일치하도록 빈칸에 알맞은 것을 골라 쓰시오.

1 ________ ________ Big Data
A. with B. Living

2 Have you ever visited an online bookstore and ________ ________ by the books that the store ________ ________ you?
A. recommended B. been C. for D. surprised

3 ________ of them ________ ________ to you.
A. looked B. many C. interesting

4 ________ how did the bookstore know ________ ________ ________?
A. you B. so C. liked D. what

5 This is ________ ________ ________ ________ big data.
A. because B. all C. of D. possible

6 ________ ________ big data?
A. is B. what

7 Big data is ________ ________ that are very ________ and ________.
A. sets B. complex C. data D. big

8 ________ information and communication technology ________, the ________ of data we have is getting ________ greater than before.
A. amount B. develops C. much D. as

9 This is ________ because ________ everything that we do online ________ a ________.
A. trace B. mainly C. leaves D. almost

10 For ________, the photos you ________ on your blog and the records of your ________ at online stores are all ________ of big data.
A. purchases B. part C. upload D. example

11 ________ ________ data, ________, is not ________.
A. collecting B. enough C. simply D. however

12 Big data ________ to be ________, and this is ________ by big data ________.
A. experts B. has C. analyzed D. done

13 Using various ________, experts ________ big data and ________ meaningful ________ from it.
A. results B. analyze C. methods D. draw

14 These ________ then can ne ________ to make ________ or to ________ the future.
A. predict B. results C. decisions D. used

15 ________ is big data ________ our ________?
A. influencing B. how C. lives

16 Big data is ________ ________ all ________ of our ________.
A. almost B. lives C. influencing D. parts

17 It helps companies understand their ________ ________ better and helps them ________ more ________.
A. customers' B. products C. needs D. sell

18 It helps people ________ ________ ________.
A. heavy B. avoid C. traffic

19 Its ________ are ________, and here are some ________ ________.
A. interesting B. endless C. examples D. uses

20 ________ ________
A. Forecast B. Disease

1 빅데이터와 함께 살아가기
2 당신은 온라인 서점을 방문해서 그 서점이 당신을 위해 추천한 책들을 보고 놀란 적이 있는가?
3 그것들 중에 많은 것들이 당신에게 흥미로워 보였다.
4 그 서점은 당신이 무엇을 좋아하는지 어떻게 알았을까?
5 이것은 모두 빅데이터 때문에 가능하다.
6 빅데이터는 무엇인가?
7 빅데이터는 매우 크고 복잡한 데이터 집합이다.
8 정보 통신 기술이 발달함에 따라 우리가 갖고 있는 정보의 양도 이전보다 훨씬 더 많아지고 있다.
9 이것은 주로 우리가 온라인상에서 하는 거의 모든 것들이 흔적을 남기기 때문이다.
10 예를 들어, 당신이 블로그에 올린 사진들과 온라인 상점에서의 구매 기록들이 모두 빅데이터의 일부가 된다.
11 하지만 단순히 데이터를 수집하는 것만으로는 충분하지 않다.
12 빅데이터는 분석되어야 하고, 이것은 빅데이터 전문가들에 의해서 이루어진다.
13 다양한 방법들을 사용하여 전문가들은 빅데이터를 분석하고, 그것으로부터 의미 있는 결과들을 도출한다.
14 그런 다음, 이런 결과들은 결정을 하거나 또는 미래를 예측하는 데 사용될 수 있다.
15 빅데이터는 어떻게 우리 삶에 영향을 미치고 있는가?
16 빅데이터는 우리 삶의 거의 모든 부분에 영향을 미치고 있다.
17 그것은 회사들이 소비자들이 필요로 하는 것을 더 잘 이해하고 그들이 더 많은 상품을 팔도록 도와준다.
18 그것은 사람들이 교통 체증을 피하도록 도와주기도 한다.
19 그것의 활용은 끝이 없고, 여기에 몇 가지 흥미로운 예들이 있다.
20 질병 예측

21 Did you know that health ________ can now ________ a ________ just as weather ________ forecast the weather?
A. forecast B. professionals C. experts D. disease

22 This is ________ ________ ________ big data.
A. to B. possible C. thanks

23 For example, when the flu season ________, people will ________ more ________ ________.
A. flu B. buy C. comes D. medicine

24 They will also ________ ________ about ________ ________ more.
A. symptoms B. search C. flu D. online

25 If this kind of data is ________ ________, the ________ of the flu can be ________.
A. spread B. wisely C. analyzed D. predicted

26 ________ ________ in Sports
A. Performance B. Improving

27 Are you a ________ ________?
A. sports B. fan

28 Well, big data is ________ the ________ of players, ________ sports more ________.
A. making B. performance C. exciting D. improving

29 A ________ ________ is ________ ________ soccer team.
A. national B. example C. Germany's D. famous

30 The team built a database by ________ and ________ a ________ ________ of data on players.
A. analyzing B. amount C. collecting D. huge

31 For example, the data ________ information about how ________ each player ________ and how ________ he had the ball.
A. included B. long C. much D. ran

32 ________ the ________ of this database, Germany's national soccer team was able to ________ its ________ and win the 2014 World Cup.
A. improve B. help C. performance D. with

33 ________ ________
A. Prevention B. Crime

34 ________ to big data, police can now ________ ________ before it ________.
A. happens B. thanks C. crime D. predict

35 ________ the ________ of big data about the type, time and place of crime, police can make a map of crime ________ ________.
A. hot B. through C. analysis D. spots

36 This map ________ when and where ________ is most ________ to ________.
A. likely B. identifies C. happen D. crime

37 Police can ________ ________ crime by ________ on the areas and the times this map ________.
A. focusing B. predicts C. further D. prevent

38 Big data ________ ________ ________ the world ________.
A. already B. greatly C. has D. changed

39 So where will the big data ________ ________ ________ ________?
A. go B. here C. industry D. from

40 Nobody knows for ________, but ________ agree that big data will ________ a more and more important ________ in our lives.
A. sure B. role C. experts D. play

---

21 당신은 날씨 전문가가 날씨를 예측하는 것과 같이 건강 전문가들이 현재 질병을 예측할 수 있다는 것을 알고 있는가?
22 이것은 빅데이터 덕분에 가능하다.
23 예를 들어서 독감의 계절이 오면, 사람들은 독감 약을 더 많이 구입할 것이다.
24 그들은 또한 온라인상에서 독감 증상들을 더 찾아볼 것이다.
25 만약 이런 종류의 데이터를 지혜롭게 분석한다면, 독감의 확산을 예측할 수 있다.
26 스포츠에서의 경기력 향상
27 당신은 스포츠 팬인가?
28 빅데이터는 스포츠를 더 흥미롭게 만들면서, 선수들의 경기력을 향상하고 있다.
29 유명한 사례로 독일 국가 대표 축구팀이 있다.
30 그 팀은 선수들에 관한 엄청난 양의 데이터를 모으고 분석함으로써, 데이터베이스를 구축했다.
31 예를 들어 데이터는 각각의 선수들이 얼마나 많이 달렸고, 얼마나 오랫동안 공을 소유했는지도 포함했다.
32 이 데이터베이스의 도움으로 독일 국가 대표 축구팀은 경기력을 향상할 수 있었고, 2014년 월드컵에서 우승할 수 있었다.
33 범죄 예방
34 빅데이터 덕분에 경찰은 이제 범죄가 발생하기 전에 범죄를 예측할 수 있다.
35 범죄의 유형, 시간 및 장소에 관한 빅데이터의 분석을 통해, 경찰은 범죄 다발 지역의 지도를 만들 수 있다.
36 이 지도는 범죄가 언제, 어디에서 가장 많이 발생할 것 같은지를 알려 준다.
37 경찰은 이 지도가 예측하는 장소들과 시간대에 집중함으로써, 추가 범죄를 예방할 수 있다.
38 빅데이터는 이미 세계를 크게 변화시켰다.
39 그러면 빅데이터 산업은 여기에서부터 어디로 가게 될까?
40 누구도 확실히 알지는 못하지만, 전문가들은 빅데이터가 우리 삶에서 더욱 더 중요한 역할을 할 것이라는 데에는 동의한다.

※ 다음 우리말과 일치하도록 빈칸에 알맞은 말을 쓰시오.

1 ________ ________ Big Data

2 Have you ever visited an online bookstore and ________ ________ by the books that the store ________ ________ you?

3 Many of them ________ ________ to you.

4 So how did the bookstore know ________ ________ ________?

5 This is all ________ ________ ________ big data.

6 ________ ________ big data?

7 Big data is ________ ________ that ________ very big and ________.

8 ________ information and communication technology ________, the ________ ________ data we have is ________ ________ ________ than before.

9 This is ________ ________ almost everything that we do online ________ ________ ________.

10 For example, the photos you ________ ________ ________ ________ and the records of ________ ________ at online stores are ________ ________ ________ big data.

11 ________ ________ ________, ________, is not enough.

12 Big data ________ ________ ________ ________, and this is ________ ________ big data experts.

13 ________ various methods, experts ________ big data and ________ ________ ________ from it.

14 These results then ________ ________ ________ to make decisions or ________ ________ the future.

15 ________ is big data ________ our ________?

16 Big data is influencing ________ ________ ________ of our lives.

17 It helps companies ________ ________ ________ ________ better and helps them ________ ________ ________.

18 It helps people ________ ________ ________.

19 Its uses are ________, and here are some ________ ________.

20 Disease ________

1 빅데이터와 함께 살아가기
2 당신은 온라인 서점을 방문해서 그 서점이 당신을 위해 추천한 책들을 보고 놀란 적이 있는가?
3 그것들 중에 많은 것들이 당신에게 흥미로워 보였다.
4 그 서점은 당신이 무엇을 좋아하는지 어떻게 알았을까?
5 이것은 모두 빅데이터 때문에 가능하다.
6 빅데이터는 무엇인가?
7 빅데이터는 매우 크고 복잡한 데이터 집합이다.
8 정보 통신 기술이 발달함에 따라 우리가 갖고 있는 정보의 양도 이전보다 훨씬 더 많아지고 있다.
9 이것은 주로 우리가 온라인상에서 하는 거의 모든 것들이 흔적을 남기기 때문이다.
10 예를 들어, 당신이 블로그에 올린 사진들과 온라인 상점에서의 구매 기록들이 모두 빅데이터의 일부가 된다.
11 하지만 단순히 데이터를 수집하는 것만으로는 충분하지 않다.
12 빅데이터는 분석되어야 하고, 이것은 빅데이터 전문가들에 의해서 이루어진다.
13 다양한 방법들을 사용하여 전문가들은 빅데이터를 분석하고, 그것으로부터 의미 있는 결과들을 도출한다.
14 그런 다음, 이런 결과들은 결정을 하거나 또는 미래를 예측하는 데 사용될 수 있다.
15 빅데이터는 어떻게 우리 삶에 영향을 미치고 있는가?
16 빅데이터는 우리 삶의 거의 모든 부분에 영향을 미치고 있다.
17 그것은 회사들이 소비자들이 필요로 하는 것을 더 잘 이해하고 그들이 더 많은 상품을 팔도록 도와준다.
18 그것은 사람들이 교통 체증을 피하도록 도와주기도 한다.
19 그것의 활용은 끝이 없고, 여기에 몇 가지 흥미로운 예들이 있다.
20 질병 예측

21 Did you know that health professionals can now forecast a disease ________ ________ weather experts ________ the weather?

22 This is possible ________ ________ big data.

23 For example, when the flu season ________, people ________ ________ more ________ ________.

24 They will also ________ ________ ________ flu symptoms more.

25 If this kind of data ________ ________ ________, the ________ of the flu can ________ ________.

26 ________ ________ in Sports

27 Are you a ________ ________?

28 Well, big data ________ ________ the performance of players, ________ sports more ________.

29 A famous example is Germany's ________ ________ ________.

30 The team ________ a database by ________ and ________ a ________ ________ of data on players.

31 For example, the data included information about ________ ________ each player ran and ________ ________ he had the ball.

32 ________ ________ ________ ________ this database, Germany's national soccer team was ________ ________ ________ its performance and win the 2014 World Cup.

33 Crime ________

34 ________ ________ big data, police can now predict crime before it ________.

35 ________ the analysis of big data about the type, time and place of crime, police can make a map of ________ ________ ________.

36 This map ________ when and where crime ________ ________ ________ ________ ________.

37 Police can prevent ________ ________ ________ ________ on the areas and the times this map ________.

38 Big data ________ ________ ________ the world ________.

39 So where will the big data industry ________ ________ ________?

40 Nobody knows for sure, but experts agree that big data will ________ a more and more important ________ in our ________.

21 당신은 날씨 전문가가 날씨를 예측하는 것과 같이 건강 전문가들이 현재 질병을 예측할 수 있다는 것을 알고 있는가?
22 이것은 빅데이터 덕분에 가능하다.
23 예를 들어서 독감의 계절이 오면, 사람들은 독감 약을 더 많이 구입할 것이다.
24 그들은 또한 온라인상에서 독감 증상들을 더 찾아볼 것이다.
25 만약 이런 종류의 데이터를 지혜롭게 분석한다면, 독감의 확산을 예측할 수 있다.
26 스포츠에서의 경기력 향상
27 당신은 스포츠 팬인가?
28 빅데이터는 스포츠를 더 흥미롭게 만들면서, 선수들의 경기력을 향상하고 있다.
29 유명한 사례로 독일 국가 대표 축구팀이 있다.
30 그 팀은 선수들에 관한 엄청난 양의 데이터를 모으고 분석함으로써, 데이터베이스를 구축했다.
31 예를 들어 데이터는 각각의 선수들이 얼마나 많이 달렸고, 얼마나 오랫동안 공을 소유했는지도 포함했다.
32 이 데이터베이스의 도움으로 독일 국가 대표 축구팀은 경기력을 향상할 수 있었고, 2014년 월드컵에서 우승할 수 있었다.
33 범죄 예방
34 빅데이터 덕분에 경찰은 이제 범죄가 발생하기 전에 범죄를 예측할 수 있다.
35 범죄의 유형, 시간 및 장소에 관한 빅데이터의 분석을 통해, 경찰은 범죄 다발 지역의 지도를 만들 수 있다.
36 이 지도는 범죄가 언제, 어디에서 가장 많이 발생할 것 같은지를 알려 준다.
37 경찰은 이 지도가 예측하는 장소들과 시간대에 집중함으로써, 추가 범죄를 예방할 수 있다.
38 빅데이터는 이미 세계를 크게 변화시켰다.
39 그러면 빅데이터 산업은 여기에서부터 어디로 가게 될까?
40 누구도 확실히 알지는 못하지만, 전문가들은 빅데이터가 우리 삶에서 더욱 더 중요한 역할을 할 것이라는 데에는 동의한다.

본문 Test

Step3

※ 다음 문장을 우리말로 쓰시오.

1 Living with Big Data

➡ ____________________

2 Have you ever visited an online bookstore and been surprised by the books that the store recommended for you?

➡ ____________________

3 Many of them looked interesting to you.

➡ ____________________

4 So how did the bookstore know what you liked?

➡ ____________________

5 This is all possible because of big data.

➡ ____________________

6 What is big data?

➡ ____________________

7 Big data is data sets that are very big and complex.

➡ ____________________

8 As information and communication technology develops, the amount of data we have is getting much greater than before.

➡ ____________________

9 This is mainly because almost everything that we do online leaves a trace.

➡ ____________________

10 For example, the photos you upload on your blog and the records of your purchases at online stores are all part of big data.

➡ ____________________

11 Simply collecting data, however, is not enough.

➡ ____________________

12 Big data has to be analyzed, and this is done by big data experts.

➡ ____________________

13 Using various methods, experts analyze big data and draw meaningful results from it.

➡ ____________________

14 These results then can be used to make decisions or to predict the future.

➡ ____________________

15 How is big data influencing our lives?

➡ ____________________

16 Big data is influencing almost all parts of our lives.

➡ ____________________

17 It helps companies understand their customers' needs better and helps them sell more products.

➡ ____________________

18 It helps people avoid heavy traffic.

➡ ____________________

19 Its uses are endless, and here are some interesting examples.

➡ ____________________

20 Disease Forecast

➡ ____________________

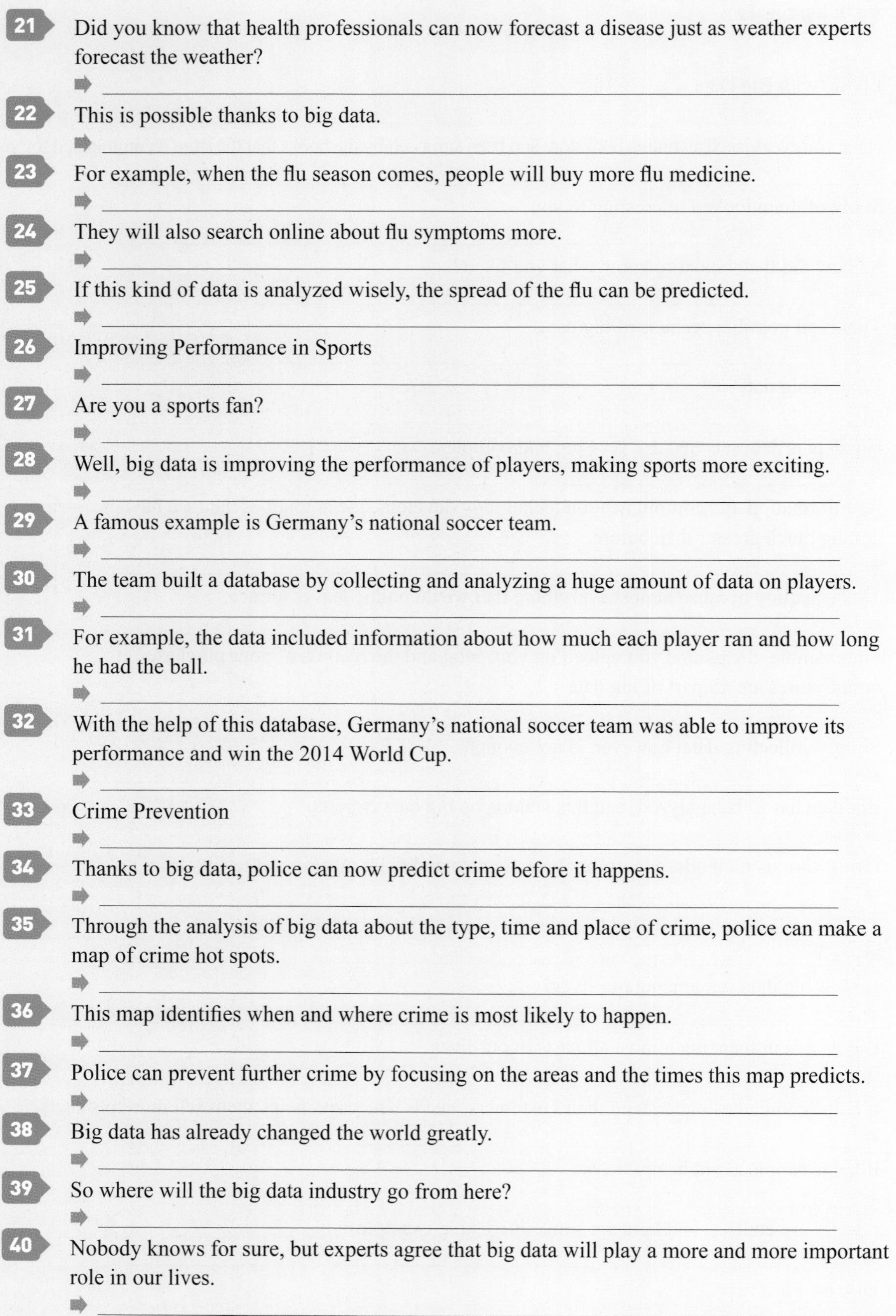

21 Did you know that health professionals can now forecast a disease just as weather experts forecast the weather?

➡ ______________________________

22 This is possible thanks to big data.

➡ ______________________________

23 For example, when the flu season comes, people will buy more flu medicine.

➡ ______________________________

24 They will also search online about flu symptoms more.

➡ ______________________________

25 If this kind of data is analyzed wisely, the spread of the flu can be predicted.

➡ ______________________________

26 Improving Performance in Sports

➡ ______________________________

27 Are you a sports fan?

➡ ______________________________

28 Well, big data is improving the performance of players, making sports more exciting.

➡ ______________________________

29 A famous example is Germany's national soccer team.

➡ ______________________________

30 The team built a database by collecting and analyzing a huge amount of data on players.

➡ ______________________________

31 For example, the data included information about how much each player ran and how long he had the ball.

➡ ______________________________

32 With the help of this database, Germany's national soccer team was able to improve its performance and win the 2014 World Cup.

➡ ______________________________

33 Crime Prevention

➡ ______________________________

34 Thanks to big data, police can now predict crime before it happens.

➡ ______________________________

35 Through the analysis of big data about the type, time and place of crime, police can make a map of crime hot spots.

➡ ______________________________

36 This map identifies when and where crime is most likely to happen.

➡ ______________________________

37 Police can prevent further crime by focusing on the areas and the times this map predicts.

➡ ______________________________

38 Big data has already changed the world greatly.

➡ ______________________________

39 So where will the big data industry go from here?

➡ ______________________________

40 Nobody knows for sure, but experts agree that big data will play a more and more important role in our lives.

➡ ______________________________

본문 Test

Step4

※ 다음 괄호 안의 단어들을 우리말에 맞도록 바르게 배열하시오.

1 (with / Living / Data / Big)

➡ ______________________________

2 (you / have / visited / ever / online / an / bookstore / been / and / by / surprised / books / the / the / that / recommended / store / you? / for)

➡ ______________________________

____

3 (of / many / looked / them / to / interesting / you.)

➡ ______________________________

4 (how / so / the / did / know / bookstore / you / what / liked?)

➡ ______________________________

5 (is / this / possible / all / of / because / data. / big)

➡ ______________________________

6 (is / what / data? / big)

➡ ______________________________

7 (data / big / data / is / that / sets / are / big / very / complex. / and)

➡ ______________________________

8 (information / as / and / technology / communication / develops, / amount / the / data / of / have / we / is / much / getting / greater / before. / than)

➡ ______________________________

____

9 (is / this / because / mainly / almost / that / everything / do / we / online / a / leaves / trace.)

➡ ______________________________

10 (example, / for / photos / the / upload / you / on / blog / your / the / and / records / your / of / at / purchases / online / are / stores / part / all / big / of / data.)

➡ ______________________________

____

11 (collecting / simply / data, / is / however, / enough. / not)

➡ ______________________________

12 (data / big / to / has / analyzed, / be / this / and / done / is / big / by / experts. / data)

➡ ______________________________

1 빅데이터와 함께 살아가기

2 당신은 온라인 서점을 방문해서 그 서점이 당신을 위해 추천한 책들을 보고 놀란 적이 있는가?

3 그것들 중에 많은 것들이 당신에게 흥미로워 보였다.

4 그 서점은 당신이 무엇을 좋아하는지 어떻게 알았을까?

5 이것은 모두 빅데이터 때문에 가능하다.

6 빅데이터는 무엇인가?

7 빅데이터는 매우 크고 복잡한 데이터 집합이다.

8 정보 통신 기술이 발달함에 따라 우리가 갖고 있는 정보의 양도 이전보다 훨씬 더 많아지고 있다.

9 이것은 주로 우리가 온라인상에서 하는 거의 모든 것들이 흔적을 남기기 때문이다.

10 예를 들어, 당신이 블로그에 올린 사진들과 온라인 상점에서의 구매 기록들이 모두 빅데이터의 일부가 된다.

11 하지만 단순히 데이터를 수집하는 것만으로는 충분하지 않다.

12 빅데이터는 분석되어야 하고, 이것은 빅데이터 전문가들에 의해서 이루어진다.

13 (various / using / methods, / analyze / experts / data / big / and / meaningful / draw / from / results / it.)

➡ ____

____

14 (results / these / can / then / used / be / to / decisions / make / to / or / the / predict / future.)

➡ ____

15 (is / how / data / big / our / influencing / lives?)

➡ ____

16 (data / is / big / influencing / all / almost / of / pasts / lives. / our)

➡ ____

17 (helps / it / understand / companies / customer's / their / better / needs / and / them / helps / more / sell / products.)

➡ ____

____

18 (helps / it / avoid / people / traffic. / heavy)

➡ ____

19 (uses / its / endless, / are / here / and / some / are / examples. / interesting)

➡ ____

20 (Forecast / Disease)

➡ ____

21 (you / did / that / know / professionals / health / now / can / a / forecast / disease / as / just / experts / weather / the / forecast / weather?)

➡ ____

____

22 (is / this / thanks / possible / big / to / data.)

➡ ____

23 (example, / for / the / when / season / flu / comes, / will / people / more / buy / medicine. / flu)

➡ ____

____

24 (will / they / search / also / about / online / symptoms / flu / more.)

➡ ____

25 (this / if / of / kind / data / analyzed / is / wisely, / spread / the / the / of / can / flu / predicted. / be)

➡ ____

____

13 다양한 방법들을 사용하여 전문가들은 빅데이터를 분석하고, 그것으로부터 의미 있는 결과들을 도출한다.

14 그런 다음, 이런 결과들은 결정을 하거나 또는 미래를 예측하는 데 사용될 수 있다.

15 빅데이터는 어떻게 우리 삶에 영향을 미치고 있는가?

16 빅데이터는 우리 삶의 거의 모든 부분에 영향을 미치고 있다.

17 그것은 회사들이 소비자들이 필요로 하는 것을 더 잘 이해하고 그들이 더 많은 상품을 팔도록 도와준다.

18 그것은 사람들이 교통 체증을 피하도록 도와주기도 한다.

19 그것의 활용은 끝이 없고, 여기에 몇 가지 흥미로운 예들이 있다.

20 질병 예측

21 당신은 날씨 전문가가 날씨를 예측하는 것과 같이 건강 전문가들이 현재 질병을 예측할 수 있다는 것을 알고 있는가?

22 이것은 빅데이터 덕분에 가능하다.

23 예를 들어서 독감의 계절이 오면, 사람들은 독감 약을 더 많이 구입할 것이다.

24 그들은 또한 온라인상에서 독감 증상들을 더 찾아볼 것이다.

25 만약 이런 종류의 데이터를 지혜롭게 분석한다면, 독감의 확산을 예측할 수 있다.

26 (Performance / Improving / Sports / in)
➡ ______________________________

27 (you / are / sports / a / fan?)
➡ ______________________________

28 (big / well, / data / improving / is / performance / the / players, / of / sports / making / exciting. / more)
➡ ______________________________
____

29 (famous / a / is / example / national / Germany's / team. / soccer)
➡ ______________________________

30 (team / the / a / built / by / database / collecting / and / a / analyzing / huge / of / amount / data / players. / on)
➡ ______________________________
____

31 (example, / for / data / the / information / included / how / about / much / player / each / and / ran / long / how / had / he / ball. / the)
➡ ______________________________
____

32 (the / with / of / help / database, / this / national / Germany's / team / soccer / able was / improve / to / performance / its / win / and / the / World / 2014 / Cup.)
➡ ______________________________
____

33 (Prevention / Crime)
➡ ______________________________

34 (to / thanks / data, / big / can / police / predict / now / before / crime / happens. / it)
➡ ______________________________

35 (the / through / analysis / big / of / about / data / type, / the / and / time / of / place / crime, / can / police / make / map / a / crime / of / spots. / hot)
➡ ______________________________
____

36 (map / this / when / identifies / and / crime / where / most / is / to / likely / happen.)
➡ ______________________________

37 (can / police / further / prevent / by / crime / focusing / the / on / areas / the / and / this / times / predicts. / map)
➡ ______________________________
____

38 (data / big / already / has / the / changed / greatly. / world)
➡ ______________________________

39 (where / so / the / will / data / big / go / industry / here? / from)
➡ ______________________________

40 (knows / nobody / sure, / for / experts / but / that / agree / big / will / data / play / more / a / and / important / more / in / role / lives. / our)
➡ ______________________________
____

26 스포츠에서의 경기력 향상
27 당신은 스포츠 팬인가?
28 빅데이터는 스포츠를 더 흥미롭게 만들면서, 선수들의 경기력을 향상하고 있다.
29 유명한 사례로 독일 국가 대표 축구팀이 있다.
30 그 팀은 선수들에 관한 엄청난 양의 데이터를 모으고 분석함으로써, 데이터베이스를 구축했다.
31 예를 들어 데이터는 각각의 선수들이 얼마나 많이 달렸고, 얼마나 오랫동안 공을 소유했는지도 포함했다.
32 이 데이터베이스의 도움으로 독일 국가 대표 축구팀은 경기력을 향상할 수 있었고, 2014년 월드컵에서 우승할 수 있었다.
33 범죄 예방
34 빅데이터 덕분에 경찰은 이제 범죄가 발생하기 전에 범죄를 예측할 수 있다.
35 범죄의 유형, 시간 및 장소에 관한 빅데이터의 분석을 통해, 경찰은 범죄 다발 지역의 지도를 만들 수 있다.
36 이 지도는 범죄가 언제, 어디에서 가장 많이 발생할 것 같은지를 알려 준다.
37 경찰은 이 지도가 예측하는 장소들과 시간대에 집중함으로써, 추가 범죄를 예방할 수 있다.
38 빅데이터는 이미 세계를 크게 변화시켰다.
39 그러면 빅데이터 산업은 여기에서부터 어디로 가게 될까?
40 누구도 확실히 알지는 못하지만, 전문가들은 빅데이터가 우리 삶에서 더욱 더 중요한 역할을 할 것이라는 데에는 동의한다.

본문 Test

※ 다음 우리말을 영어로 쓰시오.

1 빅데이터와 함께 살아가기
➡ ______

2 당신은 온라인 서점을 방문해서 그 서점이 당신을 위해 추천한 책들을 보고 놀란 적이 있는가?
➡ ______

3 그것들 중에 많은 것들이 당신에게 흥미로워 보였다.
➡ ______

4 그 서점은 당신이 무엇을 좋아하는지 어떻게 알았을까?
➡ ______

5 이것은 모두 빅데이터 때문에 가능하다.
➡ ______

6 빅데이터는 무엇인가?
➡ ______

7 빅데이터는 매우 크고 복잡한 데이터 집합이다.
➡ ______

8 정보 통신 기술이 발달함에 따라 우리가 갖고 있는 정보의 양도 이전보다 훨씬 더 많아지고 있다.
➡ ______

9 이것은 주로 우리가 온라인상에서 하는 거의 모든 것들이 흔적을 남기기 때문이다.
➡ ______

10 예를 들어, 당신이 블로그에 올린 사진들과 온라인 상점에서의 구매 기록들이 모두 빅데이터의 일부가 된다.
➡ ______

11 하지만 단순히 데이터를 수집하는 것만으로는 충분하지 않다.
➡ ______

12 빅데이터는 분석되어야 하고, 이것은 빅데이터 전문가들에 의해서 이루어진다.
➡ ______

13 다양한 방법들을 사용하여 전문가들은 빅데이터를 분석하고, 그것으로부터 의미 있는 결과들을 도출한다.
➡ ______

14 그런 다음, 이런 결과들은 결정을 하거나 또는 미래를 예측하는 데 사용될 수 있다.
➡ ______

15 빅데이터는 어떻게 우리 삶에 영향을 미치고 있는가?
➡ ______

16 빅데이터는 우리 삶의 거의 모든 부분에 영향을 미치고 있다.
➡ ______

17 그것은 회사들이 소비자들이 필요로 하는 것을 더 잘 이해하고 그들이 더 많은 상품을 팔도록 도와준다.
➡ ______

18 그것은 사람들이 교통 체증을 피하도록 도와주기도 한다.
➡ ______

19 그것의 활용은 끝이 없고, 여기에 몇 가지 흥미로운 예들이 있다.
➡ ______

20 질병 예측
➡ ______

21 당신은 날씨 전문가가 날씨를 예측하는 것과 같이 건강 전문가들이 현재 질병을 예측할 수 있다는 것을 알고 있는가?
➡

22 이것은 빅데이터 덕분에 가능하다.
➡

23 예를 들어서 독감의 계절이 오면, 사람들은 독감 약을 더 많이 구입할 것이다.
➡

24 그들은 또한 온라인상에서 독감 증상들을 더 찾아볼 것이다.
➡

25 만약 이런 종류의 데이터를 지혜롭게 분석한다면, 독감의 확산을 예측할 수 있다.
➡

26 스포츠에서의 경기력 향상
➡

27 당신은 스포츠 팬인가?
➡

28 빅데이터는 스포츠를 더 흥미롭게 만들면서, 선수들의 경기력을 향상하고 있다.
➡

29 유명한 사례로 독일 국가 대표 축구팀이 있다.
➡

30 그 팀은 선수들에 관한 엄청난 양의 데이터를 모으고 분석함으로써, 데이터베이스를 구축했다.
➡

31 예를 들어 데이터는 각각의 선수들이 얼마나 많이 달렸고, 얼마나 오랫동안 공을 소유했는지도 포함했다.
➡

32 이 데이터베이스의 도움으로 독일 국가 대표 축구팀은 경기력을 향상할 수 있었고, 2014년 월드컵에서 우승할 수 있었다.
➡

33 범죄 예방
➡

34 빅데이터 덕분에 경찰은 이제 범죄가 발생하기 전에 범죄를 예측할 수 있다.
➡

35 죄의 유형, 시간 및 장소에 관한 빅데이터의 분석을 통해, 경찰은 범죄 다발 지역의 지도를 만들 수 있다.
➡

36 이 지도는 범죄가 언제, 어디에서 가장 많이 발생할 것 같은지를 알려 준다.
➡

37 경찰은 이 지도가 예측하는 장소들과 시간대에 집중함으로써, 추가 범죄를 예방할 수 있다.
➡

38 빅데이터는 이미 세계를 크게 변화시켰다.
➡

39 그러면 빅데이터 산업은 여기에서부터 어디로 가게 될까?
➡

40 누구도 확실히 알지는 못하지만, 전문가들은 빅데이터가 우리 삶에서 더욱 더 중요한 역할을 할 것이라는 데에는 동의한다.
➡

구석구석 지문 Test

Step1

※ 다음 우리말과 일치하도록 빈칸에 알맞은 말을 쓰시오.

After You Read B Read and Complete

Example 1

1. ________ ________ can now ________ ________ ________ of the flu ________ ________ the sales of flu medicine and online searches about ________ ________.

Example 2

2. ________ ________ and ________ ________ ________ ________ ________ data on players, Germany's national soccer team ________ ________ ________ ________ its performance and win the 2014 World Cup.

Example 3

3. ________ ________ ________ of big data, police can make a map of ________ ________ ________ and use it ________ ________ ________ ________.

사례 1
1. 건강 전문가들은 독감 약 판매와 독감 증상에 관한 온라인 검색을 분석함으로써 이제 감기의 확산을 예측할 수 있다.

사례 2
2. 독일 국가 대표 축구팀은 선수들에 관한 엄청난 양의 데이터를 모으고 분석함으로써, 경기력을 향상하고 2014년 월드컵에서 우승할 수 있었다.

사례 3
3. 빅데이터의 분석을 통해서 경찰은 범죄 다발 지역의 지도를 만들 수 있고 그것을 추가 범죄를 예방하는 데에 사용할 수 있다.

Around the World

1. Yuna: We're not ________. The bus ________ ________ ________ 4 ________.
2. Computer: ________ ________, you ________ question numbers 3 and 5, ________ ________ ________ ________ first.
3. Yuna: ________ ________ ________ ________ tomorrow?
4. AI: It's ________ ________ ________. ________ your umbrella.
5. Yuna: Big data ________ ________ ________ ________ so ________ ________!

1. 유나: 늦지 않았네. 버스가 4분 후에 도착할 거야.
2. 컴퓨터: 지난번에 당신은 3번과 5번 문제를 틀렸습니다. 그러니 우선 그것들부터 복습해 봅시다.
3. 유나: 내일 날씨가 어때?
4. AI: 비가 올 예정입니다. 우산 챙기세요.
5. 유나: 빅데이터는 내 삶을 훨씬 더 쉽게 만들고 있구나!

Think and Write

1. ________ ________ Time Activities
2. We asked 100 ________ about their ________ ________ ________.
3. ________ ________ show that the free time activity the ________ ________ ________ ________ ________ ________ ________ ________.
4. 34% said that they want ________ ________ ________ ________ ________ ________.
5. However, ________ ________ ________ ________ they actually do the most ________ ________ ________.
6. 39% said that they ________ TV ________ ________ ________ ________.
7. ________ ________ the results, we see that there is ________ ________ ________ between ________ ________ ________ ________ ________ do and ________ ________ ________ ________ in their free time.

1. 청소년들의 여가 활동들
2. 우리는 100명의 청소년들에게 여가 활동에 관해 질문했습니다.
3. 그 결과 청소년들이 가장 하고 싶은 여가 활동은 여행인 것으로 나타났습니다.
4. 34%는 여가 시간에 여행을 가고 싶다고 답했습니다.
5. 하지만 그들이 실제로 가장 많이 하는 여가 활동은 TV를 보는 것입니다.
6. 39%는 여가 시간에 TV를 본다고 답했습니다.
7. 결과로 봤을 때, 우리는 청소년들이 여가 시간에 하고 싶은 활동과 실제로 하는 활동 사이에 큰 차이가 있다는 것을 알 수 있습니다

구석구석 지문 Test

Step2

※ 다음 우리말을 영어로 쓰시오.

After You Read B Read and Complete

사례 1

1. 건강 전문가들은 독감 약 판매와 독감 증상에 관한 온라인 검색을 분석함으로써 이제 감기의 확산을 예측할 수 있다.
➡ ______________________________

사례 2

2. 독일 국가 대표 축구팀은 선수들에 관한 엄청난 양의 데이터를 모으고 분석함으로써, 경기력을 향상하고 2014년 월드컵에서 우승할 수 있었다.
➡ ______________________________

사례 3

3. 빅데이터의 분석을 통해서 경찰은 범죄 다발 지역의 지도를 만들 수 있고 그것을 추가 범죄를 예방하는 데에 사용할 수 있다.
➡ ______________________________

Around the World

1. 유나: 늦지 않았네. 버스가 4분 후에 도착할 거야.
➡ ______________________________
2. 컴퓨터: 지난번에 당신은 3번과 5번 문제를 틀렸습니다. 그러니 우선 그것들부터 복습해 봅시다.
➡ ______________________________
3. 유나: 내일 날씨가 어때?
➡ ______________________________
4. AI: 비가 올 예정입니다. 우산 챙기세요.
➡ ______________________________
5. 유나: 빅데이터는 내 삶을 훨씬 더 쉽게 만들고 있구나!
➡ ______________________________

Think and Write

1. 청소년들의 여가 활동들
➡ ______________________________
2. 우리는 100명의 청소년들에게 여가 활동에 관해 질문했습니다.
➡ ______________________________
3. 그 결과 청소년들이 가장 하고 싶은 여가 활동은 여행인 것으로 나타났습니다.
➡ ______________________________
4. 34%는 여가 시간에 여행을 가고 싶다고 답했습니다.
➡ ______________________________
5. 하지만 그들이 실제로 가장 많이 하는 여가 활동은 TV를 보는 것입니다.
➡ ______________________________
6. 39%는 여가 시간에 TV를 본다고 답했습니다.
➡ ______________________________
7. 결과로 봤을 때, 우리는 청소년들이 여가 시간에 하고 싶은 활동과 실제로 하는 활동 사이에 큰 차이가 있다는 것을 알 수 있습니다.
➡ ______________________________

단어 Test

Step1

※ 다음 영어를 우리말로 쓰시오.

01 melt ____________
02 suddenly ____________
03 curvy ____________
04 thus ____________
05 bend ____________
06 represent ____________
07 despite ____________
08 cancel ____________
09 symbolize ____________
10 dynasty ____________
11 effectively ____________
12 folk painting ____________
13 value ____________
14 loyalty ____________
15 behavior ____________
16 frozen ____________
17 harmony ____________
18 ill ____________
19 appear ____________
20 influence ____________
21 attitude ____________
22 symbolic ____________
23 justice ____________
24 lotus flower ____________
25 muddy ____________
26 bloom ____________
27 carp ____________
28 will ____________
29 character ____________
30 disappointed ____________
31 respect ____________
32 society ____________
33 decoration ____________
34 difficulty ____________
35 in particular ____________
36 as follows ____________
37 get well ____________
38 once upon a time ____________
39 much more than ____________
40 remind ~ of … ____________
41 for this reason ____________
42 because of ____________
43 right after ~ ____________

단어 Test

Step2

※ 다음 우리말을 영어로 쓰시오.

01 시대, 왕조 ____________

02 효과적으로 ____________

03 ~하게 보이다, 나타나다 ____________

04 영향을 미치다 ____________

05 충성, 충실 ____________

06 정의, 공정성 ____________

07 꽃을 피우다, 꽃이 피다 ____________

08 잉어 ____________

09 나타내다, 보여 주다 ____________

10 굽다, 구부러지다 ____________

11 굴곡이 많은 ____________

12 장식 ____________

13 연꽃 ____________

14 어려움, 고난 ____________

15 갑자기 ____________

16 민화 ____________

17 존경, 경의 ____________

18 사회 ____________

19 가치, 중요성 ____________

20 글자 ____________

21 행동 ____________

22 상징하다 ____________

23 진흙투성이의, 흙탕물의 ____________

24 의지 ____________

25 취소하다 ____________

26 상징적인, 상징하는 ____________

27 조화 ____________

28 실망한, 낙담한 ____________

29 태도, 자세 ____________

30 대나무 ____________

31 얼어붙은 ____________

32 녹다 ____________

33 ~에도 불구하고 ____________

34 물건, 물체 ____________

35 병이 나아지다, 회복하다 ____________

36 ~ 직후에 ____________

37 특히, 특별히 ____________

38 다음과 같이 ____________

39 이런 이유로 ____________

40 ~보다 훨씬 많이 ____________

41 ~에게 …을 상기시키다 ____________

42 옛날에 ____________

43 너무 ~해서 …하다 ____________

단어 Test

Step3

※ 다음 영영풀이에 알맞은 단어를 <보기>에서 골라 쓴 후, 우리말 뜻을 쓰시오.

1 __________: produce or yield flowers: __________

2 __________: to show or mean something: __________

3 __________: a sign, picture, object etc. that represents something else: __________

4 __________: a thing that you can see and touch: __________

5 __________: the way you think or feel about something: __________

6 __________: to make someone remember something: __________

7 __________: the things that a person or animal does: __________

8 __________: representing a particular idea or quality: __________

9 __________: although something happens or exists: __________

10 __________: made into, covered with, or surrounded by ice: __________

11 __________: a feeling of support for someone or something: __________

12 __________: all the people who live in a country, and the way they live: __________

13 __________: to begin to be seen; come into existence or use: __________

14 __________: to shape or force something straight into a curve or angle: __________

15 __________: the quality of being fair and reasonable; fairness in the way people are treated: __________

16 __________: a period of time during which members of the same family rule a country or region: __________

보기

frozen	symbolic	loyalty	behavior
justice	object	dynasty	bloom
despite	attitude	society	remind
bend	represent	appear	symbol

대화문 Test

Step1

※ 다음 우리말과 일치하도록 빈칸에 알맞은 말을 쓰시오.

Listen and Talk A 1

G: Minho, look at these ________ ________ ________ ________ here. ________ they great?

B: Yes, they ________.

G: They ________ are good, but I like ________ ________ on the left more. How ________ you?

B: I ________ the one on the right. It ________ ________ ________ ________ the cat in it is ________. I also like the bird in it.

G: 민호야, 여기 고양이가 그려진 그림 두 점을 봐. 멋있지 않니?
B: 응, 그러네.
G: 그것들은 모두 멋있지만 난 왼쪽에 있는 그림이 더 좋아. 넌 어때?
B: 난 오른쪽에 있는 그림이 더 좋아. 그림 속 고양이가 더 귀여운 것 같아. 새도 마음에 들어.

Listen and Talk A 2

G: We can have Bibimbap or Galbitang. ________ do you ________?

B: I ________ Bibimbap. ________ ________ to me that it's the ________ ________.

G: I think ________, too. I also ________ Bibimbap ________.

B: Let's ________, then. I'm very hungry.

G: 우리는 비빔밥이나 갈비탕을 먹을 수 있어. 어떤 것이 더 좋니?
B: 난 비빔밥이 더 좋아. 그것이 더 건강에 좋은 선택인 것 같아.
G: 나도 그렇게 생각해. 난 비빔밥을 더 좋아하기도 해.
B: 그럼 주문하자. 난 정말 배고파.

Listen and Talk A 3

G: Look at these two ________ ________, Steve. Aren't they beautiful?

B: Yes. ________ ________ do you ________, the green plate or the white plate?

G: Well, it's hard ________ ________, but I like the green one ________. How ________ you?

B: ________, ________. It ________ to me ________ the green plate is more ________.

G: Steve, 이 두 개의 옛날 접시들을 봐. 아름답지 않니?
B: 응. 초록색 접시와 흰색 접시 중 무엇이 더 좋니?
G: 음, 고르기가 어렵지만 난 초록색 접시가 더 좋아. 너는 어때?
B: 나도. 초록색 접시가 더 독특한 것 같아.

Listen and Talk A 4

G: Junsu, you said ________ ________ ________ buy a ________ for your sister. ________ ________ the bags here?

B: They ________ ________.

G: ________ ________ do you ________, the one with flowers ________ the one ________ animals?

B: I ________ the one ________ flowers. ________ ________ ________ ________ that my sister will like it more.

G: 준수야, 너 여동생 줄 선물을 살 거라고 했잖아. 여기 이 가방들은 어때?
B: 좋아 보인다.
G: 가방에 꽃들이 있는 것과 동물들이 있는 것 중 무엇이 더 좋니?
B: 난 꽃들이 있는 것이 더 좋아. 내 여동생이 그것을 더 좋아할 것 같아.

Listen and Talk B

A: ________ food do you ________, Tteokbokki or Gimbap?
B: I ________ Tteokbokki. ________ seems to me ________ it's more ________. How about you?
A: I ________ Tteokbokki, too. / I ________ Gimbap. It ________ ________ ________ that it's ________.

A: ________ painting do you ________, the one on the left ________ the one on the right?
B: I ________ the one on the right. It seems to me that the cat in it is cuter. How about you?
A: I ________ the one on the right, too. / I ________ the one on the left. It seems to me that it looks ________ ________.

A: ________ plate do you prefer, the green one ________ the white one?
B: I ________ the green one. It seems to me that it's ________ ________. How about you?
A: I ________ the green one, too. / I ________ the white one. It seems to me that it's ________ ________ beautiful.

A: ________ bag do you ________, the one with fish ________ the one ________ stars?
B: I ________ the one with stars. It seems to me that it's ________ my style. How about you?
A: I ________ the one with stars, ________. / I ________ the one with fish. It seems to me that the fish are ________.

A: 떡볶이와 김밥 중에 어떤 것을 더 좋아하니?
B: 난 떡볶이를 좋아해. 그것이 더 맛있을 것 같아. 너는 어때?
A: 나도 떡볶이를 좋아해. / 난 김밥을 좋아해. 그것이 더 건강에 좋은 것 같아.

A: 왼쪽 그림과 오른쪽 그림 중 어떤 것을 더 좋아하니?
B: 난 오른쪽 그림을 더 좋아해. 그림 속 고양이가 더 귀여운 것 같아. 너는 어때?
A: 나도 오른쪽 그림이 더 좋아. / 난 왼쪽 그림을 더 좋아해. 그것이 더 평화로워 보이거든.

A: 초록색 접시와 흰색 접시 중 어떤 것을 더 좋아하니?
B: 난 초록색 접시가 더 좋아. 그것이 더 독특하다고 생각해. 너는 어때?
A: 나도 초록색 접시가 더 좋아. / 난 흰색 접시가 더 좋아. 그것이 단순하지만 아름답다고 생각해.

A: 물고기가 있는 가방과 별들이 있는 가방 중 어떤 것을 더 좋아하니?
B: 난 별들이 있는 가방을 더 좋아해. 그것이 더 내 취향이야. 너는 어때?
A: 나도 별들이 있는 가방이 더 좋아. / 난 물고기가 있는 가방을 더 좋아해. 물고기가 귀여운 것 같아.

Listen and Talk C

G: There are two ________ we can go to. ________ one do you want to see ________, Eric?
B: I ________ the Korean mask exhibition. Is ________ OK, Somi?
G: Of ________. And it seems to me that the mask exhibition will be ________ more interesting.
B: Do you think ________?
G: Yes. Look at this poster. There isn't ________ an exhibition. There's ________ a mask dance show at 4:00 and 6:00.
B: Great! I've ________ ________ a mask dance show ________.
G: Well, I've seen a show ________. I'm ________ you'll like it.
B: So where is the show?
G: It's in Dasom Hall, ________ ________ the exhibition room.
B: It's 4:30 now, so ________ ________ the 6 o'clock show.
G: OK. ________ go see the exhibition ________.

G: 우리가 갈 수 있는 전시회가 두 곳이 있어. 어느 것을 더 보고 싶니, Eric?
B: 나는 한국의 탈 전시회를 더 선호해. 소미야, 괜찮겠니?
G: 물론이지. 그리고 나도 탈 전시회가 더 흥미로울 것 같아.
B: 그렇게 생각하니?
G: 그래. 이 포스터를 봐. 단순히 전시회만 있는 것이 아니야. 탈춤 공연도 4시와 6시에 있어.
B: 좋아! 나는 전에 탈춤 공연을 본 적이 없어.
G: 음, 나는 전에 본 적이 있어. 네가 분명 좋아할 거야.
B: 그래서 공연은 어디서 해?
G: 전시관 옆 다솜 홀에서 해.
B: 지금 4시 30분이니까 6시 공연을 보자.
G: 그래. 우선 전시회부터 보자.

Listen and Talk D

I ________ science. It seems to me that it's ________ ________ ________ ________. I also ________ it because I want to be a great ________ ________ Edison.

난 과학을 더 좋아해. 그것을 배우는 것이 더 즐거운 것 같아. 난 Edison과 같은 훌륭한 발명가가 되고 싶어서 그것을 더 좋아하기도 해.

Talk and Play

A: ________ do you ________, Ramyeon or spaghetti?
B: I ________ Ramyeon. ________ ________ ________ me that it's more delicious. How about you?
A: I ________ Ramyeon, too. / I ________ spaghetti. It seems to me that it's ________.

A: 라면과 스파게티 중 어떤 걸 더 좋아하니?
B: 난 라면을 더 좋아해. 그것이 더 맛있는 것 같아. 너는 어때?
A: 나도 라면을 더 좋아해. / 난 스파게티를 더 좋아해. 그것이 건강에 더 좋을 것 같아.

Review 1

G: Joe, didn't you say you needed ________ ________ a cap? How about these caps here?
B: They look ________.
G: ________ ________ do you ________, the one with triangles ________ the one ________ flowers?
B: I ________ the one ________ ________. It seems to me that it's ________ ________.

G: Joe, 모자를 사야 한다고 하지 않았니? 여기 있는 이 모자들은 어때?
B: 그것들은 좋아 보인다.
G: 삼각형이 있는 것과 꽃이 있는 것 중 어떤 것이 좋니?
B: 난 삼각형이 있는 것이 더 좋아. 그것이 더 독특한 것 같아.

Review 2

B: We can have Gimbap or Tteokbokki. ________ do you ________, Jenny?
G: I ________ Gimbap. It seems to me that it's ________ ________ ________. How about you, Minsu?
B: I'll have Tteokbokki. ________ ________ that the Tteokbokki here is very good.
G: Let's ________, then. I'm very ________.

G: 우리는 김밥이나 떡볶이를 시킬 수 있어. 어떤 것이 더 좋니, Jenny?
B: 난 김밥이 더 좋아. 건강에 더 좋은 선택인 것 같거든. 민수야, 넌 어떠니?
G: 난 떡볶이 먹을래. 여기는 떡볶이가 더 맛있다고 들었거든.
B: 그럼 주문하자. 난 정말 배고파.

Review 3

John: There are two movies we can see. ________ ________ do you want to see ________, Somi?
Somi: I ________ *Batman*. I saw *Spider-Man* last week. Is ________ OK, John?
John: Of course. It seems to me that *Batman* will be ________ more fun.
Somi: Good. Then, ________ ________ and see it.

John: 우리가 볼 수 있는 영화가 두 개 있어. 소미야, 어떤 것이 더 보고 싶니?
Somi: 난 "배트맨"이 더 좋아. 난 "스파이더맨"을 지난주에 봤거든. John, 괜찮니?
John: 물론이지. "배트맨"이 훨씬 더 재미있을 것 같아.
Somi: 좋아. 그럼 영화 보러 가자.

대화문 Test

※ 다음 우리말에 맞도록 대화를 영어로 쓰시오.

Listen and Talk A 1

G: ________________

B: ________________

G: ________________

B: ________________

____

G: 민호야, 여기 고양이가 그려진 그림 두 점을 봐. 멋있지 않니?
B: 응, 그러네.
G: 그것들은 모두 멋있지만 난 왼쪽에 있는 그림이 더 좋아. 넌 어때?
B: 난 오른쪽에 있는 그림이 더 좋아. 그림 속 고양이가 더 귀여운 것 같아. 새도 마음에 들어.

Listen and Talk A 2

G: ________________

B: ________________

G: ________________

B: ________________

G: 우리는 비빔밥이나 갈비탕을 먹을 수 있어. 어떤 것이 더 좋니?
B: 난 비빔밥이 더 좋아. 그것이 더 건강에 좋은 선택인 것 같아.
G: 나도 그렇게 생각해. 난 비빔밥을 더 좋아하기도 해.
B: 그럼 주문하자. 난 정말 배고파.

Listen and Talk A 3

G: ________________

B: ________________

G: ________________

B: ________________

G: Steve, 이 두 개의 옛날 접시들을 봐. 아름답지 않니?
B: 응. 초록색 접시와 흰색 접시 중 무엇이 더 좋니?
G: 음, 고르기가 어렵지만 난 초록색 접시가 더 좋아. 너는 어때?
B: 나도. 초록색 접시가 더 독특한 것 같아.

Listen and Talk A 4

G: ________________

____

B: ________________

G: ________________

B: ________________

G: 준수야, 너 여동생 줄 선물을 살 거라고 했잖아. 여기 이 가방들은 어때?
B: 좋아 보인다.
G: 가방에 꽃들이 있는 것과 동물들이 있는 것 중 무엇이 더 좋니?
B: 난 꽃들이 있는 것이 더 좋아. 내 여동생이 그것을 더 좋아할 것 같아.

Listen and Talk B

A: ______
B: ______
A: ______

A: ______
B: ______
______
A: ______
______

A: ______
B: ______
A: ______
______

A: ______
B: ______
______
A: ______
______

A: 떡볶이와 김밥 중에 어떤 것을 더 좋아하니?
B: 난 떡볶이를 좋아해. 그것이 더 맛있을 것 같아. 너는 어때?
A: 나도 떡볶이를 좋아해. / 난 김밥을 좋아해. 그것이 더 건강에 좋은 것 같아.

A: 왼쪽 그림과 오른쪽 그림 중 어떤 것을 더 좋아하니?
B: 난 오른쪽 그림을 더 좋아해. 그림 속 고양이가 더 귀여운 것 같아. 너는 어때?
A: 나도 오른쪽 그림이 더 좋아. / 난 왼쪽 그림을 더 좋아해. 그것이 더 평화로워 보이거든.

A: 초록색 접시와 흰색 접시 중 어떤 것을 더 좋아하니?
B: 난 초록색 접시가 더 좋아. 그것이 더 독특하다고 생각해. 너는 어때?
A: 나도 초록색 접시가 더 좋아. / 난 흰색 접시가 더 좋아. 그것이 단순하지만 아름답다고 생각해.

A: 물고기가 있는 가방과 별들이 있는 가방 중 어떤 것을 더 좋아하니?
B: 난 별들이 있는 가방을 더 좋아해. 그것이 더 내 취향이야. 너는 어때?
A: 나도 별들이 있는 가방이 더 좋아. / 난 물고기가 있는 가방을 더 좋아해. 물고기가 귀여운 것 같아.

Listen and Talk C

G: ______
______
B: ______
G: ______
______
B: ______
G: ______
______
B: ______
G: ______
B: ______
G: ______
B: ______
G: ______

G: 우리가 갈 수 있는 전시회가 두 곳이 있어. 어느 것을 더 보고 싶니, Eric?
B: 나는 한국의 탈 전시회를 더 선호해. 소미야, 괜찮겠니?
G: 물론이지. 그리고 나도 탈 전시회가 더 흥미로울 것 같아.
B: 그렇게 생각하니?
G: 그래. 이 포스터를 봐. 단순히 전시회만 있는 것이 아니야. 탈춤 공연도 4시와 6시에 있어.
B: 좋아! 나는 전에 탈춤 공연을 본 적이 없어.
G: 음, 나는 전에 본 적이 있어. 네가 분명 좋아할 거야.
B: 그래서 공연은 어디서 해?
G: 전시관 옆 다솜 홀에서 해.
B: 지금 4시 30분이니까 6시 공연을 보자.
G: 그래. 우선 전시회부터 보자.

Listen and Talk D

난 과학을 더 좋아해. 그것을 배우는 것이 더 즐거운 것 같아. 난 Edison과 같은 훌륭한 발명가가 되고 싶어서 그것을 더 좋아하기도 해.

Talk and Play

A:

B:

A:

A: 라면과 스파게티 중 어떤 걸 더 좋아하니?

B: 난 라면을 더 좋아해. 그것이 더 맛있는 것 같아. 너는 어때?

A: 나도 라면을 더 좋아해. / 난 스파게티를 더 좋아해. 그것이 건강에 더 좋을 것 같아.

Review 1

G:

B:

G:

B:

G: Joe, 모자를 사야 한다고 하지 않았니? 여기 있는 이 모자들은 어때?

B: 그것들은 좋아 보인다.

G: 삼각형이 있는 것과 꽃이 있는 것 중 어떤 것이 좋니?

B: 난 삼각형이 있는 것이 더 좋아. 그것이 더 독특한 것 같아.

Review 2

B:

G:

B:

G:

G: 우리는 김밥이나 떡볶이를 시킬 수 있어. 어떤 것이 더 좋니, Jenny?

B: 난 김밥이 더 좋아. 건강에 더 좋은 선택인 것 같거든. 민수야, 넌 어떠니?

G: 난 떡볶이 먹을래. 여기는 떡볶이가 더 맛있다고 들었거든.

B: 그럼 주문하자. 난 정말 배고파.

Review 3

John:

Somi:

John:

Somi:

John: 우리가 볼 수 있는 영화가 두 개 있어. 소미야, 어떤 것이 더 보고 싶니?

Somi: 난 "배트맨"이 더 좋아. 난 "스파이더맨"을 지난주에 봤거든. John, 괜찮니?

John: 물론이지. "배트맨"이 훨씬 더 재미있을 것 같아.

Somi: 좋아. 그럼 영화 보러 가자.

※ 다음 우리말과 일치하도록 빈칸에 알맞은 것을 골라 쓰시오.

1 Munjado, a ________ ________ the Joseon ________
A. into B. Window C. Dynasty

2 Look ________ the painting ________ ________ ________.
A. on B. right C. at D. the

3 Do you ________ the ________ ________, *hyo*(孝)?
A. character B. see C. Chinese

4 Do you ________ ________ a ________, a geomungo, and a ________?
A. fan B. also C. carp D. see

5 This kind of painting is ________ Munjado, and it is a ________ of folk painting that was ________ in the ________ Joseon dynasty.
A. popular B. called C. late D. type

6 In Munjado, ________ is ________ a Chinese character ________ some animals or ________.
A. with B. objects C. usually D. there

7 ________ ________ eight Chinese ________ ________ in Munjado.
A. appears B. one C. characters D. of

8 They are *hyo*(孝), *je*(悌), *chung*(忠), *sin*(信), *ye*(禮), *ui*(義), *yeom*(廉), and *chi*(恥), and they ________ the ________ that were ________ to people of the Joseon ________.
A. values B. represent C. important D. dynasty

9 The ________ or ________ in Munjado are not ________ ________.
A. decorations B. objects C. animals D. just

10 They ________ are ________.
A. symbolic B. often

11 For example, carp in the ________ of *hyo* ________ ________ for parents ________ of an old story.
A. because B. symbolize C. paintings D. respect

12 The story ________ ________ ________.
A. as B. goes C. follows

13 ________ ________ a ________, a man lived ________ his old mother.
A. with B. time C. once D. upon

14 One winter, the man's mother ________ ________ and ________ eat ________.
A. anything B. ill C. couldn't D. became

15 ________ one very cold day, the mother said to the man, "It ________ be wonderful if I ________ eat ________ fish."
A. would B. on C. could D. fresh

16 The man ________ ________ to the river, but it was ________ ________.
A. frozen B. out C. completely D. went

1 문자도, 조선 시대를 보는 창

2 오른쪽에 있는 그림을 보라.

3 한자 효(孝)가 보이는가?

4 잉어, 거문고, 그리고 부채가 보이는가?

5 이런 종류의 그림은 문자도이며, 조선 시대 후기에 인기 있었던 민화의 한 종류이다.

6 문자도에는 보통 한자 하나가 동물이나 사물과 함께 있다.

7 문자도에는 여덟 개의 한자 중 하나가 나온다.

8 그것들은 효(孝), 제(悌), 충(忠), 신(信), 예(禮), 의(義), 염(廉), 치(恥)이고, 그것들은 조선 시대 사람들에게 중요했던 가치들을 나타낸다.

9 문자도에 있는 동물이나 사물은 단순한 장식이 아니다.

10 그것들은 종종 상징적이다.

11 예를 들어, '효' 그림 속에 있는 잉어는 옛이야기 때문에 부모님에 대한 존경심을 상징한다.

12 그 이야기는 다음과 같다.

13 옛날 옛적에 한 남자가 나이 드신 어머니와 살았다.

14 어느 겨울, 남자의 어머니는 병이 들어서 어떤 것도 먹을 수 없었다.

15 무척 추운 어느 날, 어머니는 남자에게 말했다. "신선한 물고기를 먹을 수 있다면 좋겠구나."

16 그 남자는 강으로 나갔지만, 강은 완전히 얼어붙어 있었다.

17 ________ was impossible ________ him ________ ________ any fish.
A. for　B. it　C. catch　D. to

18 The man was ________ ________ ________ he cried out ________ the sky, "What should I do? Please help me."
A. that　B. so　C. to　D. disappointed

19 Then the ice ________, and three carp ________ came ________ ________ the water.
A. out　B. melted　C. suddenly　D. of

20 The man ________ ________ ________ and ________ the fish for his mother.
A. home　B. cooked　C. back　D. went

21 ________ his mother ________ ________.
A. well　B. got　C. then

22 There are ________ ________ of ________ ________ in Munjado.
A. objects　B. other　C. symbolic　D. examples

23 They are ________ in the ________ of the ________ *chung*(忠) and ________ flowers in the paintings of *ui*(義).
A. character　B. bamboo　C. paintings　D. lotus

24 ________ ________ not ________.
A. bend　B. bamboo　C. does

25 It ________ ________ ________ all ________ of weather.
A. kinds　B. green　C. stays　D. in

26 ________ these ________, bamboo came to ________ ________ to the king.
A. symbolize　B. reasons　C. loyalty　D. for

27 In the ________ of lotus flowers, they ________ in ________ ponds but still ________ beautifully.
A. muddy　B. case　C. bloom　D. grow

28 They thus became a symbol of a person's ________ to ________ for justice ________ ________.
A. will　B. despite　C. fight　D. difficulties

29 Munjado was ________ ________ ________ a painting ________ people of the Joseon dynasty.
A. than　B. to　C. more　D. much

30 It ________ them of important values that greatly ________ their ________ and ________.
A. behaviors　B. reminded　C. attitudes　D. influenced

31 ________ ________, ________ children, Munjado was a study ________.
A. tool　B. in　C. for　D. particular

32 ________ it, children in the Joseon dynasty could learn the ________ of ________ in family and ________.
A. harmony　B. through　C. society　D. importance

---

17 그가 그 어떤 물고기라도 잡는 것은 불가능했다.

18 남자는 몹시 낙담해서 하늘에 대고 외쳤다. "제가 어떻게 해야 하나요? 제발 저를 도와주세요."

19 그러자 얼음이 녹았고, 잉어 세 마리가 갑자기 물 밖으로 나왔다.

20 남자는 집으로 돌아가서 어머니를 위해 물고기들을 요리했다.

21 그러자 그의 어머니는 회복되었다.

22 문자도에 있는 상징적인 사물의 또 다른 예가 있다.

23 그것들은 글자 '충(忠)' 그림에 있는 대나무와 '의(義)' 그림에 있는 연꽃이다.

24 대나무는 구부러지지 않는다.

25 그것은 어떤 날씨에서도 푸르름을 유지한다.

26 이런 이유로 대나무는 왕에 대한 충성을 상징하게 되었다.

27 연꽃의 경우, 그것들은 진흙투성이의 연못에서 자라지만 여전히 아름답게 꽃을 피운다.

28 그래서 그 꽃들은 어려움에도 불구하고 정의를 위해 싸우는 사람의 의지를 상징하게 되었다.

29 문자도는 조선 시대 사람들에게 그림 그 이상이었다.

30 그것은 그들에게 자신들의 행동과 태도에 큰 영향을 미치는 중요한 가치를 상기시켰다.

31 특히 아이들에게 문자도는 학습 도구였다.

32 그것을 통해 조선 시대의 아이들은 가족과 사회에서의 조화의 중요성을 배울 수 있었다.

본문 Test

Step2

※ 다음 우리말과 일치하도록 빈칸에 알맞은 말을 쓰시오.

1 Munjado, a Window ________ the Joseon ________

2 ________ ________ the painting ________ ________ ________.

3 Do you ________ the ________ ________, *hyo*(孝)?

4 Do you also ________ a ________, a geomungo, and a fan?

5 This kind of painting ________ ________ Munjado, and it is ________ ________ ________ ________ ________ ________ ________ ________ in the ________ Joseon dynasty.

6 In Munjado, there is ________ a Chinese character ________ some animals or ________.

7 ________ ________ eight Chinese ________ ________ in Munjado.

8 They are *hyo*(孝), *je*(悌), *chung*(忠), *sin*(信), *ye*(禮), *ui*(義), *yeom*(廉), and *chi*(恥), and they ________ the values ________ ________ ________ ________ people of the ________ ________.

9 The animals or objects in Munjado are not ________ ________.

10 They ________ are ________.

11 For example, carp in the paintings of *hyo* ________ ________ for parents ________ ________ an old story.

12 The story ________ ________ ________.

13 ________ ________ ________ ________, a man lived with his old mother.

14 One winter, the man's mother ________ ________ and couldn't eat ________.

15 ________ one very cold day, the mother said to the man, "It ________ ________ ________ ________ ________ ________ ________ ________ ________."

16 The man ________ ________ ________ the river, but it ________ ________ ________.

1 문자도, 조선 시대를 보는 창

2 오른쪽에 있는 그림을 보라.

3 한자 효(孝)가 보이는가?

4 잉어, 거문고, 그리고 부채가 보이는가?

5 이런 종류의 그림은 문자도이며, 조선 시대 후기에 인기 있었던 민화의 한 종류이다.

6 문자도에는 보통 한자 하나가 동물이나 사물과 함께 있다.

7 문자도에는 여덟 개의 한자 중 하나가 나온다.

8 그것들은 효(孝), 제(悌), 충(忠), 신(信), 예(禮), 의(義), 염(廉), 치(恥)이고, 그것들은 조선 시대 사람들에게 중요했던 가치들을 나타낸다.

9 문자도에 있는 동물이나 사물은 단순한 장식이 아니다.

10 그것들은 종종 상징적이다.

11 예를 들어, '효' 그림 속에 있는 잉어는 옛이야기 때문에 부모님에 대한 존경심을 상징한다.

12 그 이야기는 다음과 같다.

13 옛날 옛적에 한 남자가 나이 드신 어머니와 살았다.

14 어느 겨울, 남자의 어머니는 병이 들어서 어떤 것도 먹을 수 없었다.

15 무척 추운 어느 날, 어머니는 남자에게 말했다. "신선한 물고기를 먹을 수 있다면 좋겠구나."

16 그 남자는 강으로 나갔지만, 강은 완전히 얼어붙어 있었다.

17 ________ was impossible ________ ________ ________ ________ ________ fish.

18 The man was ________ ________ ________ he ________ ________ ________ the sky, "What should I do? Please help me."

19 Then the ice ________, and three carp ________ came ________ ________ the water.

20 The man went ________ ________ and cooked the fish for his mother.

21 Then his mother ________ ________.

22 There are other examples of ________ ________ in Munjado.

23 They are bamboo ________ the paintings ________ the character *chung*(忠) and ________ ________ ________ the paintings ________ *ui*(義).

24 Bamboo does not ________.

25 It ________ ________ ________ all ________ of weather.

26 ________ ________ ________, bamboo ________ ________ ________ ________ ________ the king.

27 ________ ________ ________ ________ lotus flowers, they grow in muddy ponds ________ ________ ________ ________.

28 They ________ became a symbol of a person's ________ ________ ________ ________ justice ________ ________.

29 Munjado was ________ ________ ________ a painting ________ people of the Joseon dynasty.

30 It ________ them ________ important values ________ greatly influenced their ________ and ________.

31 ________ ________, ________ children, Munjado was a study tool.

32 ________ ________, children in the Joseon dynasty could learn the ________ of ________ ________ family and ________.

17 그가 그 어떤 물고기라도 잡는 것은 불가능했다.

18 남자는 몹시 낙담해서 하늘에 대고 외쳤다. "제가 어떻게 해야 하나요? 제발 저를 도와주세요."

19 그러자 얼음이 녹았고, 잉어 세 마리가 갑자기 물 밖으로 나왔다.

20 남자는 집으로 돌아가서 어머니를 위해 물고기들을 요리했다.

21 그러자 그의 어머니는 회복되었다.

22 문자도에 있는 상징적인 사물의 또 다른 예가 있다.

23 그것들은 글자 '충(忠)' 그림에 있는 대나무와 '의(義)' 그림에 있는 연꽃이다.

24 대나무는 구부러지지 않는다.

25 그것은 어떤 날씨에서도 푸르름을 유지한다.

26 이런 이유로 대나무는 왕에 대한 충성을 상징하게 되었다.

27 연꽃의 경우, 그것들은 진흙투성이의 연못에서 자라지만 여전히 아름답게 꽃을 피운다.

28 그래서 그 꽃들은 어려움에도 불구하고 정의를 위해 싸우는 사람의 의지를 상징하게 되었다.

29 문자도는 조선 시대 사람들에게 그림 그 이상이었다.

30 그것은 그들에게 자신들의 행동과 태도에 큰 영향을 미치는 중요한 가치를 상기시켰다.

31 특히 아이들에게 문자도는 학습 도구였다.

32 그것을 통해 조선 시대의 아이들은 가족과 사회에서의 조화의 중요성을 배울 수 있었다.

본문 Test

Step3

※ 다음 문장을 우리말로 쓰시오.

1 Munjado, a Window into the Joseon Dynasty

➡ ______________________________

2 Look at the painting on the right.

➡ ______________________________

3 Do you see the Chinese character, *hyo*(孝)?

➡ ______________________________

4 Do you also see a carp, a geomungo, and a fan?

➡ ______________________________

5 This kind of painting is called Munjado, and it is a type of folk painting that was popular in the late Joseon dynasty.

➡ ______________________________

6 In Munjado, there is usually a Chinese character with some animals or objects.

➡ ______________________________

7 One of eight Chinese characters appears in Munjado.

➡ ______________________________

8 They are *hyo*(孝), *je*(悌), *chung*(忠), *sin*(信), *ye*(禮), *ui*(義), *yeom*(廉), and *chi*(恥), and they represent the values that were important to people of the Joseon dynasty.

➡ ______________________________

____

9 The animals or objects in Munjado are not just decorations.

➡ ______________________________

10 They often are symbolic.

➡ ______________________________

11 For example, carp in the paintings of *hyo* symbolize respect for parents because of an old story.

➡ ______________________________

12 The story goes as follows.

➡ ______________________________

13 Once upon a time, a man lived with his old mother.

➡ ______________________________

14 One winter, the man's mother became ill and couldn't eat anything.

➡ ______________________________

15 On one very cold day, the mother said to the man, "It would be wonderful if I could eat fresh fish."

➡ ______________________________

16 The man went out to the river, but it was completely frozen.

➡ ______________________________

17 It was impossible for him to catch any fish.

➡ ______________________________

18 The man was so disappointed that he cried out to the sky, “What should I do? Please help me.”

➡ ______________________________

19 Then the ice melted, and three carp suddenly came out of the water.

➡ ______________________________

20 The man went back home and cooked the fish for his mother.

➡ ______________________________

21 Then his mother got well.

➡ ______________________________

22 There are other examples of symbolic objects in Munjado.

➡ ______________________________

23 They are bamboo in the paintings of the character *chung*(忠) and lotus flowers in the paintings of *ui*(義).

➡ ______________________________

24 Bamboo does not bend.

➡ ______________________________

25 It stays green in all kinds of weather.

➡ ______________________________

26 For these reasons, bamboo came to symbolize loyalty to the king.

➡ ______________________________

27 In the case of lotus flowers, they grow in muddy ponds but still bloom beautifully.

➡ ______________________________

28 They thus became a symbol of a person’s will to fight for justice despite difficulties.

➡ ______________________________

29 Munjado was much more than a painting to people of the Joseon dynasty.

➡ ______________________________

30 It reminded them of important values that greatly influenced their behaviors and attitudes.

➡ ______________________________

31 In particular, for children, Munjado was a study tool.

➡ ______________________________

32 Through it, children in the Joseon dynasty could learn the importance of harmony in family and society

➡ ______________________________

Step4

※ 다음 괄호 안의 단어들을 우리말에 맞도록 바르게 배열하시오.

1 (a / Munjado / into / Window / Joseon / the / Dynasty)
➡ ______________________________

2 (at / look / painting / the / the / on / right.)
➡ ______________________________

3 (you / do / the / see / character, / Chinese / *hyo*(孝)?)
➡ ______________________________

4 (you / do / see / also / carp, / a / geomungo / a / and / fan? / a)
➡ ______________________________

5 (kind / this / painting / of / called / is / Munjado, / and / is / it / of / type / a / folk / that / painting / was / popular / the / in / Joseon / late / dynasty.)
➡ ______________________________

6 (Munjado, / in / is / there / a / usually / character / Chinese / some / with / or / animals / objects.)
➡ ______________________________

7 (of / one / Chinese / eight / appears / characters / Munjado. / in)
➡ ______________________________

8 (are / they / *je*(悌), / *hyo*(孝), / *sin*(信), / *chung*(忠), / *ui*(義), / *ye*(禮), / *chi*(恥), / and / *yeom*(廉), / and / represent / they / values / the / were / that / to / important / of / people / the / dynasty. / Joseon)
➡ ______________________________

9 (animals / the / objects / or / Munjado / in / are / just / not / decorations.)
➡ ______________________________

10 (often / they / symbolic. / are)
➡ ______________________________

11 (example, / for / in / carp / paintings / the / *hyo* / of / respect / symbolize / parents / for / of / because / old / an / story.)
➡ ______________________________

12 (story / the / as / goes / follows.)
➡ ______________________________

13 (upon / once / time, / a / man / a / with / lived / old / mother. / his)
➡ ______________________________

14 (winter, / one / man's / the / became / mother / and / ill / eat / couldn't / anything.)
➡ ______________________________

15 (one / on / cold / very / day, / mother / the / to / said / man, / the / would / "it / be / if / wonderful / eat / could / I / fish." / fresh)
➡ ______________________________

16 (man / the / out / went / the / to / river, / it / but / completely / was / frozen.)
➡ ______________________________

1 문자도, 조선 시대를 보는 창
2 오른쪽에 있는 그림을 보라.
3 한자 효(孝)가 보이는가?
4 잉어, 거문고, 그리고 부채가 보이는가?
5 이런 종류의 그림은 문자도이며, 조선 시대 후기에 인기 있었던 민화의 한 종류이다.
6 문자도에는 보통 한자 하나가 동물이나 사물과 함께 있다.
7 문자도에는 여덟 개의 한자 중 하나가 나온다.
8 그것들은 효(孝), 제(悌), 충(忠), 신(信), 예(禮), 의(義), 염(廉), 치(恥)이고, 그것들은 조선 시대 사람들에게 중요했던 가치들을 나타낸다.
9 문자도에 있는 동물이나 사물은 단순한 장식이 아니다.
10 그것들은 종종 상징적이다.
11 예를 들어, '효' 그림 속에 있는 잉어는 옛이야기 때문에 부모님에 대한 존경심을 상징한다.
12 그 이야기는 다음과 같다.
13 옛날 옛적에 한 남자가 나이 드신 어머니와 살았다.
14 어느 겨울, 남자의 어머니는 병이 들어서 어떤 것도 먹을 수 없었다.
15 무척 추운 어느 날, 어머니는 남자에게 말했다. "신선한 물고기를 먹을 수 있다면 좋겠구나."
16 그 남자는 강으로 나갔지만, 강은 완전히 얼어붙어 있었다.

17 (was / it / for / impossible / to / him / any / catch / fish.)
➡ ______________________________

18 (man / the / so / was / that / disappointed / cried / he / to / out / sky, / the / should / "what / I / do? / help / please / me.")
➡ ______________________________
____

19 (the / then / melted, / ice / three / and / suddenly / carp / out / came / the / of / water.)
➡ ______________________________

20 (man / the / back / went / home / and / the / cooked / for / fish / mother. / his)
➡ ______________________________

21 (his / then / got / mother / well.)
➡ ______________________________

22 (are / there / examples / other / symbolic / of / in / objects / Munjado.)
➡ ______________________________

23 (are / they / in / bamboo / paintings / the / the / of / *chung*(忠) / character / lotus / and / in / flowers / paintings / the / *ui*(義) / of)
➡ ______________________________
____

24 (does / bamboo / bend. / not)
➡ ______________________________

25 (stays / it / in / green / kinds / all / weather. / of)
➡ ______________________________

26 (these / for / reasons, / came / bamboo / symbolize / to / to / loyalty / king. / the)
➡ ______________________________

27 (the / in / of / case / flowers, / lotus / grow / they / muddy / in / but / ponds / still / beautifully. / bloom)
➡ ______________________________
____

28 (thus / they / a / became / symbol / of / person's / a / to / will / fight / justice / for / difficulties. / despite)
➡ ______________________________
____

29 (was / Munjado / more / much / a / than / to / painting / of / people / the / dynasty. / Joseon)
➡ ______________________________
____

30 (reminded / it / of / them / values / important / greatly / that / their / influenced / behaviors / attitudes. / and)
➡ ______________________________
____

31 (particular, / in / children, / for / was / Munjado / study / a / tool.)
➡ ______________________________

32 (it, / through / in / children / Joseon / the / could / dynasty / learn / the / of / importance / in / harmony / family / society. / and)
➡ ______________________________
____

17 그가 그 어떤 물고기라도 잡는 것은 불가능했다.

18 남자는 몹시 낙담해서 하늘에 대고 외쳤다. "제가 어떻게 해야 하나요? 제발 저를 도와주세요."

19 그러자 얼음이 녹았고, 잉어 세 마리가 갑자기 물 밖으로 나왔다.

20 남자는 집으로 돌아가서 어머니를 위해 물고기들을 요리했다.

21 그러자 그의 어머니는 회복되었다.

22 문자도에 있는 상징적인 사물의 또 다른 예가 있다.

23 그것들은 글자 '충(忠)' 그림에 있는 대나무와 '의(義)' 그림에 있는 연꽃이다.

24 대나무는 구부러지지 않는다.

25 그것은 어떤 날씨에서도 푸르름을 유지한다.

26 이런 이유로 대나무는 왕에 대한 충성을 상징하게 되었다.

27 연꽃의 경우, 그것들은 진흙투성이의 연못에서 자라지만 여전히 아름답게 꽃을 피운다.

28 그래서 그 꽃들은 어려움에도 불구하고 정의를 위해 싸우는 사람의 의지를 상징하게 되었다.

29 문자도는 조선 시대 사람들에게 그림 그 이상이었다.

30 그것은 그들에게 자신들의 행동과 태도에 큰 영향을 미치는 중요한 가치를 상기시켰다.

31 특히 아이들에게 문자도는 학습 도구였다.

32 그것을 통해 조선 시대의 아이들은 가족과 사회에서의 조화의 중요성을 배울 수 있었다.

본문 Test

Step5

※ 다음 우리말을 영어로 쓰시오.

1 문자도, 조선 시대를 보는 창

➡ ______________________________

2 오른쪽에 있는 그림을 보라.

➡ ______________________________

3 한자 효(孝)가 보이는가?

➡ ______________________________

4 잉어, 거문고, 그리고 부채가 보이는가?

➡ ______________________________

5 이런 종류의 그림은 문자도이며, 조선 시대 후기에 인기 있었던 민화의 한 종류이다.

➡ ______________________________

____

6 문자도에는 보통 한자 하나가 동물이나 사물과 함께 있다.

➡ ______________________________

7 문자도에는 여덟 개의 한자 중 하나가 나온다.

➡ ______________________________

8 그것들은 효(孝), 제(悌), 충(忠), 신(信), 예(禮), 의(義), 염(廉), 치(恥)이고, 그것들은 조선 시대 사람들에게 중요했던 가치들을 나타낸다.

➡ ______________________________

____

9 문자도에 있는 동물이나 사물은 단순한 장식이 아니다.

➡ ______________________________

10 그것들은 종종 상징적이다.

➡ ______________________________

11 예를 들어, '효' 그림 속에 있는 잉어는 옛이야기 때문에 부모님에 대한 존경심을 상징한다.

➡ ______________________________

12 그 이야기는 다음과 같다.

➡ ______________________________

13 옛날 옛적에 한 남자가 나이 드신 어머니와 살았다.

➡ ______________________________

14 어느 겨울, 남자의 어머니는 병이 들어서 어떤 것도 먹을 수 없었다.

➡ ______________________________

15 무척 추운 어느 날, 어머니는 남자에게 말했다. "신선한 물고기를 먹을 수 있다면 좋겠구나."

➡ ______________________________

16 그 남자는 강으로 나갔지만, 강은 완전히 얼어붙어 있었다.

➡ ______________________________

17 그가 그 어떤 물고기라도 잡는 것은 불가능했다.

➡ ______________________________

18 남자는 몹시 낙담해서 하늘에 대고 외쳤다. "제가 어떻게 해야 하나요? 제발 저를 도와주세요."

➡ ______________________________

19 그러자 얼음이 녹았고, 잉어 세 마리가 갑자기 물 밖으로 나왔다.

➡ ______________________________

20 남자는 집으로 돌아가서 어머니를 위해 물고기들을 요리했다.

➡ ______________________________

21 그러자 그의 어머니는 회복되었다.

➡ ______________________________

22 문자도에 있는 상징적인 사물의 또 다른 예가 있다.

➡ ______________________________

23 그것들은 글자 '충(忠)' 그림에 있는 대나무와 '의(義)' 그림에 있는 연꽃이다.

➡ ______________________________

24 대나무는 구부러지지 않는다.

➡ ______________________________

25 그것은 어떤 날씨에서도 푸르름을 유지한다.

➡ ______________________________

26 이런 이유로 대나무는 왕에 대한 충성을 상징하게 되었다.

➡ ______________________________

27 연꽃의 경우, 그것들은 진흙투성이의 연못에서 자라지만 여전히 아름답게 꽃을 피운다.

➡ ______________________________

28 그래서 그 꽃들은 어려움에도 불구하고 정의를 위해 싸우는 사람의 의지를 상징하게 되었다.

➡ ______________________________

29 문자도는 조선 시대 사람들에게 그림 그 이상이었다.

➡ ______________________________

30 그것은 그들에게 자신들의 행동과 태도에 큰 영향을 미치는 중요한 가치를 상기시켰다.

➡ ______________________________

31 특히 아이들에게 문자도는 학습 도구였다.

➡ ______________________________

32 그것을 통해 조선 시대의 아이들은 가족과 사회에서의 조화의 중요성을 배울 수 있었다.

➡ ______________________________

구석구석 지문 Test

Step1

※ 다음 우리말과 일치하도록 빈칸에 알맞은 말을 쓰시오.

After You Read B Read and Complete

1. Paintings of *Hyo*(孝): Carp ________ ________ ________ ________.
2. In an old story, a man caught ________ ________ ________ ________ ________ ________ and cooked them ________ ________ ________ ________.
3. Paintings of *Chung*(忠): Bamboo ________ ________ ________ the king.
4. It does not ________ and ________ ________ in ________ ________ ________ weather.
5. Paintings of *Ui*(義): Lotus flowers symbolize a ________ ________ ________ ________ ________ justice ________ ________.
6. They grow ________ ________ ________ but still ________ ________.

1. '효' 그림: 잉어는 부모님에 대한 존경심을 상징한다.
2. 옛이야기에서 한 남자가 얼어붙은 강에서 잉어 세 마리를 잡아 자신의 아픈 어머니를 위해 그것들을 요리했다.
3. '충' 그림: 대나무는 왕에 대한 충성을 상징한다.
4. 그것은 구부러지지 않고 어떤 날씨에서도 푸르름을 유지한다.
5. '의' 그림: 연꽃은 어려움에도 불구하고 정의를 위해 싸우는 인간의 의지를 상징한다.
6. 그 꽃들은 진흙투성이의 연못에서 자라지만 여전히 아름답게 꽃을 피운다.

Around the World

1. This painting ________ ________ ________ ________ ________ ________ ________ in Europe in the 16th century.
2. This painting shows a ssireum competition ________ ________ ________ ________ ________.
3. This painting ________ ________ ________ ________ an American farmer's daughter ________ ________ ________ ________.

1. 이 그림은 16세기 유럽 교외 지역의 수확기를 보여 준다.
2. 이 그림은 조선 시대 후기의 씨름 대회를 보여 준다.
3. 이 그림은 19세기 미국 농부의 딸의 결혼식을 보여 준다.

Think and Write

1. My ________ Painting, *Water Lillies: The Clouds*
2. ________ ________ ________ is *Water Lilies: The Clouds.*
3. It ________ ________ ________ Claude Monet.
4. In the painting, I can see ________ ________ ________ ________ in the pond ________ ________ ________ water lilies.
5. I like this painting ________ the colors are beautiful and the ________ ________ ________.
6. I think ________ was very ________ ________ ________ ________ ________ ________ the pond as a mirror ________ ________ the clouds in the sky ________ ________ in the pond.

1. 내가 가장 좋아하는 그림, '수련: 구름'
2. 내가 가장 좋아하는 그림은 '수련: 구름'이다.
3. 그것은 Claude Monet에 의해 그려졌다.
4. 그림 속에서, 나는 수련뿐만 아니라 연못에 비친 구름도 볼 수 있다.
5. 나는 색깔도 아름답고, 장면이 평화롭게 보여서 이 그림을 좋아한다.
6. 나는 화가가 연못을 거울로 해서 하늘의 구름이 연못에 비치도록 한 것이 매우 창의적이라고 생각한다.

구석구석 지문 Test

Step2

※ 다음 우리말을 영어로 쓰시오.

After You Read B Read and Complete

1. '효' 그림: 잉어는 부모님에 대한 존경심을 상징한다.
➡ ______________________________
2. 옛이야기에서 한 남자가 얼어붙은 강에서 잉어 세 마리를 잡아 자신의 아픈 어머니를 위해 그것들을 요리했다.
➡ ______________________________
3. '충' 그림: 대나무는 왕에 대한 충성을 상징한다.
➡ ______________________________
4. 그것은 구부러지지 않고 어떤 날씨에서도 푸르름을 유지한다.
➡ ______________________________
5. '의' 그림: 연꽃은 어려움에도 불구하고 정의를 위해 싸우는 인간의 의지를 상징한다.
➡ ______________________________
6. 그 꽃들은 진흙투성이의 연못에서 자라지만 여전히 아름답게 꽃을 피운다.
➡ ______________________________

Around the World

1. 이 그림은 16세기 유럽 교외 지역의 수확기를 보여 준다.
➡ ______________________________
2. 이 그림은 조선 시대 후기의 씨름 대회를 보여 준다.
➡ ______________________________
3. 이 그림은 19세기 미국 농부의 딸의 결혼식을 보여 준다.
➡ ______________________________

Think and Write

1. 내가 가장 좋아하는 그림, '수련: 구름'
➡ ______________________________
2. 내가 가장 좋아하는 그림은 '수련: 구름'이다.
➡ ______________________________
3. 그것은 Claude Monet에 의해 그려졌다.
➡ ______________________________
4. 그림 속에서, 나는 수련뿐만 아니라 연못에 비친 구름도 볼 수 있다.
➡ ______________________________
5. 나는 색깔도 아름답고, 장면이 평화롭게 보여서 이 그림을 좋아한다.
➡ ______________________________
6. 나는 화가가 연못을 거울로 해서 하늘의 구름이 연못에 비치도록 한 것이 매우 창의적이라고 생각한다.
➡ ______________________________
____

단어 Test

Step1

※ 다음 영어를 우리말로 쓰시오.

01 still ____________

02 accident ____________

03 pick ____________

04 confidently ____________

05 fair ____________

06 compliment ____________

07 list ____________

08 hesitate ____________

09 stuck ____________

10 worried ____________

11 creative ____________

12 work ____________

13 cheerful ____________

14 point ____________

15 scratch ____________

16 messy ____________

17 hurt ____________

18 pause ____________

19 scream ____________

20 air ____________

21 calm ____________

22 shyly ____________

23 bicycle stand ____________

24 except for ____________

25 all day long ____________

26 Just a minute. ____________

27 pull out ____________

28 the other day ____________

29 a piece of ____________

30 come out of ____________

31 What made you ~? ____________

단어 Test

Step2

※ 다음 우리말을 영어로 쓰시오.

01 효과가 있다 ____________
02 가만히 있는, 고요한 ____________
03 사고 ____________
04 칭찬, 찬사; 칭찬하다 ____________
05 공평한, 공정한 ____________
06 망설이다, 주저하다 ____________
07 수줍게, 부끄러워하며 ____________
08 난처한, 걱정[근심]스러운 ____________
09 자신 있게 ____________
10 목록, 명단 ____________
11 ~을 다치게 하다, 아프다 ____________
12 지저분한, 엉망인 ____________
13 창의적인, 창조적인 ____________
14 (일시적인) 중단 ____________
15 (~에 빠져) 움직일 수 없는 ____________
16 발랄한, 쾌활한 ____________
17 가리키다 ____________
18 긁다 ____________
19 공중, 허공 ____________
20 뽑다, 따다, 뜯다 ____________
21 침착한, 차분한 ____________
22 비명을 지르다 ____________
23 자전거 거치대 ____________
24 일전에, 최근에 ____________
25 빠져나가다[나오다] ____________
26 ~을 제외하고 ____________
27 하루 종일 ____________
28 잠깐만. ____________
29 하나의 ~, 한 조각의 ~ ____________
30 ~에서 나오다 ____________
31 무엇 때문에 ~했니? ____________

※ 다음 영영풀이에 알맞은 단어를 <보기>에서 골라 쓴 후, 우리말 뜻을 쓰시오.

1 __________: dirty and/or not neat: __________

2 __________: not excited, nervous, or upset: __________

3 __________: the space or sky that is filled with air: __________

4 __________: to make a very loud, high-pitched cry: __________

5 __________: feeling or showing happiness: __________

6 __________: to be successful, effective, or satisfactory: __________

7 __________: to rub your fingernails against your skin because it is itching: __________

8 __________: involving the use of imagination to produce new ideas or things: __________

9 __________: an unfortunate mishap; especially one causing damage or injury: __________

10 __________: to pause or hold back in uncertainty or unwillingness: __________

11 __________: a short period when you stop doing something before continuing: __________

12 __________: treating people in a way that does not favor some over others: __________

13 __________: to hold out your finger towards a person or thing in order to make someone notice them: __________

14 __________: a set of names or addresses which all belong to a particular category, written down one below the other: __________

15 __________: in a way that shows that you feel sure about your own ability to do things and be successful: __________

16 __________: a polite remark that you say to someone to show that you like their appearance, appreciate their qualities, or approve of what they have done: __________

보기

pause	work	hesitate	list
compliment	calm	air	messy
fair	cheerful	point	creative
accident	scream	scratch	confidently

본문 Test

※ 다음 우리말과 일치하도록 빈칸에 알맞은 것을 골라 쓰시오.

1 The ________ ________ ________
A. Best B. Ever C. Compliment

1 최고의 칭찬

2 Scene 1

2 〈장면 1〉

3 *It is* ________ ________ ________ *of school.*
A. week B. last C. the

3 이번 주는 학교의 마지막 주이다.

4 ________ *student has just* ________ a ________ *of paper* ________ *a name on it.*
A. piece B. each C. with D. picked

4 각 학생들은 이름 하나가 쓰인 종이 한 장씩을 막 뽑았다.

5 Ms. Kemp: "________ ________ Classmates" will be our ________ ________ of the school year.
A. activity B. Compliments C. last D. for

5 Ms. Kemp: '학급 친구들 칭찬하기'는 이번 학년 우리의 마지막 활동이 될 거예요.

6 Did ________ ________ a ________?
A. pick B. name C. everyone

6 모두 이름을 뽑았나요?

7 Class: ________, ________ Kemp.
A. Ms. B. yes

7 Class: 네, Kemp 선생님.

8 *Students are* ________ *to* ________ ________.
A. other B. talking C. each

8 학생들이 서로 이야기를 나누고 있다.

9 Beth: So, ________ ________ did you ________?
A. pick B. whose C. name

9 Beth: 너는 누구 이름을 뽑았니?

10 Lucy: (________) I ________ Boyd.
A. got B. smiling

10 Lucy: (웃으며) Boyd를 뽑았어.

11 I have a ________ ________ ________ about him.
A. say B. lot C. to

11 그 애에 관해 할 말이 많아.

12 ________ ________ you, Beth?
A. about B. what

12 너는 어때, Beth?

13 Beth: (________ ________) Uh, I ________ Peter's name.
A. worried B. picked C. looking

13 Beth: (걱정스러운 표정으로) 어, Peter 이름을 뽑았어.

14 Lucy: Peter? Oh, no! It won't be ________ to find ________ to ________ him ________.
A. compliment B. on C. easy D. something

14 Lucy: Peter? 아, 이런! 그 애에 관해서 칭찬할 것을 찾는 게 쉽지 않을 거야.

15 Steve: Yeah. He doesn't talk much and just ________ ________ his desk ________ day ________.
A. long B. sits C. all D. at

15 Steve: 그래. 그 애는 말을 많이 하지 않고 하루 종일 그냥 책상에 앉아만 있잖아.

16 Beth: (________ *her head*) Well, I'll ________ ________ ________ something.
A. to B. scratching C. have D. find

16 Beth: (머리를 긁적이며) 음, 무언가를 찾아야 해.

17 Scene 2

17 〈장면 2〉

18 *Beth is ________ home ________ ________ her parents about the ________.*

A. activity B. with C. at D. talking

19 Beth: Everyone has long ________ of ________ for ________ classmates, ________ for me.

A. except B. lists C. other D. compliments

20 I don't know ________ ________ ________ Peter ________.

A. to B. on C. compliment D. what

21 Mom: ________ ________.

A. carefully B. think

22 ________ ________ be ________.

A. something B. there C. should

23 Beth: Well, ________ ________.

A. clean B. he's

24 He ________ his ________ ________ day.

A. face B. washes C. every

25 Mom: That's ________ ________ ________.

A. not B. compliment C. a

26 Everybody ________ ________.

A. that B. does

27 Dad: ________ ________.

A. again B. try

28 I'm ________ you can find ________ ________ to ________ about him.

A. say B. good C. sure D. something

29 Scene 3

30 *The ________ day, ________ is ________ ________ at school.*

A. accident B. next C. there D. an

31 *Boyd's ________ ________ ________ in a bicycle ________.*

A. stand B. stuck C. is D. foot

32 Boyd: (________ ________ in the ________) Help! I need ________!

A. air B. with C. help D. arms

33 Beth: ________ ________. I'm trying to ________ your foot ________.

A. pull B. stay C. out D. still

34 Boyd: (________) Ouch! That ________!

A. hurts B. screaming

35 Peter: ________ me ________. Just a ________.

A. help B. let C. minute

18 Beth는 집에서 그 활동에 대해 자신의 부모님과 이야기를 나누고 있다.

19 Beth: 저를 제외한 모두가 다른 친구들에 대해 긴 칭찬 목록을 가지고 있어요.

20 저는 Peter에 관해 무엇을 칭찬해야 할지 모르겠어요.

21 엄마: 잘 생각해 봐.

22 뭔가 있을 거야.

23 Beth: 음, 그 애는 깔끔해요.

24 매일 세수를 해요.

25 엄마: 그건 칭찬이 아니야.

26 모든 사람들이 하는 거잖니.

27 아빠: 다시 생각해 보렴.

28 그 아이에 대해 말할 뭔가 좋은 것을 분명히 찾을 수 있을 거야.

29 〈장면 3〉

30 다음 날, 학교에서 사고가 생긴다.

31 Boyd의 발이 자전거 거치대에 끼었다.

32 Boyd: (공중에 양팔을 벌린 채) 도와줘! 도움이 필요해!

33 Beth: 가만히 있어. 네 발을 꺼내려고 노력 중이야.

34 Boyd: (비명을 지르며) 아! 아파!

35 Peter: 내가 도와줄게. 잠깐만.

36 *Peter ________ to the school's kitchen and ________ ________ ________ butter.*
A. back B. runs C. comes D. with

37 Peter: I'm ________ to ________ this butter ________ your ________.
A. on B. put C. foot D. going

38 Boyd: ________? ________?
A. butter B. what

39 Peter: Just ________ ________.
A. calm B. stay

40 Beth: (________ *to Boyd's* ________) Wow! It's ________!
A. working B. pointing C. foot

41 Boyd's foot is ________ ________ ________ the ________.
A. of B. stand C. out D. coming

42 Scene 4

43 *Beth is ________ ________ ________ her parents.*
A. with B. dinner C. eating

44 *She tells them ________ ________ ________ to Boyd.*
A. happened B. what C. about

45 Beth: ________ was a ________ ________ at school today.
A. little B. there C. accident

46 Boyd's foot ________ ________ ________ a bicycle stand.
A. stuck B. in C. got

47 Mom: Oh, no! ________ how did he ________ his foot ________?
A. get B. so C. out

48 Beth: Peter ________ butter ________ his foot and then ________ it ________.
A. on B. pulled C. put D. out

49 Dad: That was really ________. ________ ________ creative.
A. creative B. messy C. but

50 Beth: Hmm. ________? Can that ________ a ________, Dad?
A. compliment B. creative C. be

51 Dad: ________.

36 Peter가 학교 주방으로 뛰어가 버터를 가지고 온다.

37 Peter: 네 발에 이 버터를 바를 거야.

38 Boyd: 뭐? 버터를?

39 Peter: 그냥 침착하게 있어.

40 Beth: (Boyd의 발을 가리키며) 와! 효과가 있어!

41 Boyd의 발이 거치대에서 빠져나오고 있어.

42 〈장면 4〉

43 Beth는 부모님과 저녁 식사를 하고 있다.

44 그녀는 부모님께 Boyd에게 일어난 일에 대해 이야기한다.

45 Beth: 오늘 학교에서 작은 사고가 있었어요.

46 Boyd의 발이 자전거 거치대에 끼었어요.

47 엄마: 오, 저런! 그래서 발을 어떻게 뺐니?

48 Beth: Peter가 그 애 발에 버터를 바르고 나서 발을 당겨서 꺼냈어요.

49 아빠: 정말 창의적이구나. 지저분하지만 창의적이야.

50 Beth: 흠. 창의적이라고요? 아빠, 그것이 칭찬이 될 수 있어요?

51 아빠: 물론이지.

52 Scene 5

53 *It is the ________ day of school, and the students are ________ ________ ________.*

A. complimenting B. last C. other D. each

54 Ms. Kemp: Joanne, ________ ________ do you have ________ Beth?

A. what B. for C. compliment

55 Joanne: Beth, you're ________ ________.

A. cheerful B. always

56 You're also ________ and ________ to ________.

A. fair B. kind C. everybody

57 Beth: Thanks, Joanne. It's ________ nice ________ ________ ________ say so.

A. you B. to C. of D. so

58 Ms. Kemp: Beth, ________ ________ ________ you now.

A. from B. let's C. hear

59 You ________ Peter's ________.

A. name B. picked

60 Beth: (________) Well, I ________ Peter is ________. Peter, you're … uh … creative.

A. creative B. hesitating C. think

61 Peter: (________) ________?

A. really B. shyly

62 Ms. Kemp: ________ ________ ________ ________ Peter is creative?

A. think B. what C. you D. made

63 Beth: (*after a long* ________) When Boyd's foot got ________ in the bicycle stand the ________ day, Peter got it out by ________ butter.

A. using B. other C. pause D. stuck

64 ________ was ________.

A. creative B. that

65 Boyd: Yeah! ________ ________ ________ of ________ that.

A. doing B. else C. thought D. nobody

66 Steve: I didn't know that. Well, ________, I ________ think he's ________.

A. also B. creative C. then

67 Beth: (________) Yeah, Peter, you ARE ________!

A. creative B. confidently

68 Peter: Thanks, Beth! It's ________ ________ ________ ________!

A. best B. ever C. the D. compliment

52 〈장면 5〉

53 오늘은 학교의 마지막 날이고 학생들은 서로를 칭찬하고 있다.

54 Ms. Kemp: Joanne, Beth에게 무슨 칭찬을 해 주겠니?

55 Joanne: Beth, 너는 항상 쾌활해.

56 또한 친절하고 모두에게 공정해.

57 Beth: 고마워, Joanne, 그렇게 말해 주다니 친절하구나.

58 Ms. Kemp: Beth, 이제 네 말을 들어 보자.

59 Peter의 이름을 뽑았구나.

60 Beth: (주저하며) 음, Peter는 창의적이라고 생각해요. Peter, 너는… 어… 창의적이야.

61 Peter: (수줍어하며) 정말?

62 Ms. Kemp: Peter가 왜 창의적이라고 생각하니?

63 Beth: (한참 있다가) 일전에 Boyd의 발이 자전거 거치대에 끼었을 때, Peter는 버터를 사용해서 그의 발을 꺼냈어요.

64 그것은 창의적이었어요.

65 Boyd: 맞아! 어느 누구도 그렇게 하는 것을 생각하지 못했어.

66 Steve: 난 몰랐어. 음, 그래, 나도 그가 창의적이라고 생각해.

67 Beth: (자신 있게) 그래, Peter, 너는 창의적이야!

68 Peter: 고마워, Beth! 그건 최고의 칭찬이야!

본문 Test

※ 다음 우리말과 일치하도록 빈칸에 알맞은 것을 골라 쓰시오.

1 The ________ ________ Ever

2 Scene 1

3 *It is the ________ ________ of school.*

4 ________ *student has just picked* ________ ________ ________ ________ ________ *a name on it.*

5 Ms. Kemp: "________ ________ Classmates" will be our ________ ________ of the school year.

6 Did everyone ________ a name?

7 Class: Yes, Ms. Kemp.

8 *Students are* ________ *to* ________ ________.

9 Beth: So, ________ ________ did you ________?

10 Lucy: (________) I ________ Boyd.

11 I have ________ ________ ________ ________ about him.

12 ________ ________ you, Beth?

13 Beth: (________ ________) Uh, I ________ Peter's name.

14 Lucy: Peter? Oh, no! It won't be easy ________ ________ something to ________ ________ ________.

15 Steve: Yeah. He doesn't talk much and just ________ ________ ________ ________ ________ ________ ________.

16 Beth: (*scratching her head*) Well, I'll ________ ________ ________ something.

17 Scene 2

18 *Beth is at home* ________ ________ *her parents about the activity.*

19 Beth: Everyone has long lists of ________ for ________ classmates, ________ ________ me.

20 I don't know ________ ________ ________ Peter ________.

21 Mom: Think ________.

1 최고의 칭찬

2 〈장면 1〉

3 이번 주는 학교의 마지막 주이다.

4 각 학생들은 이름 하나가 쓰인 종이 한 장씩을 막 뽑았다.

5 Ms. Kemp: '학급 친구들 칭찬하기'는 이번 학년 우리의 마지막 활동이 될 거예요.

6 모두 이름을 뽑았나요?

7 Class: 네, Kemp 선생님.

8 학생들이 서로 이야기를 나누고 있다.

9 Beth: 너는 누구 이름을 뽑았니?

10 Lucy: (웃으며) Boyd를 뽑았어.

11 그 애에 관해 할 말이 많아.

12 너는 어때, Beth?

13 Beth: (걱정스러운 표정으로) 어, Peter 이름을 뽑았어.

14 Lucy: Peter? 아, 이런! 그 애에 관해서 칭찬할 것을 찾는 게 쉽지 않을 거야.

15 Steve: 그래. 그 애는 말을 많이 하지 않고 하루 종일 그냥 책상에 앉아만 있잖아.

16 Beth: (머리를 긁적이며) 음, 무언가를 찾아야 해.

17 〈장면 2〉

18 Beth는 집에서 그 활동에 대해 자신의 부모님과 이야기를 나누고 있다.

19 Beth: 저를 제외한 모두가 다른 친구들에 대해 긴 칭찬 목록을 가지고 있어요.

20 저는 Peter에 관해 무엇을 칭찬해야 할지 모르겠어요.

21 엄마: 잘 생각해 봐.

22 There ________ ________ something.

23 Beth: Well, ________ ________.

24 He ________ his face ________ ________.

25 Mom: That's not ________ ________.

26 Everybody ________ ________.

27 Dad: ________ ________.

28 ________ ________ you can find ________ ________ to say about him.

29 Scene 3

30 *The next day, there is ________ ________ at school.*

31 *Boyd's foot ________ ________ in a bicycle ________.*

32 Boyd: (________ ________ ________ ________ ________) Help! I need help!

33 Beth: ________ ________. I'm trying to ________ your foot ________.

34 Boyd: (________) Ouch! That ________!

35 Peter: ________ me help. Just a ________.

36 *Peter runs to the school's kitchen and ________ ________ with butter.*

37 Peter: I'm going to ________ this butter ________ your ________.

38 Boyd: ________? Butter?

39 Peter: Just stay ________.

40 Beth: (________ ________ *Boyd's foot*) Wow! It's ________!

41 Boyd's foot is ________ ________ ________ the stand.

42 Scene 4

43 *Beth is ________ ________ ________ her parents.*

44 *She tells them about ________ ________ to Boyd.*

45 Beth: There was ________ ________ ________ at school today.

46 Boyd's foot ________ ________ ________ a bicycle stand.

47 Mom: Oh, no! So how did he ________ his foot ________?

22 뭔가 있을 거야.
23 Beth: 음, 그 애는 깔끔해요.
24 매일 세수를 해요.
25 엄마: 그건 칭찬이 아니야.
26 모든 사람들이 하는 거잖니.
27 아빠: 다시 생각해 보렴.
28 그 아이에 대해 말할 뭔가 좋은 것을 분명히 찾을 수 있을 거야.
29 〈장면 3〉
30 다음 날, 학교에서 사고가 생긴다.
31 Boyd의 발이 자전거 거치대에 끼었다.
32 Boyd: (공중에 양팔을 벌린 채) 도와줘! 도움이 필요해!
33 Beth: 가만히 있어. 네 발을 꺼내려고 노력 중이야.
34 Boyd: (비명을 지르며) 아! 아파!
35 Peter: 내가 도와줄게. 잠깐만.
36 Peter가 학교 주방으로 뛰어가 버터를 가지고 온다.
37 Peter: 네 발에 이 버터를 바를 거야.
38 Boyd: 뭐? 버터를?
39 Peter: 그냥 침착하게 있어.
40 Beth: (Boyd의 발을 가리키며) 와! 효과가 있어!
41 Boyd의 발이 거치대에서 빠져나오고 있어.
42 〈장면 4〉
43 Beth는 부모님과 저녁 식사를 하고 있다.
44 그녀는 부모님께 Boyd에게 일어난 일에 대해 이야기한다.
45 Beth: 오늘 학교에서 작은 사고가 있었어요.
46 Boyd의 발이 자전거 거치대에 끼었어요.
47 엄마: 오, 저런! 그래서 발을 어떻게 뺐니?

48 Beth: Peter ________ butter ________ his foot and then ________ ________ ________.

49 Dad: That was really creative. ________ but ________.

50 Beth: Hmm. Creative? Can that be ________ ________, Dad?

51 Dad: ________.

52 Scene 5

53 *It is ________ ________ ________ of school, and the students are ________ ________ ________.*

54 Ms. Kemp: Joanne, ________ ________ do you have for Beth?

55 Joanne: Beth, you're always ________.

56 You're ________ kind and ________ to everybody.

57 Beth: Thanks, Joanne. It's so nice ________ ________ to say so.

58 Ms. Kemp: Beth, let's ________ ________ ________ now.

59 You ________ Peter's name.

60 Beth: (________) Well, I think Peter is ________. Peter, you're … uh … creative.

61 Peter: (________) Really?

62 Ms. Kemp: ________ ________ ________ ________ Peter is creative?

63 Beth: (*after a long* ________) When Boyd's foot ________ ________ in the bicycle stand ________ ________ ________, Peter ________ it ________ ________ ________ butter.

64 That was ________.

65 Boyd: Yeah! ________ ________ ________ ________ doing that.

66 Steve: I didn't know that. Well, then, I ________ think he's creative.

67 Beth: (________) Yeah, Peter, you ARE ________!

68 Peter: Thanks, Beth! It's ________ ________ ________ ________!

48 Beth: Peter가 그 애 발에 버터를 바르고 나서 발을 당겨서 꺼냈어요.

49 아빠: 정말 창의적이구나. 지저분하지만 창의적이야.

50 Beth: 흠. 창의적이라고요? 아빠, 그것이 칭찬이 될 수 있어요?

51 아빠: 물론이지.

52 〈장면 5〉

53 오늘은 학교의 마지막 날이고 학생들은 서로를 칭찬하고 있다.

54 Ms. Kemp: Joanne, Beth에게 무슨 칭찬을 해 주겠니?

55 Joanne: Beth, 너는 항상 쾌활해.

56 또한 친절하고 모두에게 공정해.

57 Beth: 고마워, Joanne. 그렇게 말해 주다니 친절하구나.

58 Ms. Kemp: Beth, 이제 네 말을 들어 보자.

59 Peter의 이름을 뽑았구나.

60 Beth: (주저하며) 음, Peter는 창의적이라고 생각해요. Peter, 너는… 어… 창의적이야.

61 Peter: (수줍어하며) 정말?

62 Ms. Kemp: Peter가 왜 창의적이라고 생각하니?

63 Beth: (한참 있다가) 일전에 Boyd의 발이 자전거 거치대에 끼었을 때, Peter는 버터를 사용해서 그의 발을 꺼냈어요.

64 그것은 창의적이었어요.

65 Boyd: 맞아! 어느 누구도 그렇게 하는 것을 생각하지 못했어.

66 Steve: 난 몰랐어. 음, 그래, 나도 그가 창의적이라고 생각해.

67 Beth: (자신 있게) 그래, Peter, 너는 창의적이야!

68 Peter: 고마워, Beth! 그건 최고의 칭찬이야!

본문 Test

Step3

※ 다음 문장을 우리말로 쓰시오.

1 The Best Compliment Ever
➡ ______________________

2 Scene 1
➡ ______________________

3 It is the last week of school.
➡ ______________________

4 Each student has just picked a piece of paper with a name on it.
➡ ______________________

5 Ms. Kemp: "Compliments for Classmates" will be our last activity of the school year.
➡ ______________________

6 Did everyone pick a name?
➡ ______________________

7 Class: Yes, Ms. Kemp.
➡ ______________________

8 Students are talking to each other.
➡ ______________________

9 Beth: So, whose name did you pick?
➡ ______________________

10 Lucy: (smiling) I got Boyd.
➡ ______________________

11 I have a lot to say about him.
➡ ______________________

12 What about you, Beth?
➡ ______________________

13 Beth: (looking worried) Uh, I picked Peter's name.
➡ ______________________

14 Lucy: Peter? Oh, no! It won't be easy to find something to compliment him on.
➡ ______________________

15 Steve: Yeah. He doesn't talk much and just sits at his desk all day long.
➡ ______________________

16 Beth: (scratching her head) Well, I'll have to find something.
➡ ______________________

17 Scene 2
➡ ______________________

18 Beth is at home talking with her parents about the activity.
➡ ______________________

19 Beth: Everyone has long lists of compliments for other classmates, except for me.
➡ ______________________

20 I don't know what to compliment Peter on.
➡ ______________________

21 Mom: Think carefully.
➡ ______________________

22 There should be something.
➡ ______________________

23 Beth: Well, he's clean.

➡ ______

24 He washes his face every day.

➡ ______

25 Mom: That's not a compliment.

➡ ______

26 Everybody does that.

➡ ______

27 Dad: Try again.

➡ ______

28 I'm sure you can find something good to say about him.

➡ ______

29 Scene 3

➡ ______

30 The next day, there is an accident at school.

➡ ______

31 Boyd's foot is stuck in a bicycle stand.

➡ ______

32 Boyd: (with arms in the air) Help! I need help!

➡ ______

33 Beth: Stay still. I'm trying to pull your foot out.

➡ ______

34 Boyd: (screaming) Ouch! That hurts!

➡ ______

35 Peter: Let me help. Just a minute.

➡ ______

36 Peter runs to the school's kitchen and comes back with butter.

➡ ______

37 Peter: I'm going to put this butter on your foot.

➡ ______

38 Boyd: What? Butter?

➡ ______

39 Peter: Just stay calm.

➡ ______

40 Beth: (pointing to Boyd's foot) Wow! It's working!

➡ ______

41 Boyd's foot is coming out of the stand.

➡ ______

42 Scene 4

➡ ______

43 Beth is eating dinner with her parents.

➡ ______

44 She tells them about what happened to Boyd.

➡ ______

45 Beth: There was a little accident at school today.

➡ ______

46 Boyd's foot got stuck in a bicycle stand.
➡ ______

47 Mom: Oh, no! So how did he get his foot out?
➡ ______

48 Beth: Peter put butter on his foot and then pulled it out.
➡ ______

49 Dad: That was really creative. Messy but creative.
➡ ______

50 Beth: Hmm. Creative? Can that be a compliment, Dad?
➡ ______

51 Dad: Sure.
➡ ______

52 Scene 5
➡ ______

53 It is the last day of school, and the students are complimenting each other.
➡ ______

54 Ms. Kemp: Joanne, what compliment do you have for Beth?
➡ ______

55 Joanne: Beth, you're always cheerful.
➡ ______

56 You're also kind and fair to everybody.
➡ ______

57 Beth: Thanks, Joanne. It's so nice of you to say so.
➡ ______

58 Ms. Kemp: Beth, let's hear from you now.
➡ ______

59 You picked Peter's name.
➡ ______

60 Beth: (hesitating) Well, I think Peter is creative. Peter, you're … uh … creative.
➡ ______

61 Peter: (shyly) Really?
➡ ______

62 Ms. Kemp: What made you think Peter is creative?
➡ ______

63 Beth: (after a long pause) When Boyd's foot got stuck in the bicycle stand the other day, Peter got it out by using butter.
➡ ______

64 That was creative.
➡ ______

65 Boyd: Yeah! Nobody else thought of doing that.
➡ ______

66 Steve: I didn't know that. Well, then, I also think he's creative.
➡ ______

67 Beth: (confidently) Yeah, Peter, you ARE creative!
➡ ______

68 Peter: Thanks, Beth! It's the best compliment ever!
➡ ______

본문 Test

※ 다음 괄호 안의 단어들을 우리말에 맞도록 바르게 배열하시오.

1 (Best / The / Ever / Compliment)
➡ ______________________________

2 (1 / Scene)
➡ ______________________________

3 (is / it / last / the / of / week / school.)
➡ ______________________________

4 (student / each / just / has / picked / piece / a / paper / of / with / name / a / it. / on)
➡ ______________________________

5 (Ms. Kemp: / for / "Compliments / Classmates" / be / will / last / our / of / activity / school / year. / the)
➡ ______________________________
____

6 (everyone / did / a / pick / name?)
➡ ______________________________

7 (Class: / Ms. / Yes, / Kemp.)
➡ ______________________________

8 (are / students / to / talking / other. / each)
➡ ______________________________

9 (Beth: / whose / so, / did / name / pick? / you)
➡ ______________________________

10 (Lucy: / (smiling) / got / Boyd. / I)
➡ ______________________________

11 (have / I / lot / a / about / say / to / him.)
➡ ______________________________

12 (about / what / Beth? / you,)
➡ ______________________________

13 (Beth: / worried) / (looking / I / uh, / Peter's / picked / name.)
➡ ______________________________

14 (Lucy: / Peter? // no! / oh, // won't / it / easy / be / find / to / to / something / complement / on. / him)
➡ ______________________________
____

15 (Steve: / Yeah. // doesn't / he / much / talk / and / sits / just / at / desk / his / all / long. / day)
➡ ______________________________

16 (Beth: / her / (scratching / head) / I'll / well, / to / have / something. / find)
➡ ______________________________

17 (2 / Scene)
➡ ______________________________

1 최고의 칭찬

2 〈장면 1〉

3 이번 주는 학교의 마지막 주이다.

4 각 학생들은 이름 하나가 쓰인 종이 한 장씩을 막 뽑았다.

5 Ms. Kemp: '학급 친구들 칭찬하기'는 이번 학년 우리의 마지막 활동이 될 거예요.

6 모두 이름을 뽑았나요?

7 Class: 네, Kemp 선생님.

8 학생들이 서로 이야기를 나누고 있다.

9 Beth: 너는 누구 이름을 뽑았니?

10 Lucy: (웃으며) Boyd를 뽑았어.

11 그 애에 관해 할 말이 많아.

12 너는 어때, Beth?

13 Beth: (걱정스러운 표정으로) 어, Peter 이름을 뽑았어.

14 Lucy: Peter? 아, 이런! 그 애에 관해서 칭찬할 것을 찾는 게 쉽지 않을 거야.

15 Steve: 그래. 그 애는 말을 많이 하지 않고 하루 종일 그냥 책상에 앉아만 있잖아.

16 Beth: (머리를 긁적이며) 음, 무언가를 찾아야 해.

17 〈장면 2〉

18 (is / Beth / home / at / with / talking / parents / her / the / about / activity.)
➡ ____________________

19 (Beth: / has / everyone / lists / of / long / compliments / other / for / classmates, / for / except / me.)
➡ ____________________
____

20 (don't / I / what / know / complement / to / on. / Peter)
➡ ____________________

21 (Mom: / carefully. / think)
➡ ____________________

22 (should / there / something. / be)
➡ ____________________

23 (Beth: / he's / well, / clean.)
➡ ____________________

24 (washes / he / face / his / day. / every)
➡ ____________________

25 (Mom: / not / that's / complement. / a)
➡ ____________________

26 (does / everybody / that.)
➡ ____________________

27 (Dad: / again. / try)
➡ ____________________

28 (sure / I'm / can / you / something / find / to / good / about / say / him.)
➡ ____________________

29 (3 / Scene)
➡ ____________________

30 (next / the / there / day, / an / is / accident / school. / at)
➡ ____________________

31 (foot / Boyd's / stuck / is / a / in / stand. / bicycle)
➡ ____________________

32 (Boyd: / arms / (with / the / in / air) / help! // help! / need / I)
➡ ____________________

33 (Beth: / still. / stay // trying / I'm / pull / to / foot / your / out.)
➡ ____________________

34 (Boyd: / Ouch! / (screaming) // hurts! / that)
➡ ____________________

35 (Peter: / me / let / help. // a / just / minute.)
➡ ____________________

18 Beth는 집에서 그 활동에 대해 자신의 부모님과 이야기를 나누고 있다.

19 Beth: 저를 제외한 모두가 다른 친구들에 대해 긴 칭찬 목록을 가지고 있어요.

20 저는 Peter에 관해 무엇을 칭찬해야 할지 모르겠어요.

21 엄마: 잘 생각해 봐.

22 뭔가 있을 거야.

23 Beth: 음, 그 애는 깔끔해요.

24 매일 세수를 해요.

25 엄마: 그건 칭찬이 아니야.

26 모든 사람들이 하는 거잖니.

27 아빠: 다시 생각해 보렴.

28 그 아이에 대해 말할 뭔가 좋은 것을 분명히 찾을 수 있을 거야.

29 〈장면 3〉

30 다음 날, 학교에서 사고가 생긴다.

31 Boyd의 발이 자전거 거치대에 끼었다.

32 Boyd: (공중에 양팔을 벌린 채) 도와줘! 도움이 필요해!

33 Beth: 가만히 있어. 네 발을 꺼내려고 노력 중이야.

34 Boyd: (비명을 지르며) 아! 아파!

35 Peter: 내가 도와줄게. 잠깐만.

36 (runs / Peter / the / to / kitchen / school's / comes / and / with / back / butter.)

➡ ______________________________

37 (Peter: / going / I'm / put / to / butter / this / your / on / foot.)

➡ ______________________________

38 (Boyd: / butter? // what?)

➡ ______________________________

39 (Peter: / stay / just / calm.)

➡ ______________________________

40 (Beth: / to / (pointing / foot) / Boyd's / wow! // working! / it's)

➡ ______________________________

41 (foot / Boyd's / coming / is / of / out / stand. / the)

➡ ______________________________

42 (4 / Scene)

➡ ______________________________

43 (is / Beth / dinner / eating / her / with / parents.)

➡ ______________________________

44 (tells / she / about / them / happened / what / Boyd. / to)

➡ ______________________________

45 (Beth: / was / there / little / a / at / accident / today. / school)

➡ ______________________________

46 (Boyd's / got / foot / in / stuck / a / stand. / bicycle)

➡ ______________________________

47 (Mom: / no! / oh, // how / so / he / did / his / get / out? / foot)

➡ ______________________________

48 (Beth: / put / Peter / on / butter / foot / his / then / and / it / pulled / out.)

➡ ______________________________

49 (Dad: / was / that / creative. / really // but / creative. / messy)

➡ ______________________________

50 (Beth: / Creative? // hmm. // that / can / a / be / Dad? / compliement)

➡ ______________________________

51 (Dad: / sure.)

➡ ______________________________

36 Peter가 학교 주방으로 뛰어가 버터를 가지고 온다.

37 Peter: 네 발에 이 버터를 바를 거야.

38 Boyd: 뭐? 버터를?

39 Peter: 그냥 침착하게 있어.

40 Beth: (Boyd의 발을 가리키며) 와! 효과가 있어!

41 Boyd의 발이 거치대에서 빠져 나오고 있어.

42 〈장면 4〉

43 Beth는 부모님과 저녁 식사를 하고 있다.

44 그녀는 부모님께 Boyd에게 일어난 일에 대해 이야기한다.

45 Beth: 오늘 학교에서 작은 사고가 있었어요.

46 Boyd의 발이 자전거 거치대에 끼었어요.

47 엄마: 오, 저런! 그래서 발을 어떻게 뺐니?

48 Beth: Peter가 그 애 발에 버터를 바르고 나서 발을 당겨서 꺼냈어요.

49 아빠: 정말 창의적이구나. 지저분하지만 창의적이야.

50 Beth: 흠. 창의적이라고요? 아빠, 그것이 칭찬이 될 수 있어요?

51 아빠: 물론이지.

52 (5 / Scene)
➡ ____

53 (is / it / last / the / of / day / school, / the / and / are / students / each / complementing / other.)
➡ ____

54 (Ms. Kemp: / what / Joanne, / do / compliment / have / you / Beth? / for)
➡ ____

55 (Joanne: / you're / Beth / cheerful. / always)
➡ ____

56 (also / you're / and / kind / to / fair / everybody.)
➡ ____

57 (Beth: / Joanne. / thanks, // so / it's / of / nice / to / you / so. / say)
➡ ____

58 (Ms. Kemp: / let's / Beth, / from / hear / now. / you)
➡ ____

59 (picked / you / name. / Peter's)
➡ ____

60 (Beth: / (hesitating) / I / well, / Peter / think / creative. / is // you're / Peter, / … / creative. / … / uh)
➡ ____

61 (Peter: / really? / (shyly))
➡ ____

62 (Ms. Kemp: / made / what / think / you / is / Peter / creative?)
➡ ____

63 (Beth: / a / (after / pause) / long / Boyd's / when / got / foot / stuck / the / in / stand / bicycle / other / the / Peter / day, / it / got / out / using / by / butter.)
➡ ____

64 (was / that / creative.)
➡ ____

65 (Boyd: / yeah! // else / nobody / of / thought / that. / doing)
➡ ____

66 (Steve: / didn't / I / that. / know // then, / well, / also / I / he's / think / creative.)
➡ ____

67 (Beth: / yeah, / (confidently) / you / Peter, / creative! / ARE)
➡ ____

68 (Peter: / Beth! / thanks, // the / it's / compliment / best / ever!)
➡ ____

52 〈장면 5〉

53 오늘은 학교의 마지막 날이고 학생들은 서로를 칭찬하고 있다.

54 Ms. Kemp: Joanne, Beth에게 무슨 칭찬을 해 주겠니?

55 Joanne: Beth, 너는 항상 쾌활해.

56 또한 친절하고 모두에게 공정해.

57 Beth: 고마워, Joanne. 그렇게 말해 주다니 친절하구나.

58 Ms. Kemp: Beth, 이제 네 말을 들어 보자.

59 Peter의 이름을 뽑았구나.

60 Beth: (주저하며) 음, Peter는 창의적이라고 생각해요. Peter, 너는… 어… 창의적이야.

61 Peter: (수줍어하며) 정말?

62 Ms. Kemp: Peter가 왜 창의적이라고 생각하니?

63 Beth: (한참 있다가) 일전에 Boyd의 발이 자전거 거치대에 끼었을 때, Peter는 버터를 사용해서 그의 발을 꺼냈어요.

64 그것은 창의적이었어요.

65 Boyd: 맞아! 어느 누구도 그렇게 하는 것을 생각하지 못했어.

66 Steve: 난 몰랐어. 음, 그래, 나도 그가 창의적이라고 생각해.

67 Beth: (자신 있게) 그래, Peter, 너는 창의적이야!

68 Peter: 고마워, Beth! 그건 최고의 칭찬이야!

본문 Test

※ 다음 우리말을 영어로 쓰시오.

1 최고의 칭찬
➡ ______________________

2 〈장면 1〉
➡ ______________________

3 이번 주는 학교의 마지막 주이다.
➡ ______________________

4 각 학생들은 이름 하나가 쓰인 종이 한 장씩을 막 뽑았다.
➡ ______________________

5 Ms. Kemp: '학급 친구들 칭찬하기'는 이번 학년 우리의 마지막 활동이 될 거예요.
➡ ______________________

6 모두 이름을 뽑았나요?
➡ ______________________

7 Class: 네, Kemp 선생님.
➡ ______________________

8 학생들이 서로 이야기를 나누고 있다.
➡ ______________________

9 Beth: 너는 누구 이름을 뽑았니?
➡ ______________________

10 Lucy: (웃으며) Boyd를 뽑았어.
➡ ______________________

11 그 애에 관해 할 말이 많아.
➡ ______________________

12 너는 어때, Beth?
➡ ______________________

13 Beth: (걱정스러운 표정으로) 어, Peter 이름을 뽑았어.
➡ ______________________

14 Lucy: Peter? 아, 이런! 그 애에 관해서 칭찬할 것을 찾는 게 쉽지 않을 거야.
➡ ______________________

15 Steve: 그래. 그 애는 말을 많이 하지 않고 하루 종일 그냥 책상에 앉아만 있잖아.
➡ ______________________

16 Beth: (머리를 긁적이며) 음, 무언가를 찾아야 해.
➡ ______________________

17 〈장면 2〉
➡ ______________________

18 Beth는 집에서 그 활동에 대해 자신의 부모님과 이야기를 나누고 있다.
➡ ______________________

19 Beth: 저를 제외한 모두가 다른 친구들에 대해 긴 칭찬 목록을 가지고 있어요.
➡ ______________________

20 저는 Peter에 관해 무엇을 칭찬해야 할지 모르겠어요.
➡ ______________________

21 엄마: 잘 생각해 봐.
➡ ______________________

22 뭔가 있을 거야.
➡ ______________________

23 Beth: 음, 그 애는 깔끔해요.
➡

24 매일 세수를 해요.
➡

25 엄마: 그건 칭찬이 아니야.
➡

26 모든 사람들이 하는 거잖니.
➡

27 아빠: 다시 생각해 보렴.
➡

28 그 아이에 대해 말할 뭔가 좋은 것을 분명히 찾을 수 있을 거야.
➡

29 〈장면 3〉
➡

30 다음 날, 학교에서 사고가 생긴다.
➡

31 Boyd의 발이 자전거 거치대에 끼었다.
➡

32 Boyd: (공중에 양팔을 벌린 채) 도와줘! 도움이 필요해!
➡

33 Beth: 가만히 있어. 네 발을 꺼내려고 노력 중이야.
➡

34 Boyd: (비명을 지르며) 아! 아파!
➡

35 Peter: 내가 도와줄게. 잠깐만.
➡

36 Peter가 학교 주방으로 뛰어가 버터를 가지고 온다.
➡

37 Peter: 네 발에 이 버터를 바를 거야.
➡

38 Boyd: 뭐? 버터를?
➡

39 Peter: 그냥 침착하게 있어.
➡

40 Beth: (Boyd의 발을 가리키며) 와! 효과가 있어!
➡

41 Boyd의 발이 거치대에서 빠져나오고 있어.
➡

42 〈장면 4〉
➡

43 Beth는 부모님과 저녁 식사를 하고 있다.
➡

44 그녀는 부모님께 Boyd에게 일어난 일에 대해 이야기한다.
➡

45 Beth: 오늘 학교에서 작은 사고가 있었어요.
➡

46 Boyd의 발이 자전거 거치대에 끼었어요.
➡ ______

47 엄마: 오, 저런! 그래서 발을 어떻게 뺐니?
➡ ______

48 Beth: Peter가 그 애 발에 버터를 바르고 나서 발을 당겨서 꺼냈어요.
➡ ______

49 아빠: 정말 창의적이구나. 지저분하지만 창의적이야.
➡ ______

50 Beth: 흠. 창의적이라고요? 아빠, 그것이 칭찬이 될 수 있어요?
➡ ______

51 아빠: 물론이지.
➡ ______

52 〈장면 5〉
➡ ______

53 오늘은 학교의 마지막 날이고 학생들은 서로를 칭찬하고 있다.
➡ ______

54 Ms. Kemp: Joanne, Beth에게 무슨 칭찬을 해 주겠니?
➡ ______

55 Joanne: Beth, 너는 항상 쾌활해.
➡ ______

56 또한 친절하고 모두에게 공정해.
➡ ______

57 Beth: 고마워, Joanne. 그렇게 말해 주다니 친절하구나.
➡ ______

58 Ms. Kemp: Beth, 이제 네 말을 들어 보자.
➡ ______

59 Peter의 이름을 뽑았구나.
➡ ______

60 Beth: (주저하며) 음, Peter는 창의적이라고 생각해요. Peter, 너는… 어… 창의적이야.
➡ ______

61 Peter: (수줍어하며) 정말?
➡ ______

62 Ms. Kemp: Peter가 왜 창의적이라고 생각하니?
➡ ______

63 Beth: (한참 있다가) 일전에 Boyd의 발이 자전거 거치대에 끼었을 때, Peter는 버터를 사용해서 그의 발을 꺼냈어요.
➡ ______
______

64 그것은 창의적이었어요.
➡ ______

65 Boyd: 맞아! 어느 누구도 그렇게 하는 것을 생각하지 못했어.
➡ ______

66 Steve: 난 몰랐어. 음, 그래, 나도 그가 창의적이라고 생각해.
➡ ______

67 Beth: (자신 있게) 그래, Peter, 너는 창의적이야!
➡ ______

68 Peter: 고마워, Beth! 그건 최고의 칭찬이야!
➡ ______

영어 기출 문제집

적중100

2학기

정답 및 해설

동아 | 윤정미

중3

적중100

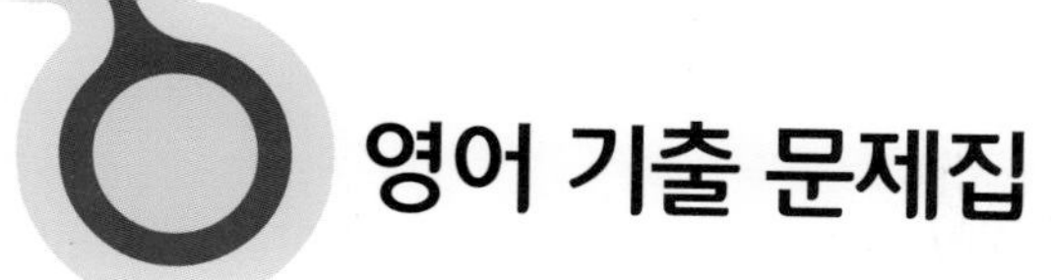
영어 기출 문제집

적중100

2학기
정답 및 해설
동아 | 윤정미
중 3

적중100

Lesson 7

Technology in Our Lives

시험대비 실력평가 p.08

01 ① 02 analyze 03 ② 04 ④
05 ③ 06 ⑤

01 동의어 관계이다. mainly: 주로 – mostly: 대개, 주로, specialist: 전문가 – expert: 전문가

02 '어떤 것을 주의 깊게 조사하다'는 'analyze(분석하다)'가 적절하다. 저는 빅데이터를 분석하고 그것으로부터 의미 있는 결과들을 도출할 수 있어요.

03 ① make a decision: 결정하다. 어떤 결정을 할 때 그들은 감정이 아니라 이성에 의지한다. ② just as ~: 꼭 ~처럼. 우리는 바로 그 연주자들이 악기를 챙기고 있을 때 도착했다. ③ thanks to ~: ~ 덕분에, ~ 때문에. 폭풍 때 문에 모든 항공편이 취소됐다. ④ get+비교급: 점점 더 ~해지다. 전문가들은 서해가 계속해서 더 따뜻해질 것이라고 말한다. ⑤ be likely to ~: ~할 것 같다. 기차 요금은 계속 변하지 않을 것 같다.

04 communication: 의사소통, 연락. 전화는 효율적인 의사전달 수단이다.

05 ① improve: 개선하다, 향상하다. 사정이 나아질 희망이 약간 있다. ② influence: 영향을 미치다. 미디어[대중 매체]는 여론에 강력한 영향력이 있다. ③ rent: 빌리다. 우리는 한 주 동안 자동차를 한 대 빌려 그 지역을 탐사할 것이다. ④ unlock: 잠금을 풀다. 문을 열려고 했지만 열쇠가 맞지 않았다. ⑤ predict: 예측하다. 최종 결과가 어떻게 될지 예견하기는 불가능하다.

06 thanks to ~: ~ 덕분에, ~ 때문에. 이젠 모든 사람들이 그것에 대해 알아, 너 때문에 말야! be used to+동사원형: ~하는 데 사용되다. 그 테스트는 다양한 질병들을 진단하는 데 이용된다. diagnose: 진단하다

서술형 시험대비 p.09

01 (1) develop (2) database (3) identify (4) predict
02 (1) wisely (2) awful
03 (1) (c)omplex (2) (c)rime (3) (f)orecast
(4) (i)nclude
04 (1) That test was focused on the prisoners alone.
(2) There is a limit to the amount of pain we can bear.
(3) More and more people are using the Internet.
(4) He'll be back on Monday, but I can't say for sure.

01 (1) develop: 발전시키다, 성장하다. 더 크고 나은, 또는 더 중요한 것으로 변화하고 성장하다 (2) database: 데이터베이스. 컴퓨터 시스템에 저장되어 있는 많은 양의 정보 (3) identify: 확인하다. 어떤 사람이 누구인지 또는 어떤 사물이 무엇인지 알아차리다 (4) predict: 예측하다. 어떤 일이 일어날 것이라고 말하다

02 (1) '형용사+ly = 부사'의 관계이다. angry: 화난 – angrily: 노하여, 성내서, wise: 현명한 – wisely: 현명하게 (2) '명사+ful = 형용사'의 관계이다. peace: 평화 – peaceful 평화로운, awe: 경외(敬畏), 두려움 – awful: 끔찍한, 지독한

03 (1) complex: 복잡한 (2) crime: 범죄 (3) forecast: 예측하다, 예보하다 (4) include: 포함하다

04 (1) focus on: ~에 초점을 맞추다. 수동태가 적절하므로 was를 추가한다. (2) the amount of: ~의 양/수량. 주어가 단수이므로 is를 추가한다. (3) more and more: 점점 더 많이, 갈수록 더. more를 추가한다. (4) for sure: 확실히, 분명히. for를 추가한다.

교과서

Conversation

핵심 Check p.10~11

1 Could you explain how to use this machine?
2 ①

교과서 대화문 익히기

Check(√) True or False p.12

1 F 2 T 3 T 4 F

교과서 확인학습 p.15~17

Listen and Talk A 1

tell, how to add, to / First, put, in, Second, choose, amount / Last, insert, into, simple

Listen and Talk A 2

know how to use / First / did, next / put in, take, out / Got it

Listen and Talk A 3

rent, tell, how to use / log in to / it / what / to unlock, with / appreciate

Listen and Talk B

return, know how to do / simple, insert, into, put, in / Then, take, out / appreciate / add, to, know how to do / simple, First, Second, amount / Then insert / appreciate / to buy, know how to do / simple, First, Second / Then / appreciate

Listen and Talk C

what's, for / that / tell, how to use / place, on / type, title, press / Is that all / Then, it / get / easy, isn't it / amazing

Listen and Talk D

how to use, First, Then, Last, out of

Talk and Play

know how to make / First, put / Then, pour / Last, take, out / got it, appreciate

Review 1

how to plant / cut, into, pieces, dig, in / put, in, cover, with / sounds simple

Review 2

tell, how to use / put, on, the number of / what / appreciate

시험대비 기본평가 p.18

01 ③
02 I really appreciate your help. 03 ⑤

01 'Are you explaining ~?'은 '~을 설명하는 중이니?'라는 의미로 방법이나 절차를 물을 때 쓰는 표현이 아니다.
02 'I really appreciate your help.'는 상대방에게 감사를 표현할 때 사용하는 말이다.
03 (a)와 나머지는 방법이나 절차를 묻는 것이지만 ⑤번은 사용법을 알려주겠다는 것이다.

시험대비 실력평가 p.19~20

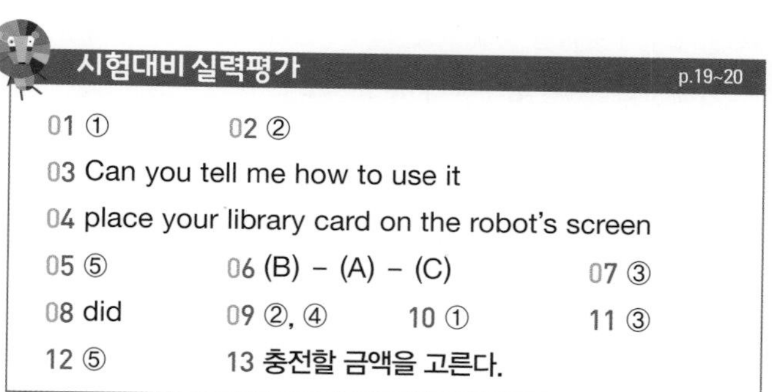
01 ① 02 ②
03 Can you tell me how to use it
04 place your library card on the robot's screen
05 ⑤ 06 (B) – (A) – (C) 07 ③
08 did 09 ②, ④ 10 ① 11 ③
12 ⑤ 13 충전할 금액을 고른다.

01 방법이나 절차를 묻는 말에 '물론'이라고 답하고 '마지막으로'라며 설명을 시작하는 것은 어색하다. Last를 First로 바꾸는 것이 적절하다.
02 용도를 나타내는 전치사 for가 적절하다.
03 'Can you tell me how to use it'은 방법이나 절차를 물을 때 쓰는 표현이다.
04 place: ~에 두다, 놓다 on the screen: 화면 위에
05 그냥 안내 데스크로 가서 책을 받을 수 있고 로봇이 책을 건네준다는 말은 없다.
06 반납에 대한 순서를 설명하는 주어진 글에 이어 (B)에서 '알았다'고 답하고, (A)에서 마지막 순서를 설명하고, (C)에서 감사하는 말이 자연스럽다.
07 뒤에 나오는 대답으로 보아 방법이나 절차를 묻는 질문이 적절하다.
08 'choose the snack I want'를 대신하는 대동사이므로 did가 적절하다.
09 'It's not a big deal.'과 'It's my pleasure.'는 모두 감사 표현에 대한 응답이다.
10 (a) put A in B: A를 B에 넣다 (b) pour A in B: A를 B에 붓다 (c) take A out: A를 꺼내다
11 방법을 아느냐는 질문에 대한 답으로 이어서 First, ~. Second ~.로 순서대로 설명하고 있으므로 ③번이 적절하다.
12 밑줄 친 문장은 감사를 나타낼 때 쓰는 표현이다. appreciate: 감사하다, 감상하다
13 'Second, choose the amount of money.'라고 하고 있다.

서술형 시험대비 p.21

01 (D) → (C) → (A) → (B) 02 isn't it
03 it's a robot that[which] finds books for you
04 This conversation happens in a library.
05 from
06 (1) **기계에 돈을 넣는다.** (2) **원하는 음료를 고른다.** (3) **기계에서 음료를 꺼낸다.**
07 appreciate 08 should I do

01 방법을 묻는 질문에 이어, (D)에서 첫 번째 순서를 설명하고, (C)에서 알겠다고 답하고 이어서, (A)에서 두 번째 순서에 대해 설명하고, (B)에서 그게 다인지 묻자 그렇다고 답하는 순서가 적절하다.
02 앞에서 긍정의 be동사 is가 쓰였으므로 isn't를 쓰고 대명사 주어 it을 쓴다.
03 주격 관계대명사로 that이나 which를 쓴다. find A for B: B를 위해 A를 찾아 주다
04 이 대화는 '당신의 도서 대출 카드(library card)를 로봇의 화면 위에 놓으라'는 말로 보아 도서관이라고 할 수 있다.

05 'out of'는 (1) ~의 안에서 밖으로, ~의 밖으로 (2) ~ 바깥에, (3) ~ 중에(서) (4) ~에서(from) 등의 뜻이 있다.
06 First: 우선, 맨 먼저, Then: 그 다음에, 그러고 나서, Last: 마지막으로
07 '누군가에게 공손하게 감사하거나 해준 것에 대해 고맙다고 말하다'를 가리키는 말은 'appreciate(감사하다)'이다.
08 다음에 무엇을 해야 하는지 묻는 것이므로 'what should I do?'에서 should I do를 생략했다고 보는 것이 적절하다.

교과서
Grammar

핵심 Check
p.22~23

1 (1) approaching (2) Feeling 2 ③

시험대비 기본평가
p.24

01 ④ 02 ⑤ 03 ③
04 (1) he was absent from school
(2) she watched Utube videos
(3) she felt excited
(4) Though[Although] he is short

01 ④는 결과의 부사절을 나타내는 접속사 that이 적절하다.
02 부사절을 분사구문으로 바꿀 때, 주어가 같으면 주어를 생략하고 분사를 쓴다. ③의 완료분사구문은 종속절의 시제가 주절의 시제보다 앞설 때 써야 한다.
03 ③ 접속사 또는 전치사로서 as가 들어갈 수 없다. 내용상 '의문사+to부정사' 형태의 구조로서 how가 적절하며, 'as to'는 '~에 대한'이라는 뜻의 전치사구로, 뒤에 명사/동명사가 와야 한다.
04 분사구문은 분사를 활용하여 부사절을 부사구로 줄인 표현이다. 대개 양보, 동시동작, 이유, 시간, 조건 등의 부사절이며, 절과 구의 전환시 동사의 시제 등에 유의해야 한다. (4)는 내용상 양보이므로 Though 외에도 Although, Even though 등의 접속사가 가능하다.

시험대비 실력평가
p.25~27

01 ④ 02 ② 03 ⑤ 04 ④
05 ② 06 Made → Making 07 ③
08 ⑤ 09 ③ 10 ④ 11 ④
12 Not wanting to get hurt in the football match
13 Strange as it may sound
14 Though having been built more than
15 ② 16 ⑤

01 ④는 전치사 as로 쓰였으며, '~로서'라는 뜻이다. 그 외에는 모두 접속사 as로 사용되었다.
02 ②는 전치사 as로 쓰였으며, '~로서'라는 뜻이다. 그 외에는 모두 접속사 as로 사용되었다.
03 'with+목적어+분사' 구문은 '목적어의 능동/수동' 여부가 중요하다. 눈이 '감겨진 것'이므로 과거분사 closed가 적절하다.
04 부사절로 영작하면, 'Though he had made many people happy, Chad died lonely.'이다. 분사구문 Having made에 분사구문의 의미를 명확하게 하기 위해 Though를 추가한 문장이 ④이다. ①의 경우, 접속사와 주어가 동시에 있는 경우에는 분사구문을 쓸 수 없음에 유의한다.
05 각 문장을 해석하면, (1) 'Jane은 거울에 비친 자신의 모습을 보고 놀라서 운동을 시작했다.', (2) 'David은 그가 더 높이 올라가려고 할수록 숨 쉬기가 더 힘들어지는 것을 느꼈다.', (3) '그 개는 훈련사가 보여준 대로 움직임을 따라했다.'가 된다.
06 '스포츠를 더욱 흥미진진하게 만들면서'(능동의 분사구문)이므로 Made를 Making으로 고치는 것이 적절하다.
07 ① 접속사로도 전치사로도 쓸 수 없다.(As → 삭제) ② 내용상 '의문사+to부정사'의 구조.(as → how 또는 when이나 where 등 의문부사가 적절하다.) ④ 명사절 접속사가 필요하다.(as → that) ⑤ '부사구'로 시작해서 완전한 절이 왔으므로, as는 접속사로도 전치사로도 무의미하다.(as → 삭제)
08 내용상 though의 역접 관계가 아닌, and 또는 so와 같은 순접 관계의 접속사가 적절하다.
09 주어진 문장의 as는 '~하는 것과 같이'라는 뜻으로서 '양태'를 나타낸다. 나머지는 각각 ① ~함에 따라서(비례) ② ~ 때문에(이유) ④ 이유 ⑤ ~할 때(시간) 등이다.
10 <보기>와 ④는 '양보'의 의미로 사용되었다.
11 완료분사구문과 양보 의미의 부사구가 쓰였으므로, 접속사는 Though 또는 Although를, 시제는 had come을 쓰는 것이 적절하다. '그 바이러스가 자국에서 왔음에도 불구하고, 그 중국 외교관은 한국의 늑장 대응을 비난했다.'
12 분사구문의 부정은 분사 앞에 not이나 never를 쓴다. 'As he didn't want to get hurt in the football match,'이다.
13 접속사 as의 양보 의미는 형용사를 앞에 두어 표현한다.
14 주절보다 종속절 시제가 앞서고, 수동태이므로 완료분사구문의 수동형인 'Having been p.p.'를 활용한다.
15 접속사 as의 용법이 알맞게 쓰였는지 묻고 있다. ②를 해석해 보면, '당신이 거짓말을 했기 때문에, 나는 그 어느 때보다도 당신을 더 믿을 수 있었다.'가 되어 어색하다. As를 양보의 접속사 Though 또는 Although 등으로 바꾸는 것이 적절하다.
16 접속사 또는 전치사로 쓰인 as와 적절하게 어법상 어울리는지 묻는 문제이다. ①은 '언니가 하듯이 엄마에게 관심을 가지라'는

내용으로서 옳다. ②와 ③은 전치사로 쓰였고, 문제없다. ④의 'couple'은 '단/복수 취급이 가능'하며, as도 알맞게 쓰였다. ⑤의 경우, '그 장난감 가게가 막 문을 닫으려할 때, 우리가 도착했다.'는 내용으로 so as는 의미가 맞지 않는다. so as → just as로 바꾸는 것이 적절하다.

서술형 시험대비 p.28~29

01 (1) Being a little tired,
(2) Finding the ring she had lost,
(3) It having rained the day before,
(4) Not having a car,
(5) **고칠 필요 없음**

02 (1) While they use various methods,
(2) If you have a problem that you cannot talk to me,
(3) Though I was sick through the weekend,
(4) Because he did not want to wake the sleeping baby up,
(5) and it makes sports more exciting
(6) When she cleaned the windows of the kitchen,

03 (1) As information and communication technology develops
(2) Just as our bodies change our minds
(3) Not having any friends in her class
(4) Using various methods, experts analyze

04 (1) Did you know that health professionals can forecast a disease just as weather experts forecast the weather?
(2) Big data helps companies understand their customers' needs better, assisting them sell more products.
(3) Can you tell me how to add money to my transportation card? (how 대신 when 또는 where도 가능)
(4) Germany's national soccer team was able to improve its performance, winning the 2014 World Cup.

05 Singing to the radio music,

06 (1) Based on our survey, we chose Gyeongju.
(2) activities are the most important when choosing a field trip place
(3) Searching for some data online,
(4) As, as

01 (1) 내용상 부사구 a little은 tired를 수식하기 때문에, 분사 being 앞에 쓰지 않는다. (2) 능동이므로 Found → Finding이 적절하다. (3) 분사구문에서의 비인칭 주어 It과 주절의 주어가 다르므로, 'It having rained'와 같이 독립분사구문 형태로 표현하는 것이 적절하다. (4) 분사구문의 부정은 Not을 분사 앞에 쓴다. *Frankly speaking:솔직히 말해서

02 문제에 쓰인 분사구문은 각각 동시동작, 조건, 양보, 이유, 병렬, 시간 등의 의미로 쓰였다. (1) 다양한 방법을 사용하여, (2) 나에게 말할 수 없는 문제가 있다면, (3) 주말 내내 아팠지만, (4) 잠자는 아기를 깨우고 싶지 않아서, (5) 그리고 스포츠를 더욱 흥미롭게 만든다. (6) 부엌 창문을 청소할 때,

03 (1), (2)는 '접속사 as'를, (3), (4)는 분사구문을 활용하는 문제이다. 의미에 맞게 단어를 배열하도록 한다.

04 (1) just if → just as (2) 내용상 as는 접속사로도 전치사로도 의미가 없으며, 생략하면 적절한 분사구문이 된다. (3) as to → how(when/where) to (4) 접속사 없이 동사 두 개가 있으므로, won을 winning으로 바꿔 분사구문을 만드는 것이 적절하다.

05 부사절의 주어와 주절의 주어가 같으므로 부사절의 접속사와 주어를 생략한다.

06 (1) 과거분사로 시작하는 분사구문이다. (2) when choosing은 분사구문 앞에 접속사를 넣어 의미를 명확하게 한 것이다. (3) 종속절과 주절의 주어가 같으므로, 접속사와 주어를 생략하고, 동사를 현재분사 형태로 전환하면 된다. (4) 접속사와 전치사 역할을 하며, 내용상 알맞은 것은 as 뿐이다.

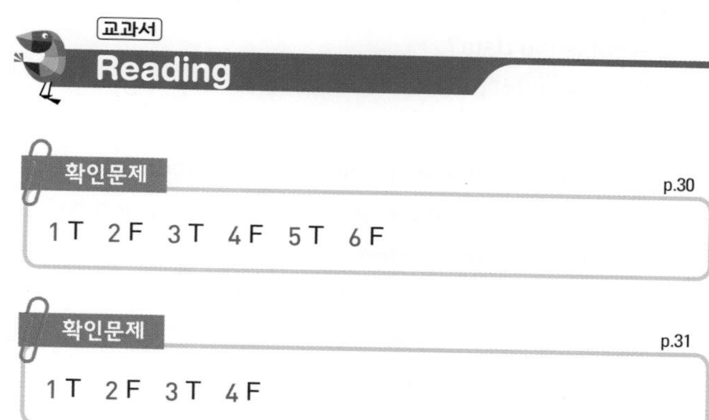

교과서 **Reading**

확인문제 p.30

1 T 2 F 3 T 4 F 5 T 6 F

확인문제 p.31

1 T 2 F 3 T 4 F

교과서 확인학습 A p.32~33

01 Living with
02 recommended for
03 looked interesting
04 what you liked
05 because of
06 What is
07 data sets, complex
08 As, getting much greater
09 leaves a trace
10 upload on your blog, your purchases, all part of
11 Simply collecting data
12 has to be analyzed
13 Using, draw
14 can be used
15 How
16 almost all parts
17 their customers' needs, sell more products
18 avoid heavy traffic
19 endless, interesting examples

20 Forecast
21 just as
22 thanks to
23 comes, will buy
24 search online about
25 is analyzed wisely
26 Improving Performance
27 sports fan
28 making, exciting
29 national soccer team
30 collecting, analyzing
31 how much, how long
32 With the help of
33 Prevention
34 Thanks to
35 Through, crime hot spots
36 is most likely to happen
37 further crime, predicts
38 has already changed
39 go from here
40 play, role

교과서 확인학습 B

p.34~35

1 Living with Big Data
2 Have you ever visited an online bookstore and been surprised by the books that the store recommended for you?
3 Many of them looked interesting to you.
4 So how did the bookstore know what you liked?
5 This is all possible because of big data.
6 What is big data?
7 Big data is data sets that are very big and complex.
8 As information and communication technology develops, the amount of data we have is getting much greater than before.
9 This is mainly because almost everything that we do online leaves a trace.
10 For example, the photos you upload on your blog and the records of your purchases at online stores are all part of big data.
11 Simply collecting data, however, is not enough.
12 Big data has to be analyzed, and this is done by big data experts.
13 Using various methods, experts analyze big data and draw meaningful results from it.
14 These results then can be used to make decisions or to predict the future.
15 How is big data influencing our lives?
16 Big data is influencing almost all parts of our lives.
17 It helps companies understand their customers' needs better and helps them sell more products.
18 It helps people avoid heavy traffic.
19 Its uses are endless, and here are some interesting examples.
20 Disease Forecast
21 Did you know that health professionals can now forecast a disease just as weather experts forecast the weather?
22 This is possible thanks to big data.
23 For example, when the flu season comes, people will buy more flu medicine.
24 They will also search online about flu symptoms more.
25 If this kind of data is analyzed wisely, the spread of the flu can be predicted.
26 Improving Performance in Sports
27 Are you a sports fan?
28 Well, big data is improving the performance of players, making sports more exciting.
29 A famous example is Germany's national soccer team.
30 The team built a database by collecting and analyzing a huge amount of data on players.
31 For example, the data included information about how much each player ran and how long he had the ball.
32 With the help of this database, Germany's national soccer team was able to improve its performance and win the 2014 World Cup.
33 Crime Prevention
34 Thanks to big data, police can now predict crime before it happens.
35 Through the analysis of big data about the type, time and place of crime, police can make a map of crime hot spots.
36 This map identifies when and where crime is most likely to happen.
37 Police can prevent further crime by focusing on the areas and the times this map predicts.
38 Big data has already changed the world greatly.
39 So where will the big data industry go from here?
40 Nobody knows for sure, but experts agree that big data will play a more and more important role in our lives.

시험대비 실력평가

p.36~39

01 ②
02 how did the bookstore know what you liked
03 온라인 서점이 당신을 위해 추천한 책들 중에 많은 것들이 당신에게 흥미로워 보이는 것

04 ④	05 ④	06 ③	07 ④
08 will come → comes		09 ④	10 ③
11 ②	12 ③	13 ③	

14 and it makes sports more exciting

15 ② 16 ②, ④ 17 crime

18 (A) Through (B) further (C) agree

19 ③ 20 ②, ⑤

21 how much each player ran and how long he had the ball

22 Big data is influencing almost all parts of our lives.

23 Big data

24 (1) 회사들이 소비자들이 필요로 하는 것을 더 잘 이해하도록 도와준다.
(2) 회사들이 더 많은 상품을 팔도록 도와준다.
(3) 사람들이 교통 체증을 피하도록 도와준다.

01 ⓐ와 ②: 경험 용법, ① 완료 용법, ③, ⑤: 계속 용법, ④ 결과 용법

02 know의 목적어를 간접의문문으로 써서 what you like로 쓰는 것이 적절하다.

03 'Many of the books that the online bookstore recommended for you looked interesting to you.'를 가리킨다.

04 이 글의 전반부는 '빅데이터 덕분에 경찰은 이제 범죄가 발생하기 전에 범죄를 예측할 수 있다'는 내용의 글이므로, 제목으로는 ④번 '범죄 예방'이 적절하다.

05 happen/occur/take place/arise/come about: (사건 등이) 발생하다, ④ cause: ~을 야기하다[초래하다]

06 ⓒ와 ②, ④: 완료 용법, ① 계속 용법, ③ 경험 용법, ⑤ 결과 용법

07 이 글은 '빅데이터가 우리 삶에 영향을 미치고 있는 부분들'에 대한 글이므로, 제목으로는 ④번 '빅데이터는 어떻게 우리 삶에 영향을 미치고 있는가?'가 적절하다. ② benefit: 혜택, 이득

08 when절에서는 미래의 일이라고 해도 현재시제로 쓰는 것이 적절하다.

09 '날씨 전문가가 어떻게 날씨를 예측하는지'는 대답할 수 없다. ① It is influencing almost all parts of our lives. ② Thanks to big data, they can do so. ③ Yes, they can. ⑤ If the data about people's behavior during the flu season is analyzed wisely, the spread of the flu can be predicted.

10 ③번 다음 문장의 Big data has to be analyzed에 주목한다. 주어진 문장의 내용을 보충 설명하는 것이므로 ③번이 적절하다.

11 이 글은 '빅 데이터에 대한 소개와 빅데이터의 수집과 분석 및 활용'에 대한 글이므로, 제목으로는 ②번 '빅데이터는 무엇인가?'가 적절하다.

12 '온라인 상점'에서의 구매 기록들이 빅데이터의 일부가 된다고 했다. street stall: 노점

13 ⓐ by ~ing: ~함으로써, ⓑ With the help of ~: ~의 도움으로

14 making을 makes로 바꿔 쓰는 것이 적절하다.

15 위 글은 '데이터베이스의 도움으로 스포츠에서 경기력을 향상시키는' 내용의 글이므로, 주제로는 ②번 '데이터베이스의 도움에 의한 팀의 경기력 향상'이 적절하다.

16 빅데이터 '때문에' 경찰은 이제 범죄가 발생하기 전에 범죄를 예측할 수 있다고 하는 것이 적절하다. ① ~에도 불구하고, ③ ~라기 보다는, ⑤ ~ 대신에

17 '범죄'를 가리킨다.

18 (A) 빅데이터의 분석을 '통해서'라고 해야 하므로 Through가 적절하다. Though: 비록 ~이지만(뒤에 주어+동사), (B) '추가' 범죄라고 해야 하므로 further가 적절하다. further: 더 이상의, 추가의, farther: (공간, 시간상으로) 더 먼, (C) 전문가들은 빅데이터가 우리 삶에서 더욱더 중요한 역할을 할 것이라는 데에 '동의한다.'고 해야 하므로 agree가 적절하다. disagree: 동의하지 않다

19 ⓐ와 ②, ⑤: 현재분사, ①, ③, ④: 동명사

20 huge: 거대한, (크기·양·정도가) 막대한, ② 작은, 조그마한, ⑤ 미소한, 미세한, ① 거대한, 막대한, 엄청난, ③ 광대한, ④ 거대한

21 전치사 about의 목적어이므로 간접의문문(의문사+주어+동사)의 어순으로 쓰는 것이 적절하다.

22 almost all parts: 거의 모든 부분

23 '빅데이터'를 가리킨다.

24 'Big data is influencing almost all parts of our lives.' 뒤에 이어지는 내용을 쓰는 것이 적절하다.

서술형 시험대비

p.40~41

01 be analyzed 02 analyzing big data

03 (A) very big and complex (B) big data experts

04 limited → endless 또는 limitless/unlimited/infinite

05 Thanks to big data.

06 If we analyze this kind of data wisely, we can predict the spread of the flu.

07 excited → exciting

08 (1) 각각의 선수들이 얼마나 많이 달렸는가?
(2) 각각의 선수들이 얼마나 오랫동안 공을 소유했는가?

09 Germany's national soccer team

10 (A) collected and (B) analyzed

11 after → before

12 (1) 범죄가 언제, 어디에서 가장 많이 발생할 것 같은지를 알려 준다.

(2) **경찰은 이 지도가 예측하는 장소들과 시간대에 집중함으로써, 추가 범죄를 예방할 수 있다.**
13 part 14 (A) analyzing (B) crime

01 '빅데이터는 분석되어야 한다.'라고 해야 하므로 수동태로 써서 'be analyzed'로 쓰는 것이 적절하다.
02 '빅데이터를 분석한 것'을 가리킨다.
03 빅데이터는 '매우 크고 복잡한' 데이터 집합이고 '빅데이터 전문가들'은 빅데이터를 분석하고, 그것으로부터 의미 있는 결과들을 도출한다.
04 '빅데이터는 우리 삶의 거의 모든 부분에 영향을 미치고 있다.'고 했으므로, '그것(빅데이터)의 활용은 끝이 없다'고 하는 것이 적절하다.
05 '빅데이터 덕분에' 가능하다.
06 this kind of data와 the spread of the flu를 각각 목적어로 사용하여 능동태로 고치는 것이 적절하다.
07 감정을 나타내는 동사는 감정을 유발할 때 현재분사를 쓰는 것이 적절하다.
08 바로 뒤에 이어지는 내용을 쓰는 것이 적절하다.
09 '독일 국가 대표 축구팀'을 가리킨다.
10 그 팀은 데이터베이스를 구축하기 위해 선수들에 관한 엄청난 양의 데이터를 '모으고' '분석했다.'
11 빅데이터 덕분에 경찰은 이제 범죄가 발생하기 '전에' 범죄를 예측할 수 있다고 하는 것이 적절하다.
12 바로 뒤에 이어지는 내용을 쓰는 것이 적절하다.
13 play a role = play a part: 역할을 맡다, 한몫을 하다
14 '범죄'의 유형, 시간 및 장소에 관한 빅데이터를 '분석'함으로써, 경찰은 범죄 다발 지역의 지도를 만들 수 있다.

영역별 핵심문제

p.43~47

01 ①
02 (s)pread / (i)ndustry / (1) spread (2) industry
03 amount
04 (A) (u)sed (B) (l)ikely (C) (h)elped(helps)
05 (1) colorful (2) useful (3) endlessly
06 Do you know how to make tea?
07 ③ 08 ② 09 ③ 10 ④
11 ⑤ 12 ③ 13 ③ 14 ④
15 (1) to eat more as she ate
(2) insects were caught as the spider
16 ② 17 trace 18 ①, ③, ④
19 health professionals can now forecast a disease just as weather experts forecast the weather
20 ④ 21 ⑤ 22 ② 23 ④

01 ①번은 '동일시하다'라는 의미로 쓰였지만 <보기>와 나머지는 모두 '알아보다'라는 의미로 쓰였다. <보기> 이 지도는 범죄가 언제, 어디에서 가장 많이 발생할 것 같은지를 알려 준다. ① 부를 행복과 동일시해서는 안 된다. ② 그녀는 자신을 공격한 범인을 알아볼 수 있었다. ③ 체포된 사람들 중 많은 이들이 자신의 신분을 밝히기를 거부했다. ④ 그들은 각기 구별되는 냄새로 구성원을 알아봅니다. ⑤ 이 중에서 당신 우산을 알아볼 수 있습니까?
02 (1) spread: 확산, 전파. 어떤 것이 더 큰 지역이나 더 많은 수의 사람들에게 영향을 주도록 성장하거나 발전하는 것 / 우리는 그 질병의 확산을 둔화시키게 되기를 바라고 있습니다. (2) industry: 산업. 특별한 종류의 상업적인 기업에 종사하는 사람들 또는 회사들 / 그의 소설들은 영화 산업을 위한 풍성한 자료의 원천이다.
03 '어떤 것의 이것은 얼마나 있는지 또는 얼마나 갖고 있거나 필요한지이다.'라는 의미로 'amount(양)'가 적절하다.
04 (A) be used to+동사원형: ~하는 데 이용되다. 이 지역에서는 소가 달구지를 끄는 데 이용된다. (B) be likely to: ~할 것 같다. 오늘은 곳에 따라 비가 오겠습니다. (C) help+A(목적어)+동사원형: A(목적어)가 ~하도록 돕다, 하게 하다. 목적격보어로 동사원형이 나왔으므로 사역동사나 준사역동사 help가 나와야 한다. 그는 그녀가 공부에만 전념할 수 있게 도와주었다.
05 (1), (2) 접미사 'ful'을 붙여 형용사가 된 어휘이다. colorful: 형형색색의. 그 정원은 형형색색의 꽃들로 가득 차 있었다. useful: 유용한, 쓸모 있는. 그는 유용한 충고를 좀 해 주었다. (3) 접미사 'ly'를 붙여 '부사'가 된 어휘이다. endlessly: 무한히, 영원히. 그녀는 자기 문제에 대해 끝도 없이 얘기를 한다.
06 뒤에 이어지는 내용으로 보아 차를 만드는 방법을 묻는 질문이 적절하다.
07 우선 컵에 티백을 넣어'라는 말에 이어 (D)에서 알겠다고 반응하고, (A)에서 Then(그런 후)으로 이어서 설명하고, (C)에서 '그러고 나서는?'이라고 묻자, (B)에서 '마지막으로 3분 후에 티백을 꺼내.'라고 한 후, 알겠다며 고맙다고 하는 주어진 문장으로 이어지는 것이 적절하다.
08 방법을 묻고 있는 질문에 '고맙다'고 답하는 것은 어색하다. Sure. 정도가 적절하다.
09 ③번 다음 문장의 So에 주목한다. 주어진 문장의 결과를 이끄는 내용이 나오고 있으므로 ③번이 적절하다.
10 로봇이 어떻게 책을 찾아서 안내 데스크로 가져다주는지는 알 수 없다.
11 분사구문의 부정은 분사 앞에 not을 쓴다. 접속사를 쓸 경우, 접속사 뒤에 주어가 오면 분사구문은 쓸 수 없다.
12 주어진 문장의 접속사 As는 '~할 때, ~하는 동안'의 의미로서 '시간'을 나타낸다. ③을 제외한 나머지는 각각 ① '양태–당신이 바라는 대로' ② '비례–날씨가 더욱 더 더워지면서' ④ '비교–그

들이 원했던 만큼' ⑤ '이유—오해를 받아서'이다.

13 주어진 문장의 접속사 As는 '이유'로 사용되었다. ③은 '~함에 따라서'로 해석되어, '비례'의 의미이다.

14 주어진 문장의 접속사 As는 '~하듯이, ~하는 것처럼'으로 해석되어 '양태'로 사용되었다. ④는 '~이기 때문에'로 해석되어, '이유'로 쓰였다.

15 접속사 as를 활용하는 문장이다. (1) '그녀는 피자 한 판을 다 먹었기 때문에 배가 너무 불러 더 먹을 수가 없었다.' (2) '거미가 계획한 대로 곤충 몇 마리가 잡혔다.'

16 ⓐ on your blog: 블로그에, ⓑ draw A from B: B로부터 A를 끌어내다

17 trace: 흔적, 어떤 것이 발생했거나 존재했다는 신호

18 (A)와 ①, ③, ④: 현재분사, ②, ⑤: 동명사

19 '날씨 전문가가 날씨를 예측하는 것과 같이 건강 전문가들이 현재 질병을 예측할 수 있다는 것'을 가리킨다.

20 이 글은 '빅데이터가 어떻게 우리 삶에 영향을 미치고 있는지'에 관한 글이므로, 주제로는 ④번 '빅데이터가 우리 삶에 끼치는 영향'이 적절하다.

21 건강 전문가들은 현재 질병을 '치유'할 수 있는 것이 아니라, 날씨 전문가가 날씨를 예측하는 것과 같이 현재 질병을 '예측'할 수 있다. cure: 치유하다

22 ② 십대들이 여가 시간에 가장 하고 싶어 하는 활동은 여행이지만 실제로 그들이 가장 많이 하는 활동은 TV 시청이므로, 십대들이 여가 시간에 가장 하고 싶어 하는 활동과 실제로 그들이 가장 많이 하는 활동 사이에는 큰 '차이'가 있다고 하는 것이 적절하다. gap: 차이, ① 합의, 일치, ③ 조화, 일치, ④ 정돈, 정리, ⑤ 상호 관련, 상관

23 ④ 39%의 학생들이 여가 시간에 TV를 시청하므로, 5분의 2 미만의 학생들(Less than two-fifths)이라고 하는 것이 적절하다. two-fifths: 5분의 2

단원별 예상문제

p.48~51

01 ②	02 ④	03 (1) focus (2) play	
04 ⓐ into ⓑ with		05 ④	
06 ②, ⑤	07 ③	08 ④	09 ④
10 ④	11 ①, ②	12 ②	13 ④
14 ⑤	15 ③	16 ②	17 ④

18 This map identifies when and where crime is most likely to happen.

19 They agree that big data will play a more and more important role in our lives.

20 ①　21 When[If] we look at the results

22 ⑤

01 ②번은 동의어의 관계이며 나머지는 모두 반의어의 관계이다. complex: 복잡한, complicated: 복잡한 ① include: 포함하다, exclude: 제외하다 ③ meaningful: 의미 있는, meaningless: 무의미한 ④ lock: 잠그다, unlock: 잠금을 풀다 ⑤ borrow: 빌리다, lend: 빌려주다

02 ① 그 사람들은 주로 쌀과 콩을 재배한다. ② 무슨 일이 일어날지 예견하기는 불가능하다. ③ 그가 IT 기술을 향상시키면 직장을 쉽게 구할 텐데. ④ prevention: 예방. 전통 의학에서는 예방이 중요한 역할을 한다. ⑤ 사전 구매 할인을 받고 싶어요.

03 (1) focus on: ~에 초점을 맞추다. 자신으로부터 더 멀리 있는 물체에 눈의 초점을 맞추어라. (2) play a role: 역할을 하다. 그는 서울의 매력을 전 세계에 알리는 데 중요한 역할을 할 것이다.

04 ⓐ cut A into small pieces: A를 잘게 썰다, ⓑ cover A with B: A를 B로 덮다

05 언제 소녀가 감자를 심는지는 알 수 없다.

06 'Don't mention it.(별일 아닌 걸요., 천만에요.)'은 상대방의 감사 표현에 대한 응답으로 주로 사용된다.

07 ⓐ add A to B: A를 B에 더하다[추가하다] ⓑ insert A into B: A를 B에 끼우다[삽입하다]

08 ④ 부사절로 고쳐보면, 'As there was no money left in her pockets'가 된다. 주어가 다르므로, 유도부사 there는 생략할 수 없다. 'Being no money left in her pockets → There being no money left in her pockets'가 적절하다.

09 종속절이 주절보다 앞선 시제이므로, 완료분사구문이 필요하다. 준동사의 부정은 not을 앞에 쓴다.

10 내용상 '오전에 밖은 추워서 뛰다가 거의 감기에 걸릴 뻔했다'라는 문장이다. 접속사 as의 위치에 유의한다.

11 ① '보고서를 제시간에 완성하기 위해 열심히 일하고 녹초가 되었다'는 내용이므로, 능동의 분사구문이 되어야 한다. 'Worked → Working' ② 'look'이 자동사로 쓰였으므로 수동태로 쓸 수 없다. 'Being looked → Looking'

12 ⓐ 앞의 내용의 예가 나오고 있으므로 For example이 가장 적절하다. ⓑ 앞에 나오는 내용과 상반되는 내용이 뒤에 이어지므로 however가 가장 적절하다.

13 very는 비교급을 강조할 수 없다.

14 이 글은 '빅 데이터에 대한 소개와 빅데이터의 수집과 분석 및 활용'에 관한 글이므로, 주제로는 ⑤번 '빅데이터의 수집과 분석 및 활용'이 적절하다.

15 건강 전문가들이 현재 질병을 예측할 수 있다고 했으므로, 이런 종류의 데이터를 지혜롭게 분석한다면, 독감의 확산을 '예측할 수 있다'고 하는 것이 적절하다. ① protect: 보호하다, ② improve: 개선되다, ④ produce: 생산하다, ⑤ increase: 증가하다

16 주어진 문장의 This에 주목한다. ②번 앞 문장의 내용을 받고 있으므로 ②번이 적절하다.

17 (A)와 ④: '~하는 것처럼'(접속사), 녹이 쇠를 좀먹듯이 근심은 마음을 좀먹는다. ① 때(접속사), ② 이유(접속사), ③ ~한 대로, ~인 채로(접속사), ⑤ (양보) ~이지만, ~이면서도(접속사, as 앞의 명사는 관사가 없음)

18 identify: 알아보다, 확인하다, 식별하다, be likely to: ~할 것 같다

19 전문가들은 '빅데이터가 우리 삶에서 더욱 더 중요한 역할을 할 것이라는 데에' 동의한다.

20 빅데이터 덕분에 경찰은 이제 범죄가 발생하기 전에 '범죄를 예측할 수 있다.' ③ the police: 복수 취급함. ④ change: 변하다, 변화시키다

21 접속사 When이나 If를 사용하여 바꿔 쓰는 것이 적절하다.

22 십대들이 여가 시간에 가장 하고 싶어 하는 활동을 하는 것이 어려운 이유는 알 수 없다. ① What they want to do the most is traveling. ② 34%. ③ Watching TV. ④ 39%.

서술형 실전문제 p.52~53

01 1. 도서 대출 카드를 로봇의 화면 위에 놓는다.
2. 찾으려는 책의 제목을 입력하고 나서 ENTER 키를 누른다.
3. 안내 데스크로 가서 책을 받는다

02 amazed → amazing

03 The robot finds books and take them to the front desk.

04 (1) Though knowing what the teacher meant
(2) There being any seats left on the train
(3) Wanting to clean my house

05 (1) she said before, the importance of big data is growing
(2) As big data has already changed the world greatly,

06 It is data sets that are very big and complex.

07 Because information and communication technology develops.

08 Using various methods, experts analyze big data and draw meaningful results from it.

09 It helps them understand their customers' needs better and helps them sell more products.

10 the flu season

11 (A) almost all parts (B) uses

01 대화의 First ~, Second ~, Then ~에 이어지는 내용을 쓰면 된다.

02 감정동사의 경우 감정을 느끼게 하면 현재분사형으로 쓰고, 감정을 느끼면 과거분사형으로 쓴다. 보통 사람이 주어인 경우 과거분사형이 나오고, 사물이 주어인 경우 현재분사형이 나온다.

03 로봇은 사람들이 찾으려는 책을 찾아 안내 데스크로 가져다준다.

04 주어진 어휘에 접속사들이 없으므로, 분사구문을 배열하는 문제이다. 각각 (1) '양보', (2) '조건', (3) '이유' 등의 부사절을 분사구문으로 만든 것이며, (2)의 경우 주절과 종속절의 주어가 다르기 때문에, 유도부사 There를 문두에 써야 한다.

05 접속사 as가 각각 (1) '양태', (2) '이유' 등의 의미로 사용된 문장들이다.

06 빅데이터는 매우 크고 복잡한 데이터 집합이다.

07 정보 통신 기술이 발달하기 때문이다.

08 Using various methods는 분사구문으로 '다양한 방법들을 사용하여'라는 의미이다.

09 그것은 회사들이 소비자들이 필요로 하는 것을 더 잘 이해하고 그들이 더 많은 상품을 팔도록 도와준다.

10 '독감 계절 동안 사람들의 행동에 관한 데이터'를 가리킨다.

11 빅데이터는 우리 삶의 '거의 모든 부분'에 영향을 미치고 있고, 빅데이터 덕분에 건강 전문가들이 현재 질병을 예측할 수 있는 것과 같이 빅데이터의 '활용'은 끝이 없다.

창의사고력 서술형 문제 p.54

|모범답안|

01 (1) ① As she was eating a sandwich, Jisu read a book.
② Eating a sandwich, Jisu read a book.
(2) ① As he watered the plants, Brian danced.
② Watering the plants, Brian danced.

02 (A) free time activities (B) traveling (C) 34%
(D) watching TV (E) 39%
(F) what the teenagers want to do
(G) what they actually do

01 단어들을 적절히 조합하여 내용과 어법에 맞게 영작한 답이면 된다.

단원별 모의고사 p.55~58

01 (i)nfluence 02 avoid 03 purchase 04 ④

05 (1) To avoid spreading or catching the flu, you should keep your distance and stay home.
(2) The wording of questions can influence how people answer

06 Can you explain to me how to use this application?

07 log in to the application

08 I'm really grateful to you for your help.

09 Can you tell me how to use this snack machine?
10 We have to wait for 3 minutes before we take out the tea bag.

11 ⑤	12 ④	13 ③	14 ②
15 **빅데이터를 분석하는 것**		16 ③	17 ④
18 experts	19 ②	20 With	21 ②

22 that big data will play a more and more important role in our lives

01 동의어 관계이다. spread: 확산, 전파 – expansion: 확장, 확대, affect: 영향을 미치다 – influence: 영향을 주다
02 '어떤 사람이나 사물로부터 떨어져 있다'는 'avoid(피하다)'가 적절하다. 그는 그녀를 만나는 것을 피하려고 급히 나갔다.
03 '무언가를 사는 행위; 산 물건'은 'purchase(구매(품))'가 적절하다. 구입한 물건이 마음에 들지 않으시면 전액 환불해 드립니다.
04 • recommend: 추천하다[권하다]. 좋은 호텔을 좀 추천해 주실 수 있으세요? • symptom: 증상[징후]. 그 질병의 초기 증세는 고열이다. sympathy: 동정
05 (1) avoid: 피하다, spreading: 확산, catch the flu: 독감에 걸리다, keep distance: 거리를 두다 (2) influence: 영향을 주다
06 explain은 4형식으로 쓰이지 않고 'explain+to 사람+목적어' 형식으로 쓰인다.
07 log in to: ~에 접속하다. 전치사 to를 빠뜨리지 않도록 주의한다.
08 be grateful to A for B: B에 대해 A에게 감사하다
09 tell은 'tell+간접목적어+직접목적어' 형식으로 쓰는 것이 일반적이다.
10 '3분 후에 티백을 꺼내.'라고 하고 있으므로 3분을 기다렸다가 꺼내야 한다.
11 A가 B에게 감사하고 있다.
12 '전에 그녀에 대해 많이 들었다.'는 내용과, '그녀에 대해 거의 알지 못했다.'는 내용은 접속사 As로 표현하면 맞지 않는다. '양보'로 표현하는 것이 좋다. As → (Al)though 또는 Even though가 적절하다.
13 ①, ④, ⑤는 주절과 종속절의 주어가 다르므로, 분사구문의 주어를 쓴다. ① Raining → It raining, ④ Eating → Bentley eating ⑤ Putting → You putting, ②번은 주절과 종속절의 주어가 같기 때문에, 주어를 생략해야 한다. William going → Going
14 각 부분은, '내가 전에 언급했듯이', '그의 상사를 설득하는 수단으로서', '그 여자가 나이를 먹어감에 따라' 등으로 해석할 수 있다. '양태'와 '비례'의 접속사, '자격, 도구'의 전치사로 모두 쓸 수 있는 것은 as뿐이다.
15 'to analyze big data'를 가리킨다.
16 ⓑ와 ①, ③: 부사적 용법, ②, ⑤: 명사적 용법, ④: 형용사적 용법
17 앞의 내용의 예가 나오고 있으므로 For example이 가장 적절하다. ① …임에 비하여[반하여], ② 그러므로, ③ 게다가, 더욱이
18 professional = expert: 전문가
19 이 글은 '데이터베이스의 도움으로 스포츠에서 경기력을 향상시키는' 내용의 글이므로, 제목으로는 ②번 '스포츠에서의 경기력 향상'이 적절하다.
20 with the help of: ~의 도움으로
21 주어진 문장의 This map에 주목한다. ②번 앞 문장의 a map of crime hot spots를 받고 있으므로 ②번이 적절하다.
22 play an important role: 중요한 역할을 하다

Lesson 8

The Joseon Dynasty Through Paintings

시험대비 실력평가 p.62

01 ④ 02 behavior[behaviour] 03 ②
04 ① 05 ⑤ 06 ③

01 동의어 관계이다. ill: 아픈 – sick: 아픈, community 지역사회, 공동체 – society 사회

02 '사람이나 동물이 하는 것들'은 'behavior(행동)'가 적절하다. Sally의 안 좋은 행동은 우리를 짜증나게 하기 시작했다.

03 ① take a walk: 산책하다. 대나무 숲에서 산책하자. ② right: 옳은. 시험 끝나고 답 맞춰 봤어요? 이 문장에서는 '~후에 옳은지' 정도의 뜻으로 'right after'가 하나의 숙어처럼 쓰인 것이 아니다. ③ despite: ~에도 불구하고. 그녀는 안전벨트를 하고 있었는데도 불구하고 앞으로 거세게 튕겨 나갔다. ④ once upon a time 옛날 옛적에. 옛날 옛적에 한 아름다운 공주가 있었다. ⑤ in particular: 특히. 특히 그 박물관은 인상주의 작품을 많이 소장하고 있다.

04 remind ~ of …: ~에게 …을 상기시키다. 네가 그런 말을 할 때에는 네 아버지가 생각나.

05 • for example: 예를 들어. 많은 언어들에, 예를 들어 프랑스어와 이탈리아어에도 비슷한 단어가 있다. • for this reason: 이런 이유로. 이런 이유로, 전문가들은 종종 스포츠를 전쟁에 비유한다.

06 ① frozen: 얼어붙은. 우리는 한번 한밤중에 얼어붙은 연못을 건너갔다. ② object: 물건. 그가 찾은 물건은 낡았다. ③ cancel: 취소하다. 열흘 이내에 취소하면 수수료가 청구되지 않는다. ④ bend: 굽다, 구부러지다. 다리 밑의 버팀대가 휘어지기 시작하고 있었다. ⑤ respect: 존경심. 우리는 선생님들에게 항상 존경심을 표한다.

서술형 시험대비 p.63

01 (1) appear (2) bend (3) dynasty (4) remind
02 (1) fascinating (2) disappointed
03 (1) (r)eminds (2) (s)ymbolizes (3) (d)espite (4) (b)loom
04 (1) Is there anything in particular you'd like for dinner?
(2) For this reason, Friday was considered to be a good day for weddings.
(3) The tiger is a common subject in Korean folk paintings.
(4) The reason he came to see me is as follows.

01 (1) appear: 나타나다. 보여지기 시작하다; 생기거나 쓰이게 되다 (2) bend: 굽다, 구부러지다. 어떤 곧은 것을 구부러지거나 각이 지게 만들거나 힘을 가하다 (3) dynasty: 왕조. 일가족이 나라나 지역을 통치하는 기간 (4) remind: 상기시키다. 어떤 사람에게 어떤 것을 기억하게 만들다

02 감정동사의 '동사+-ing'나 '동사+-ed' 형태의 형용사는 감정을 유발하는 경우에는 '동사+-ing' 형태를 쓰고, 감정을 느끼는 경우에는 '동사+-ed' 형태를 쓴다. (1) 그 지역의 지역사는 아주 흥미롭다. (2) 난 나 자신에게 몹시 실망했다.

03 (1) remind A of B: A에게 B를 상기시키다 (2) symbolize: 상징하다 (3) despite: ~에도 불구하고 (4) bloom: 꽃을 피우다, 꽃이 피다

04 (1) in particular: 특히. in을 추가한다. (2) for this reason: 이런 이유로. for를 추가한다. (3) folk painting: 민화. folk를 추가한다. (4) as follows: 다음과 같이. as를 추가한다.

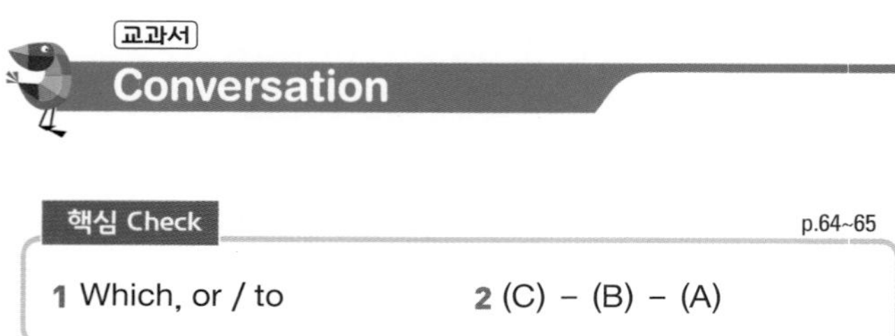

교과서

Conversation

핵심 Check p.64~65

1 Which, or / to 2 (C) – (B) – (A)

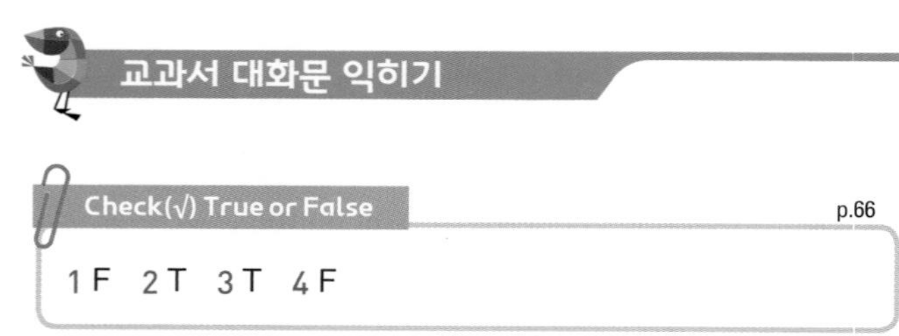

교과서 대화문 익히기

Check(√) True or False p.66

1 F 2 T 3 T 4 F

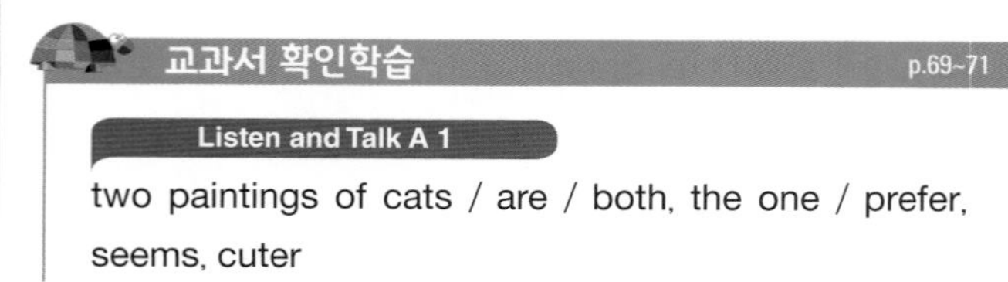

교과서 확인학습 p.69~71

Listen and Talk A 1

two paintings of cats / are / both, the one / prefer, seems, cuter

Listen and Talk A 2

Which, prefer / prefer, It seems, choice / so, like, more

Listen and Talk A 3

Which one / to choose, better / Me, too, seems, that

Listen and Talk A 4

you're going to / nice / Which one, prefer, or / prefer, with, It seems to me

Listen and Talk B

Which, prefer / prefer / prefer, prefer / Which, prefer, or / prefer / prefer, prefer, more calm / Which, or / prefer, more unique / prefer, prefer, but / Which, prefer, or / prefer, more / prefer, prefer

Listen and Talk C

Which, more / prefer, that / much / so / just, also / never, before / before, sure / next to / let's watch / first

Listen and Talk D

prefer, more fun to learn, prefer, like

Talk and Play

Which, prefer / prefer / prefer, prefer

Review 1

to buy / great / Which one, prefer, or / prefer

Review 2

Which, prefer / prefer, the healthier choice / I heard / order

Review 3

Which one, more / prefer, this / much

시험대비 기본평가 p.72

01 ③

02 It seems to me that it's more unique. 03 ⑤

01 'I would rather(I'd rather)' 다음에는 동사가 나와야 한다. 나머지는 모두 선호를 나타내는 표현이다.

02 'It seems to me that ~'은 자신의 의견을 말할 때 쓸 수 있는 표현이다.

03 (a)와 나머지는 자신의 의견을 나타내는 것이지만, ⑤번은 상대방에 대한 기대나 희망을 나타내는 것이다.

시험대비 실력평가 p.73~74

01 ①	02 Which do you prefer	03 ②
04 ⑤	05 (B) – (A) – (C)	06 ③
07 Which food do you prefer		08 ④
09 ①	10 ④ 11 ⑤	12 ②, ③

01 I like *Batman*.은 단지 좋아한다고 말하는 것이다. 선호를 묻는 말이므로 'I prefer *Batman*.' 또는 'I like *Batman* more.'로 쓰는 것이 적절하다.

02 'Which do you prefer?'는 선호를 물을 때 쓰는 표현이다.

03 선호를 묻는 질문에 대한 답이므로 more가 적절하다.

04 'I'm very hungry.'라고 말한 것은 남자 아이이다.

05 '아름답지 않니?'라는 주어진 질문에 '그렇다'고 답하며 어떤 것이 더 좋은지를 질문하는 (B)가 이어지고, (B)의 '무엇이 더 좋은지' 묻는 질문에 '초록색 접시가 더 좋다'고 답하는 (A)가 이어진 후, (C)에서 '나도.'라고 답하며 이유를 설명하는 순서가 자연스럽다.

06 (A) 선택을 나타내는 or, (B) to me: 나에게는

07 A와 B 두 가지 중 어떤 것을 선호하는지 물을 때 prefer를 사용하여 'Which (one) do you prefer, A or B?'로 표현한다.

08 'There isn't just an exhibition.(단순히 전시회만 있는 것이 아니야.)'에 이어 'There's also a mask dance show at 4:00 and 6:00.(탈춤 공연도 4시와 6시에 있어.)'가 이어지고 여기에 Great!라고 반응하는 것이 자연스럽다.

09 (a) exhibitions와 we 사이에 관계대명사가 생략된 형태이다. go는 자동사로 목적어를 취할 수 없으므로 전치사 to가 필요하다. (b) 둘 중에서 선호를 묻고 있으므로 prefer가 적절하다. like를 쓰려면 뒤에 more나 better 등이 나와야 한다. (c) ago는 현재완료와 함께 쓰이지 않는다.

10 '공연은 어디서 해?'라는 Eric의 질문에 '전시관 옆 다솜 홀에서 해.'라고 소미가 답하고 있다.

11 자신의 의견을 말할 때 'It seems (to me) that+주어+동사 ~'로 표현할 수 있다.

12 A는 '난 스파게티를 더 좋아해.'라고 하고 있다.

서술형 시험대비 p.75

01 (D) → (C) → (A) → (B)

02 Which one do you want to see more

03 They are talking about the exhibitions.

04 such as

05 (1) It seems to the writer that science is more fun to learn.

(2) The writer wants to be a great inventor like Edison.

06 are

07 Because he thinks the cat in it is cuter and he also likes the bird in it.

01 '전에 탈춤 공연을 본 적이 없다'는 말에 이어, (D)에서 '전에 본 적이 있다며. 분명 좋아할 거'라고 언급하고, (C)에서 '공연은 어디서 하는지' 묻고, 이어서 (A)에서 '다솜 홀에서' 한다고 답하고, (B)에서 약속을 정하는 순서가 적절하다.

02 which가 의문형용사로 one을 수식해 주는 구조로 which를 쓴다.
03 그들은 전시회에 관하여 이야기하고 있다.
04 '~와 같은'의 뜻을 나타내는 like는 'such as'로 바꿔 쓸 수 있다.
05 필자는 '과학을 배우는 것이 더 즐거운 것 같아.'라고 말하며 'Edison과 같은 훌륭한 발명가가 되고 싶어서 그것을 더 좋아하기도 해.'라고 하고 있다.
06 앞에서 'Aren't they great?'이라고 물었으므로 be동사 are로 답하는 것이 적절하다.
07 '그림 속 고양이가 더 귀여운 것 같아. 새도 마음에 들어.'라고 하고 있다.

교과서

Grammar

핵심 Check p.76~77

1 (1) of (2) for
2 (1) were you, I would hire me
(2) would not move away if he had some money

시험대비 기본평가 p.78

01 ③
02 (1) make → made (2) will → would
(3) can → could (4) will → would
03 It was not easy for Suji to ride a bike on the street.
04 ④

01 to부정사가 진주어가 되는 구문에서 to부정사의 의미상의 주어는 전치사 'for 또는 of+목적격'의 형태로 표현한다. to부정사의 '의미상의 주어'에 대해 '성격이나 태도'를 나타내는 형용사가 있을 때는 of를 쓴다.
02 문제에서 모든 문장이 가정법 문장이라고 했고, 모든 문장들의 구조는 '가정법 과거' 형태로 볼 수 있으므로, 조건절의 동사를 과거로, 주절의 조동사도 과거형으로 고치는 것이 적절하다.
03 to부정사의 의미상의 주어를 표현할 때 전치사 for를 쓴다. 일반적으로 '가주어-진주어' 구문에서 동명사 주어는 진주어로 쓰지 않으며, 문제의 조건에서 to부정사를 이용하라고 한 것에 유의한다.
04 주절에 조동사의 과거형이 나왔으므로, 가정법 문장이다. 가정법 과거에서 동사의 과거형 또는 조동사의 과거형을 사용하는 것이 적절하다.

시험대비 실력평가 p.79~81

01 ② 02 ③ 03 ④ 04 ①
05 ⑤
06 If I caught the fish, I would let my mom eat it.
07 If it had not been for Munjado, children couldn't have learned the importance of harmony.
08 It was easy for the boy to learn Chinese characters using Munjado.
09 It was impossible for the girl to catch fish without any help.
10 ① 11 ② 12 ④
13 It was careless of her to give the plants too much water
14 ③
15 If they learned Munjado, they could understand Korea more
16 ①, ③ 17 ④
18 didn't melt → had not melted 또는 have come → come

01 wise는 사람의 성품에 관한 형용사이다. 이때 의미상의 주어는 'for+목적격'이 아니라 'of+목적격'을 쓴다. ④는 일반적인 진리이므로 과거시제로 쓰지 않아도 괜찮다.
02 가정법 과거로서 '반대' 개념의 직설법 현재 시제와 적절하게 전환된 문장은 ③번뿐이다.
03 to부정사의 의미상의 주어는 전치사 for를 사용하는데, 사람의 성격이나 태도를 나타낼 때는 of를 쓴다. ④ 'Jimmy가 선생님께 요청한 것은 무례했다'는 내용이므로 of를 써야 하며, 다른 문장들은 모두 for를 쓴다.
04 가정법 문장이라면 won't를 wouldn't로, 직설법 문장이라면 were를 is로 쓰는 것이 적절하다.
05 to부정사의 의미상의 주어를 표현할 때 알맞은 전치사를 고르는 문제이다. ⓑ, ⓕ에는 사람의 성격이나 태도에 관한 형용사가 있으므로 전치사 of를 쓰는 것이 적절하며, 나머지는 모두 for를 쓴다.
06 가정법 과거 시제의 문장이다. If절에 과거동사 caught가 오고, 주절에 조동사의 과거형 would를 쓰되, let my mom 뒤에 동사원형을 쓴다는 것에 유의하여 배열한다.
07 가정법 과거완료 표현이다. 가정법 과거시제로서 '~가 없다면'이라는 표현은 'if it were not for ~'로, 가정법 과거완료에서 '~가 없었다면'은 'if it had not been for'로 나타내는 것이 적절하고, 주절에는 '조동사 과거형+have p.p.' 형태를 사용하여, 적절하게 배열한다.
08 가주어 It과 진주어 to부정사구를 이용하고, '문자도를 사용해서 한자를 배우는 것'이므로 현재분사 using을 to부정사구의 뒤에

쓰는 것에 유의하여 배열한다.

09 가주어 It과 진주어 to부정사구를 이용하고, 의미상의 주어는 for를 이용해서 적절하게 배열한다.

10 ①번의 It은 비인칭 주어로서 날씨, 요일, 계절, 명암 등에 사용된다. 나머지는 모두 가주어 it으로 사용되었다.

11 ②는 시간, 요일, 날짜, 날씨, 무게, 거리, 금액, 명암 등을 표현할 때 쓰는 '비인칭 주어' it이다. 나머지는 모두 to부정사구를 진주어로 하는 '가주어-진주어' 구문으로 쓰였다.

12 가정법 과거 형태의 문장들이다. If절에는 동사의 과거형을, 주절에는 조동사의 과거형을 쓰는 것이 적절하다.

13 대화 내용상 'Jane이 식물에 물을 너무 많이 준 것이 부주의했다'라는 것이므로, of를 추가하여 알맞게 배열한다.

14 ③ 성격을 나타내는 형용사를 받을 때는 to부정사의 의미상의 주어에 of를 사용한다. '그녀가 과거에 그의 부끄러운 경험을 언급한 것은 잔인했다' ① of → for, ② for → of, ④ his → him(전치사 뒤 목적격) ⑤ of → for

15 내용상 가정법의 형태로 문장이 구성되어야 한다. have동사의 과거형과 조동사 can의 과거형을 사용하되, much의 비교급을 쓰는 것에 유의하여 영작한다.

16 '~가 없다면'이라는 가정법 표현은 'If there were no ~'로 나타내며, without[but for] 또는 'If it were not for ~'로 대체할 수 있다. 'If it were not for'는 if를 생략해서 'were it not for ~'로 표현 가능하다. 주절에는 조동사의 과거형을 쓴다.

17 옳은 문장은 ⓒ, ⓔ, ⓕ, ⓖ 4개이다. ⓐ importantly → important ⓑ for → of ⓓ using → to use

18 '얼음이 녹지 않았다면, 그 잉어들이 나오지 않았을 텐데.'라는 의미의 가정법 과거완료 문장이다. if절의 didn't melt를 hadn't melted로 고친다. 가정법 과거로 볼 경우, 종속절은 그대로 두고, 주절의 wouldn't have come을 wouldn't come으로 고치는 것도 가능하다. *carp: 잉어

서술형 시험대비

p.82~83

01 (1) ate carp, she could get well
(2) were no letters, it would be difficult for us to deliver
(3) necessary for his mother to recover her health
(4) very stupid of him to try to catch fish in this cold weather

02 (1) If it were not for (2) If there were no
(3) Were it not for
(4) As there is computer, we can

03 the ice had not melted, he could not have caught three carp

04 slept well enough, she could be

05 (1) dangerous for even experts to climb up the mountain covered with snow
(2) foolish of you to attempt to kill the beast
(3) fun for him to attend the party with his boss

06 (1) am → were[was] (2) is → were[was]
(3) be → have been (4) is → were[was]
(5) have → had

07 (1) checked → to check (2) for → of
(3) of → for (4) sitting → sit (5) let → to let

08 (1) If he were[was] rich enough, he would not go fishing in this cold weather.
(2) If Bob were[was] in Venice, he would be happy.
(3) If there were[was] time left, I would not cross the road at a red light.
(4) If we had not had Munjado, it would not have been easy for children to learn Chinese characters

01 가정법과 '가주어-진주어' 구문, to부정사의 의미상의 주어 등에 유의하여, 주어진 단어들을 적절히 배열한다.

02 '컴퓨터가 없으면, 많은 정보를 쉽게 찾을 수 없다.'는 내용으로 직설법으로 표현하면, '컴퓨터가 있어서 많은 정보를 쉽게 찾을 수 있다.'가 된다. 가정법 과거 표현, 'Without = If it were not for = Were it not for'를 기억해 두는 것이 좋다.

03 직설법으로 표현하면, '얼음이 녹았기 때문에, 그가 잉어 세 마리를 잡을 수 있었다'는 것이다. 글자 수와 어법에 맞게 가정법 과거완료시제를 활용해서 melt를 had not melted로, can을 could로 변형하고, carp는 단수와 복수가 같아 carps라고 쓰지 않는 것에 유의하여, 영작한다.

04 'Stacy가 수면을 충분히 취하지 않기 때문에 상태가 좋지 않다'라는 직설법 문장을 가정법으로 표현한 것이다. If절에 과거동사, 주절에 조동사 과거형에 유의하여 영작한다.

05 (1) '전문가들조차'를 의미상의 주어로 표현할 때는 'for even experts'로 쓴다. (2) '어리석다'는 사람의 성질을 나타내므로 전치사 of를 쓴다. (3) 의미상의 주어는 for him이다.

06 문제에서 모든 문장이 가정법이라는 전제를 주었으므로, if절의 동사를 과거시제로 고치는 것이 적절하다. 단, (3)은 yesterday로 보아 내용상 '가정법 과거완료'를 이용하는 시제이므로, 주절을 '조동사+have+p.p.'로 고치는 것이 적절하다.

07 '가주어-진주어' 구문에서 to부정사의 의미상의 주어와 그에 맞는 전치사의 활용에 유의하여, 어색한 단어를 하나만 찾아서 적절하게 고치도록 한다.

08 가정법 과거는 직설법 현재 반대, 가정법 과거완료는 직설법 과거의 반대를 나타낸다. (4)는 가정법 과거완료이다.

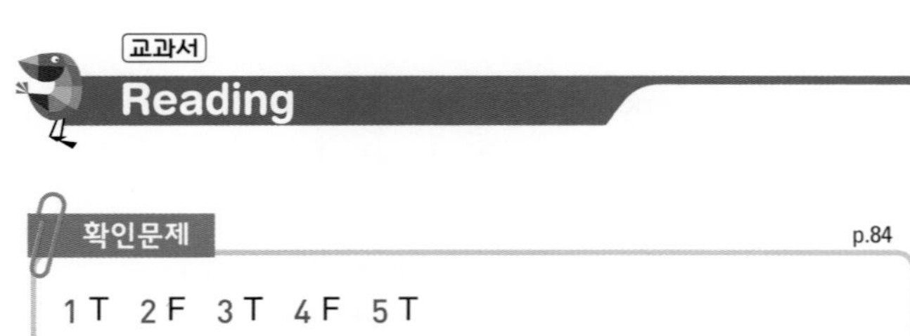

확인문제 p.84

1 T 2 F 3 T 4 F 5 T

확인문제 p.85

1 F 2 T 3 T 4 F

교과서 확인학습 A p.86~87

01 into
02 on the right
03 see, character
04 see
05 is called, a type of folk painting that was popular, late
06 usually, with
07 One of, characters appears
08 represent, that were important to
09 just decorations
10 often, symbolic
11 symbolize, because of
12 goes as follows
13 Once upon a time
14 became ill, anything
15 On, would be wonderful if I could eat
16 went out to, was completely frozen
17 It, for him to catch any
18 so disappointed that, to
19 melted, out of
20 back home
21 got well
22 symbolic objects
23 in, of, in, of
24 bend
25 stays green in
26 For these reasons, came to symbolize, to
27 In the case of, but still, beautifully
28 thus, will to fight for, despite
29 much more than, to
30 reminded, of, that
31 In particular, for
32 Through it, importance, harmony in

교과서 확인학습 B p.88~89

1 Munjado, a Window into the Joseon Dynasty
2 Look at the painting on the right.
3 Do you see the Chinese character, *hyo*(孝)?
4 Do you also see a carp, a geomungo, and a fan?
5 This kind of painting is called Munjado, and it is a type of folk painting that was popular in the late Joseon dynasty.
6 In Munjado, there is usually a Chinese character with some animals or objects.
7 One of eight Chinese characters appears in Munjado.
8 They are *hyo*(孝), *je*(悌), *chung*(忠), *sin*(信), *ye*(禮), *ui*(義), *yeom*(廉), and *chi*(恥), and they represent the values that were important to people of the Joseon dynasty.
9 The animals or objects in Munjado are not just decorations.
10 They often are symbolic.
11 For example, carp in the paintings of *hyo* symbolize respect for parents because of an old story.
12 The story goes as follows..
13 Once upon a time, a man lived with his old mother.
14 One winter, the man's mother became ill and couldn't eat anything.
15 On one very cold day, the mother said to the man, "It would be wonderful if I could eat fresh fish."
16 The man went out to the river, but it was completely frozen.
17 It was impossible for him to catch any fish.
18 The man was so disappointed that he cried out to the sky, "What should I do? Please help me."
19 Then the ice melted, and three carp suddenly came out of the water.
20 The man went back home and cooked the fish for his mother.
21 Then his mother got well.
22 There are other examples of symbolic objects in Munjado.
23 They are bamboo in the paintings of the character *chung*(忠) and lotus flowers in the paintings of *ui*(義).
24 Bamboo does not bend.
25 It stays green in all kinds of weather.
26 For these reasons, bamboo came to symbolize loyalty to the king.
27 In the case of lotus flowers, they grow in muddy ponds but still bloom beautifully.
28 They thus became a symbol of a person's will to fight for justice despite difficulties.
29 Munjado was much more than a painting to people of the Joseon dynasty.
30 It reminded them of important values that greatly influenced their behaviors and attitudes.
31 In particular, for children, Munjado was a study tool.

32 Through it, children in the Joseon dynasty could learn the importance of harmony in family and society.

시험대비 실력평가

p.90~93

01 ②

02 they represent the values that were important to people of the Joseon dynasty

03 ③ 04 ④ 05 ③ 06 ⑤

07 ① 08 In particular 09 ④

10 ② 11 ①, ⑤

12 One of eight Chinese characters appears in Munjado.

13 ③ 14 ②

15 They not only are decorations but also has symbolic meaning.

16 It stands for loyalty to the king.

17 (A) weather (B) loyalty (C) for

18 ① 19 ④

20 They could learn the importance of harmony in family and society.

21 Eight Chinese characters appear in Munjado.

22 (A) folk (B) values

23 (1) some animals or objects
(2) one of eight Chinese characters

01 ⓐ와 ②: (~한) 종류 ① (동·식물 등의) 유(類), 족(族), 종(種), ③ 성질, 본질, 특질, ④ 친절한, 상냥한, ⑤ (날씨 따위가) 쾌적한, 온화한

02 주격 관계대명사 that을 이용하고 'be important to'로 '~에게 중요하다'는 의미를 나타낸다.

03 문자도는 민화(folk painting)의 한 종류이다.

04 뒤에서 "'효' 그림 속에 있는 잉어는 옛이야기 때문에 부모님에 대한 존경심을 상징한다.'라고 하고 있으므로 '상징적'이 적절하다.

05 ⓑ와 ②, ④: 가주어, ① 비인칭 주어, ③ 인칭대명사, ⑤ 가목적어

06 out of는 '~의 안에서 밖으로, ~ 중에(서), ~에서(from)' 등의 뜻을 갖는다.

07 빈칸 ⓐ 다음에 앞 문장에 대한 결과가 이어지므로 '결과'를 이끌 수 있는 연결어구가 나오는 것이 적절하다.

08 in particular: 특히

09 '문자도에 있는 상징적인 사물의 또 다른 예가 있다.'라고 글을 시작하고 있으므로 앞에는 문자도에 있는 상징적인 사물의 예가 나왔을 것임을 추론할 수 있다.

10 주어진 문장의 also에 주목한다. 같은 것이 앞에 나왔다는 것이므로 ②번이 적절하다.

11 빈칸 ⓐ에는 주격 관계대명사가 필요하다. 선행사가 사물이므로 that이나 which가 적절하다.

12 'one of+복수 명사'는 '~ 중 하나'라는 의미로 핵심 주어가 one이므로 동사는 one과 수의 일치를 시켜 단수 동사를 써야 한다.

13 빈칸 뒤에 앞 문장의 예가 이어지고 있으므로 For example이 적절하다.

14 ⓐ once upon a time: 옛날 옛적에, ⓑ cry out to: ~에 대고 소리치다

15 '문자도에 있는 동물이나 사물은 단순한 장식이 아니다. 그것들은 종종 상징적이다.'라고 했으므로 '장식일 뿐만 아니라 상징적인 의미를 갖고 있다.'라고 쓸 수 있다. 또한 'not only A but also B'에서 A와 B는 문법적으로 대등한 것이 와야 한다.

16 '대나무는 왕에 대한 충성을 상징하게 되었다.'라고 했다. stand for = symbolize

17 (A) '어떤 '날씨'에서도 푸르름을 유지한다.'라고 해야 하므로 weather가 적절하다. whether는 접속사로 '~인지 아닌지'라는 뜻이다. (B) '이런 이유로 대나무는 왕에 대한 '충성'을 상징하게 되었다.'라고 해야 하므로 loyalty가 적절하다. royalty: 왕권, 특허권〔저작권〕 사용료, loyalty: 충성, 충실 (C) '정의를 위해 싸우는 사람'이라고 해야 하므로 for가 적절하다. fight against: ~에 대항하여 싸우다, fight for: ~을 위해 싸우다

18 '문자도는 조선 시대 사람들에게 그림 그 이상'이라고 했고 '자신들의 행동과 태도에 큰 영향을 미친다'고 했으므로 '가치'가 적절하다.

19 뒤에서 '그것을 통해 조선 시대의 아이들은 가족과 사회에서의 조화의 중요성을 배울 수 있었다.'라고 했으므로 '학습 도구'가 가장 적절하다.

20 '그것을 통해 조선 시대의 아이들은 가족과 사회에서의 조화의 중요성을 배울 수 있었다.'라고 했다.

21 '문자도에는 여덟 개의 한자 중 하나가 나온다.'라고 했으므로 8개의 한자가 있었음을 알 수 있다.

22 '조선 시대 후기에 인기 있었던 민화의 한 종류이다.'라고 하고, '그것들은 조선 시대 사람들에게 중요했던 가치들을 나타낸다.'라고 했다.

23 '문자도에는 보통 한자 하나가 동물이나 사물과 함께 있다.'라고 했고, '문자도에는 여덟 개의 한자 중 하나가 나온다.'라고 했으므로 (1) some animals or objects, (2) one of eight Chinese characters라고 쓸 수 있다.

서술형 시험대비

p.94~95

01 *hyo*

02 It would be wonderful if I could eat fresh fish.

03 (A) respect for parents (B) three carp
(C) sick mother

04 is called 05 worthless → important
06 문자도에는 보통 조선 시대 사람들에게 중요했던 가치들을 나타내는 한자 하나가 동물이나 사물과 함께 있다.
07 even, far, a lot, still 중에서 3개 이상 쓰면 정답
08 It reminded them of important values that[which] greatly influenced their behaviors and attitudes.
09 (A) Bamboo (B) lotus flowers
10 (1) 대나무는 구부러지지 않는다
(2) 그것은 어떤 날씨에서도 푸르름을 유지한다.
11 got
12 It's because lotus flowers grow in muddy ponds but still bloom beautifully.
13 got well
14 It was impossible for him to catch any fish.

01 '부모님에 대한 존경심을 상징한다'라고 했으므로 hyo(孝)가 적절하다.

02 가정법 과거는 'If+주어+동사의 과거형 ~, 주어+조동사의 과거형+동사원형 …'의 형태로 있을 법하지 않은 일을 가정하여 말할 때 쓴다.

03 잉어는 부모님에 대한 존경심을 상징한다. 옛이야기에서 한 남자가 얼어붙은 강에서 잉어 세 마리를 잡아서 병든 어머니를 위해 그것들을 요리했다. carp는 단수와 복수가 같은 형태임에 유의한다.

04 문자도가 무엇을 부르는 것이 아니라 '불리는' 것이므로 수동태로 써서 'is called'로 쓰는 것이 적절하다.

05 '그것들은 조선 시대 사람들에게 '중요했던' 가치들을 나타낸다.'고 하는 것이 적절하다.

06 '문자도에는 보통 한자 하나가 동물이나 사물과 함께 있다.' '문자도에는 여덟 개의 한자 중 하나가 나오고, 그것들은 조선 시대 사람들에게 중요했던 가치들을 나타낸다.'

07 ⓐ의 much는 비교급을 수식하고 있으며 even, still, a lot, far 등으로 대신할 수 있다.

08 remind A of B: A에게 B를 상기시키다. 주격 관계대명사 that[which]으로 important values를 수식하게 하는 것이 적절하다.

09 (A)와 (B)는 각각 그 앞에 나온 대나무와 연꽃을 가리킨다.

10 바로 앞에서 '대나무는 구부러지지 않는다. 그것은 어떤 날씨에서도 푸르름을 유지한다. 이런 이유로 대나무는 왕에 대한 충성을 상징하게 되었다.'라고 했다.

11 come to부정사 = get to부정사 = ~하게 되다

12 '연꽃의 경우, 그것들은 진흙투성이의 연못에서 자라지만 여전히 아름답게 꽃을 피운다. 그래서 그 꽃들은 어려움에도 불구하고 정의를 위해 싸우는 사람의 의지를 상징하게 되었다.'라고 했다.

13 '회복되었다'라는 의미의 'got well'이 적절하다.

14 가주어 'It', 의미상의 주어 'for 목적격', 진주어 'to부정사' 구문을 이용한다.

영역별 핵심문제

p.97~101

01 ①
02 (a)ttitude / (t)ool (1) attitude (2) tool
03 justice
04 (A) (g)et (B) (m)uch (C) (s)o
05 (1) surprised (2) disappointing (3) boring
06 Which do you like more[better]
07 ③ 08 I think that it's the healthier choice.
09 ② 10 ⑤ 11 prefer 12 ①
13 ④ 14 ④ 15 ⑤ 16 ⑤
17 (1) the carp had not come out over the ice, his mother could not have eaten them
(2) the carp came out over the ice, his mother could eat them
18 ⑤ 19 symbolize
20 (A) loyalty (B) bend (C) green
21 remained → reminded 22 ① 23 ④
24 appear → appears
25 There is usually a Chinese character with some animals or objects in Munjado.
26 They symbolize peace and happiness.
27 *The Harvesters* was painted on wood in 1565.

01 <보기>와 ①번은 '글자'라는 의미로 쓰였다. <보기> 나는 쓰여진 모든 글자가 균형 있고 아름답게 보이는 것을 알았어. ① 우리들만의 글자를 가지기 전에, 우리는 한자를 사용해야만 했어. ② 그 동네의 성격은 전혀 변하지 않았다. ③ Eddie는 그 쇼에서 가장 우스운 인물이다. ④ 성격은 오래 계속된 습관이다. (독일 속담) ⑤ 당신이 좋아하는 캐릭터가 활동하는 것을 보시려면 그저 버튼만 누르세요.

02 (1) attitude: 태도, 자세. 어떤 것에 대해 생각하거나 느끼는 방식. 네가 시험에 합격하려면 태도를 바꾸는 게 좋을 거야. (2) tool: 도구. 손에 쥐고 특정한 종류의 작업을 할 수 있는 어떤 기구나 간단한 장비. 소규모 회사에서도 컴퓨터는 필수 도구이다.

03 '공평하고 합리적인 특성: 사람들이 대우 받는 방식에서의 공정함'이라는 의미로 'justice(정의)'가 적절하다. 그들은 동등한 권리와 정의를 요구하고 있다.

04 (A) get well: 병이 낫다, 회복하다. 그는 어머니에게로 다가가 걱정하지 마시고 빨리 쾌유하시라고 말씀드린다. (B) much more than: ~보다 훨씬 많이. 그것들이 네가 생각하는 것 이상으로 가치가 있을지도 몰라. (C) so ~ that ...: 너무 ~해서 …하다. 네가 너무 빨리 걸어서 못 쫓아가겠다.

05 감정동사의 '동사+-ing'나 '동사+-ed' 형태의 형용사는 감정을 유발하는 경우에는 '동사+-ing' 형태를 쓰고, 감정을 느끼는 경우에는 '동사+-ed' 형태를 쓴다. (1) surprised: 놀란. 내가 그녀에게 말을 했을 때 그녀는 놀라는 것 같았다. (2) disappointing: 실망하게 만드는. 중요한 경기에서 패하는 것

은 매우 실망스러울 수 있다. (3) boring: 지루하게 만드는. 그의 연설은 너무 지루했다.

06 빈칸에는 선호를 묻는 표현이 적절하므로 'Which do you prefer' 또는 'Which do you like more[better]'라고 쓸 수 있다.

07 선호를 묻는 질문에 (B)에서 '김밥이 더 좋다'라고 답한 후, 이유를 말하며 '넌 어떠니?'라고 묻는 말에 이어 (C)에서 '떡볶이를 먹겠다'고 답하며 '여기는 떡볶이가 더 맛있다고 들었다'고 말하자, (A)에서 '그럼 주문하자'로 이어지는 것이 적절하다.

08 'It seems to me that it's the healthier choice.'는 의견을 나타내는 표현으로 'I think that it's the healthier choice.'라고 쓸 수 있다.

09 '그럼 주문하자.'라고 하면서 '난 아주 배불러.'라고 하는 것은 어색하다 'I'm very hungry.' 정도가 적절하다.

10 John과 소미가 언제 Batman을 볼지는 알 수 없다.

11 '누군가나 어떤 것을 다른 누군가나 어떤 것보다 더 좋아해서 할 수 있다면 그것을 선택하다'를 가리키는 말은 'prefer(~을 (더) 좋아하다, 선호하다)'이다.

12 옳은 문장은 ⓒ 1개이다. ⓐ going → go ⓑ possibly → possible ⓓ not be → not to be ⓔ they → them ⓕ of → for .

13 '과거시제의 직설법 문장'을 가정법으로 고치면 '가정법 과거완료'가 된다. If절에 'had+p.p', 주절에 '조동사 과거+have+p.p'를 쓰되, 직설법과 반대되도록 not을 뺀다.

14 비교급은 quite로 강조할 수 없고, 시간의 부사절에 will을 쓸 수 없다. 내용상 의미상의 주어는 for you이다.

15 가정법 과거에는 동사의 과거형이 온다. 이 경우 비인칭 주어 it과 동사 snowed를 쓸 수 있다는 것에 유의한다.

16 ⑤ this morning으로 봐서 내용상 가정법 과거완료 문장이다. If절에 'had+p.p.', 주절에는 '조동사 과거+have+p.p.' 형태가 와야 한다. 'succeeded'를 'had succeeded'로 고치는 것이 적절하다.

17 내용상 가정법 과거완료 문장이다. If절에 'had p.p.' 형태, 주절에는 '조동사 과거형+have p.p' 형태를 쓰고, 직설법으로 바꿀 때는 not이 없는 과거 시제로 고치는 것이 적절하다.

18 For these reasons: 이런 이유로, fight for: ~을 위해 싸우다

19 symbolize: 상징하다, 이미지, 형태 또는 모형에 의해 간접적으로 표현하다

20 대나무는 왕에 대한 충성을 상징한다. 대나무는 구부러지지 않고 어떤 날씨에서도 푸르름을 유지한다.

21 remain은 자동사로 목적어를 받을 수 없으며 의미상으로도 '상기시켰다'라고 하는 것이 적절하므로 reminded로 고치는 것이 적절하다.

22 이 글은 '문자도는 조선 시대 사람들에게 그림 그 이상이었으며 자신들의 행동과 태도에 큰 영향을 미치는 중요한 가치를 상기시켰고, 특히 아이들에게 문자도는 학습 도구였다.'는 내용의 글이므로, 주제로는 ①번 '조선시대에 문자도의 역할'이 적절하다.

23 '아이들에게 문자도는 학습 도구였다.'라고 했지 '아이들이 문자도를 학습 도구로 그렸다.'라는 말은 없다.

24 'one of+복수 명사'는 '~ 중 하나'라는 의미로 핵심 주어 one에 수를 일치시켜 단수 동사인 appears가 적절하다.

25 '문자도에는 보통 한자 하나가 동물이나 사물과 함께 있다.'라고 했다.

26 '이 새들은 평화와 행복을 상징한다.'라고 했다.

27 *The Harvesters*는 1565년에 목재 위에 그려졌다.

단원별 예상문제

p.102~105

01 ②　02 ④　03 (1) (r)emind　(d)espite

04 (1) (a)ttitude　(2) (d)ynasty

05 What do you say to these caps here?　06 ④

07 It's because the green plate seems to be more unique to him.

08 ⑤　09 ①

10 He is going to buy the bag with flowers for his sister.

11 ②　12 ①

13 (1) ⓒ　(2) ⓑ　(3) ⓐ　(4) ⓓ　(5) ⓑ　(6) ⓐ　(7) ⓓ　(8) ⓑ　(9) ⓐ　(10) ⓒ

14 (1) had your phone number, would call
(2) were[was] rich, could buy
(3) hadn't attended the meeting, couldn't have heard

15 ③　16 ⑤　17 as follows

18 ②　19 (A) ①　(B) ③

20 (A) reminded　(B) values　(C) behaviors　(D) attitudes

21 they represent the values that were important to people of the Joseon dynasty

22 ⑤

01 ②번은 동의어의 관계이며 나머지는 모두 반의어의 관계이다. represent: 나타내다, 상징하다 – symbolize: 상징하다, ~을 나타내다 ① ill: 아픈 – healthy: 건강한 ③ possible: 가능한 – impossible: 불가능한 ④ respect: 존경, 경의 – disrespect: 무례, 결례 ⑤ justice: 정의, 공정 – injustice: 불평등, 부당함

02 ① 그러므로 너는 긴장하고 집중력을 유지해야 한다. ② 이런 이유로, 이 구역에 표지판이 필요하다. ③ 그녀는 검약을 매우 중요하게 여긴다. ④ loyalty: 충성, 충실. royalty: 왕족, 왕권, 저작권 사용료. Stonehenge에 묻힌 사람들은 아마도 왕족이었을 것이다. ⑤ 네 잎 클로버는 행운의 상징이다.

03 (1) remind A of B: A에게 B를 상기시키다. 이걸 보니 지난번에 네가 실수한 거 생각 안 나니? (2) despite: ~에도 불구하

고. 일반 대중의 강한 반대에도 불구하고 그 안은 추진될 것이다.

04 (1) attitude: 태도 (2) dynasty: 왕조

05 How about ~? = What do you say to ~?

06 Joe는 '삼각형이 있는 것이 더 좋아. 그것이 더 독특한 것 같아.' 라고 말하고 있다.

07 Steve는 '초록색 접시가 더 독특한 것 같아.'라고 말하고 있다.

08 'Me, too.'는 '나도 그래.'라는 뜻으로 동의를 나타낸다. 앞에서 일반동사 like가 쓰였으므로 'So do I.'로 바꿔 쓸 수 있다

09 (a) look+형용사: ~하게 보이다 (b) 선택의문문이므로 Which (c) It seems ~ = It appears ~: ~인 것 같다

10 준수는 '여동생에게 줄 선물을 살 거라고 했'고 '꽃들이 있는 것이 더 좋아. 내 여동생이 그것을 더 좋아할 것 같아.'라고 했으므로 꽃들이 있는 가방을 살 것이라고 추측할 수 있다

11 ① they → them ③ of → for ④ playing → play ⑤ for → of

12 가정법 문장들이다. ② 종속절이 가정법 과거완료이므로 'it would be ~' → 'it would have been ~' ③ will → would ④ can → could ⑤ makes → made

13 (1), (10) 인칭대명사 (2), (5), (8) It ~ that 강조구문 (3), (6), (9) 가주어 It (4), (7) 거리, 날씨 등을 나타내는 비인칭 주어

14 (1), (2)는 가정법 과거, (3)은 가정법 과거완료이다. (3)의 경우, but 뒤에 '부정 의미'의 내용이 필요하므로 종속절과 주절 모두에 not이 와야 하는 것에 유의한다.

15 뒤에서 '잉어 세 마리가 갑자기 물 밖으로 나왔다.'라고 했으므로 '얼음이 녹았다'라고 하는 것이 적절하다. ① freeze: 얼다, ④ heighten: 높게 하다, 강화시키다, ⑤ assemble: 모으다, 집합시키다

16 주어진 문장의 the fish가 ⑤번 앞 문장의 three carp를 받고 있으므로 ⑤번이 적절하다.

17 as follows: 다음과 같이

18 앞의 내용의 결과가 나오고 있으므로 thus가 가장 적절하다.

19 (A) 대나무 그림이 있고 忠자가 있는 ①번이 적절하다. (B) 연꽃 그림이 있고 義자가 있는 ③번이 적절하다.

20 '문자도는 그들에게 자신들의 행동과 태도에 큰 영향을 미치는 중요한 가치를 상기시켰다.'라고 했다.

21 represent: 나타내다, 보여 주다 be important to: ~에게 중요하다

22 문자도에 여덟 개의 한자 중 하나가 나오는 이유는 알 수 없다. ① Yes. ② Yes. ③ Yes. ④ Yes.

서술형 실전문제 p.106~107

01 Yes, she has.

02 They will go see the exhibition.

03 very → much

04 (1) It was impossible for them to catch the tiger.
(2) It was really careless of the women to reach out to a big dog.

05 I had been in his situation, I could never have done the same thing

06 (A) the ice melted (B) came out of

07 He went out to the river to catch fish for his sick mother.

08 Because the river was completely frozen.

09 The man was so disappointed that he cried out to the sky

10 despite

11 (A) a person's will (B) despite difficulties (C) bloom beautifully

01 소미는 '나는 전에 본 적이 있어.'라고 하고 있다.

02 소미가 '우선 전시회부터 보자.'라고 하고 있다.

03 뒤에 나오는 비교급 more interesting을 수식하고 있으므로 very를 much나 even, far, a lot, still 등으로 고쳐야 한다. very는 비교급을 수식할 수 없다.

04 (1) possible은 impossible로, (2) women, careless, really 등의 활용에 주의한다. 의미상 주어에 알맞은 전치사 for와 of의 구분에 유의하여 영작한다.

05 내용상 '내가 그의 상황이었다면, 나는 결코 똑같은 일을 할 수 없었을 텐데'가 빈칸에 적절하다. 가정법 과거완료 시제이므로 'If I had been'을 종속절에, 주절에는 'could have done'인데, never는 조동사 바로 뒤에 오는 것에 유의한다.

06 남자가 하늘에 대고 외쳤을 때 얼음이 녹았고, 잉어 세 마리가 갑자기 물 밖으로 나왔다.

07 '신선한 물고기를 먹을 수 있다면 좋겠구나.'라는 어머니의 말에 남자는 물고기를 잡기 위해 강으로 나갔다. to부정사를 사용하라고 했으므로 to부정사의 부사적 용법의 '목적'을 이용한다.

08 강이 완전히 얼어붙어 있었기 때문이었다.

09 so ~ that: 너무 ~해서 …하다 cry out to: ~에 대고 소리치다

10 despite+명사(구): ~에도 불구하고

11 연꽃은 어려움에도 불구하고 정의를 위해 싸우는 사람의 의지를 상징한다. 그것들은 진흙투성이의 연못에서 자라지만 여전히 아름답게 꽃을 피운다.

창의사고력 서술형 문제 p.108

|모범답안|

01 (1) A: Which plate do you prefer, the green one or the white one?
B: I prefer the green one. It seems to me that it's more unique. How about you?
A: I prefer the green one, too.

(2) A: Which painting do you prefer, the one on the left or the one on the right?
B: I prefer the one on the right. It seems to me that the cat in it is cuter. How about you?
A: I prefer the one on the right, too.
(3) A: Which food do you prefer, Tteokbokki or Gimbap?
B: I prefer Tteokbokki. It seems to me that it's more delicious. How about you?
A: I prefer Tteokbokki, too.

02 (A) *Water Lilies*: *The Clouds*
(A) *Water Lilies*: *The Clouds*
(B) Claude Monet (C) the reflection of clouds
(D) water lilies
(E) the colors are beautiful and the scene looks peaceful
(F) as a mirror

단원별 모의고사

p.109~112

01 (s)ociety 02 loyalty 03 object 04 ⑤
05 (1) Bend your knees when you stretch.
(2) The boy suddenly appeared from behind the tree.
(3) The dove represents peace.
06 Which one do you prefer to see
07 It seems to me that *Batman* will be much more fun.
08 They will see the Korean mask exhibition.
09 They will watch the show at 6 o'clock.
10 ⑤ 11 ④ 12 ④
13 (1) It is not easy for her to move the heavy table alone.
(2) It is impossible for him to take animals on an airplane.
(3) It is rude of Angelina not to show respect for other players.
14 ⑤ 15 ⑤ 16 ⑤
17 (A) appear (B) the values
18 It was popular in the late Joseon dynasty.
19 ③
20 The ice melted, and three carp suddenly came out of the water.
21 the fish for 22 against → for 23 ④

01 동의어 관계이다. difficulty: 어려움, 고난 – hardship: 곤란, 고충, community: 지역사회, 공동체 – society: 사회
02 '어떤 사람이나 어떤 것에 대해 지지하는 감정'은 'loyalty(충성, 충실)'가 적절하다. 군인들은 국가에 충성을 맹세했다.
03 '보거나 만질 수 있는 것'은 'object(물건, 물체)'가 적절하다. 하늘에 이상한 물체가 있다.
04 • represent: 나타내다, 보여 주다, 상징하다. 음표는 악음을 나타낸다. • melt: 녹다. 눈이 녹기 시작하고 있었다. • express: 표현하다, 나타내다
05 (1) bend: 굽다, 구부리다 (2) suddenly: 갑자기 appear: 나타나다 from behind: ~ 뒤에서 (3) dove: 비둘기 represent: 나타내다, 상징하다 peace: 평화
06 prefer는 'like more[better]'나 'want more' 대신 쓸 수 있다.
07 'It seems (to me) that ~'로 자신의 의견을 말할 수 있다.
08 소미가 글의 마지막 부분에서 '그래. 우선 전시회부터 보자.'라고 하고 있다.
09 Eric이 '6시 공연을 보자.'라고 하자 소미가 '그래. 우선 전시회부터 보자.'라고 하고 있다.
10 6시 공연을 볼 것이다.
11 ④의 밑줄 친 it은 인칭대명사이다. 거리를 나타내는 비인칭 주어와 혼동하는 것에 유의한다. 나머지는 모두 가주어, 진주어의 it으로 사용되었다.
12 ④의 if만이 간접의문문의 명사절을 이끄는 접속사이며, 나머지는 모두 가정법의 부사절을 이끄는 종속접속사이다.
13 to부정사 또는 동명사가 주어인 문장을 '가주어-진주어' 구조로 표현할 때, 일반적으로 'It ~ for+의미상의 주어+to V' 형태로 표현하는데, 사람의 성질이나 태도를 나타내는 형용사가 있을 때는 for 대신 of를 쓴다. (1), (2)는 'for+의미상의 주어' 형태로, (3)은 무례하다는 뜻이므로 of를 쓴다.
14 <보기>의 would는 가정법의 주절에서 쓰이는 조동사이며, 쓰임이 같은 것은 ⑤이다. "내가 당신이라면 그 쓸모없이 비싼 가방들은 사지 않을 텐데." ① 공손한 부탁 ② will의 과거시제 ③ 과거의 습관적 행위 ④ would like to = want to
15 '잉어가 없다면, 그는 어머니가 회복하도록 도울 수 없을 텐데.'라는 문장이다. '~가 없다면'은 If it were not for = Were it not for = Without = But for 등으로 표현하며, ⑤ 'Had it not been for'는 'If it had not been for'에서 if를 생략하고 도치된 표현으로서 가정법 과거완료시제에 사용한다.
16 한자 효(孝)와 잉어, 거문고, 부채가 있는 것은 ⑤번이다.
17 그것들은 문자도에 나오는 여덟 개의 한자이고, 그것들은 조선 시대 사람들에게 중요했던 가치들을 나타낸다.
18 '이런 종류의 그림은 문자도이며, 조선 시대 후기에 인기 있었던 민화의 한 종류이다.'라고 했다.
19 문맥상 disappointed가 가장 적절하다. ② 아주 기뻐하는, ④ 만족한, ⑤ 무관심한, 냉담한
20 그러자 얼음이 녹았고, 잉어 세 마리가 갑자기 물 밖으로 나왔다.
21 cook은 간접목적어를 직접목적어 다음에 쓸 때 전치사 for를 붙인다.
22 'fight against'는 '~에 대항하여 싸우다'라는 뜻이고, 'fight for'는 '~을 위해 싸우다'라는 뜻이므로 'fight for'로 쓰는 것이 적절하다.
23 '문자도는 조선 시대 사람들에게 그림 그 이상이었다.'라고 했다.

Finding the Good in Your Friends

교과서 Reading

확인문제 p.116

1 T 2 F

확인문제 p.117

1 T 2 F

교과서 확인학습 A p.118~120

01 Compliment
03 last
04 a piece of paper
05 Compliments for, last activity
06 pick
08 each other
09 whose name
10 got
11 to say
12 What about
13 looking worried
14 compliment him on
15 sits at his desk
16 have to find
18 talking with
19 except for
20 what to compliment
21 carefully
22 should be
23 he's
24 washes
25 a compliment
26 does that
27 again
28 I'm sure
30 an accident
31 is stuck
32 with arms in the air
33 Stay still
34 hurts
35 Let
36 comes back
37 put, on
39 calm
40 working
41 coming out of
43 eating dinner
44 what happened
45 a little accident
46 got stuck in
47 get, out
48 pulled it out
49 Messy, creative
50 a compliment
51 Sure
53 complimenting each other
54 what compliment
55 cheerful
56 fair
57 of you
58 hear from you
59 picked
60 hesitating
61 shyly
62 What made you think
63 pause, the other day, by using
64 creative
65 Nobody else
66 also
67 confidently
68 the best compliment ever

교과서 확인학습 B p.121~123

1 The Best Compliment Ever
2 Scene 1
3 It is the last week of school.
4 Each student has just picked a piece of paper with a name on it.
5 Ms. Kemp: "Compliments for Classmates" will be our last activity of the school year.
6 Did everyone pick a name?
7 Class: Yes, Ms. Kemp.
8 Students are talking to each other.
9 Beth: So, whose name did you pick?
10 Lucy: (smiling) I got Boyd.
11 I have a lot to say about him.
12 What about you, Beth?
13 Beth: (looking worried) Uh, I picked Peter's name.
14 Lucy: Peter? Oh, no! It won't be easy to find something to compliment him on.
15 Steve: Yeah. He doesn't talk much and just sits at his desk all day long.
16 Beth: (scratching her head) Well, I'll have to find something.
17 Scene 2
18 Beth is at home talking with her parents about the activity.
19 Beth: Everyone has long lists of compliments for other classmates, except for me.
20 I don't know what to compliment Peter on.
21 Mom: Think carefully.
22 There should be something.
23 Beth: Well, he's clean.
24 He washes his face every day.

25 Mom: That's not a compliment.

26 Everybody does that.

27 Dad: Try again.

28 I'm sure you can find something good to say about him.

29 Scene 3

30 The next day, there is an accident at school.

31 Boyd's foot is stuck in a bicycle stand.

32 Boyd: (with arms in the air) Help! I need help!

33 Beth: Stay still. I'm trying to pull your foot out.

34 Boyd: (screaming) Ouch! That hurts!

35 Peter: Let me help. Just a minute.

36 Peter runs to the school's kitchen and comes back with butter.

37 Peter: I'm going to put this butter on your foot.

38 Boyd: What? Butter?

39 Peter: Just stay calm.

40 Beth: (pointing to Boyd's foot) Wow! It's working!

41 Boyd's foot is coming out of the stand.

42 Scene 4

43 Beth is eating dinner with her parents.

44 She tells them about what happened to Boyd.

45 Beth: There was a little accident at school today.

46 Boyd's foot got stuck in a bicycle stand.

47 Mom: Oh, no! So how did he get his foot out?

48 Beth: Peter put butter on his foot and then pulled it out.

49 Dad: That was really creative. Messy but creative.

50 Beth: Hmm. Creative? Can that be a compliment, Dad?

51 Dad: Sure.

52 Scene 5

53 It is the last day of school, and the students are complimenting each other.

54 Ms. Kemp: Joanne, what compliment do you have for Beth?

55 Joanne: Beth, you're always cheerful.

56 You're also kind and fair to everybody.

57 Beth: Thanks, Joanne. It's so nice of you to say so.

58 Ms. Kemp: Beth, let's hear from you now.

59 You picked Peter's name.

60 Beth: (hesitating) Well, I think Peter is creative. Peter, you're … uh … creative.

61 Peter: (shyly) Really?

62 Ms. Kemp: What made you think Peter is creative?

63 Beth: (after a long pause) When Boyd's foot got stuck in the bicycle stand the other day, Peter got it out by using butter.

64 That was creative.

65 Boyd: Yeah! Nobody else thought of doing that.

66 Steve: I didn't know that. Well, then, I also think he's creative.

67 Beth: (confidently) Yeah, Peter, you ARE creative!

68 Peter: Thanks, Beth! It's the best compliment ever!

서술형 실전문제

p.124~125

01 out / out　　02 accident / accident

03 (1) air (2) confidently (3) hesitate (4) scratch

04 (1) compliment (2) hurt (3) calm

05 (w)ork　　06 messy

07 (1) wonder whose name you picked

(2) what to compliment David on

(3) What made you think that

(4) about what happened to Tom

08 for → of

09 (A) last (B) Compliments (C) looking

10 a piece of paper

11 She picked Boyd's name.

12 stuck　　13 calmly → calm

14 (A) butter (B) worked

01 • come out of: ~에서 나오다. 당신이 누구든 거기서 나와. • pull out: 빠져나가다[나오다]. 그 사업은 비용이 너무 많이 들어서 우리는 손을 떼야 했다.

02 • accident: 사고. 어젯밤에 자동차 사고가 있었다. • by accident: 우연히. 우리는 공항에서 우연히 만났다.

03 (1) in the air: 공중에. 그 도시 상공에는 매연이 떠 있었다. (2) confidently: 자신 있게. 그는 모든 일을 자기가 책임지겠다고 호언했다. (3) hesitate: 망설이다, 주저하다. 나는 조금도 망설이지 않고 그 직장을 잡았다. (4) scratch: 긁다. 네가 차 긁는 거 아빠가 보셨어.

04 (1) 반의어 관계이다. deep: 깊은, shallow: 얕은, criticism: 비평, 비판, compliment: 칭찬, 찬사 (2) 반의어 관계이다. appear: 나타나다 disappear: 사라지다, heal: 고치다, 낫게 하다, hurt: 다치게 하다 (3) 동의어 관계이다. long: 긴, lengthy: 긴, 기다란, cool: 냉정한, 침착한, calm: 침착한, 차분한

05 work: 효과가 있다. 성공적이거나 효과가 있거나 만족할 만하

다. 그 약은 효험이 전혀 없었다.

06 messy: 지저분한, 엉망인

07 '의문사'가 들어가는 다양한 문장 구조이다. (1) '간접의문문'의 어순은 '의문사+주어+동사'이다. (2) '의문사+to부정사' 구조로서 'what to V'는 '무엇을 V해야 할지'라는 뜻이다. (3) '의문사 What이 주어'가 되어 'What made you think that'의 형태이다. 직역을 하면 '무엇이 당신을 그렇게 생각하게 만들었는가'라는 의미로서 '왜 그렇게 생각하게 되었는지'라는 뜻이다. (4) 간접의문문에서 '의문사가 주어'일 때는 어순이 그대로이다.

08 'to부정사'의 '의미상의 주어'는 일반적으로 전치사 for를 쓰지만, 형용사가 '사람의 성격 또는 성질'을 나타낼 때는 of를 쓴다. *thoughtful: 사려 깊은, 자상한

09 (A) '마지막' 주라고 해야 하므로 last가 적절하다. latest: 최근의, (B) 학급 친구들 '칭찬하기'라고 해야 하므로 Compliments가 적절하다. complement: 보완물, (C) look은 수동태로 쓸 수 없으므로 looking이 적절하다.

10 '종이 한 장'을 가리킨다.

11 Lucy는 'Boyd'를 뽑았다.

12 stick의 과거분사이자 형용사 형태인 stuck을 쓰는 것이 적절하다. stuck: (~에 빠져) 움직일 수 없는[꼼짝 못하는]

13 stay의 보어로 형용사를 쓰는 것이 적절하다.

14 Boyd의 발이 자전거 거치대에 끼어 더 이상 움직이지 않게 되었을 때, Peter가 Boyd의 발에 '버터'를 발랐다. 그것은 '효과가 있었고' Boyd의 발이 거치대에서 빠져나왔다.

단원별 예상문제 p.126~130

01 (1) stuck (2) creative (3) compliment
(4) work(ed)

02 ② 03 ⑤ 04 ③

05 (1) except for (2) all day long (3) shyly

06 ④

07 ⑤

08 (1) The bus bumps a tree and all the people scream and run away.
(2) What made you decide on a career as a vet?
(3) I'm awfully sorry about that problem the other day

09 will not be easy to find something to compliment her on

10 (1) how you should find something good about others
(2) what he should put on his foot to pull it out of the bicycle stand
(3) how I should open the safe

11 ⑤

12 her finger got stuck in the bottle, Brian got it out by using butter

13 including → except for

14 I should 15 **모든 사람이 매일 세수를 한다**

16 ④ 17 ③

18 putting (the) butter on Boyd's foot

19 ⑤ 20 ①

21 pulled out it → pulled it out

22 Peter put butter on his foot and then pulled it out.

23 It's so nice of you to say so.

24 Why 25 (A) creative (B) got stuck

01 (1) stuck: (~에 빠져) 움직일 수 없는. 우리는 교통 체증 속에 갇혀 있었다. (2) creative: 창의적인, 창조적인. 상상의 나래를 있는 대로 펼쳐서 창의력을 발휘해 보아라. (3) compliment: 칭찬, 찬사. 그녀는 그가 하는 말을 칭찬으로 받아들였다. (4) work: 효과가 있다. 내 계획이 효과가 있어서 그들이 동의하게 만들었다.

02 ②의 영영풀이는 point의 영영풀이이다. ① accident: 사고, 불운한 일; 특히 손상이나 부상을 일으키는 것 ② point: 가리키다. 누군가가 그것을 알아채도록 하기 위해 손가락을 사람이나 물건을 향해 내밀다 ③ compliment 칭찬, 찬사. 누군가에게 당신이 그의 외모를 좋아한다거나 그의 자질을 인정한다거나 그가 한 것을 지지한다는 것을 보여주기 위해 하는 공손한 언급 ④ scream: 비명을 지르다. 매우 크고 높은 음조로 소리치다 ⑤ hesitate: 망설이다, 주저하다. 불확실하거나 내키지 않아서 잠시 멈추거나 억제하다

03 compliment: 칭찬, praise: 칭찬, 찬양. ③ thrift: 검약, 검소

04 ③은 'ly', 나머지는 모두 '명사+y'로 형용사가 되는 어휘이다. ① stormy: 폭풍우의. 하늘은 폭풍이 올 것처럼 보인다. ② messy: 지저분한, 엉망인. 나는 이렇게 어질러진 책상에서는 아무것도 찾을 수 없다. ③ friendly: 친절한[우호적인]. 그 호텔 직원들은 친절하고 세심하다. ④ greedy: 욕심 많은. 그 탐욕스러운 남자는 가방에 대해 너무 비싼 값을 요구했다. ⑤ thrifty: 검소한. 지금 그들에게는 많은 돈이 있지만 늘 그렇듯이 여전히 검소하다.

05 (1) except for: ~을 제외하고 (2) all day long: 하루 종일 (3) shyly: 수줍게, 부끄러워하며

06 (A) pull out: 빠져나가다[나오다]. 우리 팀은 전반전 내내 부진을 면치 못했다. (B) stay calm: 침착함을 유지하다. 진정하고 참을성 있게 기다려야 해요.

07 <보기>의 'to부정사'는 '형용사적' 용법으로 쓰여서 앞의 a lot

을 뒤에서 수식한다. ⑤번의 'to부정사'는 부사적 용법으로 사용되었다.

08 (1) scream: 비명을 지르다 (2) What made you ~?: 왜 ~했니? (3) the other day: 일전에, 최근에

09 가주어로 it을 이용하고 진주어로 to부정사를 쓴다. '~에 관해'라는 의미로 on을 마지막에 붙이는 것에 주의한다.

10 '의문사+to부정사'는 '의문사+주어+should+동사원형'으로 바꿀 수 있다.

11 'What makes you think (that)+주어+동사?'를 직역하면, '무엇이 당신으로 하여금 ~하다고 생각하도록 만드는가?'가 되어 '왜 그런 생각을 하느냐'와 같은 의미이다. ⑤와 같이 think, believe 등이 있을 때, 의문사는 문두로 보내고, 간접의문문의 어순을 유지하는 것이 적절하다.

12 '병에 끼었다'는 'got stuck'으로, '빼냈다'는 'got it out'으로 표현하여, get을 두 번 쓰는 것과 '전치사 by+동명사'의 형태, 대명사 it의 위치 등에 유의하여, 영작한다.

13 저를 '제외한' 모두라고 해야 하므로 including을 except for로 고치는 것이 적절하다. including: ~을 포함하여, except for: ~을 제외하고

14 의문사 to부정사 = 의문사+주어+should+동사원형

15 do that은 앞에 나오는 washes his face every day를 받는다.

16 엄마는 Peter가 매일 세수를 한다고 말하는 것은 '칭찬이 아니라고' 했다.

17 ⓐ와 ③: 가만히 있는, 고요한(형용사), ①, ⑤: 아직(부사), ② (비교급을 강조하여) 훨씬(부사), ④ 그럼에도 불구하고(부사)

18 'Boyd의 발에 버터를 바른 것'을 가리킨다.

19 Boyd가 Peter에 대해 어떻게 느꼈는지는 대답할 수 없다. ① Boyd's foot got stuck in a bicycle stand. ② In a bicycle stand. ③ Peter did. ④ By putting butter on Boyd's foot.

20 ①번 앞 문장의 a little accident에 주목한다. 주어진 문장의 내용을 가리키는 것이므로 ①번이 적절하다.

21 'pull out'은 '동사+부사'로 이루어진 구동사로, 목적어가 명사일 경우에는 부사의 앞과 뒤에 모두 올 수 있지만 목적어가 인칭대명사일 경우에는 동사와 부사 사이에만 올 수 있다.

22 'Peter가 Boyd의 발에 버터를 바르고 나서 발을 당겨서 꺼낸 것'을 가리킨다.

23 사람의 성질을 나타내는 형용사 nice가 있으므로, to부정사의 의미상의 주어를 of you로 쓰는 것이 적절하다.

24 'What made you think ~?'는 '무엇 때문에 ~라는 생각을 하게 되었니?'라고 이유를 묻는 표현으로, 'Why did you think ~?'로 바꾸어 쓸 수 있다.

25 Beth는 일전에 Boyd의 발이 자전거 거치대에 '끼었을' 때, Peter가 버터를 사용해서 그의 발을 꺼냈기 때문에, Peter가 '창의적'이라고 생각했다.

교과서 파헤치기

Lesson 7

단어 TEST Step 1 p.02

01 총계, 총액　02 예측하다　03 영향을 미치다
04 주로　05 복잡한　06 전문가
07 독감　08 삽입하다　09 빌리다
10 자취, 발자국, 흔적　11 예측하다, 예보하다
12 분석하다　13 예방　14 범죄
15 확산, 전파　16 잠금을 풀다　17 증상
18 의미 있는, 중요한　19 산업, 공업
20 감사하다, 감상하다　21 더 이상의, 추가의
22 거대한, (크기 · 양 · 정도가) 막대한
23 알아보다, 확인하다, 식별하다　24 구매
25 개선하다, 향상하다
26 성장하다, 발달하다　27 다양한
28 끝없는, 무한한　29 피하다, 방지하다　30 방법
31 추천하다, 권하다　32 ~을 전송하다, 업로드하다
33 포함하다　34 경기력, 수행, 성과　35 확실히, 분명히
36 ~에 초점을 맞추다　37 ~함으로써
38 ~할 것 같다　39 ~의 양/수량
40 ~ 덕분에, ~ 때문에　41 결정하다
42 역할을 하다　43 ~하는 데 사용되다

단어 TEST Step 2 p.03

01 industry　02 crime　03 expert
04 flu　05 huge　06 identify
07 various　08 develop　09 prevention
10 wisely　11 improve　12 analyze
13 include　14 amount　15 forecast
16 traffic　17 purchase　18 mainly
19 further　20 predict　21 endless
22 meaningful　23 insert　24 avoid
25 recommend　26 method　27 rent
28 spread　29 influence　30 symptom
31 trace　32 appreciate　33 upload
34 unlock　35 for sure　36 play a role
37 the amount of ~　38 be likely to ~
39 focus on　40 make a decision
41 thanks to ~　42 more and more
43 be used to+동사원형

단어 TEST Step 3 p.04

1 method, 방법　2 influence, 영향을 주다
3 analyze, 분석하다　4 rent, 빌리다　5 avoid, 피하다
6 identify, 확인하다　7 predict, 예측하다
8 recommend, 추천하다, 권하다
9 performance, 수행, 성과　10 database, 데이터베이스
11 purchase, 구매, 구매품　12 symptom, 증상, 징후
13 industry, 산업　14 develop, 발전시키다, 성장하다
15 spread, 확산, 전파　16 communication, 의사소통

대화문 TEST Step 1 p.05~07

Listen and Talk A 1

tell, how to add, to, transportation / First, put, in, Second, choose, amount, to add / Last, insert, into / simple

Listen and Talk A 2

know how to use / First, choose / did, next / put in, take, out / Got it

Listen and Talk A 3

rent, tell, how to use, application / log in to, touch it / what / to unlock, with / appreciate, help

Listen and Talk B

return, know how to do / simple, insert, into, put, in / Then, take, out / appreciate / add, to, know how to do / simple, First, Second, choose, amount / Then insert / appreciate, help / to buy, know how to do / simple, First, Second, put in / Then take, out / appreciate

Listen and Talk C

what's, for / that / tell, how to use / place, on, robot's screen / type, title, looking for, press / Is that all / Then, it, front desk / get / easy, isn't it / amazing

Listen and Talk D

Let, how to use, First, insert, into, Then, Last, out of

Talk and Play

know how to make / First, put / Then, pour / Last, take, out after, minutes / got it, appreciate

Review 1

how to plant / cut, into, pieces, dig, in / put, pieces in, cover, with dirt / sounds simple

Review 2

tell, how to use / put, on, copy machine, choose, the number of / what / Press, appreciate

대화문 TEST Step 2

p.08~10

Listen and Talk A 1

B: Excuse me. Can you tell me how to add money to my transportation card?

G: Of course. First, put your card in the machine. Second, choose the amount of money you want to add.

B: OK.

G: Last, insert your money into the machine.

B: That sounds simple. Thanks.

Listen and Talk A 2

B: I want to buy a snack. Do you know how to use this snack machine?

G: Yeah. First, choose the snack you want.

B: I already did. What's next?

G: Just put in the money. Then take the snack out.

B: Got it. Thanks.

Listen and Talk A 3

G: Excuse me. I want to rent a bike. Can you tell me how to use this application?

M: Sure. First, log in to the application. Then find the RENT button and touch it.

G: Then what?

M: Then the application will give you a number to unlock a bike with.

G: Thank you. I really appreciate your help.

Listen and Talk B

A: Excuse me. I want to return these books. Do you know how to do it?

B: Sure. It's simple. First, insert the library card into the machine. Second, put the books in this box.

A: OK.

B: Then just take your card out.

A: I really appreciate your help.

A: Excuse me. I want to add money to my transportation card. Do you know how to do it?

B: Sure. It's simple. First, put your card in the machine. Second, choose the amount of money.

A: OK.

B: Then insert the money.

A: I really appreciate your help.

A: Excuse me. I want to buy a snack. Do you know how to do it?

B: Sure. It's simple. First, choose the snack. Second, put in the money.

A: OK.

B: Then take the snack out.

A: I really appreciate your help.

Listen and Talk C

G: Excuse me, but what's this robot for?

B: Oh, it's a robot that finds books for you.

G: Really? Can you tell me how to use it?

B: Sure. First, place your library card on the robot's screen.

G: OK.

B: Second, type the title of the book you're looking for and then press ENTER.

G: Is that all?

B: Yes. Then, the robot will find the book and take it to the front desk.

G: So I can just go to the front desk and get the book?

B: Right. It's so easy, isn't it?

G: Yes, it's really amazing. Thank you.

Listen and Talk D

Let me tell you how to use a drink machine. First, insert money into the machine. Then, choose the drink you want. Last, take the drink out of the machine. It's easy.

Talk and Play

A: Do you know how to make tea?

B: Sure. First, put a tea bag in a cup.

A: OK.

B: Then, pour hot water in the cup.

A: And then?

B: Last, take the tea bag out after 3 minutes.

A: I got it. I really appreciate your help.

Review 1

G: Can you tell me how to plant a potato?

B: Sure. First, cut a potato into small pieces. Second, dig holes in the ground.

G: Then?

B: Then put the potato pieces in the holes and cover the holes with dirt.

G: That sounds simple. Thanks.

Review 2

B: Excuse me. Can you tell me how to use this machine?

G: Sure. First, put the paper on the copy machine. Then choose the paper size and the number of copies.

B: Then what?

G: Press the START button.

B: Thank you. I really appreciate your help.

본문 TEST Step 1 p.11~12

01 Living with
02 been surprised, recommended for
03 Many, looked interesting 04 So, what you liked
05 all possible because of 06 What is
07 data sets, big, complex
08 As, develops, amount, much
09 mainly, almost, leaves, trace
10 example, upload, purchases, part
11 Simply collecting, however, enough
12 has, analyzed, done, experts
13 methods, analyse, draw, results
14 results, used, decisions, predict
15 How, influencing, lives
16 influencing almost, parts, lives
17 customers' needs, sell, products
18 avoid heavy traffic
19 uses, endless, interesting examples
20 Disease Forecast
21 professionals, forecast, disease, experts
22 possible thanks to
23 comes, buy, flu medicine
24 search online, flu symptoms
25 analyzed wisely, spread, predicted
26 Improving Performance 27 sports fan
28 improving, performance, making, exciting
29 famous example, Germany's national
30 collecting, analyzing, huge amount
31 included, much, ran, long
32 With, help, improve, performance
33 Crime Prevention
34 Thanks, predict crime, happens
35 Through, analysis, hot spots
36 identifies, crime, likely, happen
37 prevent further, focusing, predicts
38 has already changed, greatly
39 industry go from here
40 sure, experts, play, role

본문 TEST Step 2 p.13~14

01 Living with
02 been surprised, recommended for
03 looked interesting 04 what you liked
05 possible because of 06 What is
07 data sets, are, complex
08 As, develops, amount of, getting much greater
09 mainly because, leaves a trace
10 upload on your blog, your purchases, all part of
11 Simply collecting data, however
12 has to be analyzed, done by
13 Using, analyze, draw meaningful results
14 can be used, to predict
15 How, influencing, lives 16 almost all parts
17 understand their customers' needs, sell more products
18 avoid heavy traffic
19 endless, interesting examples
20 Forecast 21 just as, forecast
22 thanks to
23 comes, will buy, flu medicine
24 search online about
25 is analyzed wisely, spread, be predicted
26 Improving Performance 27 sports fan
28 is improving, making, exciting
29 national soccer team
30 built, collecting, analyzing, huge amount
31 how much, how long
32 With the help of, able to improve
33 Prevention 34 Thanks to, happens
35 Through, crime hot spots
36 identifies, is most likely to happen
37 further crime by focusing, predicts
38 has already changed, greatly
39 go from here 40 play, role, lives

본문 TEST Step 3 p.15~16

1 빅데이터와 함께 살아가기
2 당신은 온라인 서점을 방문해서 그 서점이 당신을 위해 추천한 책들을 보고 놀란 적이 있는가?
3 그것들 중에 많은 것들이 당신에게 흥미로워 보였다.
4 그 서점은 당신이 무엇을 좋아하는지 어떻게 알았을까?
5 이것은 모두 빅데이터 때문에 가능하다.
6 빅데이터는 무엇인가?
7 빅데이터는 매우 크고 복잡한 데이터 집합이다.
8 정보 통신 기술이 발달함에 따라 우리가 갖고 있는 정보의 양도 이전보다 훨씬 더 많아지고 있다.
9 이것은 주로 우리가 온라인상에서 하는 거의 모든 것들이 흔적을 남기기 때문이다.
10 예를 들어, 당신이 블로그에 올린 사진들과 온라인 상점에서의 구매 기록들이 모두 빅데이터의 일부가 된다.
11 하지만 단순히 데이터를 수집하는 것만으로는 충분하지 않다.
12 빅데이터는 분석되어야 하고, 이것은 빅데이터 전문가들에 의해서 이루어진다.

13 다양한 방법들을 사용하여 전문가들은 빅데이터를 분석하고, 그것으로부터 의미 있는 결과들을 도출한다.
14 그런 다음, 이런 결과들은 결정을 하거나 또는 미래를 예측하는 데 사용될 수 있다.
15 빅데이터는 어떻게 우리 삶에 영향을 미치고 있는가?
16 빅데이터는 우리 삶의 거의 모든 부분에 영향을 미치고 있다.
17 그것은 회사들이 소비자들이 필요로 하는 것을 더 잘 이해하고 그들이 더 많은 상품을 팔도록 도와준다.
18 그것은 사람들이 교통 체증을 피하도록 도와주기도 한다.
19 그것의 활용은 끝이 없고, 여기에 몇 가지 흥미로운 예들이 있다.
20 질병 예측
21 당신은 날씨 전문가가 날씨를 예측하는 것과 같이 건강 전문가들이 현재 질병을 예측할 수 있다는 것을 알고 있는가?
22 이것은 빅데이터 덕분에 가능하다.
23 예를 들어서 독감의 계절이 오면, 사람들은 독감 약을 더 많이 구입할 것이다.
24 그들은 또한 온라인상에서 독감 증상들을 더 찾아볼 것이다.
25 만약 이런 종류의 데이터를 지혜롭게 분석한다면, 독감의 확산을 예측할 수 있다.
26 스포츠에서의 경기력 향상
27 당신은 스포츠 팬인가?
28 빅데이터는 스포츠를 더 흥미롭게 만들면서, 선수들의 경기력을 향상하고 있다.
29 유명한 사례로 독일 국가 대표 축구팀이 있다.
30 그 팀은 선수들에 관한 엄청난 양의 데이터를 모으고 분석함으로써, 데이터베이스를 구축했다.
31 예를 들어 데이터는 각각의 선수들이 얼마나 많이 달렸고, 얼마나 오랫동안 공을 소유했는지도 포함했다.
32 이 데이터베이스의 도움으로 독일 국가 대표 축구팀은 경기력을 향상할 수 있었고, 2014년 월드컵에서 우승할 수 있었다.
33 범죄 예방
34 빅데이터 덕분에 경찰은 이제 범죄가 발생하기 전에 범죄를 예측할 수 있다.
35 범죄의 유형, 시간 및 장소에 관한 빅데이터의 분석을 통해, 경찰은 범죄 다발 지역의 지도를 만들 수 있다.
36 이 지도는 범죄가 언제, 어디에서 가장 많이 발생할 것 같은지를 알려 준다.
37 경찰은 이 지도가 예측하는 장소들과 시간대에 집중함으로써, 추가 범죄를 예방할 수 있다.
38 빅데이터는 이미 세계를 크게 변화시켰다.
39 그러면 빅데이터 산업은 여기에서부터 어디로 가게 될까?
40 누구도 확실히 알지는 못하지만, 전문가들은 빅데이터가 우리 삶에서 더욱 더 중요한 역할을 할 것이라는 데에는 동의한다.

본문 TEST Step 4-Step 5

p.17~21

1 Living with Big Data
2 Have you ever visited an online bookstore and been surprised by the books that the store recommended for you?
3 Many of them looked interesting to you.
4 So how did the bookstore know what you liked?
5 This is all possible because of big data.
6 What is big data?
7 Big data is data sets that are very big and complex.
8 As information and communication technology develops, the amount of data we have is getting much greater than before.
9 This is mainly because almost everything that we do online leaves a trace.
10 For example, the photos you upload on your blog and the records of your purchases at online stores are all part of big data.
11 Simply collecting data, however, is not enough.
12 Big data has to be analyzed, and this is done by big data experts.
13 Using various methods, experts analyze big data and draw meaningful results from it.
14 These results then can be used to make decisions or to predict the future.
15 How is big data influencing our lives?
16 Big data is influencing almost all parts of our lives.
17 It helps companies understand their customers' needs better and helps them sell more products.
18 It helps people avoid heavy traffic.
19 Its uses are endless, and here are some interesting examples.
20 Disease Forecast
21 Did you know that health professionals can now forecast a disease just as weather experts forecast the weather?
22 This is possible thanks to big data.
23 For example, when the flu season comes, people will buy more flu medicine.
24 They will also search online about flu symptoms more.
25 If this kind of data is analyzed wisely, the spread of the flu can be predicted.
26 Improving Performance in Sports
27 Are you a sports fan?
28 Well, big data is improving the performance of players, making sports more exciting.

29 A famous example is Germany's national soccer team.
30 The team built a database by collecting and analyzing a huge amount of data on players.
31 For example, the data included information about how much each player ran and how long he had the ball.
32 With the help of this database, Germany's national soccer team was able to improve its performance and win the 2014 World Cup.
33 Crime Prevention
34 Thanks to big data, police can now predict crime before it happens.
35 Through the analysis of big data about the type, time and place of crime, police can make a map of crime hot spots.
36 This map identifies when and where crime is most likely to happen.
37 Police can prevent further crime by focusing on the areas and the times this map predicts.
38 Big data has already changed the world greatly.
39 So where will the big data industry go from here?
40 Nobody knows for sure, but experts agree that big data will play a more and more important role in our lives.

구석구석지문 TEST Step 1 p.22

After You Read A Read and Complete

1. Health professionals, forecast the spread, by analyzing, flu symptoms
2. By collecting, analyzing a huge amount of, was able to improve
3. Through the analysis, crime hot spots, to prevent further crime

Around the World

1. late, will arrive in, minutes
2. Last time, missed, so let's review them
3. What's the weather like
4. going to rain, Take
5. is making my life, much easier

Think and Write

1. Teens' Free
2. teemagers, free time activities
3. The results, teenagers want to do the most is traveling
4. to travel in their free time
5. the free time activity, is watching TV
6. watch, in their free time
7. Looking at, a big gap, what the teenagers want to, what they actually do

구석구석지문 TEST Step 2 p.23

After You Read A Read and Complete

1. Health professionals can now forecast the spread of the flu by analyzing the sales of flu medicine and online searches about flu symptoms.
2. By collecting and analyzing a huge amount of data on players, Germany's national soccer team was able to improve its performance and win the 2014 World Cup.
3. Through the analysis of big data, police can make a map of crime hot spots and use it to prevent further crime.

Around the World

1. Yuna: We're not late. The bus will arrive in 4 minutes.
2. Computer: Last time, you missed question numbers 3 and 5, so let's review them first.
3. Yuna: What's the weather like tomorrow?
4. AI: It's going to rain. Take your umbrella.
5. Yuna: Big data is making my life so much easier!

Think and Write

1. Teens' Free Time Activities
2. We asked 100 teemagers about their free time activities.
3. The results show that the free time activity the teenagers want to do the most is traveling.
4. 34% said that they want to travel in their free time.
5. However, the free time activity they actually do the most is watching TV.
6. 39% said that they watch TV in their free time.
7. Looking at the results, we see that there is a big gap between what the teenagers want to do and what they actually do in their free time.

Lesson 8

단어 TEST Step 1 p.24

01 녹다 02 갑자기 03 굴곡이 많은
04 따라서, 그러므로 05 굽다, 구부러지다
06 나타내다, 보여 주다, 상징하다 07 ~에도 불구하고
08 취소하다 09 상징하다 10 시대, 왕조
11 효과적으로 12 민화 13 가치, 중요성
14 충성, 충실 15 행동 16 얼어붙은
17 조화 18 아픈, 병든
19 ~하게 보이다, 나타나다 20 영향을 미치다
21 태도, 자세 22 상징적인, 상징하는
23 정의, 공정성 24 연꽃
25 진흙투성이의, 탁한, 흙탕물의
26 꽃을 피우다, 꽃이 피다 27 잉어
28 의지 29 글자 30 실망한, 낙담한
31 존경, 경의 32 사회 33 장식
34 어려움, 고난 35 특히, 특별히 36 다음과 같이
37 병이 나아지다, 회복하다 38 옛날에
39 ~보다 훨씬 많이 40 ~에게 …을 상기시키다
41 이런 이유로 42 ~ 때문에 43 ~ 직후에

단어 TEST Step 2 p.25

01 dynasty 02 effectively 03 appear
04 influence 05 loyalty 06 justice
07 bloom 08 carp 09 represent
10 bend 11 curvy 12 decoration
13 lotus flower 14 difficulty 15 suddenly
16 folk painting 17 respect 18 society
19 value 20 character 21 behavior
22 symbolize 23 muddy 24 will
25 cancel 26 symbolic 27 harmony
28 disappointed 29 attitude 30 bamboo
31 frozen 32 melt 33 despite
34 object 35 get well 36 right after ~
37 in particular 38 as follows 39 for this reason
40 much more than 41 remind ~ of …
42 once upon a time 43 so ~ that …

단어 TEST Step 3 p.26

1 bloom, 꽃을 피우다, 꽃이 피다 2 represent, 나타내다
3 symbol, 상징, 기호 4 object, 물건, 물체
5 attitude, 태도, 자세 6 remind, 상기시키다
7 behavior, 행동 8 symbolic, 상징적인
9 despite, ~에도 불구하고 10 frozen, 얼어붙은
11 loyalty, 충성, 충실 12 society, 사회
13 appear, 나타나다 14 bend, 굽다, 구부러지다
15 justice, 정의 16 dynasty, 왕조

대화문 TEST Step 1 p.27~29

Listen and Talk A 1

two paintings of cats, Aren't / are / both, the one, about / prefer, seems to me that, cuter

Listen and Talk A 2

Which, prefer / prefer, It seems, healthier choice / so, like, more / other

Listen and Talk A 3

old plates / Which one, prefer / to choose, better, about / Me, too, seems, that, unique

Listen and Talk A 4

you're going to, gift, How about / look nice / Which one, prefer, or, with / prefer, with, It seems to me

Listen and Talk B

Which, prefer / prefer, It, that, delicious / prefer, prefer, seems to me, healthier / Which, prefer, or / prefer / prefer, prefer, more calm / Which, or / prefer, more unique / prefer, prefer, simple but / Which, prefer, or, with / prefer, more / prefer, too, prefer, cute

Listen and Talk C

exhibitions, Which, more / prefer, that / course, much / so / just, also / never seen, before / before, sure / next to / let's watch / Let's, first

Listen and Talk D

prefer, more fun to learn, prefer, inventor like

Talk and Play

Which, prefer / prefer, It seems to / prefer, prefer, healthier

Review 1

to buy / great / Which one, prefer, or, with / prefer, with triangles, more unique

Review 2

Which, prefer / prefer, the healthier choice / I heard / order, hungry

Review 3

Which one, more / prefer, this / much / let's go

대화문 TEST Step 2 p.30~32

Listen and Talk A 1

G: Minho, look at these two paintings of cats here. Aren't they great?

B: Yes, they are.

G: They both are good, but I like the one on the left more. How about you?

B: I prefer the one on the right. It seems to me that the cat in it is cuter. I also like the bird in it.

Listen and Talk A 2

G: We can have Bibimbap or Galbitang. Which do you prefer?

B: I prefer Bibimbap. It seems to me that it's the healthier choice.

G: I think so, too. I also like Bibimbap more.

B: Let's order, then. I'm very hungry.

Listen and Talk A 3

G: Look at these two old plates, Steve. Aren't they beautiful?

B: Yes. Which one do you prefer, the green plate or the white plate?

G: Well, it's hard to choose, but I like the green one better. How about you?

B: Me, too. It seems to me that the green plate is more unique.

Listen and Talk A 4

G: Junsu, you said you're going to buy a gift for your sister. How about the bags here?

B: They look nice.

G: Which one do you prefer, the one with flowers or the one with animals?

B: I prefer the one with flowers. It seems to me that my sister will like it more.

Listen and Talk B

A: Which food do you prefer, Tteokbokki or Gimbap?

B: I prefer Tteokbokki. It seems to me that it's more delicious. How about you?

A: I prefer Tteokbokki, too. / I prefer Gimbap. It seems to me that it's healthier.

A: Which painting do you prefer, the one on the left or the one on the right?

B: I prefer the one on the right. It seems to me that the cat in it is cuter. How about you?

A: I prefer the one on the right, too. / I prefer the one on the left. It seems to me that it looks more calm.

A: Which plate do you prefer, the green one or the white one?

B: I prefer the green one. It seems to me that it's more unique. How about you?

A: I prefer the green one, too. / I prefer the white one. It seems to me that it's simple but beautiful.

A: Which bag do you prefer, the one with fish or the one with stars?

B: I prefer the one with stars. It seems to me that it's more my style. How about you?

A: I prefer the one with stars, too. / I prefer the one with fish. It seems to me that the fish are cute.

Listen and Talk C

G: There are two exhibitions we can go to. Which one do you want to see more, Eric?

B: I prefer the Korean mask exhibition. Is that OK, Somi?

G: Of course. And it seems to me that the mask exhibition will be much more interesting.

B: Do you think so?

G: Yes. Look at this poster. There isn't just an exhibition. There's also a mask dance show at 4:00 and 6:00.

B: Great! I've never seen a mask dance show before.

G: Well, I've seen a show before. I'm sure you'll like it.

B: So where is the show?

G: It's in Dasom Hall, next to the exhibition room.

B: It's 4:30 now, so let's watch the 6 o'clock show.

G: OK. Let's go see the exhibition first.

Listen and Talk D

I prefer science. It seems to me that it's more fun to learn. I also prefer it becauseI want to be a great inventor like Edison.

Talk and Play

A: Which do you prefer, Ramyeon or spaghetti?

B: I prefer Ramyeon. It seems to me that it's more delicious. How about you?

A: I prefer Ramyeon, too. / I prefer spaghetti. It seems to me that it's healthier.

Review 1

G: Joe, didn't you say you needed to buy a cap? How about these caps here?

B: They look great.

G: Which one do you prefer, the one with triangles or the one with flowers?

B: I prefer the one with triangles. It seems to me that it's more unique.

Review 2

B: We can have Gimbap or Tteokbokki. Which do you prefer, Jenny?

G: I prefer Gimbap. It seems to me that it's the healthier choice. How about you, Minsu?

B: I'll have Tteokbokki. I heard that the Tteokbokki here is very good.

G: Let's order, then. I'm very hungry.

Review 3

John: There are two movies we can see. Which one do you want to see more, Somi?

Somi: I prefer *Batman*. I saw *Spider-Man* last week. Is this OK, John?

John: Of course. It seems to me that *Batman* will be much more fun.

Somi: Good. Then, let's go and see it.

본문 TEST Step 1 p.33~34

01 Window into, Dynasty
02 at, on the right
03 see, Chinese character
04 also see, carp, fan
05 called, type, popular, late
06 there, usually, with, objects
07 One of, characters appears
08 represent, values, important, dynasty
09 animals, objects, just decorations
10 often, symbolic
11 paintings, symbolize respect, because
12 goes as follows
13 Once upon, time, with
14 became ill, couldn't, anything
15 On, would, could, fresh
16 went out, completely frozen
17 It, for, to catch
18 so disappointed that, to
19 melted, suddenly, out of
20 went back home, cooked
21 Then, got well
22 other examples, symbolic objects
23 bamboo, paintings, character, lotus
24 Bamboo does, bend
25 stays green in, kinds
26 For, reasons, symbolize loyalty
27 case, grow, muddy, bloom
28 will, fight, despite difficulties
29 much more than, to
30 reminded, influenced, behaviors, attitudes
31 In particular, for, tool
32 Through, importance, harmony, society

본문 TEST Step 2 p.35~36

01 into, Dynasty
02 Look at, on the right
03 see, Chinese character
04 see, carp
05 is called, a type of folk painting that was popular, late
06 usually, with, objects
07 One of, characters appears
08 represent, that were important to, Joseon dynasty
09 just decorations
10 often, symbolic
11 symbolize respect, because of
12 goes as follows
13 Once upon a time
14 became ill, anything
15 On, would be wonderful if I could eat fresh fish
16 went out to, was completely frozen
17 It, for him to catch any
18 so disappointed that, cried out to
19 melted, suddenly, out of
20 back home
21 got well
22 symbolic objects
23 in, of, lotus flowers in, of
24 bend
25 stays green in, kinds
26 For these reasons, came to symbolize loyalty to
27 In the case of, but still bloom beautifully
28 thus, will to fight for, despite difficulties
29 much more than, to
30 reminded, of, that, behaviors, attitudes
31 In particular, for
32 Through it, importance, harmony in, society

본문 TEST Step 3 p.37~38

1 문자도, 조선 시대를 보는 창
2 오른쪽에 있는 그림을 보라.
3 한자 효(孝)가 보이는가?
4 잉어, 거문고, 그리고 부채가 보이는가?
5 이런 종류의 그림은 문자도이며, 조선 시대 후기에 인기 있었던 민화의 한 종류이다.
6 문자도에는 보통 한자 하나가 동물이나 사물과 함께 있다.
7 문자도에는 여덟 개의 한자 중 하나가 나온다.
8 그것들은 효(孝), 제(悌), 충(忠), 신(信), 예(禮), 의(義), 염(廉), 치(恥)이고, 그것들은 조선 시대 사람들에게 중요했던 가치들을 나타낸다.
9 문자도에 있는 동물이나 사물은 단순한 장식이 아니다.
10 그것들은 종종 상징적이다.
11 예를 들어, '효' 그림 속에 있는 잉어는 옛이야기 때문에 부모님에 대한 존경심을 상징한다.

12 그 이야기는 다음과 같다.
13 옛날 옛적에 한 남자가 나이 드신 어머니와 살았다.
14 어느 겨울, 남자의 어머니는 병이 들어서 어떤 것도 먹을 수 없었다.
15 무척 추운 어느 날, 어머니는 남자에게 말했다. "신선한 물고기를 먹을 수 있다면 좋겠구나."
16 그 남자는 강으로 나갔지만, 강은 완전히 얼어붙어 있었다.
17 그가 그 어떤 물고기라도 잡는 것은 불가능했다.
18 남자는 몹시 낙담해서 하늘에 대고 외쳤다. "제가 어떻게 해야 하나요? 제발 저를 도와주세요."
19 그러자 얼음이 녹았고, 잉어 세 마리가 갑자기 물 밖으로 나왔다.
20 남자는 집으로 돌아가서 어머니를 위해 물고기들을 요리했다.
21 그러자 그의 어머니는 회복되었다.
22 문자도에 있는 상징적인 사물의 또 다른 예가 있다.
23 그것들은 글자 '충(忠)' 그림에 있는 대나무와 '의(義)' 그림에 있는 연꽃이다.
24 대나무는 구부러지지 않는다.
25 그것은 어떤 날씨에서도 푸르름을 유지한다.
26 이런 이유로 대나무는 왕에 대한 충성을 상징하게 되었다.
27 연꽃의 경우, 그것들은 진흙투성이의 연못에서 자라지만 여전히 아름답게 꽃을 피운다.
28 그래서 그 꽃들은 어려움에도 불구하고 정의를 위해 싸우는 사람의 의지를 상징하게 되었다.
29 문자도는 조선 시대 사람들에게 그림 그 이상이었다.
30 그것은 그들에게 자신들의 행동과 태도에 큰 영향을 미치는 중요한 가치를 상기시켰다.
31 특히 아이들에게 문자도는 학습 도구였다.
32 그것을 통해 조선 시대의 아이들은 가족과 사회에서의 조화의 중요성을 배울 수 있었다.

본문 TEST Step 4-Step 5 p.39~42

1 Munjado, a Window into the Joseon Dynasty
2 Look at the painting on the right.
3 Do you see the Chinese character, *hyo*(孝)?
4 Do you also see a carp, a geomungo, and a fan?
5 This kind of painting is called Munjado, and it is a type of folk painting that was popular in the late Joseon dynasty.
6 In Munjado, there is usually a Chinese character with some animals or objects.
7 One of eight Chinese characters appears in Munjado.
8 They are *hyo*(孝), *je*(悌), *chung*(忠), *sin*(信), *ye*(禮), *ui*(義), *yeom*(廉), and *chi*(恥), and they represent the values that were important to people of the Joseon dynasty.
9 The animals or objects in Munjado are not just decorations.
10 They often are symbolic.
11 For example, carp in the paintings of *hyo* symbolize respect for parents because of an old story.
12 The story goes as follows..
13 Once upon a time, a man lived with his old mother.
14 One winter, the man's mother became ill and couldn't eat anything.
15 On one very cold day, the mother said to the man, "It would be wonderful if I could eat fresh fish."
16 The man went out to the river, but it was completely frozen.
17 It was impossible for him to catch any fish.
18 The man was so disappointed that he cried out to the sky, "What should I do? Please help me."
19 Then the ice melted, and three carp suddenly came out of the water.
20 The man went back home and cooked the fish for his mother.
21 Then his mother got well.
22 There are other examples of symbolic objects in Munjado.
23 They are bamboo in the paintings of the character *chung*(忠) and lotus flowers in the paintings of *ui*(義).
24 Bamboo does not bend.
25 It stays green in all kinds of weather.
26 For these reasons, bamboo came to symbolize loyalty to the king.
27 In the case of lotus flowers, they grow in muddy ponds but still bloom beautifully.
28 They thus became a symbol of a person's will to fight for justice despite difficulties.
29 Munjado was much more than a painting to people of the Joseon dynasty.
30 It reminded them of important values that greatly influenced their behaviors and attitudes.
31 In particular, for children, Munjado was a study tool.
32 Through it, children in the Joseon dynasty could learn the importance of harmony in family and society.

구석구석지문 TEST Step 1 p.43

After You Read A Read and Complete

1. symbolize respect for parents
2. three carp in a frozen river, for his sick mother
3. symbolizes loyalty to
4. bend, stays green, all kinds of
5. person's will to fight for, despite difficulties
6. in muddy ponds, bloom beautifully

Around the World

1. shows the harvest time of a countryside
2. in the late Joseon dynasty
3. shows the marriage of, in the 19th century

Think and Write

1. Favorite
2. My favorite painting
3. was painted by
4. the reflection of clouds, as well as
5. because, scene looks peaceful
6. it, creative of the painter to draw, so that, are reflected

구석구석지문 TEST Step 2 p.44

After You Read A Read and Complete

1. Paintings of *Hyo*(孝): Carp symbolize respect for parents.
2. In an old story, a man caught three carp in a frozen river and cooked them for his sick mother.
3. Paintings of *Chung*(忠): Bamboo symbolizes loyalty to the king.
4. It does not bend and stays green in all kinds of weather.
5. Paintings of *Ui*(義): Lotus flowers symbolize a person's will to fight for justice despite difficulties.
6. They grow in muddy ponds but still bloom beautifully.

Around the World

1. This painting shows the harvest time of a countryside in Europe in the 16th century.
2. This painting shows a ssireum competition in the late Joseon dynasty.
3. This painting shows the marriage of an American farmer's daughter in the 19th century.

Think and Write

1. My Favorite Painting, *Water Lillies: The Clouds*
2. My favorite painting is *Water Lillies: The Clouds*.
3. It was painted by Claude Monet.
4. In the painting, I can see the reflection of clouds in the pond as well as water lilies.
5. I like this painting because the colors are beautiful and the scene looks peaceful.
6. I think it was very creative of the painter to draw the pond as a mirror so that the clouds in the sky are reflected in the pond.

단어 TEST Step 1 p.45

01 가만히 있는, 고요한 02 사고
03 뽑다, 따다, 뜯다 04 자신 있게 05 공평한, 공정한
06 칭찬, 찬사; 칭찬하다 07 목록, 명단
08 망설이다, 주저하다
09 (~에 빠져) 움직일 수 없는
10 난처한, 딱한, 걱정[근심]스러운 11 창의적인, 창조적인
12 효과가 있다 13 발랄한, 쾌활한 14 가리키다
15 긁다 16 지저분한, 엉망인
17 ~을 다치게 하다, 아프다 18 (일시적인) 중단
19 비명을 지르다 20 공중, 허공 21 침착한, 차분한
22 수줍게, 부끄러워하며 23 자전거 거치대
24 ~을 제외하고 25 하루 종일 26 잠깐만.
27 빠져나가다[나오다] 28 일전에, 최근에
29 하나의 ~, 한 조각의 ~ 30 ~에서 나오다
31 무엇 때문에 ~했니?

단어 TEST Step 2 p.46

01 work 02 still 03 accident
04 compliment 05 fair 06 hesitate
07 shyly 08 worried 09 confidently
10 list 11 hurt 12 messy
13 creative 14 pause 15 stuck
16 cheerful 17 point 18 scratch
19 air 20 pick 21 calm
22 scream 23 bicycle stand 24 the other day
25 pull out 26 except for 27 all day long
28 Just a minute. 29 a piece of 30 come out of
31 What made you ~?

단어 TEST Step 3 p.47

1 messy, 지저분한, 엉망인 2 calm, 침착한 3 air, 공중
4 scream, 비명을 지르다 5 cheerful, 발랄한, 쾌활한
6 work, 효과가 있다 7 scratch, 긁다
8 creative, 창조적인 9 accident, 사고
10 hesitate, 망설이다, 주저하다 11 pause, 중단
12 fair, 공평한, 공정한 13 point, 가리키다
14 list, 목록, 명단 15 confidently, 자신 있게
16 compliment, 칭찬, 찬사

본문 TEST Step 1 p.48~51

01 Best Compliment Ever 03 the last week
04 Each, picked, piece, with
05 Compliments for, last activity
06 everyone pick, name 07 Yes, Ms.
08 talking, each other 09 whose name, pick
10 smiling, got 11 lot to say
12 What about
13 looking worried, picked
14 easy, something, compliment, on
15 sits at, all, long
16 scratching, have to find
18 at, talking with, activity
19 lists, compliments, other, except
20 what to compliment, on 21 Think carefully
22 There should, something 23 he's clean
24 washes, face every 25 not a compliment
26 does that 27 Try again
28 sure, something good, say
30 next, there, an accident
31 foot is stuck, stand 32 with arms, air, help
33 Stay still, pull, out 34 screaming, hurts
35 Let, help, minute
36 runs, comes back with
37 going, put, on, foot 38 What, Butter
39 stay calm
40 pointing, foot, working
41 coming out of, stand 43 eating dinner with
44 about what happened 45 There, little accident
46 got stuck in 47 So, get, out
48 put, on, pulled, out 49 creative, Messy but
50 Creative, be, compliment 51 Sure
53 last, complimenting, each other
54 what compliment, for 55 always cheerful
56 kind, fair, everybody 57 so, of you to
58 let's hear from 59 picked, name
60 hesitating, think, creative 61 shyly, Really
62 What made you think
63 pause, stuck, other, using 64 That, creative
65 Nobody else thought, doing
66 then, also, creative 67 confidently, creative
68 the best compliment ever

본문 TEST Step 2

p.52~54

01 Best Compliment
03 last week
04 Each, a piece of paper with
05 Compliments for, last activity
06 pick
08 talking, each other
09 whose name, pick
10 smiling, got
11 a lot to say
12 What about
13 looking worried, picked
14 to find, compliment him on
15 sits at his desk all day long
16 have to find
18 talking with
19 compliments, other, except for
20 what to compliment, on
21 carefully
22 should be
23 he's clean
24 washes, every day
25 a compliment
26 does that
27 Try again
28 I'm sure, something good
30 an accident
31 is stuck, stand
32 with arms in the air
33 Stay still, pull, out
34 screaming, hurts
35 Let, minute
36 comes back
37 put, on, foot
38 What
39 calm
40 pointing to, working
41 coming out of
43 eating dinner with
44 what happened
45 a little accident
46 got stuck in
47 get, out
48 put, on, pulled it out
49 Messy, creative
50 a compliment
51 Sure
53 the last day, complimenting each other
54 what compliment
55 cheerful
56 also, fair
57 of you
58 hear from you
59 picked
60 hesitating, creative
61 shyly
62 What made you think
63 pause, got stuck, the other day, got, out by using
64 creative
65 Nobody else thought of
66 also
67 confidently, creative
68 the best compliment ever

본문 TEST Step 3

p.55~57

1 최고의 칭찬
2 〈장면 1〉
3 이번 주는 학교의 마지막 주이다.
4 각 학생들은 이름 하나가 쓰인 종이 한 장씩을 막 뽑았다.
5 Ms. Kemp: '학급 친구들 칭찬하기'는 이번 학년 우리의 마지막 활동이 될 거예요.
6 모두 이름을 뽑았나요?
7 Class: 네, Kemp 선생님.
8 학생들이 서로 이야기를 나누고 있다.
9 Beth: 너는 누구 이름을 뽑았니?
10 Lucy: (웃으며) Boyd를 뽑았어.
11 그 애에 관해 할 말이 많아.
12 너는 어때, Beth?
13 Beth: (걱정스러운 표정으로) 어, Peter 이름을 뽑았어.
14 Lucy: Peter? 아, 이런! 그 애에 관해서 칭찬할 것을 찾는 게 쉽지 않을 거야.
15 Steve: 그래. 그 애는 말을 많이 하지 않고 하루 종일 그냥 책상에 앉아만 있잖아.
16 Beth: (머리를 긁적이며) 음, 무언가를 찾아야 해.
17 〈장면 2〉
18 Beth는 집에서 그 활동에 대해 자신의 부모님과 이야기를 나누고 있다.
19 Beth: 저를 제외한 모두가 다른 친구들에 대해 긴 칭찬 목록을 가지고 있어요.
20 저는 Peter에 관해 무엇을 칭찬해야 할지 모르겠어요.
21 엄마: 잘 생각해 봐.
22 뭔가 있을 거야.
23 Beth: 음, 그 애는 깔끔해요.
24 매일 세수를 해요.
25 엄마: 그건 칭찬이 아니야.
26 모든 사람들이 하는 거잖니.
27 아빠: 다시 생각해 보렴.
28 그 아이에 대해 말할 뭔가 좋은 것을 분명히 찾을 수 있을 거야.
29 〈장면 3〉
30 다음 날, 학교에서 사고가 생긴다.
31 Boyd의 발이 자전거 거치대에 끼었다.
32 Boyd: (공중에 양팔을 벌린 채) 도와줘! 도움이 필요해!
33 Beth: 가만히 있어. 네 발을 꺼내려고 노력 중이야.
34 Boyd: (비명을 지르며) 아! 아파!
35 Peter: 내가 도와줄게. 잠깐만.
36 Peter가 학교 주방으로 뛰어가 버터를 가지고 온다.
37 Peter: 네 발에 이 버터를 바를 거야.
38 Boyd: 뭐? 버터를?
39 Peter: 그냥 침착하게 있어.
40 Beth: (Boyd의 발을 가리키며) 와! 효과가 있어!
41 Boyd의 발이 거치대에서 빠져나오고 있어.
42 〈장면 4〉
43 Beth는 부모님과 저녁 식사를 하고 있다.
44 그녀는 부모님께 Boyd에게 일어난 일에 대해 이야기한다.
45 Beth: 오늘 학교에서 작은 사고가 있었어요.
46 Boyd의 발이 자전거 거치대에 끼었어요.
47 엄마: 오, 저런! 그래서 발을 어떻게 뺐니?

48 Beth: Peter가 그 애 발에 버터를 바르고 나서 발을 당겨서 꺼냈어요.
49 아빠: 정말 창의적이구나. 지저분하지만 창의적이야.
50 Beth: 흠. 창의적이라고요? 아빠, 그것이 칭찬이 될 수 있어요?
51 아빠: 물론이지.
52 〈장면 5〉
53 오늘은 학교의 마지막 날이고 학생들은 서로를 칭찬하고 있다.
54 Ms. Kemp: Joanne, Beth에게 무슨 칭찬을 해 주겠니?
55 Joanne: Beth, 너는 항상 쾌활해.
56 또한 친절하고 모두에게 공정해.
57 Beth: 고마워, Joanne. 그렇게 말해 주다니 친절하구나.
58 Ms. Kemp: Beth, 이제 네 말을 들어 보자.
59 Peter의 이름을 뽑았구나.
60 Beth: (주저하며) 음, Peter는 창의적이라고 생각해요. Peter, 너는… 어… 창의적이야.
61 Peter: (수줍어하며) 정말?
62 Ms. Kemp: Peter가 왜 창의적이라고 생각하니?
63 Beth: (한참 있다가) 일전에 Boyd의 발이 자전거 거치대에 끼었을 때, Peter는 버터를 사용해서 그의 발을 꺼냈어요.
64 그것은 창의적이었어요.
65 Boyd: 맞아! 어느 누구도 그렇게 하는 것을 생각하지 못했어.
66 Steve: 난 몰랐어. 음, 그래, 나도 그가 창의적이라고 생각해.
67 Beth: (자신 있게) 그래, Peter, 너는 창의적이야!
68 Peter: 고마워, Beth! 그건 최고의 칭찬이야!

본문 TEST Step 4-Step 5 p.58~64

1 The Best Compliment Ever
2 Scene 1
3 It is the last week of school.
4 Each student has just picked a piece of paper with a name on it.
5 Ms. Kemp: "Compliments for Classmates" will be our last activity of the school year.
6 Did everyone pick a name?
7 Class: Yes, Ms. Kemp.
8 Students are talking to each other.
9 Beth: So, whose name did you pick?
10 Lucy: (smiling) I got Boyd.
11 I have a lot to say about him.
12 What about you, Beth?
13 Beth: (looking worried) Uh, I picked Peter's name.
14 Lucy: Peter? Oh, no! It won't be easy to find something to compliment him on.
15 Steve: Yeah. He doesn't talk much and just sits at his desk all day long.
16 Beth: (scratching her head) Well, I'll have to find something.
17 Scene 2
18 Beth is at home talking with her parents about the activity.
19 Beth: Everyone has long lists of compliments for other classmates, except for me.
20 I don't know what to compliment Peter on.
21 Mom: Think carefully.
22 There should be something.
23 Beth: Well, he's clean.
24 He washes his face every day.
25 Mom: That's not a compliment.
26 Everybody does that.
27 Dad: Try again.
28 I'm sure you can find something good to say about him.
29 Scene 3
30 The next day, there is an accident at school.
31 Boyd's foot is stuck in a bicycle stand.
32 Boyd: (with arms in the air) Help! I need help!
33 Beth: Stay still. I'm trying to pull your foot out.
34 Boyd: (screaming) Ouch! That hurts!
35 Peter: Let me help. Just a minute.
36 Peter runs to the school's kitchen and comes back with butter.
37 Peter: I'm going to put this butter on your foot.
38 Boyd: What? Butter?
39 Peter: Just stay calm.
40 Beth: (pointing to Boyd's foot) Wow! It's working!
41 Boyd's foot is coming out of the stand.
42 Scene 4
43 Beth is eating dinner with her parents.
44 She tells them about what happened to Boyd.
45 Beth: There was a little accident at school today.
46 Boyd's foot got stuck in a bicycle stand.
47 Mom: Oh, no! So how did he get his foot out?
48 Beth: Peter put butter on his foot and then pulled it out.
49 Dad: That was really creative. Messy but creative.
50 Beth: Hmm. Creative? Can that be a compliment, Dad?
51 Dad: Sure.
52 Scene 5

53 It is the last day of school, and the students are complimenting each other.

54 Ms. Kemp: Joanne, what compliment do you have for Beth?

55 Joanne: Beth, you're always cheerful.

56 You're also kind and fair to everybody.

57 Beth: Thanks, Joanne. It's so nice of you to say so.

58 Ms. Kemp: Beth, let's hear from you now.

59 You picked Peter's name.

60 Beth: (hesitating) Well, I think Peter is creative. Peter, you're … uh … creative.

61 Peter: (shyly) Really?

62 Ms. Kemp: What made you think Peter is creative?

63 Beth: (after a long pause) When Boyd's foot got stuck in the bicycle stand the other day, Peter got it out by using butter.

64 That was creative.

65 Boyd: Yeah! Nobody else thought of doing that.

66 Steve: I didn't know that. Well, then, I also think he's creative.

67 Beth: (confidently) Yeah, Peter, you ARE creative!

68 Peter: Thanks, Beth! It's the best compliment ever!

MEMO

적중100

영어 기출 문제집

정답 및 해설

동아 | 윤정미